MW00799539

The Past as Prologue:

"Over There" in American History

by John Tierney

DORRANCE
PUBLISHING CO
EST. 1920
PITTSBURGH, PENNSYLVANIA 15238

Dorrance Publishing Co
585 Alpha Drive
Suite 103
Pittsburgh, PA 15238
Visit our website at *www.dorrancebookstore.com*

ISBN: 978-1-6480-4628-5
eISBN: 978-1-6480-4647-6

To the Future: Monica, Lauren, John

Preface

The subtitle *Over There* is the name of a 1917 song by George M. Cohan that served as a patriotic inspiration for the American role in World War I to "make the world safe for democracy" (President Wilson's famous slogan). Like other songs during America's difficult moments, *The Star Spangled Banner*, 1814, *Happy Days Are Here Again*, 1932, the song has remained as a near-timeless reminder of what the word "American" meant and what once defined the character of its people.

Equally, such lasting lyrics in all these tributes were also intended to remind others what it might mean, to quote Cohan's lyrics, when "we'll be over, we're coming over, and we won't come back till it's over, over there."

Today, such lines must seem nostalgic to a country whose character and history are in question. In judicial terms, the country is "suspect" whose content is under "interrogation." To use the dominant symbol of America in today's culture, it is difficult to write happy songs for a nation embedded with "systemic racism." Better pray the Act of Contrition.

Notwithstanding this reflection, this book has two main themes, both drawn from history. First is that the future replaces the past ("Prologue") and that inescapably it will be either influenced or even determined by it. Second that America has spent most of its history consumed by foreign policies, either isolated from or absorbed by.

Both themes may seem rather obvious but the implications and consequences of each have served to shape this nation's destiny and will be expected to do the same as far as the eye can see.

While I personally consider this to be my final "report" on a life involving both in and out periods the book is anything but an autobiography. It is only "personal" insofar as it tries to relate both historic and current themes that have affected my life, and my country's, since I have been around (1940). Events that I have experienced in government (1976-1993) are first-hand, those that happened earlier I have at least taught (1966 to 1975 and since 1998 at several universities).

Either way, first or second hand, the group of essays (162) is an attempt to summarize the main facets of America and the world and how one has affected the other. Occasionally, I even venture further to show what "might" have happened had alternative histories been chosen.

At the outset, a central belief underpins the entire project that, from the beginning, the American Revolution was meant to be universal, with potentially more lasting and positive consequences for the political globe than at home in North America. In this context, the full affects of 1776 will be judged more on how they have shaped the political world than how they have structured the society within.

The metaphoric answer to the question, "what is the lasting effect of the American Revolution"? Answer, "it's too soon to tell" contains more prophetic insight than political amusement. Put another way, "foreign" policies will always take precedence over domestic policies just as war itself, by definition, will dominate any and all demands for either "justice" or "equality" at home.

With war the issue is usually survival, at home it is convenience and comfort. Results of war are usually immediate and decisive; results at home can absorb centuries.

Thus, it was no contradiction that the original Patriots fought for "Liberty" on behalf of a society that tolerated slavery, a limited suffrage and domestic inequities inside. These could wait while liberty would either survive or die on how the soldiers did, either now, tomorrow or not at all. Similarly, in 1942 Franklin D. Roosevelt imprisoned 120,000 Americans, not just because they were Japanese but because we were at war. His decision contradicted liberty, but it was made on behalf of survival (rightly or wrongly).

Roosevelt was not a "tyrant," and his decision was symbolic of what all regimes, from time eternal, do when survival is the issue.

Conversely, any society that is dominated by itself, that is by domestic troubles, cannot by definition conduct a sustained foreign policy. In 1863 President Lincoln was urged by the Cabinet to declare war on Great Britain for its support of the Confederacy. Lincoln's reply, "Gentleman, please, one war at a time" (attributed). Lincoln also suspended habeas corpus (unlawful detention) during the Civil War, as did George W. Bush in 2006.

Theologian John Courtney Murray once (1960) summarized the need for self-identity and self-confidence as a necessary precursor for any ambitions beyond domestic shores:

"What is at stake is America's understanding of itself. Self-understanding is the necessary condition of a sense of self-identity and self-confidence, whether in the case of an individual or in the case of a people. If the American people can no longer base this sense on naïve assumptions of self-evidence, it is imperative that they find more reasoned grounds for their essential affirmation that they are uniquely a people, uniquely a free society. Otherwise, the peril is great. The complete loss of one's identity is, with all propriety of theological definition, Hell. In diminished forms, it is insanity. And it would not be well for the American giant to go lumbering about the world today, lost and mad."

Thus, it is not unusual that since 1991 we have witnessed a deliberate and sustained American "disengagement" from most of the previous ambitious and "superpower" global policies that carried this country through both world wars and the Cold War. How can the political globe compete with either police brutality or "white privilege"?

As on December 7, 1941 and 9/11/2001 we may well find out.

Overall, the whole task, by nature, is completely "arbitrary." I alone have chosen what to include and what to omit and, again by nature, "mistakes" are unavoidable. This, at least, has the virtue of permitting the reader to find interest in the subject, or to get frustrated for either an omission or selection. Of course there is the vice of insisting on my own interpretation. Either way, it is more like a "conversation" than a lecture.

The content, like the title, also has themes. One is that history "matters." This, too, may seem obvious but it is almost the opposite. Americans, for various reasons, have often been labeled "a-historical," at best, "anti-historical" at worst. The first means indifference, the second means hostile. The first is tolerable (why should foreign wars affect my career?), the second is a "revolution" and, as such, has both hidden and open dangers.

It is the second part that I am most concerned with, as it seems to have taken hold of the more recent popular culture and may define the future as well.

By "hostile" I mean that observers become opposed to the subject as presented and offer, instead, interpretations contrary to what has been believed and taught over centuries. Invariably, these become the basis for current and future directions. Thus, history turns on its head and serves as an intellectual "revolution" requiring a wholesale "remake" of society. In effect, the country starts over, "born again."

While America has not reached this stage yet it is becoming perilously close. Tearing down of statues and other reminders of history are but a beginning.

Wholesale revamping of both the nature and conduct of American society, as in the *New York Times* Project 1619, offers a more mature stage, while the full effects of a total makeover is becoming less and less of a secret goal.

These topics are taken up in several essays. While I oppose history as ideology it is still true that no country is "without sin." But full "confessions" should not condemn the sinner to Hell. Nor should the defects of humanity itself (crime, discrimination, group distinctions, wealth, poverty etc.) be seen as confined to one -and only one - locale. While southern governors certainly promoted "racism" in America, comparisons to Genghis Khan or to Hitler are, shall we say, "overblown."

In short, using global comparisons to the American political culture confuses Sociology with Political Science. Liberty is a rare political virtue earned by very few; group behaviors are sociological, universal and pervasive. Both, as well, can co-exist together, and without contradiction.

Thus, history in the US today is "comatose," somewhere between both "dead" and "alive." Alive as a popular reference but dead as an accurate or objective reflection. The subject as used in the popular culture degenerates into a mass-conversion for current or generic frustrations, with the passions that only ideologies can support (faith-based and selective belief systems).

A close parallel was the persistence of the "Lost Cause" issue in southern circles post-Civil War. Although Vicksburg refused to celebrate July 4th until 1945 the experience had little impact on the Day everywhere else. But if Vicksburg's example was widespread we would almost certainly have a different country today (or several, or none).

Reparations for slavery is another symptom. The thesis maintains that current populations must take responsibility for the past, including paying for it. But slavery is highly selective and if the thesis were fully developed it would stretch beyond a single issue to all causes that the past might provoke, with current populations going broke paying for the calamities of the past 6,000 years. On an individual level: in preparing your resume would you highlight that you once stole money or that you once served as an Altar Boy? Again, tearing down reminders of history may satisfy the inner emotions, but does nothing against reality.

Still, the use/abuse of history can be contagious and, if not appreciated, fatal.

A key element in history's "repetition" is the similarity between separate eras, not the differences. In the Civil War General Grant had neither tanks nor planes, whereas General Eisenhower in World War II had both. The differences can be noted but the similarities are critical: both men fought, advanced and won. They waged "war," and that is what unites history. How they did it, by comparison, is interesting but fairly irrelevant in history's grand "scheme."

Other themes, drawn from the above, run through the essays. One is an appreciation of both sides of the American experience, the earlier (isolationist, Washington) and the subsequent (crusader state, Wilson). Both sides reacted to the twin themes of security and liberty that pervaded all generations of American statesmen. And they both came from the same source, ie. we stole money on Saturday and went to Church on Sunday. We tear down Lee's image on Monday; on Tuesday his place in life remains the same.

A second theme is the deterioration of the felt-need to revive the country's role in structuring a new and improved "World Order" since the end of the Cold War. The decline of any and all interest in foreign policies and the near-total absorption in domestic, "group" interests ("isms," ideologies) has overtaken most of the concentration in world politics that stopped at the doorstep of Ronald Reagan.

(Full Discloser: I served in both terms of his administrations and am unapologetically "biased." Reagan apologized for nothing.)

A final theme, almost inevitably, is the need for somebody, sometime to revive the spirit of an"exceptional"nation that motivated America's great statesmen from George Washington, through Jefferson, Monroe, Polk, Lincoln, Wilson, both Roosevelts, and those Cold War presidents from Truman, IKE, JFK to Reagan who saw this country through its worst – and boldest – moments: history's greatest world wars and the protracted conflict with world communism.

Both Hitler and Stalin are buried and (mostly) forgotten while the USA, afterward, spent a year in bitter anguish over what a Supreme Court nominee did at a booze party in High School.

Now, police kill somebody somewhere and the country nearly stops. Thus, George Floyd represents all history and the American character, as if Ben Franklin becomes Simon Legree and the Pilgrims Nazi brownshirts. All logic and perspective transforms into ideology, with the passions and rage that ideology demands.

In the meantime, homicides inside cities rise 25 to 50 percent; 300 to 600 annually, while "defund the police" gathers cultural momentum.

Is "hysteria" an appropriate description? How about "national insanity"? If so it's nothing new. Germany and Japan kept the world at war for half-a-century; they both have since become models of peace and prosperity. Most of Europe, China, Japan and Mongolia had colonies all over the globe . Now, they have none. Can Devils turn into Angels overnight?

Nor is the American past and present free of deviations from any proscribed "norm." Consider this sampling from then to now: a Civil War that took nearly 3 percent of the population, an economic Depression that saw 9,000 Bank closures, a country remote from global politics on Sunday, leader of civilization on Monday, two bombs that killed over 100,000 innocent civilians in minutes, a Red Scare "hysteria" that is still named after an obscure Senator ("McCarthyism") and, now, a realtor-president who is defying electoral defeat and threatening the nature of the country itself (something neither Jeff Davis, Hitler nor Stalin could do in a lifetime).

True, there is always "light at the end of the tunnel."

Until February 1947 America was committed to isolationism. By June of that year it was already engaged on a global crusade to save western civilization. It took fifteen weeks.

As I concluded in one essay, If only some statesman, man or woman, president, Secretary of something would only, just once, announce a new and attractive goal for humanity it would do.

Whether he/she meant it bothers me not in the least.

As a Congressman I knew once reflected on his latest speech: "it even had the added advantage of being true."

Better than nothing.

PS. The essays have occasional repetitions of both factual materials and actual quotations of key personnel. This is both the by-product of a book written within a seven year timespan (2015 - 2021) and my own personal memory shortcomings. In either case the repetitions make the point that there are many factual situations that deserve appreciation and widespread acknowledgement, including repetition, again, again, again and again.

John J. Tierney Jr.

Acknowledgments

As a faculty member of The Institute of World Politics (IWP), Washington DC, since 1998 I owe my first public recognition to this institution and its personnel. Chief among these are Founder (1990) and past President Dr. John Lenczowski, Board of Trustees Chairman John Lovewell, past Chairs Owen Smith and the late Ambassador Faith Ryan Whittlesey.

IWP is a unique organization, led by "scholar-practitioners" who have experience in both academic and government careers and who are dedicated to the continuity and clarification of American history and those rare political values that have made this country "exceptional." This includes both its devotion to liberty and to the export of the values that liberty bestows, as far as possible, to the remainder of the world.

IWP was formed to explore the "non-material dimensions of power and politics, such as: intelligence and counter-intelligence, information, strategic communications, ideas and belief systems … the dignity of foreign peoples … leadership … patriotism, civic virtue, moral and strategic clarity … and certain first principles." (Mission Statement)

This book reflects those values and the people who engage them. This includes, from Vice President level to the student body, full and part-time faculty (about 50), Board members, donors and supporters of many kinds.

In particular, I wish to mention IWP Vice President Jason Johnsrud who has supervised the student body for over a quarter century. Mrs. Katie Bridges, IWP Communications and Events Director, who has supervised over 100 annual events and, in turn, has carefully monitored all 162 essays herein since the beginning in 2015.

My family members have contributed greatly by just reading (maybe) all the essays that I sent them, with daughter Lauren especially noted as prompting and promoting when I just wanted to "call it a day."

I would also like to point out the constructive work that my publisher, *Dorrance Publishing* (Pittsburgh), did in the near-two years that it took to bring a manuscript into a book. It is not easy to assemble and construct 550 pages and 162 essays but the task is over and done, and done quite well, thank you. Special appreciation goes to my "coordinators" at *Dorrance*, Sara Lewis and

Dannielle Pendzich, who picked up the pieces when they were still scattered and brought them together to final form.

All mistakes (such as my opinion everywhere) are, of course, solely my responsibility.

Finally, should copyrights exist on any pictures in this book the author refers to Title 17 U.S.C. Section 106A-117, the USA Copyright Law, "fair use, educational purposes only."

History: Alive (but not Well)

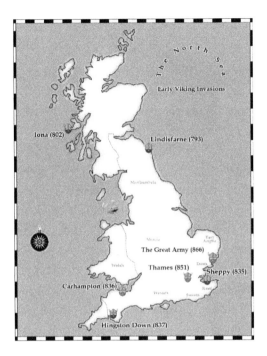

March 1, 2022

The day after Russia's invasion of Ukraine my students asked me what I "thought" of it. I replied that I was opposed to the invasion, that Vladimir Putin was too aggressive, militaristic and imperialistic and that Ukraine had the misfortune of living next to a great power and that geopolitics ruled that small countries owe their existence to larger ones.

Then I reflected on what I had said. I had a PhD in International Relations (U of Pennsylvania) for over fifty years, was a professor of World Politics since 1966 with almost twenty years in-between as staff in the House of Representatives and as a political appointee in the State Department. And that's all I could say about the biggest thing to hit Europe since Germany's surrender in 1945? What would be the difference between what I had said and that of some "drunk" at the end of the bar who just wanted to shout-out? Or what 1,000 commentators were saying on local TV all across the country?

Slinking back behind the desk I wondered what the class had thought of my "insights"? Then I wondered what I thought about my own education, or was it, to remember English class, "full of sound and fury, signifying nothing" (Macbeth)?

Well, at least I knew more Shakespeare than them. But this was a History class in US foreign policy? The "Bard" would have to wait.

What could I say relevant to the day and the event?

Then I remembered the essential subject, History. The room, it seemed, brightened.

Yesterday, February 24, 2022, I began (I almost said that it was a day that would "live in infamy"), Russia invaded Ukraine without warning or provocation. Taking a larger perspective, I went on, there were a grand total of 50,000 unprovoked invasions in human history (a number totally invented but fitting the purpose; there were certainly much more). Yesterday, I continued, Putin's action was, exactly, number 50,001.

Then came my question: class, what is your opinion of the first 50,000 ?

After a minute of silence, with no answer, I tried to draw some point. Was this particular one "unique" by some standard? If so, what is the standard? General Grant had neither planes nor tanks, while Eisenhower had both. Does that make their actions "different" or "similar" in kind but not method? The Confederacy bombed an American island (Sumter) and started a war. Japan did the same (Hawaii) a bit later-on. Were these the same or different?

If Putin's behavior is the same, why the attention? If the two of you had sex 1,000 times, why elaborate on 999? If the boss screamed at the staff thousands of days in a row, what's critical about this morning?

And so it goes, ad infinitum.

But the class seemed not to notice my point, or it seemed somehow "out-of-place." So I tried "comparison." In 1847 the American army invaded Mexico and a year later took 50% of their territory (Including Texas, California, Arizona and New Mexico), a geography about the size of Western Europe. We've kept it since with no intention of returning it.

On April 30, 1975, almost half-a-century ago, the North Vietnam Army occupied Saigon, South Vietnam, thus ending an earlier quarter-century (since 1950) of American war in that country. Vietnam was about 10,000 miles from the Golder Gate Bridge, with the war taking 58,000 American soldier's lives plus about three million Vietnamese. Within several years later the United States became "sole remaining superpower" on earth, with full recognition of the new communist Vietnam state.

Twenty years ago another American army crossed the Atlantic Ocean, through the Strait of Gibraltar, across the Mediterranean Sea, down the Red Sea and invaded a place spelled Afghanistan, about 12,000 miles from Manhattan. We stayed until last August, then left. That place remains about the same as it did before Christ.

Comparison seemed not to arouse much attention either, so I gave up and left the subject. If three invasions over time was unimpressive then, I suppose, the other 49, 997 wouldn't do either.

But the episode left me somewhat empty. The public is fully preoccupied with what happened this morning or last night and has no interest, appreciation or even speculation of what happened in the years, decades, or centuries before. Speculation is entirely for the future, the "unknown." Whether today is completely unique or part of a larger pattern is dismissed and we are no closer to appreciate human behavior than before.

Churchill was a historian and often called World War II "unnecessary" or "there never was a war more easy to stop." History means "perspective," which could lead to "anticipation" and even "prevention." As before, almost anything done in perspective would have been better than the tragedy of Ukraine today. One does not begin to watch the ball game in the bottom of the ninth.

Americans have often been called "ahistorical." Henry Ford summarized this part of "Americana" when he said that "history is bunk," by which he meant that "we want to live in the present." Synonyms for "bunk" are (in alphabetical order) balderdash, baloney, blather, crock, drivel, folly, garbage, hogwash, hooey, humbug, malarkey, nonsense, rubbish, trash, twaddle.

So I went home and watched a DVD on World War I, where I knew the end.

Only one problem: it *never* ends.

The American Worldview

January 1, 2022

In 2016 my book *Conceived in Liberty* (Transaction) was published. My intent was to assess the origin and nature of why, and how, Americans have viewed the political world from their beginnings in 1776. The title, taken from Lincoln's Gettysburg Address (1863), attempted to show that the political principles of the American "Cause" have antecedents that go deep within history and philosophy and why they should be prominent in the modern world.

My inspiration for the book came as a result of the many challenges that these principles had to endure in the post-Cold War period (1991), how the country had strayed from the core element of these ideas and why it needed to restore them if, for no other reason than to provide "sanity" to the emerging and ongoing debate.

The word "sanity" implies that I thought that the country had gone "insane," at least temporarily. "Insanity," as an adjective, is not at all that uncommon or illogical, as in "he seemed to have gone insane at least at the time." It is also a normal legal defense to avoid jail time and for "rehabilitation." In effect, I was hoping to "restore" the USA back on course at the least and toward a more normal and traditional "rehab." I also believed that this was the best way to avoid global war and to interject the American First Principles toward World Order.

Needless, to say, *Conceived in Liberty* had zero impact on the current state of the Republic while the overall political culture continued on its "insanity" course. All this time "aided and abetted" by a cooperative and co-dependent media, entertainment, sports, business and similar interests. The political culture, it seemed to me, had been "hijacked."

Such, at least, was my "worldview." Needless to say as well, it was particularly "lonely." Especially within the context of an energetic and breathless "social media" onslaught from seemingly all corners coupled with the "endless wars" of three straight administrations, the Afghanistan debacle and continuous presidential debates that held Harvey Weinstein and George Floyd over "national security" issues.

Not to mention the "border crisis," a crisis that goes back several centuries. Then came Trump, and now Joe (nothing personal but I still miss JFK).

Without domestic consensus nothing external is either possible or enduring. This reflection was brought out back in 1960 by the great theologian John Courtney Murray. His insight appears in other essays below so I might as well begin with him in this INTRO:

"What is at stake is America's understanding of itself. Self- understanding is the necessary condition of a sense of self-identity and self-confidence, whether in the case of an individual or a people. If the American people can no longer base this sense on naïve assumptions of self-evidence, it is imperative that they find other more reasoned grounds for their essential affirmation that they are uniquely a people, uniquely a free society. Otherwise, the peril is great. The complete loss of one's identity is, with all propriety of theological definition Hell. In diminished forms it is insanity. And it would not be well for the American giant to go lumbering about the world today, lost and mad."

One would have to read *Conceived in Liberty* cover to cover to appreciate the depth of the American political culture, its aspirations, ambitions and even setbacks. Suffice to note that the so-called American "Cause" has been developed over history and philosophy that can go as far back as ancient Greece, Roman law and the English political heritage beginning with the Magna Carta.

The great "architect" of modern Nationalism, Hans Kohn (d. 1971) has noted in his book *American Nationalism* (1957) that, apart from all other nations of Europe and Asia, the American nation was conceived and developed upon ideas based upon political liberty and individual rights rather than geographic or sociological distinctions. The words "Fatherland," "Motherland," do not appear as American descriptions, compared to the ideals of "liberty, equality and pursuit of happiness."

Equally, while most Americans identify themselves with "hyphens" showing their home origins (Irish, German, Italian, Hispanic, Asian, Black etc.) there is no such thing as an "English-American." As Kohn explains, they kept the political virtues of their enemies but still desired full and separate identity:

"From England came the tradition of constitutional liberty and common law. Mother Country and colony grew from the same roots – the Magna Carta, the Puritan and Glorious revolutions, Milton and Locke."

Yet at the same time, Kohn understood how the fabric and core of nationalism could turn on itself and destroy its very existence:

"In the word liberty vibrates the message which pervades all human history and makes it human: the promise of the dignity of man, of his rights as an individual, of his duties to his fellow men. … Compared with it, nationalism is only a passing form of integration, beneficial and vitalizing yet by its own exaggerations and dynamism easily destructive of human liberty."

Sound familiar?

I recently visited Jefferson's home, Monticello, in central Virginia. The guide was very animated, not about the owner's contributions to the American Nation, but to his relationship with his slave/mistress, Sally Hemmings.

To me, this was a form of insanity.

But a "sign of the times."

Apocalypse

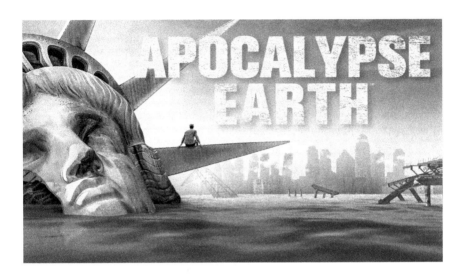

January 11, 2022

The strict definition, from ancient Christian and Jewish texts, means God's intervention against the evil of mankind, an "imminent cosmic cataclysm," the "final judgment," end of the world, the collapse of civilization etc. Apocalypse is always meant as a prophetic revelation rather than a reflection of the past. Synonyms include "armageddon," "disaster," "calamity" etc.

Thus far, in the over 6,000 years of recorded history, there has never been a true "apocalypse" by the strict and theological meaning. Debacles there have been, and many, coupled by the collapse of whole civilizations, defeats on grand scales, man-made and natural disasters.

There is probably no time in recorded history that has not experienced some sort of event that approached the meaning but none either theological or definitive. Does today's "Pandemic" conform to the definition? Answer: Not even close! Somehow, there is a universal conviction that the Pandemic, one, will end and, second, that it does not mean the "end."

If there is Hope there is no Apocalypse. And there has always been Hope.

But, conversely, in the American political "climate" today (or "culture") is it fair to define the ruling "atmosphere" as approaching an "Apocalyptic" level? Certainly not on the level of theology, as today's American society is far removed from the Christian-based culture of the nineteenth century.

Nor is the US united on any single theme that would corral all the separate parts together as One. But in the divisions that have arisen in the past several years there has emerged an "Apocalyptic" interpretation of the future that, minus the theology, closely conforms to something that we can all appreciate as meaning "The End." In this connection, the new target of the ancient word "Apocalypse" is "Democracy." Without qualification, nor apology, if one conviction unites all sides of today's political culture it is the word "Final," and Final is but another meaning of The End," ie. "Apocalypse.

There is no dismissing this stark reality, it is encompassing, enveloping and universal (to cite "entry" words). Nor am I being judgmental. Just descriptive.

The fundamental issue between the sides has become much deeper than "party loyalty" versus the essential interpretation of the word "American," its past content and future ambitions. As in "Final Judgment," it identifies the core meaning of man-on-earth, specifically "American Man, American Earth." Translated into politics this means "Democracy," and especially that word as practiced (or not) by Americans from the beginning to now.

Prior to recent times, the word was normally applied (usually subconsciously) to events that went far beyond typical party and political manipulations. A "nuclear holocaust" from the spread of nuclear weapons and the more-doctrinaire side of the environmental movement both represent "apocalyptic" visions of the end of humanity. Neither of these visions have yet to appear on the human scene, and both remain unlikely. Still, that reality does not rule-out the possibility that, sometime in the future, a time when one no-one on earth has foreseen, our earth might yet collapse from either a man-made or climatic Finality.

But as expressed by the news media and political/academic class the challenge today is purely political. This remains central to the future visions from both the political Left and Right. This "cultural" reality" was recently expressed best by Fox News commentator Mark Levin, whose book *American Marxism* (2021) predicts "The End" coming from European thought (Karl Marx):

"The counterrevolution to the American Revolution is in full force. And it can no longer be dismissed or ignored, for it is devouring our society and culture, swirling around our everyday lives, and ubiquitous in our politics, schools, media and entertainment."

From a similar perspective former Nixon speechwriter and presidential candidate, Patrick J. Buchanan, has noted in his *The Death of the West* (2002) that the basic causation of the "end" of Western civilization is demographic decline:

"As a growing population has long been a mark of healthy nations and rising civilizations, falling populations have been a sign of nations and civilizations in decline. If that holds true, Western civilization … is in critical condition. For, like the Cheshire Cat, the people of the West have begun to fade away."

From totally opposite perspectives, the political Left notes "Apocalypse" coming from within society itself but arrives at nearly identical conclusions as to The End. The end of democracy, from this position, is inherent inside the country and, indeed, can be attributed to the personality of even single individuals, Donald Trump in particular.

Like the earlier case (above), it remains true that individuals, as opposed to movements, can, indeed, ruin civilizations. This may, as well, occur again but, like an environmental collapse, it remains far-fetched but politically attractive. Hitler, Stalin, Mussolini and Napoleon did their best in this regard, but civilization, somehow, has apparently survived (so far).

The *Washington Post*, among a host of media and political allies, is most "outspoken" in this perspective. Since the 2016 election the Post has printed *"Democracy Dies in Darkness"* on the top of page one of each and every edition, night and day, week and week-ends. Next would be the *New York Times*, with its "1619 Project," to remind Americans that July 4 is a phony birthdate and that slavery, not Liberty, has defined the country, which is entitled to a new "Beginning," with an End to the "Old."

As Mark Levin (above) has written, the message of "Apocalypse" has dominated almost all aspects of US society since, but is rarely identified in name. The Post's Pulitzer-winning analyst, Carlos Lozada, has reminded us exactly how deep the divisions go. "To glimpse the coming dismemberment of the United States of America", he wrote (January 9, 2022), just stop by your local bookstore." He then reviewed several books with similar themes: *How Civil Wars Start, Divided We Fall, American War* and *The Next Civil War.*

These are not hopeful times, but is all hope gone?

If it is then Apocalypse is upon us.

PS. The great conservative writer, James Burnham, wrote *Suicide of the West*, which predicted the coming demise of Liberty, Democracy and the American Way.

The year was 1964, long before a former Hollywood actor then President announced "Morning in America." Nobody proclaimed Apocalypse for the Soviet Union. It took less than a decade!

I was there!

A Nation of ... what?

December 29, 2021

Two of the most influential books in the history of the United States, although mostly forgotten now, began with the expression "A Nation of ....." The concluding word was meant to convey what each author declared as the nation's most critical trait at the time.

For those of you under fifty (or sixty) the exact word should pass you by. For those of us somewhat older than that, how could we forget them? They were both number one best-sellers of the time and defined for most of us what the word "America" had come to mean. One was meant to convey a positive image, the second not quite so. One was descriptive, the other interpretive. One was a domestic image, the other foreign policy.

Give up? The first ended its title with "Immigrants," the second with "Sheep." Needless to say, the disparity in the descriptions created quite a stir within the American intelligentsia and an equal divide as to what the country (nation), its history and character, meant to the general public.

A Nation of Immigrants was published in 1958 by Senator John F. Kennedy, who went on to become president only to be assassinated in 1963. The book was published by the Anti-Defamation League (ADL) a group founded in 1913 to oppose anti-Semitism and other forms of anti-immigration bigotry. In re-publishing Kennedy's book in 2018 ADL Chairman Jonathan Greenblatt hoped to carry the original message to the new century:

" It was an act of courage when ADL published this book in 1958. It helped to shape the conversation of the time and shape our country's history. Hopefully, it can shape both of them again in our own time."

In his opening chapter Kennedy defined the message he wanted to convey and how the title conformed to the character of America and why it was unique throughout world history. The US was, he explained:

" … a society of immigrants, each of whom had begun life anew, on an equal footing. This was the secret of America: a nation of people with the fresh memory of old traditions who dared to explore new frontiers, people eager to build lives for themselves in a spacious society that did not restrict their freedom of choice and action."

No wonder Kennedy entitled his Administration "The New Frontier."

"The perfect is the enemy of the good" is a philosophical aphorism, attributed originally to French liberal-democrat Voltaire, which notes that perfection may be a constant goal even if it cannot be realized in the present tense. Obviously, American society carried "restrictions" on new immigrants but Kennedy's main purpose was to describe the general attributes of the "New World" as opposed to the "Old" and to relate the aspirations of the millions who flocked to these shores in earlier centuries.

The fact that they continue to do so today reflects the validity of the expression and to the wisdom of ancient philosophy as opposed to current ideologies. It also exposes those who prefer to emphasize the bright side of life, against the dark.

A Nation of Sheep, the second book, was published in 1961 by a retired Naval officer William J. Lederer, who graduated from the Naval Academy in 1936 and had an expansive career as a Captain in the Navy with vast experience in Europe and Southeast Asia. Lederer also was a novelist who co-authored *The Ugly American* with Eugene Burdick (1958) and wrote script for Hollywood naval adventures, *McHale's Navy* and *Ensign O'Toole*. Lederer died in 2009, age 97.

The main thesis in *A Nation of Sheep*, as in most of Lederer's other writings, was the gap that existed between what politicians and journalists convey to the public versus the truth as it really is, or-was from history. Citing a number of examples, mostly from Southeast Asia, Taiwan, Korea, Vietnam, China plus many others from US foreign policies, Lederer's "Sheep" designation was meant to convey a population able-and-willing to accept whatever is forced down their throats.

Normally this is done blindly and without qualification. Today, this is simply called "fake news."

In examining this situation in 1961, and before, Lederer's "Sheep" characterization was not intended as a compliment: "In a democracy, where so many are inarticulate, the voices that do speak carry enormous weight." In assessing this disparity between the "people" (Sheep) and their leaders, he notes that "the cult of government secrecy is growing," and that "the practice has become widespread and routine."

Conclusion: the ending will be two questions, rather than a final, concluding note.

1) Sixty years later, after Vietnam, Watergate, "endless wars" (as the press defines them), especially Afghanistan, the impeachments, over 30,000 lies (attributed to Trump), the Border "crisis," etc. etc. the question remains: are the conditions in America the same or different from those written in 1958 and 1961?

2) Should you attempt a brand new book beginning with "A Nation of …. what would be your final image?

(For "what it's worth" Department, would it be positive or negative? As for mine? Read on!)

Oh, I forgot: do you give a damn?

Memo to the World: Party's Over

December 27, 2021

Office "memos" are meant to impart guidelines or instruction to the rest of the staff from the Boss regarding proper (improper) behavior. They may address business conduct, office decorum, sales techniques, timeliness or any other conduct that may (may not) affect the business. They should normally be taken seriously especially if one wants (likes) his job or position. One need not agree at all with a single sentence of the message but be warned: if you want to stay in your job or continue to "put bread on the table" obey the memo!

In addressing your new "memo" to the "People of the World" regarding American conduct in the "World place" what would be the message that you ("Boss") should impart.

First, what are your choices?

1) You could congratulate the staff on their most recent performance. Sales are up, behavior is good, no complaints, most are pleased. Result: Christmas bonus, raises projected, better vacations, increase in staff plus possibly new and better locations.

2) You might give warnings about "problems" in the workplace, a decline in productivity and sales, poor business techniques, increased tardiness, sloppy dress codes, bad "attitudes." Result: your memo is meant to "turn the situation around," to offer incentives, advice and encouragement for a better output and conduct. Your advice is to inspire rather than to punish or shut-down.

3) The situation has become intolerable, beyond redemption. Personnel ignore all advice, conduct has gone from "bad" to "unruly," sales have dropped to near-nothing, staff seems not to care in the least, competition has overtaken the firm in areas where we once led. Result: memo indicates that the "party is over," the business must drop all pretentions to leadership in the field, staff reductions are imminent. A new and smaller location is needed and the possibility of "closure" is now real.

Regarding the condition of American foreign policy in the world how would your memo address the issue? Which of the three (or more) choices would your memo use?

Result: Choice One is automatically eliminated. Nothing's that good and US foreign policy, even under the best conditions, never reached this degree of satisfaction.

Perhaps the closest was the original instruction from the original president: Washington's "Farewell Address" (1796) that guided the nation until it grew into the Twentieth Century "superpower." Next would be the immediate post World War II years (1945 – 1950) under Truman where the World Order that still governs the globe first emerged. Third might be Reagan's first Administration (1981 – 1985) wherein the Soviet Union and world Communism was eliminated peacefully under the "gun" of tens of thousands of nuclear weapons and an indifferent if not hostile political climate.

Aside from those three historic chapters we are left with the post-Cold War era (since 1991). In considering options two or three, the following main points governing the political globe should guide our thought:

- The United States military has not won a war since 1945. It has become the best financed, equipped and "overworked" military in peacetime US history. It has been involved in dozens of interventions, occupations and excursions all over the globe. But it has yet to win a war!

- With the demise of world Communism (1991) the United States, military and political, has enjoyed the luxury of living in a strategic global environment that, minus incipient terrorism, has never, repeat never, been engaged in a rival, state or coalition, that challenges anything remotely close to "survival." This means both literally or figuratively. When asked what was the greatest challenge to American "survival" President Obama replied "the climate." That view is also pervasive within the culture: the weather is "public enemy number one."

- Since the end of the Cold War every political administration, without a single exception, has been directed by an overall domestic agenda as evidenced by Inaugural Addresses, thousands of political speeches and the political attention and personnel throughout the body politic. This doesn't imply that there was NO foreign policy. It simply implies that the domestic agenda occupied first place, with foreign policy somewhere near the bottom ten. (for further proof, review the 2016 and 2020 televised presidential debates and count the times "foreign affairs" was covered).

- While there has been high-level attention to the idea of a foreign "threat," coming from such as China alone or China and Russia together, one is reminded of the isolationist 1930's when nearly all of American public attention was "survival" from the Great Depression. In a similar way popular concentration has focused almost exclusively on domestic issues, especially "people of color" including "Black Lives," and "White Supremacy," plus ideological items, inequity, inequalities, injustice with a myriad of other related issues that can only be solved (or delayed) at home.

Under such, inarguable, conditions (at the least) and without either rancor or remorse, how would your memo to the world on American foreign policy read? Final result:

To: John (Jane) Q Public

From: Boss Man (Woman)

Re.: Future US Foreign Policy

Ladies and Gentlemen of the World:

For the past several decades this country, as promised from our beginnings, has done all that could be expected to keep a global peace and a promised order in the world-at-large.

As most of you know, certain conditions, or "circumstances," have arisen that have come to our attention and the attention of our shareholders ("allies"). In recent years, but especially in our new century, these conditions have come to dominate our approach to both the American staff (people) and to our business and products throughout the globe.

Without belaboring these conditions, of which you all are very well aware, it has become necessary for America to adjust our strategies and output in several critical ways. In the next few months, and into the near future, America will have to take a number of very reluctant steps to adjust our business practices and world strategies to the challenges of a new era.

These will emphasize greater attention on domestic priorities as the public has demanded, including a relaxation in our global obligations and responsibilities. The demands on home issues have become so great that they have all-but eclipsed earlier American efforts, many made reluctantly, to fix the destructive efforts of others to destroy world order, liberty and stability.

We sincerely regret these necessities and fervently hope that they will be temporary.

In the hope that these changes will be both respected by the global public and may, in their own way, contribute to both stability and order throughout the world.

I remain.
Your loving Boss and Colleague,

The American People at-large

What's Wrong With US(A)?

December 16, 2021

Pardon me but I'm almost 82, been around a "long long time," and keep thinking that "IT" has to be me. Am I too old, impatient, cranky, selfish and satisfied that everything that happens in the country is labeled both unprecedented and catastrophic?

So what is "IT"?

Good question! Answer: the country, that's what is "IT."

So … what's wrong with the country?

Again, good question! Answer: I don't know, but something.

Some things have bothered me.

A criminal is killed by police, shut down the Cops! Everywhere! After the civil rights revolution, Martin Luther King and "affirmative action" we are "systemically racist." As the world's only "superpower," that won the greatest wars in human history, the Cold War and forged history's only Democratic World Order, we are "White Supremacists." After the greatest prosperity in all of history the businessmen who created this become "oppressive." The values created by the most important political event in all history, even the country's Birthday, are challenged as irrelevant and dated.

I keep wondering: what would I do if everyone else wanted to change my Birthday (March 1) and call me nasty names?

I don't really know but it would certainly make me think: why the Hell go on? Which is about where I am now.

Certainly the country had experienced bad times before. And survived them all.

How about the thing called "Civil War"? Killed 750,000 white boys (estimate) in four years. With 30 million white people that's about 2.5 percent of that population. The Civil War ended slavery but aroused "Jim Crow" and post-slave lynching. In the one hundred years since (1865 to 1965) an estimated 3,000 Black men were hung. So, do the math. What characterizes the culture more: the war that ended slavery or its aftermath? Some more math: what if 2.5 percent of today's population died in a war since 2017? How would George Floyd or Harvey Weinstein "play" in the media against a background of 8 million body bags sent home from somewhere overseas?

Then there was the Great Depression. Over 9,000 Bank closings in ten years, 25 percent unemployment, bread lines, caravans of trucks headed west, soldiers camping out in DC demanding their war bonuses (forced out by Hoover and MacArthur), tent-towns ("Hooverville's") of unemployed families all across the land, farm foreclosures (with 45 percent of the population on farms), labor strikes everywhere, socialism and communism dominating the culture.

Those were bad times but, like the Civil War, life went on and the country flourished. Hitler and Japan ended the Depression. America won the greatest war in history (76 million total killed, about 35,000 men, women and children each day) and by war's end (1945) the country had recorded the greatest prosperity system in the history of mankind.

It still goes on, despite the "troubles" (old Irish saying).

But what about these "troubles." How "bad" can they be? Are they "real" or "contrived"?

Or is it me?

Even I can remember the terrible 1960's: civil rights, Vietnam, 250 universities closed in '68, assassinations, the Democratic Convention of '68, riots, vandalism, anti-war protests almost everywhere. The country seemed "on the brink."

Then came "Watergate," Nixon (yesterday's Trump), Gerry Ford and Jimmy Carter ("malaise" in America). On April 30, 1975 the North Vietnam Army occupied Saigon, thus ending America's 25-year commitment against Communism in Southeast Asia. Over 58,000 dead American soldiers, over a decade of daily combat in a mountainous jungle 12,000 miles away, two million Vietnamese dead, revolution and protest at home, three times the bomb tonnage dropped by the US Air Force compared to all combatants in all (repeat all) theatres of World War Two. Against a jungle target no larger than the state of New Jersey!

Talk about strategy!

If there was to be a revolt in the country why didn't it happen then? Why is democracy "threatened" so much right now?

Again, it must be me.

Then, almost from the "Blue," a former actor won in 1980, declared "morning in America," devised a strategy against the Soviet Union and, almost overnight, world Communism came to an abrupt halt, the USSR died, the Berlin Wall came down with Gorbachev and Reagan as heroes plus a final photo of Bill Clinton with his arms around a drunken (what else?) Boris Yeltsin.

And the media went crazy when Trump "played nice" with Vladimir Putin! (BTW: Gorbachev had twelve (repeat twelve) summits with Reagan-Bush).

So what's wrong now?

Answer: everything!

Caveat: "seemingly."

I still cling to the issue as me: I'm just too old to "understand" the issues as they are presented day-after-day, all across the country, in print, on the air, everywhere one goes. On page one of the *Washington Post*, day after day, after day, after day. Forget Gettysburg, Appomattox, the 1929 Market "Crash," a full decade of "Great" Depression, Tojo, Hitler, Stalin, the Cuban missile crisis, Kennedy's assassination, the others.

The list goes on, as momentum.

In searching for explanations beyond myself I try the "Social Sciences."

Can it be "Demography,": since my birth (1940) the population has tripled, to 330 million. Wonder if your family tripled: how do you control twelve kids if you only had four? (someone just has to "do drugs.")

How about "Economics," : the country has been generally prosperous, certainly compared to other countries and our own past. Is this an inducement for protest? Again, IDK.

"Sociology,": "isms" dominate the culture. They take simple nouns (race, sex) and inflate them to "worldviews" that explain everything (and nothing). They create "targets" (men, whites, systems etc.) and wage "holy war" against them; no holds barred.

"Psychology": the "inner self" can spawn wholesale protest, both real and imagined.

"Politics": does the lack of "survival" issues, as in war/peace, serve only to exaggerate issues that normally would be either bipartisan or even- tempered. By and large, the US has been spared a survival issue since the end of the Twentieth Century, which might explain why otherwise normality becomes catastrophe.

Conclusion: basically there is none. It is either myself or one of the "social scientific" areas mentioned. Perhaps it is even Biology: the Pandemic or the diffusion between races, nations and peoples that so dominate the American psyche. It is, after all, not coincidental that America is the only country on earth dominated by "hyphenated" personalities.

I am an "Irish-American."

Maybe that's the reason!

National Purpose, "Going, Going, Gone"

September 6, 2021

When I ask friends whether the country is "going or gone" they usually look at me quizzically and ask "what do you mean"?

Admittedly, the question is both pessimistic and unnatural as it presupposes that the USA is, indeed, on a trajectory and that this trajectory is headed, at best, nowhere, at worse, to oblivion. Actually, the phrase comes from baseball and is always full of optimism and progress, when a hit-ball heads toward the upper deck while the broadcaster follows its course with the expression, "going, going, gone."

That expression is probably the most "optimistic" in all of baseball as a home run may well represent the epitome of singular accomplishment in the entire sport. (The one exception is a no-hitter, but who is the "greatest" name in the sport, Babe Ruth or Nolan Ryan?)

On a "trajectory" itself implies something that few observers seem to acknowledge in American cultural momentum: is the country on a "path" or headed in a direction, like a home run, that is clearly discernible and even predictable to the average citizen ? Even a cursory coverage of the media, TV, radio, print, and despite intense coverage and opinion from all sides, one rarely gets the feeling that the whole edifice (races, genders. regions, religions etc.) is united on a decided and deliberate "course." To the contrary, one cannot help appreciate that "something, somewhere" is definitely "off-course" but, at bottom, what is the "main course," or are the "sides" all that's on the menu?

Where "the Hell" are we going? To put it another way, if we're supposed to be on Interstate 95, what are we doing on "Circle Drive", downtown Peoria?

Which brings up the central point of this essay, what, if any, "purpose" does American society have, both together and given the diversity of the "separate but equals" ? Is there anything remotely connected to "purpose" that is able to encompass the multiple divides into a whole and deliberative unit ? Literally, the term purpose is defined as "an object or end to be obtained," synonyms being "intention, resolution, determination."

Central to "purpose" is "national" since we are addressing the whole versus its separate parts. Within this notion is the difference between "nation" and "country." The first is sociological, "a group of people that has a common history, language and culture." "Country", by comparison, is mostly political, "the area or region controlled by its government."

Which is the USA? Which should it be?

A related question involves what part of nation/country are we addressing: its inside or its outside, ie. its domestic or its foreign policies? Or, are such distinctions "arbitrary"?

A brief glance backwards might add substance to the questions? As put in another essay here ("America Needs an Enemy") the single greatest incentive for "nation" (or unity) occurred when the threat was "existential," whether it came from within (Civil War) or without (foreign). In this regard perhaps the single most "unified" moment came the day after Pearl Harbor (December 8, 1941) when President Franklin D. Roosevelt proclaimed December 7 a "date which will live in infamy." Perhaps equal in this regard was Abraham Lincoln's second Inaugural, March 4, 1865, when the Civil War was over and Lincoln promised "malice toward none, charity for all."

In the midst of the Cold War, January 20, 1961, President John F. Kennedy's Inaugural speech has gone down in history as possibly the greatest "nationalistic" or unifying declaration of all. Noting that "Liberty" was the single-most prominent identification of American political culture, JFK challenged his nation and the world that the threat was both total and final:

"Let every nation know, whether it wishes us well or ill, that we shall pay any price, bear any burden, meet any hardship, support any friend, oppose any foe to assure the survival and success of Liberty."

At the close, Kennedy raised a question that appears completely contrary to anything remotely relevant in our contemporary political culture: "And so my fellow Americans, ask not what your country can do for you, ask what you can do for your country."

Within this perspective, today's America might just as well reverse the lessons of its greatest leaders: against Lincoln, malice "for all" with charity "toward none"; against Kennedy, asking what your "country can do for you."

It is difficult, if not impossible, to escape the conclusion that today's America is a "country" not a "nation." This is not, necessarily, an "indictment" as a "description." With due regard for the several "sociologies" (racial, gender, area, religious etc.) that comprise our "country" nationalism is, decidedly, not high on the list. The culture is nearly total "domestic" and self-absorbed in its directions and certainly not "existential" minus contrived "threats" (Trump as Hitler). To the contrary, it is almost wholly divisive, internalized and "ideological" in its political behaviors.

Lincoln's famous dictum of 1858, "a house divided against itself cannot stand," is as true now as it was then.

Perhaps this is both intentional and welcomed. Perhaps it may even develop a better society, at least sometime in future centuries. But a country without a decided "purpose," conceived in its infancy and developed over time cannot – by definition -- save its national identity and that of its allies in a global system still defined by nationalism, sovereignty and war.

While the world appears the same since time began, America, by choice, has, once again, turned inward.

Come on in Terror and China, we've been expecting you.

Afghanistan in Perspective

August 16, 2021

Today, August 16, 2021, will probably not go down in history as did Pearl Harbor, declared by President Franklin D. Roosevelt as a "day that will live in infamy." That particular day, December 7, 1941, has, in fact, stood the test of time. But today's day, in 2021, is being declared as much by a host of media pundits, politicians from both parties and most of the public as similar. Why? Because today is the first official acknowledgement that Afghanistan has fallen to the Afghan rebel group, Taliban, after twenty years of American occupation.

Typically, the media now devotes full coverage to the event. As if the ball game began in the ninth inning.

The repercussions of this day, to be sure, are important. A nation does not place its soldiers and its reputation on-the-line in such a faraway and relatively obscure location without expecting at least some measure of compensation or reward. Nor does the "Leader of the Free World" expect its dignity and credibility to remain amidst defeat from a rough-hewn and irregular mob of guerrillas. Worse, the Taliban had already been defeated earlier and had taken the entire country within several days, compared to the overall US occupation.

The spectacle of the US defeat rises higher than mere embarrassment: the loss of effort and finances (estimated two trillion dollars), the commitment of soldiers and their families, especially combat deaths (2,400), the legacy of physical and mental ailments that will burden the country for years and decades, the global repercussions from the notion that the American commitment, under any circumstance, has little or no credibility and, finally, the companion notion that "superpower" status as the creator of "world order" will inevitably be occupied by someone else (China?).

These are the potential consequences for the United States. Consequences for Afghanistan are immeasurable by western standards, but "tragic" by any comparable or historic criteria. For the US, with global responsibilities and centuries of involvement, it was a strategic and costly mistake; for Afghanistan it could well be the "end of the line."

But in assessing the lasting consequences of Afghanistan a degree of historic perspective might help.

Consider the beginnings of the USA as a country. Within five years (1776-1781) a relative handful of American irregular soldiers (less than one quarter of the population), led by a comparative few "radical" Patriots had ousted the world's ranking "superpower" from control of much of the American continent. They went-on to establish an independent nation with political principles that continue to this day as the singular inspiration for freedom and liberty the world over.

The "losers," on the other hand, themselves went-on to develop the greatest Navy in world history and, at its peak, controlled all seven major oceans and twenty-five percent of the globe's geography and population. Within one hundred years they had allied with their former enemies to win the two greatest world wars in all history plus the Cold War with World Communism.

Not bad for a few million islanders isolated on a northern corner of the European continent.

After the Spanish-American War (1898) the US took responsibility for "democracy" and stability throughout the region, with over twenty-five military occupations, especially in Haiti, Panama, The Dominican Republic and Nicaragua. Decades later they had all failed miserably, especially in Nicaragua which the Marines had governed since 1912. To change this President-elect Hoover made a "good will" tour of Latin America (1928) while his Secretary of State (Henry L. Stimson) told reporters (1932) that the time for US interventions was through. When asked if he would intervene again, he responded "Not on your life." At the same time the State Department issued a memo that in Nicaragua it was "preferable to run the risk of revolutionary disturbances now and let the strong man emerge without further waste of time." The Marines felt the same, with a private memo concerning "the good name of the Navy and Marine Corps, which would be getting out with the stigma of having failed in its job and withdrawing in the face of reverses."

The net result of these events came with Franklin D. Roosevelt's "Good Neighbor Policy (1933) and the subsequent creation of the Organization of American States (OAS, 1948), two of the greatest achievements in the history of American diplomacy.

Do we recall April 30, 1975, the day when North Vietnamese regular soldiers first entered Saigon, South Vietnam, thus ending the US twenty-five year engagement (back to the Truman Administration) to "contain" Communism in that country? By its end the Vietnam War took the lives of over 58,000 American soldiers, several times that figure crippled plus over two million Vietnamese and cost the American taxpayer close to one trillion dollars (in today's value). Bombing tonnage by the US Air Force exceeded three times the tonnage of all theaters of World War Two. Not to mention the many years of domestic unrest and protest against the war, including the suspension of classes in over 250 colleges in one year alone (1968). The image of that day, April 30, is now being compared to Afghanistan in the current media machine as a reminder of the "doomsday" consequences of failed foreign "entanglements."

Personally, I remember the "day" as if it were yesterday. Walter Cronkite made the announcement on his nightly show as did all other networks. Graphic scenes of Vietnamese clinging to helicopters and planes dominated, the lines of civilians trying to exit were shown as they are today. Scenes of NVA soldiers entering embassy and other buildings gave no doubt as to what was happening. Vietnam was over, and they all "moved on."

The networks then showed weather and sports. The Malls stayed busy, traffic was heavy, schools open and business was "usual."

The next day was May 1, nothing to report. Within a few years movie actor Ronald Reagan declared "morning in America." He held five summits with Gorbachev of the Soviet Union. In 1989 the Berlin Wall came down, two years later so did the Soviet Union. The Governor of Arkansas won election in '92 on the slogan "it's the economy stupid" (and he probably meant both parts). Most the world declared America the new "superpower."

The rest, so they say, is "history." Vietnam today is with the US and other countries against China.

Conclusion: Will August 16 be remembered next month, the next six, next year? Ten years away? There are 193 countries in the world (UN), Afghanistan is one.

There is an old saying: "Success is never final, failure is never fatal."

What is "final"? What is "never"? How will each influence how the US responds to August 16, 2021?

Why Do They Hate This Country?

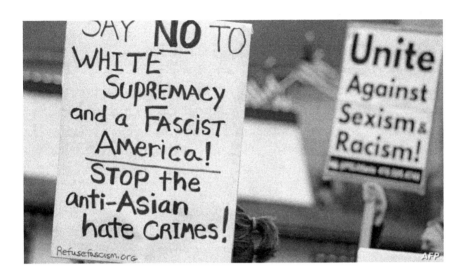

June 27, 2021

Of all the countries in the history of the world one might think that the United States of America would be the most loved, respected and even exalted compared to all others. This is not just a sentimental and biased reflection from an American national but can be amply supported by a host of data, indicators and the overall historic record.

Nor does the assertion ignore or gloss over the multiplication of mistakes, errors of policy and judgment plus social experience that has plagued the American past.

The first, and probably most critical, task is to uncover the fundamental meaning of the word "hate" and to appreciate if it belongs in the cultural milieu. The key expressions of the strict dictionary meaning is "intense and passionate dislike," which defines "love" as the same without the preface "dis" at the end. They both can be easily demonstrated in the public arena but neither definition explains reasons why.

Foregoing the sociological "whys" of the love-hate scenario, one would have to be both blind and deaf to contradict that both sentiments now dominate popular discourse, no matter where or when each emotion surfaces. Emotion, as well, must also be recognized as the dominate persuasion in this discourse, as opposed to "intellectual," "reflective" or "dispassionate."

Defined as the "… instinctive state of mind deriving from circumstances, mood or relationships," emotion prevails when and wherever such discussions arise, either at a sporting event, TV or newspaper op-ed, campus talk or dinner chatter. Evident of this phenomenon was a recent Virginia Board of Education meeting that ended with fist-fights between both sides of an educational issue (Critical Race Theory). The national disruptions from the symbolic death of George Floyd last year only highlights this national mania. Also symbolic is the literature itself, such as the feminist tract *Rage Becomes Her, the Power of Women's Anger* (Soraya Chemaly). At one point in 2020 the New York Times top ten bestsellers (nonfiction) were all, repeat all, on the issue of American "racism."

To ask "why" all of this requires a psychiatrist's couch (and I don't have one). But the cause of today's issues can be traced to the beginning of the Republic, as our first president once (1796) wrote in his Farewell Address on the subject "spirit of party":

"This spirit, unfortunately, is inseparable from our nature, having its roots in the strongest passions of the human mind. … It serves always to distract the public councils and enfeeble the public administration. It agitates the community with ill-founded jealousies and false alarms, kindles the animosity of one part against another, foments occasional riot and insurrection. It opens the door to foreign influence and corruption …"

Sound familiar?

If there is anything "systemic" in this country (as opposed to "racism") it would be this.

Yet all of this belies the otherwise beneficial history of the USA, despite the many faults one can find in its "sociology." As representative of the "human condition," the American "people" reflect the self-same shortcomings that geopolitical realities have visited upon the remainder of humanity, to include poverty, slavery, dictatorship, social division, depression, crime, sectional jealously, gang rivalries, geographical distinctions etc etc.

The distinct American contribution to this "human condition" has been the political: "life, liberty, the pursuit of happiness" and all that followed this declaration through civil war, depression, inequity and, now, cultural distinctions based on emotion and ideology.

Can the country overcome the current cultural outpourings and survive? History says yes:

Item, the American contribution in warfare may well be the greatest in all history: victory in the two greatest wars of all time by a nation embedded with isolationism, divided at home and with an anti-military cultural past;

Item, near half-century of "Cold War" against world Communism, ending with the dissolution of the Soviet Union, without a "shot being fired" amidst tens of thousands of nuclear weapons;

Item, the introduction of a "democratic" mission in the political world and the establishment of a "world order" based on that principle and still evident seventy years afterward;

Item, survival of a civil war that took nearly 3% of the population but restored a unity that has held together since;

Item, survival of an economic depression that saw 25% unemployed and the closure of 9,000 banks in a decade, resulting afterward in the greatest prosperity regime of all history;

Item, arrival of an unprecedented historical "superpower" status (1991) by acclamation despite a deep history of isolation from world politics and deep social divisions at home.

Item, Domestic concentration on a single group (Black) since the end of World War II with about 12% of the population, which at times can occupy almost 100% media and government concentration (with an array of programs, plans and policies), a concentration either unprecedented in all history or profoundly rare.

To answer the (above) questions on the future remains a speculation. The weight of "evidence" (above) suggests a positive response, but the "human condition" (above) is a "jury still out."

Conclusion: I once had a deep cut on my arm. When asked if it was serious, I replied, "it depends on how much I scratch."

Does History "Repeat"?

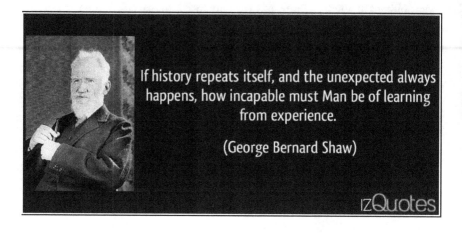

If history repeats itself, and the unexpected always happens, how incapable must Man be of learning from experience.

(George Bernard Shaw)

IZQuotes

March 28, 2021

The title of this book already answers the question in the affirmative, ie. there is a natural momentum between the past, present and future and they are all inter-related, not just by convenience, but by necessity. How else could it possibly be?

Perhaps the most quoted expression on the topic came in 1931 when a Spanish philosopher (although he taught at Harvard) laid down this maxim for eternity: "those who do not remember the past are condemned to repeat it" (Jorge Santayana).

Yet what did he mean by "repeat"? There are at least two meanings to the term. Did he mean that specific events occur in repetition? Then, we shall expect Germany to invade France again, for the US to invade Mexico, for America to fall as with Rome etc. etc. *ad infinitum*. This is much too exact to be of any use.

Second, is an endless and cyclical "pattern" of events that occur in such regularity that they may be said to "repeat." Indeed, there are many of such "events" that have occurred so often that they can be labeled as "repetitive," "cyclical" or in such patterns that they constitute the essence of history itself.

It is not difficult to identify such occurrences and the very first would almost always be "war." There have been so many wars in recorded history that it makes little difference exactly how many. Some may say 10,000, others 100,000 but the number pales compared to the "pattern." Wars "repeat" always and everywhere, and that, alone, is sufficient.

Santayana also mentioned those who do not "remember" history. Does this imply that, au contraire, only those who study history are able to avoid war? But this too cannot be the case since wars have occurred in rapid succession and often by the same leaders and the same soldiers. Thus, warfare, by definition, either has no "lessons" whatsoever or that they have been ignored throughout time and experience.

Finally, Santayana declared that we are "condemned" to repeat history, implying that this ignorance is both determined and tragic. Yet, warfare is a decision that rational beings have been undertaking since time began and, likewise, is often held as the highest nobility.

War may be "mass murder" but why is there Memorial Day and why do nations honor their soldiers and send them off with parades and welcome them back with flowers? Why are all veterans "thanked" for their "service" and why do so many books/movies celebrate their killing behaviors? Why is "anti" war sentiment called "protest"?

Still, when all is said and done, we are left with Santayana and that remains true now, yesterday and tomorrow.

But war is hardly alone in its "repetitive" quality. What else is? Answer: almost everything. Peace is repetitive, just as well as war. So is marriage, divorce, the family, group, nation, state, empire, crime, punishment, emotion, intellect, birthdays, life, death. What else? Answer (again): everything.

So life repeats, what else is new? More importantly, what is to be gained by the knowledge? History may be taught but there is no record of it having been "learned."

Answer (again): "perspective." Defined precisely as "meaningful proportion ... to perceive things in their actual interrelations or comparative importance." Indeed, perspective may well be the most important (only?) "lesson" that history teaches.

Such lessons can apply to cultural life as well as incessant warfare.

Perhaps an example from daily American life will suffice. It will come as no surprise that "racism" has replaced all other words in the current American political culture, probably ahead of number two, "terrorism." But there have been race and terror since time began. The difference is the "ism" attached.

Each share qualities that, in effect, define the nature and content of the culture as it has emerged. But there are caveats.

First, they defy precise definition but attempt to explain almost everything. Second, they use simple nouns (race, sex,) and add "ism" to become "worldviews." This allows them to define life itself, target enemies, plan programs, elevate normal events and promulgate. Third, although definitions are avoided both racism and terrorism need no such precision. One "knows" them when one "sees" them, from conversations ("N" word) to alleged murders (George Floyd), to massacres (9/11).

Yet, both expressions have precedents and are related, more explicitly, "adopted," in America today. From this background, how does "racism" have any "perspective"?

A simple fact might help. Before 1870 French armies invaded German territory on about 30 occasions. After 1870 (Franco-Prussian War) Germany returned the favor twice, producing the greatest wars in human history with over 100 million dead. All these armies represented countries from the same ("white") race, yet they killed on a scale unknown to any aspect of "racism" here or elsewhere. By far! The American Civil War itself killed about 750,000 soldiers, nearly all white. Incessant warfare since time began has been between mostly the "same" racial groupings. This fact alone makes the term "nationalism" a far more powerful explanation for human behavior than mere "racism." Terms such as "chosen people" or "master race" come to mind.

Race, in turn, is a mere derivative of nation, a noun that historically has been used with language, location, clothes, food, history, theater, sports, religion etc. as a definition of "people."

Today in America, nationalism is identified solely with the adjective "white." This is both artificial, simplistic and grossly misleading, as is the contemporary "Black Lives Matter." Nationalism has been, and still is, the most powerful sociological factor since man first settled into groups. America today remains the only country on earth dominated by hyphenated "sub-groups", each reflecting "quasi" nations. So why invent "new" terms when we are dealing with ancient realities?

From this perspective, would not "African" nationalism better describe the domestic cultural situation than mere "racism"? The word "nation" connotes a comprehensive and optimistic people united within itself and sharing far more than just race with the same history and future goals. "Racism," by contrast, connotes a defensive sociology ("oppressed"), united by enemies and dependent upon change by others for both its past and future. Would it not be better to advance on your own virtues rather than on the vices attributed to all others?

To put perspective into colloquial terms: millions have been killed for centuries on either side of the Rhine River, while a recent death in Minneapolis has paralyzed America with "systemic racism." This replaces history and reflection with ideology for the explanation of human behavior.

With a degree of perspective, how does current US public life compare? Or do words have no more meaning than their own time and circumstance? We can "war" on drugs, crime, poverty and terror but how do these words relate to Pearl Harbor, to Gettysburg to Vietnam? How does George Floyd compare to the Holocaust, to 600 murders every year in Chicago?

The net result of such stupendous confusion boggles the mind and questions if there is coherence and consistency still remaining in any public human endeavor. Do "words" have any lasting meaning?

Is the US unique in this or do all other countries behave within the same circular pattern?

Do we just move on and ask "so what" does anything before have to do with me? Do I just "invent" new realities hoping that they might appear unique? In this sense, we risk becoming "ahistorical," nothing counts, only "here and now."

Does this mean that, as Francis Fukuyama famously put it, that history has "ended"?

Ask the families of victims after 9/11. Ask Black Lives Matter which basically reinvents the commandment "thou shalt not kill."

There is a depressing corollary to these modern notions, as if after 6,000 years all we have for hope is that we be spared more brutalities .

History repeats but cannot be erased.

There is "nothing new under the sun".

Is Unity Necessary?

March 24, 2021

Embedded within the American populace, and as a general proposition, is the notion that "unity" as a societal goal is needed for nearly everything. Conversely, disunity, or synonyms "anarchy, dissent, schism, discord" etc., is generally considered as a lasting impediment to progress of any kind and as symbolic of decline, erosion or actual disappearance.

These notions are commonplace through human institutions of any variety and appear to be both inarguable, obvious and universal.

Even within an atmosphere of profound disarray the call for unity will often appear, if only as a "last resort" before the "roof caves in." President Biden made unity the theme of his Inaugural, especially in the face of widespread opposition to the validity of his election and, equally, as a need of national renewal for his own future.

Indeed, as a possible salvation for *any* future whatsoever.

Biden could not help noting the dominance of disunion, "We must end this uncivil war that pits red against blue, rural versus urban, conservative versus liberal." In identifying the "causes" of the discord he located three "faults" within the body politic: "political extremism, white supremacy, domestic terrorism."

Yet, by identifying causes, the new president was merely listing (unknowingly) elements of the "human condition" that have dominated the history of life from the very beginning, either in America itself or universal in both time and place. Ie. "what else is new"?

While his intentions must be acknowledged as positive, President Biden came no closer to solutions than any leader from Caesar to Napoleon to Roosevelt in history. Rather than stop the drift toward collapse, he may unwittingly have advanced it, if for no other reason than by identifying the faults of the political culture itself, he risks hardening those who may have fit his own personal descriptions.

Specifically:

Colors: "blue-gray" in the Civil War is now "red-blue," as "white" overnight is disparaged as a source for all things divisive while "black" becomes the object of contrition, sentiment and reward from percentage allowances to cash endowments. "Red" as in "skin" is removed as an identity while "people of color" advance under any definition so long as it is neither white or black (beige may fit). "Yellow" as an earlier immigrant "peril" (Chinese) now loses its image and answers to "Asian" only, with the self-same color ID changed to a geopolitical region. "Lavender" has been symbolic as a color-description of the "gay community," while "bluebloods" represent an inherited aristocracy now replaced by merely "rich" (color not yet assigned).

But America as "color-coded" may have just begun, as the Crayola box is quite large.

Sectional: by noting the "rural versus urban" distinction, we only are identifying that those two remain as the most dominant (only?) sectional descriptions used throughout history. Of course there is "suburban" but that has yet to catch on as a civil "divide" (although mostly Republican).

In the nineteenth century America was 90% farm; it is now 1.3%, but this profound shift has yet to affect the political expressions, still the symbol of division.

Political Expressions: by listing "conservative-liberal" as a division President Biden (inadvertantly) has tried to eliminate the term "Political Science" altogether, either as a term for division or as an attribute of the subject itself. Without this "division" there is no democratic politics at all, only a false "unity" derived from single-party rule.

True, politics as it has developed from ancient Greece would stop in its footsteps as would any form of liberal government mankind has known.

On the positive side: no argument, no divisions.

Faults: by identifying the three political "vices," "extremism, supremacy, terrorism" as exclusively "domestic" and identified by "groups" President Biden, as before, has only "reinvented the wheel."

Theoretically, under his regime, he promised, in turn, a priority of results that fit, exactly, into the same pattern of semantical "solutions" that could accommodate any and all ideals of political and human perfection. Specifically, he proposed to end American divisions with the promise to "right wrongs, put people to work [and] teach our children."

Such a fine-tuned profile of blatant sophistry may satisfy the voting public as turning ideals into results but any reflection must expose the design as fraught with dangers of promises unfulfilled. Cynics might politely ask, were "wrongs" "righted" before his Inaugural, did people "work" or were children ever "taught"?

Two months into the Biden Administration the divisions that plagued the country in its history seemed to have gone nowhere, "same old same old." This is not (necessarily) to blame the President; his fault is as ancient as those he so earnestly attacked. The issue, likewise, is equally ancient: idealist designs versus stubborn (human) realities.

But the lasting question still remains: can America, any country, perform its basic duties and privileges minus a unification deemed necessary for bare survival? This is particularly appropriate in foreign policy.

The record will indicate that America has already done this, with results unprecedented in history.

America was conceived and born within a society wherein less than one-third supported revolution. It has survived these divisions inside Civil War, economic depression, sectional, class and party divides and has won the greatest wars in human history plus the Cold War long before the terms "racist," "white privilege" or "Me Too" became the fashion.

How could a country where women couldn't vote, where Blacks were segregated and lynched, where unemployment savaged the poor while millions lived in tenements and women and children worked twelve-hour days (but "privileged") do all this in the political world?

America in the Twentieth Century did more for humanity than any single sovereignty in all of recorded history (assertion). And from an isolated, politically divided, backwater ex-colony that was nearly cut in-half by Civil War (See essay, "America Needs an Enemy" below).

Answer: leadership promoted the basic and essential values of the nation, from the beginning, that lifted it to "supremacy" home and abroad in the first place and kept it there until the "time had come."

Where is "leadership" today?

When will the "time come" (again, ever)?

Or, has anyone seen "Honest Abe"?

America Needs an Enemy

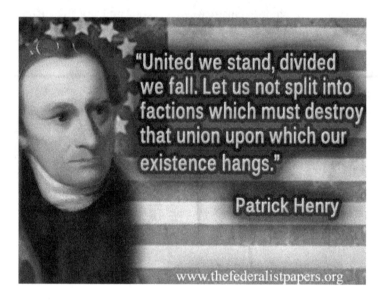

"United we stand, divided we fall. Let us not split into factions which must destroy that union upon which our existence hangs."

Patrick Henry

www.thefederalistpapers.org

March 8, 2021

After their fifth (and last) summit Premier Gorbachev of the old Soviet Union is alleged to have told President Reagan something like this: "I have done you a disservice, I have deprived you of an enemy."

This story is probably true in one form or another as it has become nearly iconic in retelling. But whether it is true or not is basically irrelevant since the story reveals an ancient truth of the American past: that division has been an essential reality of US history and that the only unity ever derived came from outside threats.

Americans apparently do not know this, but Gorbachev, at least, did.

True enough, the quest for unity has been a theme from the very beginning of the Republic, including President Biden's inspiring Inaugural. But upon reflection what political entity has ever, just once, devoted itself for a divided populace? Has anyone ever proclaimed the inverted slogan "divided we stand, united we fall."? Of all the human conceptual designs from the Declaration of Independence to the movement for "inclusion" in current rhetoric the word "equality" stands, alone, above all others.

While equality may not actually be "self-evident" (quite the opposite) it remains a symbol that has inspired generations of Americans to strive for a unity that has for at least 250 years proven elusive by their own definitions. Failure to attain the desired result has by-no-means dampened the quest but, ironically, has served only to double the effort. Today, "equality" instead of "liberty" has become the American "cause," despite contrary evidence from the very beginning.

But "Faith" (from Theology) overrules evidence every time.

Encouraged by such expressions as "give me liberty or give me death," Americans fought a long and protracted war for independence that succeeded as much from foreign help than from themselves. The active assistance from France, Spain and other enemies of Great Britain proved too much for the British Crown, which finally gave way to the Patriots amidst an exhaustive war on global fronts rather than from the colonies alone.

This aspect of America's beginning has been presented in the landmark book by William Wegner, *The Key To American Independence* (2018) which details over 69 billion dollars of aid from France and over 16 billion from Spain, the Netherlands and Sweden (in current values). The critical assistance from the French Navy at Yorktown (1781) proved to be the "nail in the coffin" from the British perspective.

But not only were foreign countries friendly to the colonists but the victory was accomplished within a divided populace in which most "Americans" were at least "neutral," if not "hostile." The American Revolution was won despite an "inequality" that saw approximately 75% of the populace refuse to support or service the revolt. The issue of "Loyalists" inside the country proved to be a problem to the opposing "Patriots" that matched the issue of Redcoats invading the home soil. In this respect, the Revolution was America's first "civil" war, as the following reflection of a British Chaplin attests:

> "These Americans so soft, pacific and benevolent by nature, are here transformed into monsters, implacably bloody and ravenous; party rage has kindled the spirit of hatred between them, they attack and rob each other by turns, destroy dwelling houses or establish themselves therein by driving out those who had before dispossessed others."

Off to a "bad" start.

In 1796 George Washington, in his Farewell Address, noted how party and sectional differences have shaped the new nation into bitter divisions:

> "It serves always to distract the public councils and enfeeble the public administration. It agitates the community with ill-founded jealousies and false alarms, kindles the animosity of one part against another, foments occasionally riot and insurrection. It opens the door to foreign influence and corruption, which finds a facilitated access to the government itself through the channels of party passion."

Sound familiar?

The history of America since the very beginning has demonstrated the multiple sectional and human divides that have occupied the country since. Despite a facade of unity these divides include Civil War itself, sectional and political separations, economic depression, class and racial distinctions, the very sexual and gender composition of humanity, the replacement of pronouns, place names and school districts and an entire "sub-culture" intent on the displacement of American history itself. Being "born again" means "starting over," as though there was no past in the first place.

National disruption in the name of unity is no accident; it is both intentional and the objective.

Together these, at a minimum, have removed any and all pretenses of a unified populace into what is now color-coordinated ("red, blue") that has replaced the "blue-gray" divide of the Civil War, an event that killed more soldiers than all foreign conflicts combined (with less than one tenth of the current population).

Gorbachev may have overstated his reference, but he had a point. Americans may well have reached the pinnacle of unity on December 8, 1941 when Franklin D. Roosevelt declared Pearl Harbor a "date that will live in infamy."

There have been three distinct reasons for American unity in the past (however temporal): Germany, Japan and Russia.

Apparently fear is a greater motivation than hope.

Remembering the Kellogg Briand Pact

February 21, 2021

Readers will be forgiven if they have no idea about the subject of this essay. Yet, at one point in time, the "Pact" was signed by 62 countries of the world and most people, especially in the US and France, believed that it would lead to an eventual "peace on earth" based on political liberty.

Kellogg was Francis Kellogg the American Secretary of State under Calvin Coolidge and Briand was Aristide Briand, French Prime Minister for eleven governments in the early twentieth century. Kellogg served before as Republican Senator from Minnesota and as such voted for ratification of the 1919 Treaty of Versailles. Briand, in his long tenure as PM of France, received the 1926 Nobel Peace Prize for the Locarno Treaty bringing Germany into the League of Nations. He also introduced a memorandum into the League in 1929 advocating a "Regime of European Federal Union," which, in retrospect, was the original forerunner of today's "European Union."

The legacy of The Great War (World War I) that took 10 million lives without solving anything was so consuming, especially in France, that countries continued to seek any number of alternatives so that it would never happen again. In April 1927 Briand wrote to the Coolidge Administration for a joint, bilateral treaty outlawing war between the two countries. The US agreed but insisted that it become universal so as not to resemble an "alliance." The result, called the "Pact of Paris," came on August 27, 1928 when Germany, France and the US signed the agreement not to use war to resolve "disputes or conflicts of whatever nature or of whatever origin they may be."

Within a short time all major countries in the world signed on, including all three eventual Axis countries and the Soviet Union. The US Senate approved 85 – 1. Enacted outside of the League of Nations, the Pact of Paris remains "legal" to this day, the last member, Barbados, joining in 1971.

Today, the Pact is notable only for what it *didn't* do, and it remains as a lasting reminder of the incapacity of "legal-moral" persuasions to control interstate conflict. Typical was commentator Eric Sevareid's assessment of the Pact on national television as "a worthless piece of paper." Historian Ian Kershaw summarized history's verdict on the Pact as "vacuous," and that it "was a dead letter from the moment it was signed" (*To Hell and Back*, p. 181, 2016).

Obviously, the Pact failed in its central (and only) mission, to prevent war. True, but a major question remains: was it the treaty that failed or the enforcement? For it is also true that, beyond the Pact itself, all other attempts to prevent World War II, to include appeasement, isolation, alliances, occupation, reparations, diplomacy, trade, aid, etc etc , failed equally if not more-so.

Although the legacy of the 1928 Pact remains buried under the demands of, first, the Cold War, and now global anarchy, terrorism, emigration and intra-state violence a case can be made that its "burial" as a force for peace, quoting Mark Twain, may be a bit "premature."

Recent examinations of the Pact give a much broader and more general assessment of its lasting effects. Political Scientists Scott Shapiro and Oona Hathaway conclude that it paved the way for the more familiar and modern aspects of world politics: "As its effects reverberated across the globe, .it reshaped the world map, catalyzed the human rights revolution, enabled the use of economic sanctions … and ignited the explosion of international organizations." (*The Internationalists*, 2017, p. xv). Similarly, Julie Bunck and Michael Fowler have noted that "In criminalizing war Kellogg-Briand played a role in the development of a new norm of behavior in international relations, a norm that continues to play a role in our current international order." (*Tulane Journal of International Law*, 2018).

The main reason for the failure of the Pact was the rise of the militaristic nations in the interwar period. Both Germany and Japan were original signatories but in the 1930's economic depression and national Fascism drove both toward military regimes intent on war for expansion and survival. Both walked out of the League of Nations and began a series of military conquests that, by 1942, saw each in control of most the political globe save Britain and the Western Hemisphere. Under such circumstances the western democracies had no choice but to fight back, while the Pact blended into historic oblivion.

Is there a chance for a revival of the Kellogg-Briand Pact?

The legacy is the first hurdle to overcome. The notoriety of the Pact to stop aggression is widespread and "rule by law" has become a dated anachronism for western statesmanship.

Second, to succeed any new Pact has to be universal. That means both Russia and China, the only two countries who conceivably could overthrow today's international order. While both exhibit ambitions and expansionist tendencies there is no indication (yet) that they might behave in Fascistic or militaristic designs reminiscent of Hitler or Tojo.

Is it worth the gamble for western leaders? Since the end of the Cold War (1991) there have been few if any bold and deliberate vehicles presented to make warfare "illegal." That would be the single and "only" purpose of any new Pact. Not to end rivalry, ambition, expansion, alliances but to end warfare as an "instrument of national policy" (original language).

Of course there is always the possibility that it might not work.

Then again, it might. But the same can be said of war.

What are the odds?

Is there another Aristide Briand somewhere on planet earth?

Irish Pride

November 21, 2020

According to the census, there are over 36 million Irish Americans living in the United States, approximately 11.9 % of the total. Practically all of these are Roman Catholics but if the 3.5 million Protestant Irish from Ulster were added ("Scotch Irish") the figure would be over 12%. This exceeds ten times the current population of Ireland itself.

The Irish contribution to American life began very early. Approximately 50,000 to 100,000 Irish arrived in the New World in the 1600's, 75% of them Catholic. In the 1700's another 100,000 arrived. While most of the Catholics gathered in urban areas such as Boston and New York, where they would dominate big-city politics for centuries, the Scotch Irish tended to settle in the Appalachian Mountain regions where they would influence cultural strains ranging from to folk and country music, military skills and, later on, stock car racing.

Despite ingrained discrimination against newcomers, the Irish contribution was felt from the beginnings of the American nation. Eight Irish Americans signed the Declaration of Independence and large numbers served in

Washington's armies, prompting one British General to tell the House of Commons that, "half the rebel Continental Army were from Ireland."

But the great influx of Irish immigrants, almost all of them Catholic, began in the nineteenth century and continued throughout, particularly after the Great Potato Famine of the late 1840's. Between 1820 and 1860 approximately 2 million arrived, where they labored in canal building, lumbering, police and fire work and urban construction in the cities of the northeast, Chicago, St. Louis and San Francisco. During the Civil War hundreds of thousands of Irish served, especially with the Union where over 38 regiments had the word "Irish" in their title. The great General Phil Sheridan himself was descendant from Irish parents.

Between 1860 and 1900 still another 2 million arrived, with Annie Moore from Cork being the first person in history to enter Ellis Island. By 1910 there were more Irish in New York than in Dublin itself.

But the nineteenth century was a period of both discrimination and assimilation for Irish-Americans. Prejudice against Irish Catholics reached a peak in the mid-1850's with the "Know Nothing" movement, which tried to oust Catholics from public office and to restrict Irish (and foreign) immigration. Later, other forms of prejudice, including violence, made Irish-American life nearly intolerable. In 1871, for example, New York's "Orange" riots, incited by Protestant mobs, celebrated the battle of the Boyne by marching through Irish neighborhoods, resulting in over 60 deaths.

But the worst part of discrimination was far more subtle and sophisticated. The sign "No Irish Need Apply" became a symbol of the nineteenth century refusal of employers to hire Irish for little more than menial jobs. Irish Catholics were stereotyped in the media of the time as being controlled by the Papacy and as being violent drunks. Political cartoonist Thomas Nast played to these sentiments by portraying New York's Irish political machine Tammany Hall as a ferocious tiger.

The Irish responded by creating institutions that sought to change such images and to assimilate themselves into American life. In 1882 the Knights of Columbus was founded by Father Michael McGivney to provide insurance for Catholic families whose husbands and fathers were killed on the job. The nationwide Catholic parochial school system was largely an effort to teach (largely) Irish children to compete against the WASP world on equal terms. The result was strict discipline in the classroom, uniformed and regimented students but future generations of Irish Americans that would help shape America in the twentieth century.

The contributions of the Irish to America in modern times cannot be adequately summarized in a short editorial. They are, as well, common knowledge and imbedded in American culture in every imaginable walk of life: politics and government, religion, sports, literature, the arts, police and fire work, the judicial system etc. The Honor Roll would include thousands of Irish American leaders, such as John F. Kennedy, Fulton J. Sheen, Mother Jones, George M. Cohan, James J. Braddock, James Michael Curley, Victor Herbert, Eugene O'Neill, Ed Sullivan, Grace Kelly, Georgia O'Keefe, Maureen O'Hara, James Cagney, Spencer Tracy, Pierce Brosnan, Jackie Gleason, the "fighting Sullivans" of World War II, F. Scott Fitzgerald, John O'Sullivan, Flannery O'Connor, Walter O'Malley and to bring it up to our current political climate: President-elect Joe Biden and commentators such as Pat Buchanan, Sean Hannity and Bill O' Reilly.

The Irish heritage, however, has deeper roots in the culture than its luminaries; it comprises the tens of millions of otherwise unknown Irish Americans (such as myself) who contribute on a daily basis to the movement of American society in all of its manifestations.

As a symbol of the Irish contribution to American culture there is probably none better than the golden dome of Notre Dame, South Bend, Indiana, where generations of football fans have spent their Saturday afternoons passionately rooting for the "Fighting Irish." Most of today's Irish rarely fight, but probably few are bothered by the mascot.

Crusader State

May 11, 2020

In his classic 1997 study on American foreign policies, Walter McDougall (University of Pennsylvania) divides the subject into old and new "testaments," between the time when the country was young and weak and since it became a global power (*Promised Land, Crusader State*). Both time periods were derived from the same geopolitical and ideological sources, and both are still alive today, pandemic or not.

In short, the division McDougall asserts is simply between an isolationist country unable to affect events beyond its shores and the internationalist nation that won two consecutive world wars and a Cold War and maintains whatever "world order" is still alive today.

The division is both appropriate and relevant and will stay that way indefinitely. In some ways, this disparity goes beyond human decision, regardless of whether or not one approves of President Trump or joins either political party.

The men who governed America in the nineteenth century did not choose isolation; it was forced on them by circumstance. In 1823, the Monroe Doctrine was proclaimed to allow the U.S. to supervise the entire Western Hemisphere.

Nine years earlier, the British Army burned Washington, D.C. (1814). Can a country that cannot protect its own Capitol supervise Brazil or Argentina? During the Civil War, British shipyards were supplying Confederate "blockade runners" against the Union Navy. When the Cabinet suggested declaring war on Britain, President Lincoln replied, "Gentlemen, please, one war at a time."

The time when America began an assertive global reach is called "Wilsonian" since President Woodrow Wilson used U.S. entry into World War I as a design to "make the world safe for democracy." Yet Wilson could not even persuade the Senate to pass the peace treaty, and America descended into another period of intense isolation, broken only in 1941 at Pearl Harbor.

With the end of World War II (1945), the U.S. began the process all over again, demobilizing nearly all of its 16 million military personnel and passing the "GI Bill" for an anticipated war-free world. Not so fast, USA.

As Foreign Service Officer Joseph M. Jones described in his classic book, *The Fifteen Weeks*, it took just that long for the U.S. to dispense with any pretensions of neutrality or isolation to come to the rescue of Britain and western Europe against the potential of a world dominated by communism and the Soviet Union. Within that time period came four historic events that transformed a "promised land" into an authentic "crusader state" that forever (perhaps) cast American power on to a global landscape, for "better or for worse."

The first was the Truman Doctrine (March 12, 1947) that promised aid and assistance to Greece and Turkey against the Soviet Union and on behalf of "free peoples everywhere." The second was the Marshall Plan announced at Harvard June 5, 1947, which provided history's largest foreign aid package against a war-ravaged Europe and, literally, saved the entire area from starvation and occupation. The third was the Berlin Airlift (June 24, 1948 – September 30, 1949) that saved the two million people of West Berlin from the same and, to this day, represents maybe the greatest voluntary contribution any democracies made for another country, a former enemy twice removed. On one day alone, April 15-16, 1949, U.S. and Allied airplanes made over 1,383 round trips to that beleaguered city, one landing every 30 seconds. The total mileage for the whole operation was 92 million miles, the distance from the earth to the sun. The fourth was the North Atlantic Treaty, April 4, 1949, that for the first time in history guaranteed a peacetime American military role in any world strategic event.

That was seventy years ago. NATO still stands with 30 members and still represents the vestiges of a world order that was the culmination of the sudden, "revolutionary" transformation of a formerly domestic-engaged nation whose "Manifest Destiny" was once fulfilled at the shoreline of the Pacific Ocean.

What has changed? Or, more appropriately, what's new? The answer: nothing – same old, same old.

In 1991, after the collapse of the Soviet Union and world communism as well, the United States began "doing it all over again," as if nothing had happened. Taking the advice of former Reagan UN Ambassador Jeanne Kirkpatrick, the U.S. went back into a "normal country in a normal time," an invitation to return to the original plan (when there were thirteen states and a whole continent left).

As if to reinforce the new plan, the Governor of Arkansas was elected in 1992 on the slogan "it's the economy stupid," while the incumbent (Bush I) forgot his pledge against "new taxes" with an apology that he was troubled with foreign policies, or "that vision thing."

It's been "downhill" since, with "assertive multilateralism," "leading from behind," and "MAGA" all reflecting that neither "crusader" nor "promised land" are designs that reflect any tradition or purpose from the Founding Fathers, or any subsequent thoughts on America's role in the world.

At this point in time, it may be appropriate to remind ourselves that America was conceived in "revolution," one whose final destination is yet undetermined. Nor did the Founding thoughts rest on the notion that revolution was a passive or empty pursuit, that the break from England was but a change in authority. From the very beginning, it was assumed that America's "cause" in the political globe was to affect change, and, like the Jesuit Order, the goal was to "convert" rather than stand alone, "a city upon a hill."

As early as 1780, Jefferson made this mission clear in his "Empire of Liberty" address, "as she has never surveyed since the creation and I am persuaded no constitution was ever before so well calculated as ours for extensive empire and self-government."

It is past time that we recognize that we are the heirs of Jefferson and the generations who were equally "persuaded," so that America's mission in the world rises far above the resentments and accusations that have come to dominate today's public discourse.

Maybe someone could just give a speech on that, even if he doesn't really mean it.

The Only Game in Town

(with QB Bart Starr) May 27, 2020

When asked about "winning," legendary football coach Vince Lombardi replied, "it's not just the most important question, it's the only one."

If asked about American foreign policy today, what would be a comparable answer? What is "winning" to America in the world? Undoubtedly, the answers would be as different and as contentious as the personalities and their backgrounds. But there must be a favorable and useful response that would provide a bare consensus to both the history and values that have supported the American experience from the beginning. Otherwise, there is nothing there, as though each football team plays for sheer pleasure or money.

The answer goes deeper than simply "national interest," a concept that every country in the world shares with comparable degree, according to circumstance. A common denominator of "interest" is security and sovereignty. Are those the "only" components that comprise the American purpose, putting this country on the same plateau as Ecuador or Pakistan? If that's the case, all are "winners."

Or, is the American experience on a higher plane, rising to a level shared by either no one else or by so few that it doesn't matter? To continue the football example, it matters little if all teams share equally in "winning," it only matters to the team that actually wins the title. Even second place is a "loser." Equally, does anyone care if Hungary wants to "make the world safe for democracy," or if Morocco wants to convert all nations to Islam?

Throughout history, countries with a "purpose" have created bedlam, revolution, and war that has both killed in the millions and has created world orders, if only for a moment. Consider these contestants: all history's empires, especially Mongol, Roman, British, Ottoman, Byzantine, French, Dutch, Belgian, Chinese, Austrian, Russian, Japanese, Spanish, Portuguese, Islamic, etc. Then, the leaders of these things: Caesar, Genghis Kahn, Charlemagne, Napoleon, Bismarck, Elizabeth I, George III, Queen Victoria, Gladstone, Disraeli, The Kaiser, Hitler, Lenin, Stalin, Mao, Mussolini, Tojo, Churchill.

Nor does a leader of "purpose" need the resources of a great power. In tiny Cuba, an island of eleven million, Fidel Castro managed to supervise a guerrilla assault on the rest of Latin America that caused chaos for years, hosted a missile crisis (1962) that might have killed hundreds of millions, and sent over 20,000 soldiers to Africa to foment revolutions. More recently, an obscure Islamic preacher, Osama Bin Laden, sent nine terrorists to hit two American cities. The operation took several minutes. Decades later, the American superpower is still recovering, with no end in sight.

All these movements, to name some, had one thing in common: they had a purpose, an objective, and it was meant to change history, if not the world. Nor were they meant as expedients, nor as temporary, but forever and everywhere. Moralists will distinguish between the "good" and "bad." That is their prerogative, but even at the time they were too late. Nor is it relevant to judge their outcomes. All of them, no exception, failed to accomplish their original purpose: whether it took years or centuries, they all ended in "rack and ruin."

Today there is no empire left in the world, no "Thousand Year Reich," no "proletariat" world, no Islamic empire, no anything that began before. Left in all their wakes, millions of body bags and millions more of broken (and fulfilled) promises. Purpose is morally free: the Nazis may be the rare political party that truly kept their promises.

All that's left is a world in constant chaos, in perpetual anarchy with a few "great powers" manipulating each other for some kind of dominance, always left undefined. What does China want, Asia, the world? Does Vladimir Putin want to take over America through "meddling" in local elections? What would he do if he got it? Will the Coronavirus see the world "plunge" into even darker anarchy? Darker than the Great Depression?

Questions abound, but the leadership of these countries may not even know their own directions. If so, it would hardly be new. Adolph Hitler, despite his planning and dedicated purpose, could not even anticipate Germany's future. When Britain finally declared war in 1939, he turned to his Foreign Secretary and asked, "now what?"

That's a fair question, appropriate across the board. What's left for an American purpose in the world? If one watches recent political debates, going back as far as 1992, the answer is far from obvious. If one goes no further back than the 2019 Democratic debates, the answer becomes more than obvious: nothing.

In 1903, Vladimir Lenin wrote a pamphlet *What Is To Be Done*, outlining his future plans to overthrow the Czar and occupy Russia. At the time, there were about a dozen Bolsheviks. It took fourteen years, but he finally did it. The rest is history. What is the answer to the same question for the American purpose in the world?

There is no scarcity of answers. The record of a "purpose" to the original revolution runs like a thread weaved through history, from the Founding Fathers through Monroe, Polk, Lincoln, both Roosevelts, Wilson, Truman, IKE, JFK to Reagan. Then it ends, and that is about where we are now, deaf and dumb, wandering through dark alleys.

Some would either deny or alter purpose, eliminate the Declaration of Independence, re-write the Constitution, and reverse the focus from liberty to slavery. If that takes hold, the quest for purpose effectively ends, from vision to apology, from a nation to quarreling "identities," from the future to history.

But if America is to revive a purpose in the world then, like Coach Lombardi, it must define what it means to "win." What are we here for, what is the "goal," do we have any purpose at all? The country must also rise "to the occasion," from micro to macro, from incidentals to a larger strategic picture.

Any foreign policy should be judged by how it has advanced its strategic vision. Usually, they have names. For the U.S.: isolation, neutrality, Monroe Doctrine, Manifest Destiny, Open Door, "making the world safe for democracy," Good Neighbor, containment, Cold War. What is the name of U.S. foreign policy now (guess)?

Without direction, the public becomes consumed by "current events," both foreign and domestic: "fast-breaking news," "this just in." Current affairs lack depth but arouse emotions and for each reason are popular.

Minus a purpose, policy becomes tomorrow's headline. Any nation that defines itself by its relations with an obscure and distant entity absorbs both those qualities itself. Likewise, a nation that judges itself in the world to what transpired in a phone conversation effectively declares that its head is "in the sand." Like all the other "Ostriches," it is both ugly and ungainly.

This is not a pretty picture, and it's getting worse.

But if all others, good and bad, have failed, why bother? Good question (just don't ask Vince Lombardi).

World Without Order

June 24, 2020

The field of Political Science is divided into four parts. First, and fundamental, is "Theory," the study of thoughts, ideas, theses, and analyses of politics as it has evolved from ancient times to today. Theory ("Philosophy") is fundamental since it provides the origins (and results) of all political movements that have graced the earth since man first descended into groups. The word "govern" is critical, since all politics is about the multiple methods of how humanity has resolved to control itself, either against or for itself, both from within and from without.

John Lennon once said, "before Elvis there was nothing." True enough! And, likewise, before Theory, there was also nothing. One cannot, by definition, begin to study the vast variety of political movements unless one first appreciates the equally vast multitude and divisions of ideas that gave these movements life in the first place.

Thus, we know that all (repeat "all") politics first springs from ancient Greece, where society originally gave credence to the types of political organizations and divisions that man envisioned, either before "in fact" or for the future, as "utopian."

In this regard, there is a line of succession from Plato, Socrates, and Aristotle to the American presidency, Josef Stalin, Adolph Hitler, and Vladimir Putin. Just as in economic theory there, is a line of succession from Adam Smith (*The Wealth of Nations*, 1776) to John D. Rockefeller, J.P. Morgan, Cornelius Vanderbilt, and modern Capitalism.

Nobody escapes history. Just as Thomas Jefferson used British philosopher John Locke (1632-1704) to write the Declaration of Independence (some say Jefferson "copied" Locke) so, too, do all political events somewhere, somehow repeat the past.

My field is "International Politics." In graduate school, we were asked once to name the one book that would best describe the Cold War, then reaching its peak of intensity. The correct answer: Thucydides, *The Peloponnesian War*, being the account of the long contest between the Greek city-states, Athens and Sparta, which ended in 404 BC.

After Theory, the remainder of Political Science is composed of several "tactical" applications of the theoretical foundations: Domestic, Comparative, and International. In Domestic, one studies the Home state and its methods of behavior, elections, parties, revolutions, movements, rights and privileges, ideas of moral vs. immoral, and the daily personalities and endless op-eds that dominate all opinion pages and media coverage. Comparative covers foreign politics, normally divided between Democratic, Dictatorship, and Totalitarian. There are subtle distinctions between these categories, as there is between Italian democracy and British and between Napoleon, Hitler, Stalin, Putin, Trump, Juan Peron, and Mussolini.

The last is International, which contains a unique feature that sets it apart from all else and places it in a category unique to any comparable "system" on earth. A "system," political or not, is always singular, i.e., controlled from top to bottom and tied together by a coherent unity. Thus, we speak of transportation, solar, economic, social, behavioral, racial, mechanical systems, etc. in colloquial terms that require single identifications. They may last forever or collapse instantly, but they are always (repeat "always") defined by their singular property, as "one."

International ("World") Politics is exactly the opposite: it has no "form," no unity nor authority to "govern," much less function. If there is one essential that ties together all domestic or foreign political systems on earth, it is "unity." All of them, democratic or dictatorial, have at least this in common: they have a top, a middle, and a bottom. If the top goes, by any method, it is automatically (eventually) replaced. If the middle or bottom goes, the system, in effect, disappears, like ancient Rome.

The defining term for "International" Politics is "anarchy," officially "absence of government, lawlessness, disorder." This has been true since time began. No country, no empire, no nation, no movement, no revolution, no anything has ever, ever, been able to control more than a small portion of the globe for more than a fraction of time. The closest, ironically, is the oldest democracy, Britain, whose empire governed about one-fifth of the world for a few centuries.

The closest conceptual tool for international control has been termed the "Balance of Power," a historic reality that defined Europe until the Twentieth Century. Essentially, the "Balance" was a crude substitute for government whereby nations existed as sovereign units in constant alignment with each other, back and forth, settling issues by war or conversation, but permanently on something called a "war footing."

As a representative of the old Balance, consider that one country, France, invaded its neighbor, Germany, on thirty separate occasions before 1870. Then it became Germany's turn, we now call this the Franco-Prussian War and the two world wars that defined our last century.

Did the Balance of Power work? Of course, if one accepts its premise and methods.

What "works" today? Anarchy remains the defining conceptual reality of world politics, with no end in sight. Nor does there seem to exist anything on the horizon to challenge that reality. The U.S. has long since given up and is now consumed with domestic and moralizing politics that appear to determine not only American history but its future as well.

Can China fill the void (as many think)?

If one knows only the history described above and nothing else, nothing about China, its past, or its future intentions, what are the odds?

August 4,

The Day Edward Grey Changed the World

August 4, 2020

The title of this essay today (August 4, 2020) will probably not draw a great deal of attention and may well seem so obscure as to throw away. I cannot blame anyone since neither the day nor the name has thus far captured much American attention (I really mean "any.")

But they should!

Americans would undoubtedly define a historic "day," typically and understandably, as to how it affected their own history. For "non-historians": July 4, 1776, (Declaration of Independence), April 9, 1865 (Confederacy surrenders), November 11, 1918 (Armistice Day), December 7, 1941 (Pearl Harbor).

There may well be others since the choice is quite subjective. In case one has not noticed, my own selections revolve around wars in history, as I consider warfare as not only the most tragic (and probably stupidest) human activity but equally the most significant and enduring. In my view, everything (repeat "everything") is the result of war, both in the short and long runs of historic momentum. For example, who is the most significant figure in the "women's movement," Betty Friedan (author of *The Feminine Mystique*) or *Rosie the Riveter*, mythical heroine of women factory workers in World War II? Without hesitation: before Rosie "there was nothing" (I did write "subjective").

Pearl Harbor may have been the last "great" day, by this definition, in U.S. history. But I would be remiss by my own career not to mention December 26, 1991, the day the Soviet Union collapsed and global Communism lost its historic mission (I was a "Cold Warrior").

"Historic days" are neither frivolous nor arbitrary; they mean a great deal to societies. Nearly two-and-one-half centuries later, July 4th remains the quintessential American "birthday." Few Americans can forget FDR's definition of Pearl Harbor as "a date that will live in infamy."

Nor is the point lost on our current "cultures" (used advisedly). *The New York Times*, arguably our most influential media machine, wants July 4 changed to August 20, 1619 (when the first slave ship landed) and claims that over 4,500 U.S. school districts have agreed to change their curricula accordingly. Judging from the current social/political climate, it would not be surprising that May 25, 2020 (when George Floyd expired) be promoted as "most important date" (but we should wait, maybe another two hundred years, before pronouncing on this). But it is symbolic of the times that last week all (repeat "all") top-ten non-fiction books were on the subject "racism."

But what is the significance of August 4, 1914, and who (in hell) is Edward Grey? In my long teaching career (1966), I always highlighted World War I as the most important event in history and June 28, 1914 (when the Austrian Archduke was assassinated) as the most important single day. I still believe in the war as "most" important (a general consensus anyway) but have moved the day up to August 4, primarily to accommodate the United States.

Edward Grey (Viscount Grey of Fallodon) was the British Foreign Secretary in 1914 and a prominent member of the Foreign Service and of the Liberal Party. He still holds the British career record of the longest service as Foreign Secretary (1905-1916) and was appointed Ambassador to the U.S., 1919-1920. Ironically, he also holds the record for the shortest term as American Ambassador (five months). He never even met President Woodrow Wilson and left due to eyesight issues which resulted in near-total blindness in the years prior to his death, 1933. Grey was a writer and sportsman as well. His *Fly Fishing* (1899) is still considered definitive, while his *The Charm of Birds*

(1927) was a best-seller on the "music" of birds, containing chapters entitled *Early Song, Return of the Warblers*, and *Nests and Eggs*.

One might not consider someone who wrote on "return of the warblers" to have helped start the greatest war in history (to 1914), but Grey qualifies. A noted *"Germanic-phobe"* Grey conspired with the young *First Sealord*, Winston S. Churchill, to steer British foreign policy decidedly against Germany and on behalf of France in the years before 1914 and was instrumental in solidifying the Triple Entente that formed the Western coalition throughout the long and brutal contest.

While both the House of Commons and the Cabinet were either undecided or outright opposed to depart from long-standing British "isolation," Grey (and Churchill) were able to draft the war message and convince the House that British intervention was needed to save Europe (France) from Germanic domination.

Recall that in 1870 a similar situation arose: Prussia defeated France in a few months, Germany was created as a nation, and Britain did nothing, while Europe, Britain, America, and the world adjusted over time to the event.

But in 1914, Britain, thanks to Grey as Foreign Secretary, declared war on Germany, theoretically because the Kaiser had violated an 1839 treaty to secure Belgian neutrality. The German Army was given twelve hours to leave Belgium by midnight. Grey didn't even wait and issued the Declaration of War an hour earlier, at 11.

The greatest consequence was that it became a "world" war. Grey's decision also committed the full Commonwealth: Canada, Australia, New Zealand, South Africa, much of Black Africa and the Islamic world, India, Pakistan, Burma, Malaya. On August 23, Japan (which had a 1902 security treaty with Britain) also declared war on Germany and quickly occupied German Far Eastern islands (that U.S. Marines had to invade later) and took over most of mainland China (laying the background for Pearl Harbor).

Thus, what started as a small quarrel in the Balkans overnight became the first global war in history, involving the entire British Commonwealth and the USA, a former colony.

All done by a birdwatcher.

There were other considerations:

First, the 1839 treaty did not require war.

Second, nor did the 1904 *Entente Cordial* with France.

Third, America declared Neutrality on the same day (August 4).

Fourth, the "neutrality" of the U.S. was one of the greatest myths ("lies" in today's language) in world history, as American banks, financiers, factories, and sympathies completely dropped Germany from support and developed total submission to the British war effort and refused even to approach continental waters against the British blockade. By 1916, aid/trade to Germany was near zero; to Britain, in the billions.

Fifth, Woodrow Wilson's Cabinet (nine members) was 100% pro-Britain, several having been born there. The entire American culture was carefully developed against the "Hun," creating the favorable climate for Wilson's eventual war declaration, April 6, 1917.

Ask yourself one, last question. What would have happened had Britain, as in 1870, remained neutral in the war? And stayed neutral to the end?

Who would the Americans support to the point of war? France? Belgium? Russia?

Ask a second question: how would that have affected world history (especially German)?

After drafting his war message, Grey looked down on the street below and saw one of London's "lamplighters" igniting the kerosene bulbs. Turning to his staff, he uttered the most prophetic sentence in world history: "The lamps are going out all over Europe, we shall not see them lit again in our lifetime."

Little did he know that he was the main reason for the enveloping darkness.

After America, Who?

June 5, 2020

These citizens ("kids") have absolutely no recall of the powerful domestic demonstrations against the Vietnam War that closed hundreds of universities and produced hundreds of thousands of protesters at a time. These went on literally for years as the U.S. war in Vietnam remains to this day the longest conflict, by far, in U.S. history (1959- 1973 actual combat).

Vietnam, in retrospect, was also the only war the U.S. ever lost. Although few in America seemed to care when North Vietnam finally entered Saigon (April 30, 1975), that date might just be the "beginning of the end" for America as a superpower. But few knew it, as within a decade the Soviet Union was about to collapse, the Cold War terminated (December 1991), and nobody on planet earth seemed to be around to challenge American influence. The era of "sole remaining superpower" came and went in a flash as the Governor of Arkansas became president on the motto "it's the economy stupid."

Few Americans more (over 80) can even remotely recall the heady days after World War II when Harry Truman changed the world order 180 degrees, brought the country out of its endemic isolationism, saved western Europe, created NATO, saved South Korea, and entered the historic challenge against global Communism that took nearly half a century to finish. Most Americans, especially under 50, have little or no remembrance of what it's like to be a "superpower," at the top of the global power structure and influencing events from the Congo, Vietnam, Egypt, Cuba, Korea, not to mention living within a world order made by and supervised by Americans

World War II, Pearl Harbor, Normandy, Iwo Jima? Forget it, even I can't remember them.

But I do recall a Saturday in 2008 when we went to West Virginia for a day with the last "Doughboy" to fight World War I. He was Frank Buckles, 108, and regaled us all day about driving General Pershing to and fro around the Western Front (died 2011, buried in Arlington, President Obama officiated).

To quote the great Welsh singer, Mary Hopkin, "Those were the days my friend, we thought they'd never end."

Alas, they did. Now what about it?

In an apocryphal sense, I might imagine bringing up this past to a *millennial* with an equally fancied response: wasn't the Army segregated, didn't women work in the factories, could they vote, and weren't gays forbidden? Fictitious? No, but certainly reality close to the political/social culture that has come to dominate the national discourse of the recent past. And, likely to continue into the foreseeable (and beyond) future.

Thus, the central factual point of the American political system over the last quarter-century has been the slow, but certain, demise of any and all American interest/concentration on the world order into a similar but opposite absorption to the domestic order.

This is more than a casual turnover; it amounts to a profound and probably lasting shift of what was once the greatest global phenomenon in world history to the same people adopting a near-total reversal into themselves.

This observation is neither judgmental nor imagined. If one needs evidence, wake up and smell the coffee (or move out of New Guinea). Nor does it matter to the system whether or not the domestic order is either pursued forever or achieved immediately. It's the "chase" (preoccupation) that matters, the results can, and will, wait.

Nor should this phenomenon come as a surprise. America was founded on isolationism and experienced a global mission only during the last half of the last century. From this perspective, the country is only "coming home." Or, as Reagan's Ambassador to the UN, Jeanne Kirkpatrick, once put it, becoming "a normal country in a normal time" (1991).

So, under the "new normal," what happens to the world when the superpower "cancels" the culture and divides itself into several parts based on color, gender, and historic definitions of what "we" are? As statues come tearing down and place-names are erased, who, if anyone, takes our place in the world (and who may care anyway)?

There are several options.

First, is nothing. The world has sailed along since the end of the Cold War with nobody in charge and can continue, indefinitely, this way. Of course, this eliminates nothing we have known for the last 6,000 years (wars, crimes, pandemics, crises, "meddling," etc.) Recall the nineteenth century when the Congress of Vienna (1815) created the "Concert of Europe" that kept Great Power peace until the whole thing exploded in 1914.

Second, someone takes over. The top candidate is China and most speculation, ranging from the hysterical to the "expert," will bet on them. How this could come about, what it may mean, and how it will be effected remains deeply in the speculative phase.

Third, someone else. Who might that be? This requires more than speculation; it requires an imagination. Russia, India, The European Union? We might as well speculate on an alien invasion, some kind of re-make of *The Day the Earth Stood Still* (1951).

Finally, what are we left with? Many of us from the Cold War based the future on an American and democratic global "Concert" that would be open to invited member-states and might – just *might* – translate American political values into a benign and peaceful world order.

Maybe later, say 2120.

World Anarchy

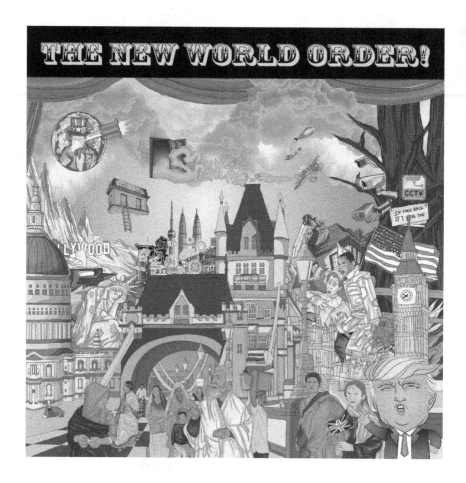

July 3, 2020

When nation-states behave as "nation-states," that is, since time began, the American media and public react in horror. Like, "this is unheard of," or "how dare they." It might help to open a book.

The Russians are "meddling," there is "collusion" between Putin and Trump, they seem to get along, Trump is too friendly with "dictators," China is reckless, wants more power, demands control of sea-lanes, some countries threaten others, some invade neighbors, smuggle dope, spy on each other, say nasty things, withdraw from treaties, cheat on them, oppose democracy and liberty, some want to control their regions, some want the whole world, etc.

I could write this whole essay, plus others, to list the sins committed under the term "world politics." But, under a political microscope, are the faults of sovereignties fundamentally different than those of local or domestic regimes? The immediate answer is "of course not," but then why distinguish between the world and the locale? Governors, Mayors, Senators, Representatives, Dictators, Generals, Admirals, Mafia Bosses, petty thieves, outlaws, husbands and wives do the same things all the time.

So what's the difference?

There are several, which makes world wars and local quarrels placed in different categories.

First, most local regimes do not have militaries. The Mafia and street thugs have "gangs," dictators and other local despots have the "police," "white collar" thieves have laws to bend. There is a profound and lasting difference between a regime that has a professional military and one that must resort to *ad hoc* or "amateur" persuasion for its ambitions.

All Latin American countries have what they call "armies," but none are true militaries. They exist to control within, not to expand out. The Falklands War (1982) between Britain and Argentina demonstrates the point: Britain had a navy, which traveled 10,000 miles. Argentina had the police, which couldn't even win off-shore.

When was the last true Latin American war (you will have to look it up)? On the positive side, Latin American geopolitics have been relatively stable since the early nineteenth century, unlike most other areas.

The second difference is legal. Nation-states are "sovereign" entities, meaning that they are responsible to no other higher authority than themselves. There are presently 193 sovereignties in the world (UN) which makes all other entities, tribes, races, nationalities, terrorists, ideologies, etc., technically unable to wage "war" in a formal sense. Thus, they do not need militaries and rarely have one in any authentic mode.

This does not mean that they cannot create damage or havoc. It took nine *Al Qaeda* members to level the World Trade Center; it looks like a few Chinese officials in Wuhan province unleashed the current pandemic.

Even minus warfare, mankind remains in perpetual danger ("don't go there at night").

The third difference is called "geopolitics." Nation-states, as the name indicates, control territories, some of them mammoth. Individual states in the U.S. – Montana, California, Texas, Alaska – are larger than most countries in the UN. Small regimes rarely cause trouble alone. Even if they wanted to, they couldn't. But, when attached to larger countries, they can. Great-power wars and other conflicts have often involved quarrels in small areas: Serbia, Poland, Berlin, Taiwan, South Korea, South Vietnam, Cuba, Kuwait, etc.

Almost all the important wars of history involved great states or their allies. You may even count them on one hand: France, Germany, Russia, UK-USA (as one). In the future, you may want to add China (still one hand). The geopolitical structure of the political globe rewards only those who have grown beyond their original locations, literally and figuratively.

The U.S. began on the east coast and, within two generations, went as far west as possible. Had the land-mass extended beyond the Pacific shore, California would now locate where Hawaii is. After both world wars, there were high-level efforts to restrict Germany to within tiny borders without resources (both obviously failed).

Geopolitics "influences" behavior but cannot "determine" it. India, Canada, Australia, and Brazil are all very big but largely tranquil.

The fourth difference is the "determining" element. In the last analysis, the decisive factor between war/peace and world vs. local regimes is the factor of control, i.e. political. Warfare, as a noun, can mean various things and has been used in liberal ways for practically everything: poverty, drugs, crime, etc. But in the original sense, not "borrowed," war means the clash of nation-states and their militaries. This has been the meaning throughout history and remains the critical usage even today.

The essential distinguishing point between local and world wars lies in the absence or presence of political control. There are few societies that have avoided "civil" war, i.e. military conflict within the same polity. But civil war has never, repeat never, dominated a domestic polity and, in fact, has usually occurred only once.

By definition, world politics is exactly the opposite. Not only does war regulate the global system, it defines its very nature. Indeed, the world political regime contains "incessant" war, i.e. non-stop, while all, repeat all, domestic regimes depend on stability/peace for very existence. This includes democracies, dictatorships, and all else in-between.

The word "anarchy," by definition, cannot exist within a country, but defines the existence of world politics. And *that* is the difference.

In the final analysis, what do we want in foreign policies? There are at least two choices:

1. Advance the cause of world stability and peace based upon western political values of liberty, democracy, and legality.
2. Support the foreign policy of my country "right or wrong."

As an avowed "American nationalist," I vote for the first. And you?

Utopian Thoughts

July 20, 2020

In a world that remains in political "anarchy," 6,000 years later, one might think that a truly global organization might arise to supervise the lurid activities of the membership. Not so. After thousands of years with incessant warfare, alliances that come and go eternally, spying, rivalry, sustained suspicion, "sovereignty," "territoriality," we might, at last, find common bond for something new. Not so again.

As the great baseball manager Casey Stengel once said of his new team, "doesn't anybody around here know how to play this game?"

Isn't anyone tired of this "same old, same old"? So A invades B, C spies on D, E allies against F, G expands against H, and I "meddles" inside J. Who needs names, but the alphabet is only so long. Even after an hour, all games grow tired.

It's not as though nobody has tried. The "nation-state" system formally began in 1648 with the end of the Holy Roman Empire, making the present "system" about 350 years old. Count the number of wars since (but stop at 100).

Within the widest perspective (6,000 years of recorded history), almost all of political history has consisted of organizational units we call "empires." This makes nation-states about five percent of history. Empires can be counted as well: Chinese, Mongol, Persian, Roman, Byzantine, Indian, Russian, Austrian, Ottoman, Islamic (and most religions), British, French, German, Italian, Spanish, Portuguese, Dutch, Japanese, Belgian, Inca, Aztec, Zulu, to name the most prominent.

Politicians often refer to an American Empire, yet ironically the U.S. may be the only great power that rarely pursued empire and spent most of its diplomatic history railing against the empires of others. This may sound disingenuous to Mexico, which lost nearly half of its land to the U.S. (1848) or to Indian tribes, who lost their own to the federal government. Still, much of America's territorial advances were real estate deals (Louisiana Purchase, Alaska), while the very objects of "Manifest Destiny" clamored against each other to join the union as "states."

(Should politicians still rage against American "imperialism," we can always give it back, just don't tell anyone living west of Maryland).

Yet the word "empire" itself connotes the very opposite of what we know as the values of "western" society: liberty, democracy, equality, rule of law. Without exception, empire means rule by a few, arbitrarily and at the very top. In effect, all citizens become "slaves" minus the term and remain indefinitely conditioned to the whims of the inherited rulers.

In democratic terminology, the differences between "subject" and "citizen," with all the rights and privileges contained therein, defines the differences between empires and free societies. There is no word for "majesty" in a democratic dictionary.

But even within the definitions of political governance, empires still lacked the capacity to influence more than a relative few. Without exception, again, they all had severe territorial limits to their rule.

Probably the largest land-mass was the Mongol Empire of Genghis Kahn, which covered most of China and the Far East plus south Asia and southern Europe. This was big but still remote and small compared to empires based on the seven seas. The largest maritime empire was the British which, together, once covered large portions of North America, Africa, the Middle East, south and southeast Asia, and the Far East.

To discover the impact of the British Empire alone, reflect on the geopolitical vocabulary used in the United States today. Standing on the Atlantic coast, looking at the ocean, which direction are you facing? East. Then why is NATO our "western" allies? On the Pacific coast, you're looking west, but China is the "Far East." Why, because that's the geopolitical perspective from London.

Yet, as in most things, empires were "short-lived." But only if centuries can be defined as "short." It depends on one's perspective but is largely irrelevant. They are now long-gone, which brings up the question, what next?

Over time, there have many efforts in the "west" to create new and better organizations to forge at least some semblance of "world order." Many have been American-inspired, from Woodrow Wilson's League of Nations to Franklin Roosevelt's United Nations. They have had many successes in many quarters (the League not so much), but in essentially changing the global political system, they haven't even come close. Try counting the wars since 1945 (and stop at 100 again).

Is failure final? No more than "success." Many in the U.S. (myself included) have argued for long-range efforts to fundamentally alter the global political system toward a more-ordered arrangement based upon the political values of the American Founding. The book *World Peace Through World Law* (Clark/Sohn, 1958) represents perhaps the best-known single volume toward that effort, but still remains only representative.

While it is fair to label such images as "utopian," the label should in no way discount, nor stop, the effort.

"Rome wasn't built in a day," "a journey of a thousand miles begins with one step" are more than empty slogans if they inspire effort. Effort, in turn, requires commitment, persistence, patience, determination, and dedication. These are all virtues, and it behooves today's America to use some of these in advancing the interests of a world better than the one we have inherited.

There's still another slogan that has relevance: "Keep your feet on the ground, your eyes on the horizon."

As criteria for U.S. foreign policies over time, especially since the Cold War, we can use a number of indicators, ranging from geopolitics and national interests to diplomacy and warfare itself. These all belong in the first part of the above quote and are in the "realist" category.

The second part belongs in the "utopian" category and should have relevance, maybe even dominance, as a priority.

The first is relatively "easy" and easy also to judge. Just have an opinion, pick up a newspaper, watch TV.

On the other hand, how is the "better world" coming along?

Reviving SEATO

August 25, 2020

While the North Atlantic Treaty (NATO) is alive and well after seventy years, now with thirty members, SEATO has long-since been forgotten. As a distant "cousin" of NATO, SEATO (Southeast Asian Treaty Organization) was intended to provide the same rationale in Asia as NATO did in western Europe, i.e. to provide a collective defense against the spread of global communism.

As a reminder, SEATO began in 1954 after the expulsion of France from Vietnam (Battle of Dien Bien Phu) and was used by the Eisenhower Administration as cover for the growing U.S. commitment to South Vietnam, particularly against Communist China. SEATO had eight members, including three from NATO (the U.S., France, Britain), and the rest were from Asia, the Philippines, Australia, New Zealand, Thailand, and Pakistan.

But as a vehicle for collective defense, SEATO was a poor substitute. It neither provided for true common security, with no joint military command, no standing armed forces, and had only a vague and ineffective commitment against a "common danger." Only Thailand was technically located in

Southeast Asia, but Vietnam, Laos, and Cambodia were given "observer" status and were included within SEATO's geopolitical range.

But SEATO had internal issues that were absent in NATO. Only the U.S. believed in the threat, while the others either sent token forces or ignored the issue altogether. Laos and Cambodia actually became U.S. targets, while Thailand, New Zealand, Australia, and Pakistan joined for purely political, as opposed to security, reasons.

But the main reason for SEATO's eventual collapse was the nature of the existing threat, an internal insurgency from Hanoi as opposed to a conventional threat from Moscow. As a functioning alliance, SEATO was purely American, and, as the U.S. stayed in Vietnam and as the war dragged on without end, the alliance simply became irrelevant. As British security expert Sir James Cable put it, SEATO was "a fig leaf for the nakedness of American power ...a zoo of paper tigers."

While members either ignored it and some (Pakistan, France) dropped out, the fall of Saigon in 1975 exposed the hollow shell of the American Asian commitment. SEATO was formally dissolved on June 30, 1977, never to be heard from again (until now).

Then what would be the purpose of reviving the memory of such a regional disaster? While history is supposed to "repeat," the admonition can be taken too far, as well. The circumstances for SEATO's demise have long since disappeared, while alliances continue to remain necessary pillars of national, and regional, security. SEATO failed, NATO succeeded, so what?

The Trump Administration heralds MAGA as its prime *raison d'état* for national security. While a colorful slogan, the notion has practically no meaning outside our shoreline. If anything, it recalls the isolationist organization formed in 1939 to keep the U.S. out of war. And we all know how that went ("America First").

Seventy-five years after World War II, NATO is alive, well, and expanded; the EU (minus Britain) is the same. How has the world changed?

For most of its history, the threat against the U.S., existential and geopolitical, has originated in Europe. If it wasn't our British "cousins," it was Germany (twice), then Russia, which became the Soviet Union, but is back as Russia again.

Where is that threat now? The original motivation for NATO, 1949, has, like SEATO, long since disappeared. If it wasn't so culturally accepted, the newest threat from Europe, Russian "meddling" in local elections, would be laughable, even if true.

Even if Putin intervenes in, say, Milwaukee's election, how does that compare to Stalin and the millions of Red Army legions reaching the channel ports of France and Belgium? How do the election results in Cleveland compare to the Cuban Missile Crisis? To juxtapose today's Russia in the same breath as the Cold War is to confuse American security issues with those of Ukraine, Croatia, and the Baltic states. It is also to confuse the dimensions of a world war, with thousands of nuclear weapons, against a nuisance on our doorstep ("rats in the closet").

The world's geopolitical interests have, as predicted, moved from Europe to Asia, where China holds sway and threatens the new, and future, order.

This is not only an Asian issue; it is global. China is the new threat to American and world stability, and the United States, as in 1949, has reached a crossroads to go one way or another.

True, we have bilateral agreements to protect vital interests, especially with Japan and Taiwan. But neither of those obligate the U.S. to automatically use military force. Nor are there existing arrangements to use force in the rest of Asia. As policy analyst Robert Kagan put it recently (regarding Taiwan), "Are we prepared to go beyond statements and sanctions if the Chinese call our bluff?"

In effect, the U.S. is "isolated." Again.

Historically, isolated countries rarely act alone, which is why there are alliances. MAGA cannot deal with China and Asia. It will be necessary for a new American administration to take historic steps and create an innovative security arrangement between ourselves and related, and relevant, Asian partners. Who shall be involved, under what circumstances, for how long, and with what will have to be settled. But it is needed.

This year, the Trump Administration made concrete moves in this direction. On March 26, it signed the Taiwan Allies International Protection and Enhancement Initiative (TAIPEI) and advanced new arms sales to Taiwan. On July 23, Secretary of State Pompeo asked in a speech that "every leader of every nation insist on reciprocity ... transparency and accountability from the Chinese Communist Party."

In November, members of the four-power Asian "Quad" (the U.S., Japan, Australia, India) will hold joint naval exercises for the first time, a step that

U.S. officials see as a significant move toward a formal alliance. Communist Vietnam, a target of Chinese pressure, also agreed to align with the Quad for economic and military security. While most experts on the issue maintain an official skepticism, the grand diplomatic trajectory in Asia appears headed toward some sort of historic realignment.

A decent beginning, so long as we don't "repeat" SEATO.

Kipling is Back: History Returns

August 30, 2020

While it is fashionable in the modern United States to disparage any and all recall of history, it is equally possible that, without knowing it, modern Americans are simply bringing forgotten history back to life.

This is particularly so in left-wing ideological circles, much of academia, the media, and the "politically correct" culture. The disruptions following the death of George Floyd and the near-unanimous emphasis on the modern campus toward "diversity and inclusion" emphasize this critical shift in modern American culture. The drive to "cancel" tradition, to replace statues and other reminders of history, and to turn around the memory of the Founding Fathers from saviors to villains marks a profound and, possibly, lasting stamp on what this country is becoming.

From a nation "proud of its ancient heritage" (JFK's Inaugural) and during the Great Depression reminded that "the only thing we have to fear is fear itself" (FDR's Inaugural), the modern American political culture has turned into a public afraid of itself and what it might represent and fearful of what it did in the past and why.

Representative of this are *The New York Times* project to change the national birth date from July 4, 1776 to August 20, 1619, when the first slave ship arrived (allegedly adopted in 4,500 school districts) to the prominence of best-selling non-fiction books on American racism (sometimes 10 out of 10 on the list).

The great irony of this fashion is that, instead of erasing history as they profess, the leadership of this new phenomenon is not dreaming of a future without the past; they are having "nightmares" and "sleeping" under the illusion that they are somehow unique.

Quite the opposite, they are as old as life itself but, unbeknownst to each other, are repeating life, albeit under a modern guise. The actual source of this, now and then, may (for want of another word) be labeled "paternalism." Described in dictionary language as when "an authority undertakes to supply needs or regulate conduct of those under its control ... in their relations to authority and to each other."

This definition is simple and straightforward and may explain much of life itself, from cradle to grave. But when it becomes a national political purpose, "obsession," it can amount to a term called "tyranny," which, in turn, is defined as "cruel, unreasonable or arbitrary use of power or control."

One may quarrel with the above adjectives, "cruel, unreasonable," but paternalism is always and everywhere "arbitrary." Synonyms "domination, authoritarian, coercion, imperious, absolute" can as well be used in the description, which cancels a subjective version with an objective one.

Thus, paternal, or tyrannical, need not be "cruel," and, like beauty, can exist in the "eye of the beholder." As employed by authorities, therefore, they can behave with the best of intentions toward societal horizons whose wonders still lie ahead. This may be just great but makes them no less tyrannical by any term.

This was true throughout history, people acting with the best of intentions with tools of authority observers can rightly judge as "tyrannical." Yet liberals, progressives, and all social reformers do not like "tyrants." This is a quarrel of words, and little more. In colonial America, British taxes ("without representation") were "tyranny" and are still remembered on today's D.C. license plates.

Ultimate irony: colonialism's memory is on every car registered in the Capitol City yet pervades the entire social culture ...everywhere (do I hear Paul Revere?).

Case in point: remember Rudyard Kipling? He was one of England's greatest poets in the nineteenth century, but what was he universally known for?

Have you ever heard of the "white man's burden," i.e. the responsibility of Caucasian people to discipline, educate, elevate, etc. all others under their jurisdiction? Today, they are called "people of color," but in history they were referred to as "subjects" in a vast colonial dominion that covered most of the political earth.

What was the "white man's burden" if not paternalism? Kipling lived for years in the United States and wrote that particular poem in 1899 to urge the U.S. to adopt the Philippine Islands, just taken from Spain. His objective was never to raise the power of America: he was British! His objective was actually "benevolent," to raise the native subjects so that they, too, might benefit from the advantages of what now we call "white supremacy."

The difference: Kipling saw "supremacy" as a virtue; today it is a vice. Go figure.

Read some of his most famous lines:

Take up the White Man's burden—
Send forth the best ye breed—
Go bind your sons to exile
To serve your captives' need; ...
By open speech and simple,
An hundred times made plain.
To seek another's profit,
And work another's gain...
Fill full the mouth of Famine
And bid the sickness cease...
Take up the White Man's burden—
Ye dare not stoop to less—
Nor call too loud on Freedom
To cloak your weariness; ...

Filipino leaders didn't exactly see the virtues of "white supremacy" either, as they fought a lengthy guerrilla war against the U.S. occupation that, irregularly, went on for over a decade.

Today, the Philippine Insurrection, like the Vietnam War, is also lost to history, but, like many other episodes in life, began with a progressive and positive intent.

Many today view the new cultural mandates with utmost suspicion, regardless of honest intentions. That was true before as well.

The Philippine occupation had its detractors, as the 1900 presidential election (McKinley vs. Bryan) became a national referendum on the issue. Mark Twain viewed the occupation as a disaster, "I cannot for the life of me comprehend how we got into that mess." Senator George F. Hoar (R-MA) was outspoken against his own party and President McKinley as well, calling the whole affair a "doctrine of purest ruffianism and tyranny."

Kipling himself noted how the purest of intentions could well backfire:
And when your goal is nearest
The end for others sought,
Watch Sloth and heathen Folly
Bring all your hopes to nought.

What's that about history repeating?

Divisions

September 12, 2020

Lincoln first brought up the danger of "a house divided" when he announced it "cannot stand" in the 1858 Senate debate in Illinois. Although he was referring to slavery, the analogy is timeless and universal and has been proven accurate in countless situations, from families to governments to societies. In drawing attention to division, Lincoln also noted that the divide would eventually end with "all one thing or another." While Lincoln, like many other Americans at the time, did not predict civil war, he still understood that the current situation was intolerable. War was a chance he was willing to take.

The end of anything, social or not, is both highly contentious and subjective, but necessary for reflection at a time when the self-same metaphor ("end") is universally applied to politics, particularly the "Trump" variety. Nary a day goes by that some commentator predicts an "end" to democracy under Trump's supervision, that he has resurrected Hitler, or that he will convert the country into his personal estate. Since he won in 2016, the *Washington Post* has published "Democracy Dies in Darkness" on the top of page one, every issue, day after day.

Yet the President, whoever he/she may be, is scarcely the source of this analogy. Hitler himself can be used, if appropriate, since he, practically alone, raised the Weimar Republic from a defeated and depressed society to history's greatest and most dangerous belligerent. But a single man, however powerful, cannot be responsible for whole societies. Just as Trump was fairly and freely elected, so, too, did Hitler come from a society that at least tolerated his rule or embraced it. To understand Hitler, one needs to start with German history, especially World War I. To understand Trump (or his enemies), one needs to start with something prior to him or deeply embedded within society itself.

Like America in 1858, today's divisions have roots that, in retrospect, have to be inherent.

It may also be asserted that the warning is overblown, or that, while divided today, American society has suffered before and survived and will do so again. Examples of the first revolution, the Civil War, the Great Depression, and a sustained inequality between levels of society can be, and have been, asserted to demonstrate the stability of the society. Fair enough, and as in all "medicine," it depends on the diagnosis. But to err on the safe side has the disadvantage of being fatal by neglect. To err on the critical side has, at least, the advantage of being, rather, "safe than sorry."

There has been, from the very beginning, a potentially fatal flaw within American society that stems both from the highly "liberal" and, thus, open nature of the society combined with the mass of the geopolitical expanse. President John F. Kennedy's great book, *A Nation of Immigrants* (1958) has explained this quality in brilliant prose. But his story emphasized the positive side of the narrative, while the very size and the societal freedom could well become the country's fatal "Achilles heel." The country's population has tripled since 1940, to 330 million. What if this repeats, with nearly a billion by 2100? Would discontent rise or decline? (Guess.)

Division, in all aspects, has dogged American society from the beginning. At the creation, 1776, barely one-fifth of colonial subjects wanted separation from Britain. The vast majority either were neutral or loyal ("Loyalists" or "Tories") and lived comfortably within the British socio/political system. The internal war between "Patriots" (rebels) and Loyalists forecast the bitter and lasting separation that would grow to plague all Americans through civil war, anti-immigration riots, economic disparities, and social/geopolitical identities. A Chaplain, observing this phenomenon in the revolution, was moved to write

"These Americans, so soft, pacific and benevolent by nature, are here transformed into monsters, implacable, bloody and ravenous; party rage has kindled the spirit of hatred between them, they attack and rob each other by turns, destroying dwelling houses, or establish themselves therein by driving out those who had before dispossessed others."

In his classic Farewell Address (1796), George Washington described the tensions and hatreds that political parties, even then, had grown to divide society:

"It serves always to distract the public councils and enfeeble the public administration. It agitates the community with ill-founded jealousies and false alarms, kindles the animosity of one part against another, foments occasionally riot and insurrection."

Still, Washington felt, "This spirit, unfortunately, is inseparable from our nature."

"As the twig is bent, so grows the tree."

Political parties, as Washington noted, are not the *cause* of division; they only reflect division. Parties did not cause most of the subsequent divides that wrenched the country from generation to generation. Factors stemming from different sociological, economic, geopolitical, racial, and other differences continued to separate Americans from each other. In some form, this has always been the case, from the revolution through the Civil War to the current climate that finds the White House surrounded by a protest movement, with street letters ordered there by none other than the Mayor of the Capitol.

It could be argued that the single moment of true American unity was December 8, 1941, after a foreign country bombed Hawaii and forced millions of Americans together to fight an unwanted war. As the saying goes, it's been "downhill since."

Paul Revere is famous for warning the Minutemen that the "British are coming." Apparently, he faced the same dilemma that plagues almost all Americans in assessing the divisions of our times. Perhaps he should have added this from his galloping horse, "They've also been here for two hundred years."

In assessing division, it is very possible that it is overdone. But recalling Lincoln, he was right, but no one in the country had the slightest idea of the cost. But neither Lincoln nor Robert E. Lee was responsible for the Civil War; the cause was there before their birth.

To discover the cause of today's divisions, don't look at the present, look in the past. To prepare for the future, remember the past, don't erase or re-invent it.

The Boston Police Strike

October 18, 2020

On September 9, 1919, the Boston police force went on strike against what the police union called poor labor and wage conditions. The strike lasted five days and to this day represents the first and only organized police strike in American history. But considering the conditions in cities today, with calls for defunding and elimination of police, the situation in Boston 101 years ago bears another look. The nature of the conditions in Boston then, and the outcome of the strike, may well give us a clue to the dangers and results of what happens when citizens are forced to take the law into their own hands.

Like now, the strike had a political background and a history of left-wing, communist influence in society. Actual conditions for the over- 1,500 Boston officers were miserable even under the standards of 1919. They typically worked 10-hour days, slept in 19 station houses that dated to pre-Civil War, and shared typically four toilets and one bathtub for an average of 135 men. The highest salary was $1,400 a year, equivalent to $23,000 today, and they made half the pay of carpenters and mechanics and less than streetcar conductors.

Despite their conditions, the police were forbidden to organize or strike. But in 1919, the nationwide labor union *American Federation of Labor* (AFL) began granting charters to police in U.S. cities, including Washington, Miami, Los Angeles, and St. Paul. This was met with protests throughout the country, including Boston's Police Commissioner, Edwin Curtis, who proclaimed that "it should be apparent to any thinking person" that police "cannot serve two masters," their own citizens and "an organization existing outside the department."

Nevertheless, on August 15, the Boston Police joined the AFL; on September 8, they voted 1,134 to 2 to strike, commencing the next day.

Of the 1,544 officers, 1,117 (72%) failed to report to work, while Massachusetts Governor Calvin Coolidge promptly hired 100 Park Police to replace them. Most of these, in turn, also failed to appear. Strikebreakers, mostly Harvard students, were recruited that evening, but they too quickly disappeared.

By the night of September 9, widespread rioting and looting began throughout Boston. Rocks were thrown at streetcars, stores were vandalized, fires and false alarms created havoc with the Fire Department. The following day, Governor Coolidge provided 5,000 State Guards to replace the absent police, prompting Commissioner Curtis to proclaim "the universal chorus of commendation that has greeted their work." The morning papers were in full agreement, calling the police "deserters" and "agents of Lenin."

Violence peaked the following day. Most businesses stayed up all night to board their stores, women were threatened, and hundreds had their handbags snatched. During the day, the Guards had to "charge" into Scollay Square, cavalry-like, to break up a riot. A total of nine civilians were killed by the Guards, but by the 12th, Boston had settled under their watch.

The next day, Commissioner Curtis fired most of the strikers and hired 1,574 replacements, most unemployed world war veterans. Salaries, vacation time, and work conditions were greatly expanded, while citizens raised $472,000 to help pay the Guards. Still, members of the *United Garments Union* refused to sew new uniforms for recruits, who initially had to wear civilian clothes. On December 21, the State Guard was relieved, and Boston went back to normal.

That was the last police strike ever to occur in the U.S., but the lessons from Boston shaped subsequent American history.

The single most critical lesson was to beware "foreign," read "Bolshevik," influence that was just starting from the 1917 revolution that created the Soviet Union. Labor Unions were often the target, and, throughout the 1920s, thousands of "Bolshevik" unionists and Soviet agents were shipped home by Attorney General A. Mitchell Palmer. This continued almost unchecked through the Great Depression, World War II, and Cold War to include the next wave of "McCarthyism" that pervaded the 1950s.

The immediate aftermath of the Boston strike began this political culture with great enthusiasm. This, ironically, was led, then as now, by a *New York Times* that might not be too comfortable with its original patriotism. Declaring the Boston strike to be "an essay in Bolshevism," the *Times* declared the strike "an imported revolutionary idea that may spread to various cities. There should be a plain and stern law against it. ... It ought to be punished suitably and repressed."

This was nearly a unanimous national view. The *Philadelphia Ledger* wrote that "Bolshevism in the United States is no longer a specter. Boston in chaos reveals its sinister substance." President Wilson called the strike "a crime against civilization" that left Boston "at the mercy of an army of thugs." A Senate Report headline read "Senators Think Effort to Sovietize the Government Is Started," while Senator Henry Cabot Lodge, Chairman of the Foreign Relations Committee, believed that "we shall be in measurable distance of Soviet government by labor unions."

The whole affair led to a great rise in prominence for both Massachusetts and its Governor. The *Boston Transcript* reported, "Massachusetts is hailed today from Maine to California as the winner of a shining triumph for straight Americanism. The voting booths of the Old Bay State were a battleground for the nation. ...the issue was America, and in the triumph of that issue all America triumphs." Governor Calvin Coolidge was catapulted overnight to national prominence, leading almost immediately to Vice President and President. Not bad for a "silent" conservative from Vermont.

Today's harbinger from a nation convulsed with anti-police sentiment: mess with the cops if you want, but this could be a hornet's nest you just might want to let alone.

Guilty As Charged

October 16, 2020

The quality of being "guilty" is a pervasive accusation, whether true or not, that can have a powerful effect on the behavior of anything so charged, be it individuals or nations. The precise definition of the term is "feelings of deserving blame for imagined offensives or from a sense of inadequacy." Synonyms are "contrition, penitence, regret, remorse, self-reproach, shame."

Note that the concept does not require accuracy or any particular behavior, meaning that it is a self-applied psychological condition, whether derived from within or without. A serial killer may have absolutely zero guilt; a pickpocket may well become absorbed by it. The charge could be completely baseless or well-deserved.

Either way, the notion of "guilt" is a powerful one, whether accepted or not. There is practically no limitation on its application, and the impact of the notion has defined humanity from Adam and Eve to the infamous "war guilt" clause after World War I, which essentially created both Hitler and the Second World War.

Guilt is also related to religion, from the Crucifixion to the Christian concept of "penance," to the ultimate theological design between eternal life or death.

The concept has placed an enormous burden on political life as well, be it the politics between members of the same family, state, or nation, or between the sociologies, religions, races, genders, tribes, and all else that comprise the vast human "family."

It does not require an enormous imagination to define the current American political "culture" to be nearly dominated by guilt. The key expression is "culture," particularly by the degree of attention that the idea has been advanced by those social elements that "define" culture.

That may mean that less than one percent of 330 million actually claim guilt, whereas their media, political, and protester elite have succeeded in imposing the notion throughout the "body politic." This, as well, is not unique to current events, as it has defined the nature and conduct of political behavior from the beginning. No more than twenty percent of original Americans wanted revolution in 1776; there were about twelve Bolsheviks in the years before the 1917 Russian revolution, while Adolph Hitler and around 800 Nazis controlled eighty million Germans in the 1930s. As they say, "that's politics."

That's also "politics" in modern America, where the "guilt complexion" has come to define the country over the past several years. The accumulation of several "isms" (racism, sexism, white nationalism) that have surfaced are sufficient evidence of the growing dominance of national, or "sub"-national, guilt applied almost universally.

Regardless of their merit, even if they are fully justified, they at least share a common and singular denominator: they have imposed a widespread psychosis of guilt upon the concept "America," and what it has purported to represent. This applies especially to Caucasian males, who have been primarily responsible for all that has comprised the national experience.

As in the theological guilt, the national guilt will likewise require "contrition," which could mean a total overhaul of the American experience long before the original revolution. This is already underway, as protest movements stemming from guilt have come to dominate the culture: to change the birthdate from 1776 to 1619, to define slavery as essential to the "experience," to develop "anti-racism" as a national imperative, to impose "identity" classes on institutional behaviors, to the change in academic curricula from explanatory to apologetic, to the emergence of protest groups as social definers, and to the destruction of historic statues and landmarks that may contradict select ideologies.

This background will not surprise any reader who has been awake since 2016 (or who can read and watch). Yet, what are the consequences/implications of such movements, assuming that they may well prevail?

The first is both apparent and obvious. Any society, individual, or group, cannot possibly advance itself or have goals or ambitions if it is perpetually trying to repent for itself, apologize, or otherwise try to make up for its past sins. These would have come in two phases, of either "commission" or "omission." If it is commission, it must repent for what has been done; if omission, it must supply what was denied. In either case, the effort would be monumental, involving a whole reconstruction of society, including its history, social composition, and, indeed, a near-reversal of the values and culture that were guilty from day one.

Typical is the projection of Professor Candace Rondeaux (Arizona State): "If this system remains the same for the next few decades, everything about Americans' way of life will be on a collision course with political institutions that have been unable to keep pace."

The second consequence would involve a social movement that might best compare to the wholesale evacuation of populations that were forced out of their homes or had to flee regimes that threatened lifestyles that were considered safe and dependable. From acceptance to rejection, the implications of guilt contain a vast spectrum in between. Many would resist, many would seek safety elsewhere, while others would have to adjust to what, some would say, they "had coming."

"Revolutions are not tea parties," has been said to justify actions taken in the name of "progress" throughout history. "Extremism in the name of liberty is no vice" was once a major American political slogan, now applied for "justice" and "equality" as well.

The phenomenon described above is an American reality. It is not a "passing fancy" nor a "mid-life crisis." It has roots elsewhere, notably in European political doctrine (Marxism, Frankfurt School, Gramsci). It is essentially "collectivist," socialistic, or communistic and, as in previous movements of that nature, decidedly "totalitarian" in political behavior. Nor is it a revisit of Fascism, which is heightened nationalism and militarism, a doctrine exactly opposite from the present danger. Fascists invade neighbors and do not tolerate opposition; this movement is internal and is the opposition.

The movement is probably in a "beginning" stage. Should it advance to a "middle," we might well predict what "The End" could be.

In the debate of 9/29, President Trump may have revealed a greater perspective than we all knew: "This is not going to end well."

What did he have in mind, the evening or the country?

Top Ten Inaugurals

November 2, 2020

Probably the most important speech ever given by any President of the United States was his first official one. While all the subsequent addresses, some in the thousands, related to situations, circumstances, and events, the Inaugural Address has an importance that is all its own. Not only does it define where the country is at any given time, but it likewise sets a follow-on definition for what, often precisely, he intends to do about it. This is more than just an agenda, it usually proclaims, in the most grandeur and astute language, goals and intentions that deliberately appeal to the basic instincts of the electorate, while drawing upon the fundamental virtues of the Republic from the beginning.

Inaugurals that fail to inspire are failures. Inaugurals that are forgotten also fail. Thus, the best Inaugurals are those that inspire and are remembered. Drawing upon the Inaugural Addresses of all forty-five Presidents, plus several by many (one president four times) we can apply both of these two criteria to select the top ten since the beginning, in 1789.

While the task is fully subjective, there is also a general consensus about the subject. So it's fairly easy not to go wrong. The trick is to select

the ones that have lasting value for both the past and future of the country
– those that people will remember and look back and say "why don't we do
what he said."

The following rank, in order, may be subjective, but, objectively, it should
be a criterion for either Joe Biden or Donald Trump when they approach the
podium on January 20th. Neither can help be aware that they are going to be
judged by what their predecessors said, and they had better be up to the task.
Otherwise, it's "all downhill from here."

1. Abraham Lincoln, 1865

The Civil War was about over: four years of unrelenting tragedy,
720,000 dead soldiers. The last thing Lincoln wanted was more of the
same. His appeal (in 700 words) was to show "malice toward none,
charity for all."

Today, we are tearing down the nation's history and its images, showing "malice toward all, charity for none."

2. Franklin D. Roosevelt, 1933

With the Great Depression now into its fourth year, widespread unemployment, banks closing left and right, FDR offered hope with "the only
thing we have to fear is fear itself." Rather than offering new schemes, he
offered inspiration and asked for authority "as if we were invaded by a foreign foe."

Amidst today's pandemic and cultural divisions, where are the inspiration and hope coming from?

3. John F. Kennedy, 1961

With the Cold War raging around the world, with the Soviet Union ahead
in technology, with Communism now in the Caribbean, JFK rallied the
nation, noting that "the torch has been passed" and placed the burden on
the shoulders of his electorate: "'ask not what your country can do for you,
ask what you can do for your country."

Would anyone dare that today?

4. **Thomas Jefferson, 1801**
    With party differences splitting the nation in half (as warned by Washington), Jefferson proclaimed that "We have called by different names brethren of the same principles. We are all Republicans, we are all Federalists."
    But he had politicians; we have to deal against "colors," red, blue, black, white, "people of color" ("all" colors).

5. **Ronald Reagan, 1981**
    With the Cold War into its fourth decade, a nuclear policy called "MAD," Vietnam a disaster, Jimmy Carter proclaiming "malaise," Reagan, like others before him, appealed to the "people" for the answers, both home and abroad: "Today we can declare: Government is not the problem, and government is not the solution. We, the American people, we are the solution."
    Can we speak of a "people" in the singular today?

6. **Woodrow Wilson, 1917**
    The greatest war in history was in its fourth year. He had campaigned on U.S. neutrality, but events forced Wilson's hand to prepare Americans for their first venture as a global power, a reality that is still ongoing today. "There can be no turning back," he offered, "our own fortunes as a nation are involved whether we would have it so or not."
    Again, "fortunes as a nation" appears nostalgic today.

7. **Theodore Roosevelt, 1905**
    "TR" harnessed the nation for world leadership, beginning in the Western Hemisphere and extending outward, with the Spanish War, Panama Canal, the Philippines, the "Great White Fleet." "Upon the success of our experiment much depends," he announced, "not only as regards our own welfare, but as regards the welfare of mankind."
    Today, the war would be "militarism," the canal "imperialism," the Philippines "colonialism," and the Fleet "racism." (Take any noun, add "ism" and, behold, you have life explained.)

8. **Abraham Lincoln, 1861**
    In his first Inaugural, Lincoln tried at the last minute to avoid the oncoming war. He failed, but his words still echo as a plea for unity lest the "roof

cave in." It caved all right, but, despite his best effort to appeal to "the better angels of our nature. ...We are not enemies, but friends. We must not be enemies. Though passion may have strained, it must not break our bonds of affection."

Good advice for any future Lincoln.

9. Harry S. Truman, 1949

After winning his first (and only) presidential election, Harry Truman reminded the nation of its newly-found global responsibilities and of the vast differences between ourselves and our enemies ("exceptionalism"). "The United States and other like-minded nations," he declared, "find themselves directly opposed by a regime with contrary aims and a totally different concept of life."

Question: can the same point be offered today?

10. Warren G. Harding, 1921

With the world war over, Americans questioned the bitter aftermath, without resolution or reason. Warren G. Harding promised "Normalcy" and a return to basics. "Our supreme task," he announced, "is the resumption of our onward, normal way. Envy and jealousy would have no soil for their menacing development, and revolution would be without the passion that engenders it."

What happened to that country?

11. Left open, since no immediate candidate arises.

Will get back on January 21, 2021.

It's the Education Stupid

November 11, 2020

In 1992, after nearly a century winning world wars and forging world orders, America finally gave up. In winning the presidency that year the Governor of Arkansas campaigned on the slogan "it's the economy stupid." With this motto on almost every poster and campaign circular Bill Clinton rode to power against the grain of every presidential election since the Great Depression. His Inaugural Address announced that the country has "drifted," that he would "reinvent America" with "dramatic change," against an economy "weakened by business failures, stagnant wages, increasing inequality and deep divisions."

In turning the country inward, Clinton began a momentum that has dominated into the new century. Barak Obama, particularly, ingrained even further the notion that the United States was in dire need of "repair" and that this would have to come through Washington and its political operatives. Through his campaign book, *Change We Can Believe In* and his first Inaugural Address, Obama stressed that "we must pick ourselves up, dust ourselves off and begin again the work of remaking America."

Four years of Donald Trump have served to highlight the divisions Clinton first announced. By "Making America Great Again" Trump opened the deep wounds left unattended for all to see. The divisive nation left over from the Cold War to the "economy stupid" has come full-circle to define the country as never before since the great Civil War. The vote count in 2020 has left indelible the notion that "Red-Blue" now defines the country nearly as did "Blue-Gray" when Abraham Lincoln took the oath of office.

Question: is Joe Biden the new Lincoln?

These are not transparent nor ephemeral conditions. While actual military war is ridiculous, the "war" definition can apply. While Trump brought history back to "restore" the country the overwhelming cultural/media/dissident attention has been focused on "remake." Essentially, this means that, into its fourth century, the USA is "broken" beyond repair and needs to "begin anew." Basically, this phenomenon appeals to "group" behaviors, which confuses sociology with political science.

Aspects of the new directions have been in-play for decades but the momentum has gathered power, despite (or maybe because of) Trump. The destruction of statues, place-names and other historic memorabilia, the influence of protest, reject and regret as national identities, the target of "white" populations as responsible for everything bad, geographic divides between regional voting and cultural locations now dominate the country. Nowhere is this direction more apparent than the *New York Times* "Project 1619" which is a full-court effort to "reframe the country's history by placing the consequences of slavery and the contributions of black Americans at the very center of the national narrative."

Good luck with that, but they may not need "luck." The schools will do.

These might be passing-fancies, or aspects of social democracy, were it not for the fact that, taken together, they have all either been integrated into the national educational system or are next-in-line.

Alone, Project 1619 has been incorporated into the curricular of 4,500 local school districts (claimed) while President Trump has threatened to withhold federal funds from those that have already done so. Even in education, a "civil war" rages.

Yet that is the precise locale where the issue began, and eventually where it will be resolved. For at bottom, by definition, "ideas have consequences," and the clash of ideas between "Reds vs Blues" begins, as necessary, in the classroom.

Examples have become "mainstream." Typical is the presence of Howard Zinn's *A Popular History of the United States* (1980), an openly Marxist tome now by far the bestseller on US campuses. The overwhelming emphasis of the university as sociological primer, emphasizing "inclusion-diversity" and "identity," has come to define the core nature of the national academy.

This, essentially, is the "battleground" where the "war" for America's future will be (and has been) fought. The conflict goes beyond the mere academic "search for truth," it will define what the country believes it has been and will remain: either apologize for the vices and destroy the old or appreciate the virtues and build forward. Between those extremes there is very little "no man's land."

It is also oxymoronic, why would anyone's biography highlight their worse traits?

At the bottom of this clash is the timeless idea of "nationalism," by-far the most dominate idea in recorded history. Unlike most other nationalisms, defined by biology and geography ("fatherland," "motherland"), American nationalism has always been defined by its "ideas."

The late Hans Kohn, the essential historian of nationalism, has defined "American nationalism" as derived from its English heritage as the "roots and origins of the republic," by English liberalism, rationalism and from figures such as Locke, Milton and Cromwell (*American Nationalism*, 1957). Such notions prompted John Adams to once proclaim this apocalyptic vision of the American purpose, as "Our pure, virtuous, public spirited, federative republic to last forever, govern the globe and introduce the perfection of man."

Adams may be forgiven for his own hyperbole but his proclamation, as another enduring "social myth," serves to highlight in exaggerated form what modern critics do today. Their own interpretations from "racism" to a "privileged" few currently dominate the political landscape, and will eventually destroy nationalism.

Already, the term itself has been qualified to "white" only. This, by itself, divides the idea beyond recovery.

American nationalism cannot be found in ethnics, ancestries or separate from the Founding ideals. If one rejects the ideas that formed the country one is something else by definition, a singular part against a much larger whole ("Me Too, Black Lives, Privileged.")

The essential lessons from history are the ideas that formed and governed the country, that developed growth, belief in progress, the several motivations that provided American prosperity, liberty and success. One does not become a "superpower" by accident.

And since when does a superpower need to be torn apart and "remade"?

In opposition to these notions are the ideologies that relentlessly condemn the nature and conduct of the country, turning "one" into "many" and "nation" into "self," a history neither appreciated, liked nor even understood.

In 1940 the US population was 120 million; it is now triple that. Should this continue there will be 900 million Americans in 2100. What are the prospects of a country that large and taught a steady diet of lessons that degrade their adopted country's nature and conduct, everywhere and always?

There is a profound distinction between political liberty and sociology, between ideas and people. Liberty, the Constitution, Bill of Rights, has little or no bearing upon the political behaviors of whole populations or their politicians. Liberty cannot stop tweets from the president, supervise his personality or force disparate groups to like each other. It will, however, keep the President from closing the *New York Times*, dissolving Congress and invading Canada (things real dictators do in an afternoon).

In the final analysis what we believe is what we are and if trends continue we will begin American Studies from a negative and apologetic definition. It will be difficult, perhaps impossible, to overcome that perspective. The result will be a "Balkanized" continent, sooner or later.

Either way it's the education stupid.

Building the Atlantic World

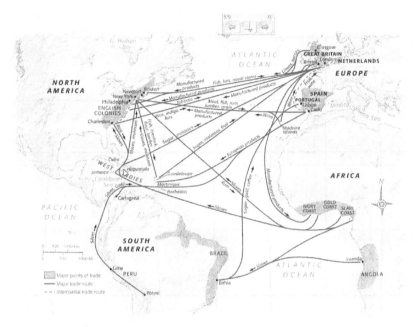

Map 5-3 p84

November 18, 2020

In 1963 a group of scholars at the University of Pennsylvania's *Foreign Policy Research Institute* (FPRI) wrote a book with the same title as this essay (Robert Strausz-Hupe et al) that argued for a greater common political relationship that would unite the sovereign nations of the "Atlantic World." Just fourteen years after NATO and within the time of the Common Market and other post-war unions, Strausz-Hupe and his team (James E. Dougherty, William R. Kintner and many others) felt that the nation-state, as it had existed for centuries, was an anachronism that would, eventually, give way to greater unions of shared values.

Strausz-Hupe, a native of Austria who would later serve as US Ambassador to five separate posts including NATO, had long-held this view in his writings. In 1942, as world war raged throughout the globe, he predicted that "As policy evolves toward several continental systems and technology accentuates the importance of large, contiguous areas, the national state will be a thing of the past" (*Geopolitics: The Struggle for Space and Power*).

Such a vision, held for centuries by others but never realized in full, still remains a theoretical construct despite the European Union (1992), several trade groups and other associated but "fraternal" unities. England's "Brexit" departure and the move toward centralized regimes in eastern Europe demonstrates the tensions that still dominate between national vs transnational political allegiance.

The "status quo" remains an alive and powerful intellectual mindset that continues to retard the momentum that "Atlantic Union" adherents still seek. "Rome wasn't built in a day" may serve as a reminder for patience and deliberation but slogans do not necessarily serve causation.

One who believed in "causes greater than oneself" was none-other than Winston Churchill, perhaps the world's best embodiment of national perseverance and salvation. Not only did he (almost alone) keep England alive in its worst hour but he also did his best for France, offering them a political union to forestall a possible defeat by Hitler's Army (May-June 1940). Under Churchill both British and French civil servants drafted a memorandum on "Franco-British Union" that read, in part, "the Governments of the United Kingdom and the French Republic make this declaration of indissoluble union and unyielding resolution." From his office Churchill declared that "We had before us the bridge toward a new world, the first elements of European or even World Federation."

While skeptical, French leaders endorsed the proposal, even as German Armies were crossing the frontier. Charles de Gaulle, the *persona* of French nationalism, agreed, noting that "The gesture must be immediate." But defeatism soon destroyed the future as the French Parliament and other politicians sought accommodation with Hitler. Prime Minister Paul Reynaud stepped down with these bitter regrets, "Those who rose indignation at the idea of union with our ally were the same individuals who were getting ready to bow and scrape to Hitler."

But Churchill wasn't done. In one of the century's greatest orations, March 5, 1946, he gave his famous "Iron Curtain" speech in Independence, Missouri warning Americans that Europe "from Stettin on the Baltic to Trieste on the Adriatic" was now under control of the Soviet Union. Thus began the "Cold War," but Churchill's actual intention, largely ignored, was how both countries should wage it.

Obscured, somehow, inside the message was Churchill's real purpose, not dissimilar from his earlier one with France. Alluding to the common political inheritance uniquely shared by the US and England, the Magna Carta, Bill of Rights, Habeas Corpus, trial by jury, English common law which "find their most famous expression in the American Declaration of Independence," Churchill proposed political union. "Eventually there may come," he noted,

I feel eventually there will come, the principle of common citizenship, but that we may be content to leave to destiny, whose outstretched arm many of us can already clearly see."

Generations have come and gone, the United Nations has multiplied to 193 members, NATO is 70 and has almost tripled, the EU almost 30 years old (but minus one member), and a host of economic, social and cultural entities dot the globe. But "Building the Atlantic World" remains a distant and seldom-mentioned vision.

But not forgotten.

On November 17 the Foreign Ministers of both France and Germany publically called on the US (assuming President Biden) to "make transatlantic unity possible" (*Washington Post*, A25). In calling for a transatlantic "New Deal," the two Ministers urged both sides of the ocean to "adapt our partnership to global upheavals and in line with the depth of our bonds, common values and shared interests."

While stopping short of Churchill's "common citizenship" they both recognized the need for "a more balanced transatlantic partnership" to include global issues, from Iran to China, to "preserve our way of life and to pursue our never-ending quest for individual freedom and collective progress."

There is an old saying, "some see things that are and ask why, others see things that never were and ask why not."

So ... in starting a global "New Deal," why not?

To Lose a Country

Bundesarchiv, Bild 121-0822
Foto: o.Ang. | 1940 Mai - Juni

November 12, 2020

The title is taken from the third volume of Alistair Horne's trilogy on French-German relations (wars) between 1870 and 1940. France lost two and won the middle (1918), but, in the last (1940), France, in effect, lost itself, i.e. its "country." What does the loss of "country" imply and does it occur every time a war is lost?

Many countries absorb losses quite well. Britain lost the American colonies in 1781 but went on to a greater naval and colonial empire. The U.S. lost Vietnam in 1975; a few years later, it was the world's "sole remaining superpower." Then why did France lose itself in 1940 and not earlier? Horne's actual title for the third book is *To Lose a Battle*: *France 1940*. Substitute "country" for "battle," and that is what he *really* means. And that is what *really* happened.

As British Prime Minister, Churchill made several trips to France in order to stave off defeat, as he knew what that would mean. He even proposed a

Franco-British political union to hold together. Nothing worked. After the surrender, he told the people, "...the Battle of France is over. The Battle of Britain is about to begin."

Words are deceptive. France "won" in 1918, but the effects of that trauma paralyzed the country until the final blow in 1940. The same army that held Germany at bay for four devastating years came apart in six weeks before the surrender on June 24, 1940.

World War II was "total" war, which means that victory and defeat were also total. To "lose" a country, therefore, is to lose heart and soul. Territory, army, colonies, casualties, and other tangible manifestations can be recovered or compensated over time, but a country's nature, purpose, and being, once lost, cannot be recovered.

Total defeat, in this case, meant the end of France in the global strategic balance; replacing historic *grandeur* with a more modest and restrained world-view; the priority of domestic versus global ambitions; the threat of immigration as potentially fatal, acceptance of status rather than leadership, the realities of occupation and a German Army parade down the *Champs-Élysées*.

Finally, the personality of Charles de Gaulle, in this perspective, is more nostalgic than substantive, almost pure memory. In his attempt to revive France as a great power, he demanded the removal of all American troops from French soil (1964). At the press conference, he was asked this question: "Does that include the ones buried here?"

Rubbing it in, yes, but that's what "loss of country" means (dependence).

Does this case have any bearing upon the United States today?

France was defeated in battle by a neighbor but faced decades of internal erosion before the defeat. The experience of World War I was so traumatic that France simply could not bear a repetition. Germany profited from the same experience, improvised, and won in a few weeks a victory that escaped them years earlier. What occurred *internally*, thus, decided the difference between victory and defeat. Germany (Nazis) was eventually defeated (1945), but solely from without (should anyone doubt this, just examine pictures of post-war Berlin).

In the final analysis, it makes little difference whether "loss" comes from military defeat or political/cultural erosion. In either case, the result is the same. Just as boxers retire after their prime, countries, also, reach a "peak" before final decline.

Where does the U.S. stand today? After the experience of winning two world wars and the Cold War, former UN Ambassador under Reagan, Jeanne Kirkpatrick, declared it was time for America to "become a normal country in a normal time" (1991). By the end of the Cold War, Soviet Premier Mikhail Gorbachev confided to President Reagan, "We have done a terrible thing to you, we have deprived you of an enemy."

Gorbachev was right but probably did not see the full implications. But the Governor of Arkansas, Bill Clinton, did. By campaigning on the slogan "it's the economy stupid," Clinton saw that America's time as world hegemon was over, to be replaced by a well-worn but reliable turn inward. While still promising to "remake the world," Clinton promised to do this through the new phenomenon of "globalization," as an equal country with others toward a shared goal of "more growth, more equality, better preservation of the environment and a greater possibility of world peace."

In the ensuing decades, neither equality, growth, nor peace have prevailed while the turn inward has been exacerbated to the point where a subsequent administration pledged to "lead from behind," while the current one has ignored the existing world order through domestic "greatness."

In the 2020 presidential race, neither candidate cared to even discuss the subject "foreign policy," much less any new world orders. With the death of a black man in Minneapolis by police in May, the concentration of American political/social order has been fully devoted to the twin abstractions, "justice, equality," while the president's personal conversations with world leaders came the closest to anything remotely "foreign" to the public.

The attention of the voting public has now come full-circle to unveil new and innovative ways to achieve both equality and justice between home-grown identities and to determine if the domestic order will be socialist or capitalist. Judging from history (about 6,000 recorded years of it), this may occupy whole generations, if not centuries, to decide. It may just as well never end.

In the meantime, world order, if there is to be one, will almost certainly be determined by someone else. Judging from recent and current directions, it may well make little difference to Americans as to whom.

In any case, we are certain neither to like nor to accept it. But Police reform requires total attention.

If history is any guide, again, an injured America, as in 1941 and 2001, might just survive another "day of infamy" and rise to the occasion. But this historical repetition has probably run its course.

In the meantime, it might be instructive to see how France has done since 1940. Once "lost," it has re-emerged, but not by itself nor as before (not even remotely).

Who would be around the help America?

Outer Space: The Last Frontier

September 8, 2020

President's are prone to elevate their policies to the highest levels, using words, "great," "new" etc. to advertise how unique they're going to be in the world. Franklin D. Roosevelt and John F. Kennedy introduced us to a "New Deal" and "New Frontier" respectively and now Congresswoman Octavia Cortez (AOC to us) has added color to the combination, "Green New Deal." Lyndon Johnson sought a "Great Society" that now Trump is restoring with "MAGA," identified on the street with red hats.

Not that each politician was insincere or that the public didn't buy-in. They were not and they did. Nor does it make much difference: the New Deal didn't end the Depression and JFK died too soon to realize his Frontier. Johnson's society was anything but great and Trump's MAGA and AOC's Green New Deal remain to-be-seen. Just don't hold your breath.

But the main point about such flattering language is that it offered the voting public some sort of hope that the next time-around the place would be better than it is now. "Hope springs eternal" goes the saying and without hope the attention and the patience of the electorate vanishes quickly. True, it's all a "play on words" but it's effective and without hope life soon becomes the "same old same old."

What would be the fate of a candidate who promised "vote for me and we all stay still?"

Kennedy's Inaugural Address offered hope out of the depressing Cold War, reminding Americans of their mission on earth with his assurance that "I do not shrink from this responsibility, I welcome it." Roosevelt gave hope within the worst economic depression, proclaiming that "the only thing we have to fear is fear itself."

A little-remembered part of Kennedy's Inaugural was the ambition to "let us explore the stars." This promise came-and-went until he told Congress that one of his primary missions was "landing a man on the moon and returning him safely to earth." Of course, this promise fell mostly on deaf-ears. The public had a bit more on their mind than any such rhetoric that put the country into the solar system (a Gallup Poll indicated 58% opposed).

Kennedy went into more detail on September 12, 1962, when he addressed Rice University on the higher ambition to put America first-and-foremost into the "Space Race." This remains one of the greatest oratories in American history; a promise that needs recall now more than even then.

At the time the US was decidedly inferior to the Soviet Union in Outer Space, as Americans still had the memory of the Soviet "Sputnik" visibly circling the earth every 40 hours (1957). Not-to-mention Yuri Gagarin, the first human to orbit the earth (1961).

At Rice Kennedy did not pull punches. "Why go to the moon in this decade and do the other things" he asked rhetorically. "not because they are easy but because they are hard; because that goal will serve to organize and measure the best of our energies and skills, because that challenge is one that we are willing to accept, one we are unwilling to postpone, and one we intend to win ..."

Kennedy went on to put this new effort into context, "... Why climb the highest mountain? Why, 35 years ago, fly the Atlantic? Why does Rice play Texas?" In doing so, he condensed history into brief time eras, "only last week did we develop penicillin and television and nuclear power," ending with the present moment when Mariner 2 was heading for Venus: "and now if America's new spacecraft succeeds in reaching Venus, we will have literally reached the stars before midnight tonight."

With such metaphors Kennedy sought to create a sense of urgency, purpose and change into the audience, and the country itself. He deliberately injected a sense of romance coupled with patriotic history in his appeal. He talked of space as literally his "New Frontier," implicitly invoking those of the past, "Manifest Destiny," Lewis and Clark, "54/40 or fight," make the world "safe for democracy," Pearl Harbor, Berlin Airlift etc.

He also emphasized that space travel was both affordable and doable while using the pronoun "we" throughout to enroll the public into the endeavor.

Kennedy succeeded beyond imagination as seven years after Rice, with over 400,000 working on the effort, Neil Armstrong stepped out of Apollo Eleven to the surface of the moon.

Kennedy never lived to see the reward for his ambition, while the "space race", such as it was, ended in 1972 when the last (of five) lunar landings from the US occurred. The period since has been occupied by a "Vietnam syndrome," end of the cold war and the descent of American political ambitions into ideology, race, gender and other purely domestic designs.

Today the country faces a critical election with nothing on the horizon remotely close to what was conceived sixty years ago. Nearly the opposite, the country appears on the brink of destruction as buildings burn, cities occupied and attention totally focused on what internal groups demand here- and- now, but all on planet earth.

With nothing outside left to conquer, with external ambitions long-since gone the American "dream" has turned into itself again. Even Trump's "MAGA" rhetoric has an isolationist memory. But the administration has, to its credit, created a "space force", whose ambitions remain promising but little more.

In the meantime others are not so inhibited. Ye Peijian, head of China's Lunar Program, spoke to his country this way in 2018: "The universe is an ocean, the moon is the Diaoyu Islands, Mars is Huangyan Island. If we don't get there now ... then we will be blamed by our descendants.

If others go there, then they will take over, and you won't be able to go even if you want to. This is reason enough" [for china's space project].

Is there another JFK out there? Again, don't hold your breath.

Polarities (we have known)

GLOBAL ECONOMY 2018

Article and Sources:

August 29, 2020

In political terms a "pole" is a center of power, expressed in the familiar terms of national strength, military, diplomatic, economic, sociology, stability, leadership, determination etc. There are three, and only three, ways in which to examine world politics through "poles": unipolar (one center), bipolar (two) and multipolar (three or more). Those are the only alternatives and it makes no difference whether "multipolar" has three or thirty centers, it remains "multi" throughout.

Historically, the main definition of "power center" has been "unipolar," insofar as most political regimes from ancient times to the seventeenth century have consisted of "empires" wherein government ran directly from the top down to the central and distant regions. The Roman and British Empires probably constitute the clearest examples of a land and a sea-based system each, with both Rome and London as classic "imperial" centers of great political authority.

While empires still existed until the mid-twentieth century the gravity-center of world politics took a sharp turn against imperial rule in 1648, when the Peace of Westphalia (Germany) ended the Holy Roman Empire in Europe. The result not only ended the religious war between Catholic Rome and Protestant Europe but it also inaugurated the "nation-state," wherein political "sovereignties" based their authority on both their people (nation) and their unique political association (state). Thereafter, world politics became both Europe-centered and multipolar, while as many as fifteen "countries" (nation-states) began competing with each other for supremacy through near-endless alliances and wars.

The modern nation-state was both homogenous and aggressive, against itself and others abroad. Internally, they were "British," "French," "Dutch," "Spanish" etc. while overseas they combined to carve the remainder of the globe into particular regions with little left to digest.

The great wars of the last century were essentially the result of latecomers to the system, mainly Germany and Japan, bent on finding their own "place in the sun" between the vast expanse of territories, from central Europe, Africa through the Middle East to the Far East, already taken by the rest of Imperial Europe. As collisions and near-wars produced history's greatest conflicts, (world wars) the newcomers soon found-out that beneath the imperial "sun" there was precious little room left "on the beach."

Multipolarity as a system ended in the Twentieth Century, pushed over in 1914 and finally laid to rest by 1945 when the USA first entered the fray and, in effect, replaced Great Britain as the "holder" of the historic Balance of Power that governed European society for centuries.

This was a historic moment, memorialized by the American Foreign Service Officer, Joseph M. Jones, in his classic, *The Fifteen Weeks*. It was within this time period, February through June 1947, when the "torch was passed to a new generation of Americans, born in this century, disciplined by a hard and bitter peace" (John F. Kennedy) who took on the responsibility to preserve the hard-won peace, create a new world order and "stay the course" (Ronald Reagan) until the Soviet Union was gone and another world order promised a new "lease" on an old and already-dead multipolarity.

In between, the world witnessed, and lived, a precarious order in which nuclear stalemate kept a global stability based eventually on the doctrine that, if fulfilled, meant a possible termination of any order to the world, old or new. While "Mutual Assured Destruction" ("MAD") secured the end of a potential communist order, the "bipolar" world lived day-by-day in which small points on the globe promised to erupt into the end of humanity. As crises passed and went, from Korea, to Taiwan, Vietnam, Israel, Egypt, Lebanon, Cuba, Panama, Iraq, Suez, Hungary, Berlin, the political order seemed just one-step away from the vanishing point.

But by late 1991 the Soviet Union, exhausted by competition from America and NATO, and under the combined guidance of Reagan, Gorbachev, Thatcher and the Pope, "threw in the towel" and returned as an old-friend from multipolar days. Under its "baptized" name, Mother Russia came back to life but was not exactly welcomed under the wing of the brand-new American emergence as guardian of western civilization.

First introduced by the late journalist, Charles Krauthammer in 1990, the "Unipolar Moment," according to him was "a unique historical phenomenon ... called the moment of unipolarity" and caused by the emergence of modern history's first "superpower." Krauthammer acknowledged that the "moment" would "be brief" and confidently assured us that the US would, sooner rather than later, be joined by rivals from both Asia (Japan, China) and Europe (Germany).

The emergence of America as the unipolar savior of peace in the world was certainly not unique to Krauthammer. None other than British Prime Minister William Gladstone wrote in 1878 that "while we have been advancing with portentous rapidity, America is passing us by as if a canter. ... she will probably become what we are now, head servant in the great household of the world." French demographer Vacher de Lapouge predicted both the eventual Cold War and American supremacy, noting that "the United States is the true adversary of Russia in the great struggle to come ... I also believe that the United States is appealed to triumph. Otherwise, the universe would be Russian" (1899). British novelist H.G. Wells in *Anticipations* (1900) wrote that "the great urban region between Chicago and the Atlantic" will emerge by the year 2000 to "strangle the serpents of war and national animosity in its cradle," while his compatriot, William Thomas Stead, entitled his 1900 book, *The Americanization of the World, The Trend of the Twentieth Century.*

So much for a unipolar "moment," which, as Krauthammer saw, came and went in a flash in the American political culture.

Clue: while all other great imperial regimes came from homogeneous societies, perhaps only Krauthammer knew that American heterogeneity would savage any efforts to control outsiders and, almost inevitably, force Americans inward time and again. If a society tolerates chronic quarrelling inside it can hardly expect to govern order outside.

As the country approaches another election minus any thought on world order, and as the riots between and among identity groups clog our cities, note please the re-emergence of world politics as between several sovereigns all bent on similar paths toward their own versions of what and who should govern. China heads this list but it's anyone's game.

For a reminder of potential results from such chaos, suggest *The Peloponnesian War* (Thucydides), on polarity four hundred years before Christ.

Then go riot for your cause back home, and watch the world go to hell in a handbasket, for the 1,450th time (rough guess).

Acceptance

September 12, 2020

Words have meaning. To misuse a word or an expression may turn around the entire content of what one is trying to relate. Precision in language, written or vocal, is often scrutinized carefully so as not to convey a wrong impression.

In world politics examples of such confusion are legion. During the Cold War Premier Nikita Khrushchev of the Soviet Union once declared (1956) that "we will bury you," interpreted in the west that he was preparing nuclear war. Khrushchev later explained that he meant in economic competition, but this was too late to avert a major US arms increase and fear throughout the entire world.

The word "détente" has more than one meaning. In its original French it means a "release from tension" but as it was interpreted in the west it was often defined as a Soviet tactical policy to disarm NATO into a false complacency. Policy disagreements in the 1970's between Secretary of State Henry Kissinger, who pursued détente, and his opponents, including Secretary of Defense James Schlesinger, often reflected this semantic confusion. The Reagan Administration abandoned détente altogether, with President Ronald Reagan calling the USSR an "evil empire" while building up a vast offensive and defensive arms machine. Ironically, Reagan later implicitly pursued a form of détente himself, minus the word, while negotiating with Mikhail Gorbachev to end the Cold War.

In the political world, domestic and foreign, the word "acceptance," and its opposite, "rejection" are often invoked, if just implicitly, to determine policies. Whether or not a country accepts the *status quo* or rejects it may well define the difference between peace and war.

Briefly, acceptance means consent, agreement or to accede. Rejection means dismiss, repudiate or refuse. While the degrees of difference between both are substantial, they are often disguised in the so-called "gray" areas of political discourse. Sometimes, these disguises are real, ie. meant to "deceive" the other party. Precedents abound:

> few in Britain before 1775 understood how deeply Americans rejected "taxation without representation." The result was a war for independence that changed the course of history.

> the expression "states-rights" in the political vocabulary, including slavery, was defined by the southern states as essential to their life. The North, including President-elect Lincoln, rejected this. The North was taken by surprise when South Carolina seceded in December 1860. Civil War was declared three months later because, for one side, the situation was unacceptable.

> In 1919 the Versailles Treaty blamed Germany as solely responsible for World War I, deprived it of its colonies, no military and forced enormous reparations on the population. The Treaty was wholly unacceptable to almost all Germans, which allowed Adolph Hitler and the Nazis to take over.

> "Containment" as a foreign policy was adopted in 1947 by the Truman Administration but was later critiqued by his Republican opponents as too defensive and reactive to produce any result. By 1981 the Reagan Administration found containment unacceptable, abandoned it for a policy of "rollback" and terminated the Soviet Union within a decade.

These examples are from American foreign policy but can be applied to domestic political life as well. Here too can be found similar semantical distinctions that have defined world politics since time immemorial. The same definitions of "accept and "reject" that have directed the world are likewise present here-at-home.

Today, two months before the next presidential election, the group *Black Lives Matter* (BLM) has taken center-stage by directing a nationwide set of urban disturbances stemming from the death of a man named George Floyd in Minneapolis (May 25). Normally, the death of a single person would not attract much attention, since in history tens of millions have been executed by the home regime. But BLM has succeeded in elevating this death as symbolic of the country itself, putting the USA in the same category as Soviet Russia (40 million civilians murdered) or Communist China (60 million). This is quite some political "deception" but it has, somehow, captured the public imagination, including millions of dollars from business. The Mayor of the Capitol City has surrounded the White House with the name of the movement in bold letters.

Thus, instead of a civil rights issue the movement has skyrocketed into a question of the very character of the people and their history, with a deliberate intention to expunge both character and history. In short, the country itself is "unacceptable."

The deception occurs when BLM and allied groups pretend that they "accept" the content and nature of the country they, simultaneously, are trying to replace. By calling the deficiencies of the American culture and its people "systemic" they are declaring that the entire enterprise, not just the policies, the times nor the individuals, have become unacceptable and thus rejected and, ultimately, replaced.

Behind the rhetoric for the late Mr. Floyd there is a "hidden agenda" that surpasses any reference to individuals or racial beliefs, now or before. BLM was founded by three Black women in 2013 who are professed "trained Marxists." While its public persona belies this ideological origin the website proclaims causes that have little to do with standard civil rights issues, including but not limited to: "colonialism, sexism, trans-gender-antagonistic violence, misogyny, defunding police, western nuclear family, queer affirming network, heteronormative thinking, ageism, environments where men are not centered."

In the short-term BLM tactics appear momently disruptive but their long-term goals are, indeed, "systemic" and, by definition, revolutionary.

Just as America rejected the British, as the South rejected the North, as the Germans rejected the Versailles Treaty and as Reagan rejected containment so, too, does BLM reject America.

Immediately prior to each event in history: did anyone know that the British would lose America, that the South would secede and over 700,000 soldiers die, that Versailles would disappear and history's greatest war take over 76 million lives, that the Soviet Union would collapse without a single shot?

Even more remarkable was that all this was done by a relatively few: a small group of New England and Virginia Patriots, several hundred plantation-owners, basically one man (the *Fuhrer*) and a tiny group of Reagan National Security advisors.

In all cases the status-quo was unacceptable but few living within the status quo knew it or believed it. As the late Harvard historian Bernard Bailyn wrote of the "Loyalists" (pro British) inside the American Revolution, "they were outplayed, overtaken, by-passed."

Question: where do we stand in this perspective?

Can the Congress of Vienna Be Restored?

November 15, 2020

If the main purpose of international organizations is to prevent war the only one worth examining is the historic congress held in Vienna, Austria, 1814-1815. The others, League of Nations, United Nations, are worth examining only if one wants to appreciate how world bodies typically fail from their main purpose. Not to undercut the valuable social and economic aspects of global meetings, but if war prevention is our singular object they have all, with minor exceptions, proven empty.

Perhaps the best example of the "exception" would be the Organization of American States (OAS), founded in 1948. Yet this valuable body reflects the range and influence of American power in the Western Hemisphere, going back to the Monroe Doctrine (1823). There have been few wars in the area over history, none major, but the reason is the overwhelming American dominance and geopolitical realities (Andes mountains). The OAS reflects this reality but did not cause it.

The world is another matter. From the beginnings of the nation-state system (1648) the global arena has been dominated by an incessant warfare "system" that has created the world "orders" that have come and gone since then. At the same time they have killed untold millions, the latest ending in 1945 leaving 76 million dead in its wake (estimate).

But the system continued and to this day still represents the diplomatic anatomy that was first constructed in the seventeenth century. Minor wars have become our daily and accepted reality, "minor" defined as wars incapable of transforming the order of the day. Yet this definition avoids the human cost of such a world. And maybe worse, it has a fatal defect if we assume that history's tragedies on a global scale remain confined to the past.

"Those who do not remember the past are condemned to repeat it" (Jorge Santayana, 1931) might be a guide for our time rather than naïve assumptions that, somehow, the new century has left the old ones dead and buried. The precarious great-power peace that has prevailed since World War II has grown more fragile since the US has turned inward and since Europe has united within itself. The rise of China in Asia, Russia under Putin and continued global anarchy testifies that history is neither old nor irrelevant and could yet surprise us how quickly it can return.

But a "return" to history might well be worth examining if we want to "do something" about the present rather than just abdicating to subterranean forces. America, as architect of the current global order, has a unique responsibility to lead the world down this path. Who else?

Yet America must use a distant and fairly obscure example to emulate. At the same time the country's most famous diplomat/scholar, Henry Kissinger, himself a German émigré, has provided the prime (perhaps only) way to-go. His first book was itself a historic inquiry as to why the nineteenth century provided great-power peace until its lessons were forgotten in the tragic beginnings of the First World War, 1914. We have all gone "downhill" since.

The book, *A World Restored* (1957), reviewed how the major European statesmen met at the end of the quarter-century of Napoleonic wars that had devastated the continent (and the world). The title "restored" implied a return to the political stability that monarchy had provided before the French Revolution and rescued the political "legitimacy" that was required for an enduring peace.

In effect, Vienna created a renewed world order based upon "legitimacy," which Kissinger meant as "acceptance of the framework of the international order by all major powers." Vienna eliminated neither human nature nor war but even minor wars, from Kissinger, "may occur, but they will be fought in the name of the existing structure."

The result was called the "Concert of Europe," and defined how great powers avoided major war for a century, unprecedented in European history, before or since. "Concert," in this regard, is defined as "an agreement in design or plan ... act in harmony or conjunction."

But peace may have created a false sense of security, or an illusion, that it was to be lasting. As Kissinger noted in his Introduction that was precisely the problem of 1914: they had forgotten what war was like. "Those ages," he wrote, "which in retrospect seem most peaceful were least in search of peace." The answer, then and perhaps now, is the idea of political "concert," "an international agreement about the future of workable arrangements and about the permissible aims of foreign policy" (Introduction)

No two periods of history are identical, but parallels exist. When asked recently about the merits of a renewed global concert, Kissinger, now 97, emphasized the presence of three conditions, an "architecture" for mutual security, a "common purpose" to avoid war and "an intellectual framework" that embraces philosophy and technology. (*Washington Post*, November 13, A21).

Since the end of the Cold War America has receded both its global ambitions and its interests in constructing world orders. But the "past is prologue" and the same country that tried this in 1919 and 1945 still has the time and the resources to start over.

All we need is an architecture, a purpose and the intellect.

One Hundred Years Apart:

Overstretch in World Politics, 1839-1939

November 5, 2020

The word "overstretch" first came to prominence in 1987 when Professor Paul Kennedy (Yale) defined it as the cause of great power decline in his book, *The Tragedy of Great Power Politics*. The theme was applied later by Professor Walter McDougall (Pennsylvania) in *The Tragedy of US Foreign Policy* (2016). It is no coincidence that both used the word "tragedy" in describing the results from overstretch, Kennedy for the decline of countries in history such as Spain, McDougall with regard to the US especially since World War II.

With regard to recent, post-Cold War America, McDougall noted that "Americans bore responsibility to engage in regime change wherever necessary and possible." The resultant military interventions by the US, beginning in 1982 through 2016, produced at least nineteen separate episodes, mostly in the Middle East and Afghanistan. The political symbolism for these cases has been termed "endless wars," with the exception of Trump, who has withdrawn from most and started none. But that is history.

The Dictionary term to describe "overstretch" is "beyond normal," a label that begs the question, what is "normal." Thus, the term remains subjective, ie. variable and independent. Perhaps the only way to grade "normal" (vs "abnormal") is the result obtained. Was the effort worth it and successful or unsuccessful and unnecessary. Was it within the geopolitical and resource limits of the occasion? Did it produce appropriate results or have we come to regret them? Were the commitments the result of frustration or desperation?

Some situations are obvious. There can be no overstretch between neighbors. Thus, it can be determined that France and Germany, whose wars spanned centuries including both world wars, behaved "normally," that is they always fought (until recently). Nor was it overstretch for Teddy Roosevelt to take Panama from Columbia and build a canal. On the other hand, the Monroe Doctrine (1823) was a clear overstretch. How could one country declare supervision over an entire hemisphere when it couldn't even defend its own Capitol (British burned Washington, 1814)?

Fortunately for the hemisphere, the Monroe Doctrine did not result in tragedy, but overstretch, as both Kennedy and McDougall have shown, often does.

In judging the long (25 year) American involvement in Vietnam, would it be appropriate to judge it as "overstretch"? There are two answers, both the same, the "personal" and the "strategic." One might ask the families of the 58,000 soldiers who returned in body bags. Or we can judge the result of the US retreat when several years later America became the "world's sole remaining superpower." Irrespective of Vietnam.

By 1781 the British found that the war in America was another overstretch. They soon granted independence, went on to defeat Napoleon and became the reigning "superpower" of the time, with colonies all over the world. But not in America.

Yet the full story of British foreign policy, almost completely overlooked, produced an "overstretch" that changed the course of history and resulted in the two greatest human "tragedies" of all-time, World War I and World War II. Ironically, both occasions came with near-identical circumstances and exactly one hundred years apart.

In 1839 Britain, France and other European countries signed the Treaty of London which guaranteed Belgian neutrality, without specifics, should Belgium be threatened. In July 1914 the German Foreign Minister, Bethmann-Hollweg, informed Britain that the German Army might invade Belgium and that they should not intervene because of a "mere scrap of paper." On August

1 the Germans did just that and on the fourth British Foreign Secretary Edward Grey issued an ultimatum, giving the German Army twelve hours to leave. Grey did not even wait until midnight but declared war at 11 PM.

A similar situation occurred earlier (1870) when the Germans (Prussia) invaded France, resulting in a French surrender and the emergence of modern Germany. In that case the two were left alone and Britain and the rest of the world accepted the result.

By intervening in 1914 Britain also enrolled its full Commonwealth, including Australia, New Zealand, most of Africa, the Middle East, India, Pakistan, Malaya and on 23 August Japan (by treaty with England). In 1917 the US joined the allies, thus guaranteeing what Britain did in the first place: make the German attack a world war.

It would be entertaining to speculate on what "might have happened" otherwise. But this should suffice: could it have been much worse?

Having failed to "appease" Hitler at Munich in 1938, British Prime Minister Neville Chamberlain "guaranteed" Poland in April 1939, again without specifics. On September 1 Hitler invaded Poland and on the third Chamberlain (the "appeaser") declared war, just as his predecessor did before. Like Belgium in 1914 Poland fell in a few weeks, but the conflict was now worldwide and within two years, again, the US was in for-good.

For Hitler, as with Bethmann-Hollweg, the reasoning seemed distant, removed. When he was told of the British declaration he turned to his Foreign Secretary, von Ribbentrop, and asked pointedly, "now what"?

Was Britain "overstretched" in either case? Neither Belgium nor Poland were saved, they both suffered occupation for years thereafter. Nor did Britain even attempt to rescue each, any more than it had either the intention or resources to do so.

For its own sake, the net result of world war saw the final chapter of the British Empire, the rise of totalitarian regimes throughout, the emergence of a bipolar world between the US and USSR, nuclear threats and the final decline of Europe as center of the political globe.

World War II took 76 million lives (estimate), that's 35,000 each day for six years. Were Belgium or Poland worth it?

Most will probably say "yes." Today the US is in turmoil over the death of one man in Minnesota. Is he worth it, again apparently "yes." Or, are these cases merely symbolic of greater causes?

But in each case "overstretch" is equivalent to "exaggeration," both being the opposite of "normal."

Or is world politics similar to domestic, like living in an asylum?

May 15, 2020

In his classic study, *Anatomy of Revolution* (1938) Harvard Professor Crane Brinton compared the four great political revolutions (English, American, French, Russian) to a "fever" that contained several stages, eventually ending in a new and invigorated society but still based upon cultures inherited from the past. That is to say, revolution was a sickness of the body, cleansed and healed, but within the same inherited physiology. For example, Russia's political structure and ideology can be overturned but Russia's geopolitical reality is permanent. Russian soldiers facing German armies in 1941 cared little whether or not the leadership was Stalin or Nicholas.

Brinton was also careful not to condemn revolution as a phenomenon itself, noting how the phrase has innate connotations that depend on cultures, philosophies and locations. The British were proud of their own Magna Carta (1215) but far-less charitable of the American one (1776). Americans, similarly, were conceived in revolution but condemned both the French (1789) and Russian (1917) ones. As Brinton himself wrote, "biologically, fever in itself is a good thing rather than a bad thing for the organism that survives it. ... the fever burns up the wicked germs ..."

Brinton was most famous for his contribution that revolution, rather than being derived from oppression and dominion, actually was conceived at the precise time that society had achieved a degree of movement or "progress." Cruel and unusual regimes cannot be overthrown precisely due to their nature; it is only when that nature retreats that opportunity for change begins. To apply a metaphor: with no light at the end the tunnel stays "dark," movement can only begin when light appears. After that, it's "off to the races."

Acknowledging that "untouchables very rarely revolt," Brinton found that a "cross-section of common humanity" actually inspire revolt and that economics were never critical. This was certainly true in eighteenth century America, probably the wealthiest place on earth at the time, where, "general economic conditions ... show increasing wealth, ... no class ground down in poverty."

Far more important than objective conditions for revolution were the *subjective* factors, particularly among the intellectual class. The term *alienation* was found to be a common catalyst for class action in the four major revolutions that Brinton uncovered: "the desertion of the intellectuals is a real uniformity in the societies herein studied." While noting that intellectual alienation is "normal in the modern west," he nevertheless identified this phenomena as the true springboard for wholesale societal change:

"... if he has a full or tolerably full belly and a grievance, a sense of being treated undeservedly, unjustly, if something inspires in him that feeling that, it would seem no other animal can have, that of moral indignation, he will revolt; or rather he will make a revolution, not a mere revolt."

All these observations apply to the past, what is their merit now? Ie. is history relevant or not? If not then we all start each day brand new; if so the "past is prologue," ie. guides the present and future.

Is there "alienation" in American culture today? Has anyone read the papers? Are the American universities calm and studious or hotbeds of unrest and revolt? The most popular American history book is Howard Zinn's *A People's History of the United States* (1980), a Marxist tract that excoriates US history and culture each step of the way. Nothing, repeat nothing, is positive or even benign. Yet this book has sold over 2.6 million copies for American schools and has reached "an almost iconic status" according to one reviewer. Among other things, Zinn compares Franklin D. Roosevelt with Adolph Hitler and the atomic bombings of Japan to Japanese atrocities in China. Despite horrible reviews by most traditional historians ("incoherent," "deeply pessimistic," "a scissors and paste pot job," "a Manichean fable," - to name some -) Zinn was also labeled by the great historian Arthur Schlesinger, Jr. as "a polemicist, not a historian."

But, was Zinn's purpose history ... or revolution? By his own account he had no inclination toward "disinterested scholarship," but wanted foremost to bring on "a revolution in the academy."

That he has done, along with a number of other "alienated" personages and institutions whose primary aim is change ... that is "revolutionary" change.

Today's political culture in the United States is widely "infected" with the revolutionary "fever," from the academy, theater to the media. "Identity" politics has replaced analysis and scholarship with a series of radical "isms" that effectively place history, biology and sociology (with most other studies) into neat "compartments" in a continuous struggle for either "equality" or "supremacy" or a combination thereof.

"White supremacy" confuses the two, is it descriptive or disparaging? If one is truly, "truly," opposed show the world and throw out your computer (among another ten thousand items).

Crane Brinton foresaw this resentment in 1938 by noting that "one of the hardest things to do on this earth is to describe men or institutions without wanting to change them." He, thus, would not be surprised to learn of today's *New York Times* "Project 1619" that intends to change the "birth" of America from July 4, 1776 to August 20, 1619, when the first slave ship arrived in North America (alleged). By reversing the American "experiment" from the hope of liberty to the despair of slavery the *Times* has gone from reporting events to making them. The newspaper, thus, is now an agent of revolution.

A "fever" is not a rational or a coherent conception, it does not answer to "reason." "Moral indignation" will not be calmed by laws or sympathies. This insight was captured by another Harvard historian, Bernard Bailyn, in describing how the revolutionaries of 1776 were viewed by "Loyalists":

"Committed to the moral as well as the political integrity of the Anglo-American system as it existed, the Loyalists were insensitive to the moral basis of the protests that arose against it ... they could find only persistent irrationality in the arguments of the discontented ... they did not sense the constriction of the existing order, often because they lived so deeply within it ... They were outplayed, overtaken, bypassed."

Is there a "fever" today? What is America's "temperature"?

Will it live? As what?

Wilsonianism

July 16, 2020

I normally do not favor "isms" as the suffix changes a simple noun into a raging and defiant "worldview" on the loose, aimed at targets to erase and societies to subvert. But for this I can make an exception, since the subject, President Woodrow Wilson, made the first, and most definitive, American contribution to world order.

The notion itself has been, and rightly so, the subject of notoriety and ridicule since Wilson went to great lengths to change the world but failed miserably in the implementation. After declaring "he kept us out of war" (which he did) in the 1916 election he found himself declaring war on Imperial Germany five months later. Wilson didn't lie, he just found himself captive to events, a fate that destroyed his world order soon afterward.

With the American contribution decisive, after four dreadful years, Wilson turned victory into an American crusade, establishing the war aim to "make the world safe for democracy" and creating the organization, League of Nations, to do just that. Then came the tragedy, of the century most likely.

While the Allies (Britain, France) reluctantly agreed to Wilson's conception, and the "Fourteen Points" that accompanied it, he forgot to maintain his home base. This was his signal mistake, but more a monstrous tragedy given his profound background.

Woodrow Wilson may have been the most distinguished political personality to ever grace the White House. A distinguished professor, with revered publications on history and law, he was, in turn, President of the American Academy of Political Science, President of Princeton University, Governor of New Jersey and twice elected President of the United States, beating out challengers such as Theodore Roosevelt and William Howard Taft.

Yet when it came to the decisive event of his lifetime he failed to even make an effort to obtain the necessary domestic political backing that would have crowned his war aims. First, he failed to include even a single member of the opposition on the US negotiating team, thus snubbing not only the entire Republican Party, that controlled the Senate, but Henry Cabot Lodge (R-MA) as well, Chairman of the Foreign Relations Committee (upon innocent reflection, did anyone, anywhere whisper in his ear, "don't piss-off Henry").

Second, Wilson refused to compromise on anything that might alter the Versailles Peace Treaty (and the League). In assessing the Republicans he famously called them "a little group of willful men" and, again, refused negotiations. Third, he took a final, fateful step in forbidding any Senate Democrat to vote for the Treaty, even including a set of Republican "amendments" that would have permitted passage (these were quite innocuous, recognizing the Monroe Doctrine, American right to declare war etc.).

Finally, with the Treaty certain to fail in the Senate Wilson took "to the road," in a non-stop, whirlwind train campaign intended to enlist popular support. Then came his last mistake: he got sick. After suffering a stroke in Pueblo, Colorado he was rushed back to Washington, whereupon he suffered an even more massive stroke, leaving both himself and the League destitute. For the remainder of his term his wife, Edith, ran the White House, as the Treaty, and with it the League, went down "for the count."

Thus we have the figure of President Woodrow Wilson, a truly great man who commanded both the most daring and adventurous American intrusion into world politics and, simultaneously, the most dramatic and catastrophic fall.

What may have happened if the US joined the League of Nations is anyone's guess. The only certainty: with American power and commitment to the integrity of the Peace Treaty the history of the interwar period would have been much different. For the record, there remains this question: could it have been any worse?

Today, we have Wilson's name in total disgrace. Once rejected as failing to accomplish the most daring American adventure on the world stage, he is now labeled a personal "racist." Thus, he fails on both fronts, home and abroad. Can anyone go lower?

The one saving grace: as a "racist" (variously defined) he probably joins all or at least most presidents and probably most Americans who had anything to do with the country from the Puritans to Trump.

Yet the name "Wilson" also contains a singular distinction that still serves as the American "cause" in the world. For all his failings, Woodrow Wilson was the first, but not the last, to develop the principles of liberty, justice and democracy as the ultimate goals to be pursued in foreign policies. Like the personality himself, these remain ideas only, not necessarily realities, but theoretical, "idealistic," "utopian," with the failings, defeats, hypocrisies and tragedies of the man himself.

Wilson's demise portends another, disturbing feature of the current culture ("cancel"). The decision of the Princeton School of International Affairs to remove his name from their masthead may well be the final "nail in the coffin" of any American intentions to influence future structures toward world order.

In the final analysis "Wilsonianism" is an idea, the only one that has been identified with this country from the beginnings until the present day. If the ultimate criterion of American presidents is the degree of "racism" in their heart we are on the cusp of a new age, a new value structure; indeed a new country. "What's past is prologue" becomes "what's past is past."

The urge to create democratic order out of global anarchy may well be ancient history, a faint memory to be erased in a "new humanity" where race, gender and identity prevail worldwide. Three possible scenarios (not beyond the imagination):

1) Statues of Franklin D. Roosevelt and Harry Truman, Wilsonian architects of world order, are torn down;

2) Princeton replaces Wilson's name on the School of International Affairs with Frederick Douglass;

3) NATO is replaced with The "Anti-Racist Alliance" (only Norway, Denmark and Iceland qualify).

League of Nations, Woodrow Wilson, R.I.P.

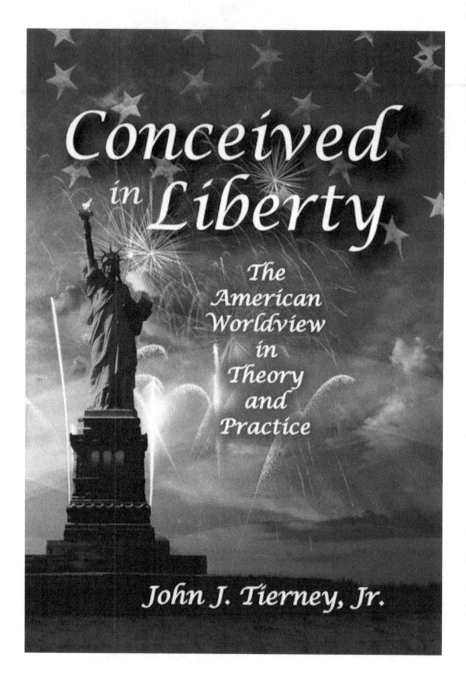

June 20, 2020

In 2016 my book *Conceived in Liberty* was published (Transaction). The title was deliberately chosen to emphasize the two terms, "conceived" and "liberty," being careful not to extrapolate more from the title than was intended. This was not a "historical" study to determine whether or not Americans, from the start to 2016, lived up to the promises begun in 1776. Nor was it a "sociology" to determine what faults resided within the population or whether or not the people deserved the title.

A key reference used in the beginning was the response given by Benjamin Franklin to those who asked him what the Constitutional Convention had accomplished. "A Republic," he noted. "if you can keep it."

Franklin's answer is more important for the second half than the first. The definitions of a "Republic" go back as far as the ancient Greeks and Romans, whose qualities were carefully referenced by the Founders. These are theoretical, actually "Political Science," and elaborate the "designs" and nature of a republican political system and its variety of duties from both the government and the governed. Franklin had no intention to describe these in his answer, rather to warn the listener (and his successors) that there is a profound difference between ideas and reality.

It is one thing to design a beautiful or magnificent structure. It is altogether another to put people into it to live and work. How they accomplish these tasks in their daily life may or may not have any bearing upon the carefully presented design. They may ruin it in a day, they may keep it as-is for a generation, it may deteriorate over time or they may develop it to heights not even imagined by its builders. They may well be content to let it stay as-is without regard to the neighbors, a single beauty within a slum. Conversely, they might want to show others how to do the same, eventually producing not only one structure but a beautiful and thriving village.

All these options apply precisely to how Americans have treated their own Founding, for better or worse. All these options, as well, depend upon a consensus that the "structure" was both original and magnificent from its inception. If there is no consensus on this there is no further need to develop the thesis; it was "DoA."

Proceding from a consensus that the American Founding was, indeed, both original, creative and positive, we can then proceed as to how it has been implemented. If one rejects the thesis one must start all over again (as some propose).

As in any well-developed artifice (house, car, city, farm, nation, family, economy, political system) the original design cannot possibly dictate or even indicate how it will be implemented. How, then, do we judge its value or strength?

Perhaps the first criterion is durability. Has it endured? Take marriage: one that lasted 50 years is defined as a success; one that dissolves after two years a failure. That's sufficient, no further questions.

By that standard the American system is both powerful and lasting. Perhaps 250 years is too short to determine, knowing that empires have lasted many more centuries before collapsing.

Maybe so, but compared to most other countries the US system comes out quite strong. Just observe recent history. Russia: revolutions, occupation, from czar to communist to Putin; Germany: from Kaiser to democracy to Nazi to democratic again; Japan: monarchy to military, to democracy; Spain: from monarchy, to revolution to Fascist to democratic; Italy: monarchy, Fascist, democratic; France: monarchy, revolution, monarchy, democratic, occupied, democratic. Etc., the list goes on. Most countries that show stability have been one-party or totalitarian, with democracies fairly scarce.

The second criterion, and the one most used, is "observance" (for want of a better term). Here the standards break down so much as to be nearly impossible to judge. It is currently fashionable to critique the American Founding as not "living up" to its potential. Inside this critique must be asked: what/who has, Denmark, Nigeria, Indonesia?

One reason for the US to be so "observable" is the lasting image of the "city upon a hill" standing so far above the rest. In this regard, America stands "accused" by its own lofty promise, with a political revolution not only the first but the most pronounced in terms both of its original design and the hopes inherent within the design itself. Has anyone heard of the Australian "dream"?

One can judge the US by a single criteria: probably the only country in history that has a problem keeping people out, rather than in.

A question often asked is about the significance of the American Revolution. The apocryphal answer, "it's too soon to tell" contains more truth than hypocrisy.

Utopia rarely translates to reality. There are 193 countries in the world but few (if any) are so routinely critiqued for systemic failure. Some in the US want to "overhaul" the political system due to its many sociological shortcomings. All of these shortcomings, however, are universal; none are derived from the American Founding but, rather, are the result of the character issues that have infected the Creator's humanity from Adam and Eve to Hitler.

Liberty is a" conception," synonyms of "conceived" are cause, think, begin, imagine, envision. Liberty is also an "ideal," ie. a revolution "in progress," a "choice" that can be made. There is no incompatibility between Liberty and general human behavior; like Original Sin it coexists alongside "Free Will." It also means "freedom" and has co-existed with or without equality: with slavery, with income inequality, with voting privilege, with poverty, discrimination, slums, tenement life, child labor, the draft, crime, suicide, lockdowns, war casualties, undeclared wars etc. etc.

There is little relationship between equality and liberty, they can or cannot co-exist. Another analogy: prisons are equal inside by definition. Outside the walls may be massive inequality. Take your choice. Probably only those who have been denied liberty appreciate what it is.

Liberty is extremely rare in history, almost unknown until 1776. It is incompatible with most human experience, including empire, colonies, occupation, invasion, slavery, dictatorship, socialism, ideologies. It can survive with both the seven "deadly" sins as well as the three "cardinal" virtues. Its values are also largely confined to English, both the novels of George Orwell or the philosophy of Isiah Berlin.

It is fashionable for history to be judged against equality. Again we have a choice. Some historians prefer to expose life's "dark" side rather than the bright, often confusing sociology (equality) with political science. This is hardly uncommon and is present throughout the American academy today.

Fair enough, but just make sure we don't confuse conception with whatever comes after; it's a difference between life and birth. Or, put another way: between building your "dreamhouse" and living in it.

Division, Diversity, Unity

May 27, 2020

The first two words overlap and have a common understanding in the colloquial sense. But in the American popular culture there is a distinction, whereas division implies separation ("portion," "piece," "unit") diversity implies variety within a whole ("assortment," "heterogeneity"). By any definition, however, both words are the exact opposite of "unity," best defined by its inherent virtues, "balance," "accord," "coherence," "symphony."

Thus, even within a strict dictionary definition, the term "unity" connotes a superior reference of existence, while division always connotes a lower form. *Merriam-Webster* even begins its unity definition by separating it from division: "not being multiple." It is fair to say, therefore, that between the two unity is always superior than division (or diversity) for the simple reason that one is easier to count than two.

Starting from that simplicity to humanity the word "system," often assigned to humanity, takes on profound meaning precisely because of its "unity." In short, system connotes singularity rather than multiplicity. Practically, everything on earth is some form of "system." This is often used sub-consciously, as in the full spectrum of systems used everyday: political, solar, transportation, biological, economic etc.

All systems are "macro," rather than "micro," which means that the full system must function as a unit and that even a small, slight deviation could cause the whole to malfunction. This is manifest throughout life. An automobile is a system. A carburetor represents a tiny segment of the whole but if the carburetor stops the entire car stops as well. Politics is also "systemic" with the Army a portion. But if a General removes a President then the whole system turns into a dictatorship, ie. the "system" breaks down, becomes something else. Senator Bernie Sanders campaigned as a "socialist," an economic system opposite from capitalism. As opposed to most other candidates, Sanders sought "systemic" change, ie. a whole new form of organization and behavior.

World politics is, likewise, considered "systemic" based upon merely the number of "players." When someone refers to the United States as the "sole remaining superpower" they mean that the world is governed by a "unipolar" system. The Cold War was between the USA and the USSR, thus it was "bipolar." The old European "Balance of Power" consisted of around twenty countries, thus it was "multipolar."

Like all other systems, the world system can collapse from the smallest breakdown. In 1914 a Serbian terrorist killed the heir to the Austrian throne. The result was World War I, systemic change throughout the Twentieth Century, wholesale mass-murder and by some standards the "end of history." In 1939 Germany invaded Poland. Six years later, 76 million deaths, the atomic bomb, the Cold War and the world system divided in half. In 2001 nine terrorists destroyed two buildings. Notice anything different (been to an airport)?

Domestic political systems are equally vulnerable. In 1765, ten years before the revolution, there were about a dozen Americans that wished to break with the British Crown (most from Massachusetts). In 1903, when Lenin gathered his "Bolsheviks" in a Swiss hotel, he had around ten co-conspirators. When Hitler took power in 1933 he had about 800 uniformed Nazis with him, against 80 million Germans. And so it goes.

Today, America is often defined as in a "revolutionary" condition, either as a description or as a prescription. If the virus won't get us, then the repercussions from police "brutality" will. Either way, it's at least certain that all 330 million Americans cannot possibly wish or prepare for "systemic" change. It must, therefore, come from somewhere else. Even an orchestra needs a leader.

But, like the British before us, the Russian Czar or the Weimar Republic, who can define where revolution originates? They all had at least one thing in common: they were all caught by surprise.

Statistically, the death of one person cannot possibly cause the demonstrations that have convulsed American cities since. It must be both symbolic and orchestrated and, by definition, cannot be either spontaneous or incoherent. Nothing occurs in a vacuum.

These questions may not be known, but, in the longer term, they remain secondary. The primary concern is the unity that every country requires for bare existence. At stake is actually the continuing existence of the American "system," as it has existed for 250 years and, of equal importance, as leader of the "Free World" for nearly a century. Both cases, within and without, may well be decided inside the near future.

Nor can the future be determined through dispassionate analysis or reflection. Whether George Floyd was typical or a-typical, whether Blacks are better off here or in Kenya, whether "whiteness" is a virtue or a vice, whether slavery or liberty represents America will all be lost amidst the challenges between the emergence of a unified versus a divided people. That is the "bottom line," or as Coach Lombardi put it, the "only question." No entity, nation or not, can function divided for long. Sooner or later, it will be "surprised."

As the world can turn with just a pistol shot, so can the American "experiment" end in a fraction of a second somewhere inside an obscure location.

I once had a cut on my arm. Someone asked me, is it serious? "It depends," I replied, "on how much I scratch."

Born Again

March 1, 2020

To be "Born Again," in Christian theology, means to be "renewed" in belief, ie. to gain a newer and more committed faith in the meaning of Christianity. In Biblical terms it expresses a rebirth "in spirit and water" to Christ and the path to Heaven. Born Again, thus, is a spiritual renewal and certainly not a new "birthday" in the original, physical sense of the term.

Everybody, no exceptions, has a "birthday," the day when they entered the world. This cannot be changed, either to "conception" or any other biological phenomenon. Nor can birthday be changed to either a sociological or psychological phenomenon, such as graduation, wedding, promotion etc. It is biological and, thus, immutable to hypothetical or artificial interference.

Countries, plus other secular institutions, also have "birthdays, or what they normally call "Independence Day." There are 193 official countries in the United Nations and each one has a day when it became one-unto-itself and, usually, the day it broke free from another nationality. Thus, Uganda's is October 9, 1962, Argentina's July 9, 1816, Morocco's April 7, 1956. As with personal birthdays, these are sacred in national histories, are celebrated each year and remain a testimonial to what the country and people stand for in popular culture and politics. There are no exceptions, every country has an independence or "national" day when it was, so-to-speak, "born."

No country on earth, none, has ever changed its "birthday" peacefully. This has always required a phenomenon call "revolution," ie. Bolshevik, French, American.

To distinguish, this is different from "born again," or renewal, ie. when the country was involved in a higher calling than before or when it was upon a new and dangerous adventure. In the United States, the birthday is July 4, 1776, but "born again" could be a number of events, the Bill of Rights, Battle of New Orleans, the transcontinental railroad, end of the Civil War, victory in World War I, Woman's suffrage, Pearl Harbor, civil rights movement, end of the Cold War etc.

In America today there is a movement, sponsored by the New York Times, to move the actual birthday back over 150 years to August 20, 1619. Why would a newspaper attempt to overturn 250 years of official testimony and change the day in which America first entered the political world? Answer: allegedly, that was the day in which the first slave ship entered the so-called "New World" of British America. The reason is not because the ship entered unexplored British territory but because the ship carried slaves from Africa and, thereby, represented what the New World had, in effect, become, ie. a slave dominion and nothing else worth remembering.

Whether or not the date is, in fact, accurate is irrelevant, at least to the newspaper. The date, in reality, is symbolic since slave ships had been arriving into the New World since Columbus first landed in 1492. But the symbolism is critical since the factual basis pales against the actual purpose of the newspaper's objective, ie. to transform the nature and image of what the country represents both to itself and to outsiders.

Thus, the intent is a political overhaul as powerful and as lasting as the one enshrined in Jefferson's Declaration of July 4, 1776. The newspaper's spokeswoman, Nicole Hannah-Jones, has called the Declaration of Independence "nice words" against a reality she described as "a constant reminder of the lie of our origins."

Project 1619 represents a direct challenge to the American national heritage as open and flagrant as Howard Zinn's popular, quasi-Marxist history, *A People's History of the United States* (1980). It also represents the new and growing phenomena of "identity" politics as typified with the several ideological "isms" that have become fashionable in "mainstream" media and national politics.

The intent is comprehensive and total, to make slavery and African-Americans the centerpiece of historic American existence. Although they have represented around ten percent of the total populace overall, Ms. Jones entertains an encompassing vision of both slavery and Black history as both the original and lasting explanation of the nature and record of the country, from 1619 to 2020, and, of course, into the unknown.

By placing slavery as the main reason for independence in the first place, she intends to "reframe the country's history" around that institution from, seemingly, everything that has occurred to that which has not. Her list of phenomena that slavery determined includes today's traffic patterns, intake of foods and sugar, health care, capitalism, socialism, insurance, manufacturing, banking, rum consumption, surgery, medicine etc. in order to "force us to confront how slavery has impacted the country."

As a newspaper and as a reporter *The Times* and Ms. Jones have taken on the responsibilities that generations of historians have apparently overlooked. One can easily anticipate their response that all the others were "white" as symptomatic of the new ideologies that have filtered through the country and are now S.O.P. in polite (and not-so-polite) company.

One wonders how all the other "minorities" of the USA, which means almost everyone else, would react to this, shall we say, "one-sided" interpretation of life. With little to-do in the nation's existence, we might just-as-well sit back and pay a subscription to *The Times*, not just to see what we *did* but to see what we are going to do tomorrow.

In the national history, Hitler and Stalin notwithstanding, the greatest challenges to American existence have come from within, especially the great Civil War.

Now we face a rising China, a "meddling" Russia and Islamic terrorism as the chief threats from outside. At the same time, and right under our noses, is what J. Edgar Hoover once called *The Enemy Within*, that eats away at the vitals of national life and existence all under the pretense of "social justice," "progress" or some other benevolent term. But like both Jefferson Davis and *ISIS*, they remain open and free in both pretension and intent.

We may have been "born" on July 4 but we may soon become "born again" without even knowing it. Worse, we may even assist in our own demise.

PS. While watching an interview with Ms. Jones I soon asked myself what "on earth" was she talking about, only to realize that "earth" had absolutely nothing to do with it. She is, authentically, "out of this world." But, why is our greatest newspaper?

To some, it seems, reality is an exclusively internal design (or is there something else at play?).

Pandemics We Have Known

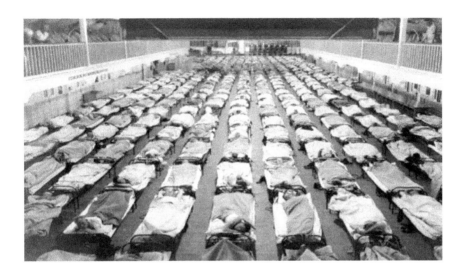

March 16, 2020

Now the entire country is in a "pandemic." The word has a combined meaning. One is sociological, "panic," "hysteria," chaos." The second is biological, "fever," "virus," "spread." Combined, they represent what might be called a national "lockdown," meaning everything geared toward a single purpose, no deviation.

The last time the country experienced a lockdown was in World War II, when all 120 million Americans lived to win the war. Food was rationed, over 16 million were in uniforms, no commercial production allowed, and "V for victory" a daily slogan. "Don't you know there's a war on" was the common response to even the slightest hesitation. An example of what "lockdown" meant then: in 1941, the country produced over 3 million passenger automobiles. From 1942 until 1946, the total was 29.

Not that citizens even slightly appreciate the larger perspective. This, too, is commonplace. On December 7, 1941, Japanese carrier-based planes attacked Hawaii; the following day, enlistment offices across America were inundated with millions of boys lining up for blocks waiting to enlist against the "day of infamy." They were inspired by the attack, but few appreciated the diplomacy that led to the event, which could be traced as far back as the mid-nineteenth century.

Today, within the span of days, the whole country has reversed "gears" against an unseen enemy, spawned somewhere in China and which has, within the same time period, taken some 100 American lives. Is the response appropriate? Could the whole thing have been avoided?

Would such questions have been entertained on December 8, 1941? Without opinion polls, a good guess is that anyone harboring such "dark" thoughts in those circumstances would have been labeled "treasonous." Today, the issue is "moot," but a universal answer (minus TV's "experts") would undoubtedly be "how should I know?"

Yet, the condition escalates with no end in sight. Are we all "blind mice"? Is there an alternative?

The answer to each question has to be probably "No," while the most appropriate and the first step toward such a circumstance reminds one of how Britain handled the first wave of German bombers that began pounding British cities. With as many as 800 to 1000 *Luftwaffe* warplanes over London day and night through 1940 and 1941, the government issued a poster telling the people to "Keep Calm and Carry On." Churchill used this message throughout the war.

President Trump has said this also but has met ridicule from much of the press. While the administration is doing much more, it seems still impossible to keep "politics" out of a national pandemic. Yet politics was largely absent from both the world wars and the Cold War, demonstrating how "visible" enemies can overcome even base political emotions.

At first, the current pandemic appears somewhat "overblown," given comparisons. The common flu, for example, takes about 30,000 American lives each year, yet this statistic is rarely mentioned. Nor is it defined as an "epidemic."

Yet the refrain to "keep calm ..." is fully appropriate if only to address the sociological dimensions of the above definition. To avoid panic, keep calm. Maybe easier said than done, but essential as a first step. The remainder, like war itself, will take time, resolve, resource, and perseverance.

Like any other panic, the current one needs perspective, the basic gift of history. Like war and conflict themselves, pandemics are common throughout history.

The Black Death, 14th century, wiped out nearly half of Europe, approximately 200 million people. The Spanish Flu, 1918-1926, took many more lives than even the Great War, about 60 million. A smallpox epidemic in Europe,

1520, took over 50 million lives. In 735 AD, Japan lost 30% of its population to disease. The "Justian Plague," 541 AD, claimed 40 million.

Closer to home, in 1957, an Asian Flu took 116,000 American lives, yet President Eisenhower refused to even recognize it until the very end. Since 1981, the HIV/AIDS crisis has a toll of 30 million worldwide, while the "Swine Flu" in 2009 took about 200,000 American lives.

These are but samples out of dozens-more historical plagues. But panic-attacks are not confined to disease only. They can spread to war itself and economics.

The current coronavirus has seen a precipitous drop in the stock market, compounding the death toll itself. But the Great Depression of the 1930s, in this context, exceeds all comparison. With a high of 25% unemployed throughout the decade, there were 744 bank closures in 1930 alone. In 1933, there were 4,000 closures, with a total of 9,000 bank closures for the full decade. Hundreds of billions of personal account-dollars were lost to "thin air," as millions of American families saw their entire savings disappear for reasons unknown to them.

Franklin D. Roosevelt, legend to the contrary, never ended the depression; it was as severe in 1940 as when he first took office. But he provided "hope" through a series of "New Deal" programs, including Social Security, that allowed the country to survive the great "pandemic" called the "Depression."

Hitler, Japan, and the world war brought Americans back to work, but they could never have survived unless they "kept calm and carried on."

In his first Inaugural Address FDR appealed to hope against the crisis: "The only thing we have to fear is fear itself." This is still considered the greatest line of all Inaugural speeches.

Is there a lesson here?

The Blame Game

March 19, 2020

Whenever anything occurs there is "responsibility." If it's bad it's called "blame," if good it's "taking credit." With the COVID 19 virus there is, as always, both.

First the blame. The American president, again as always, is the final arbiter of everything that happened here and the first to blame. That is nearly always the case. Southerners still blame Lincoln for the Civil War, Hoover is everywhere blamed for the Depression, Truman for the Cold War, Johnson for Vietnam etc. This is all correct, to a degree. Even if they happened to be in office when the event occurred that is sufficient for blame. Or, in a greater context, "responsibility."

President Harry Truman famously had a motto on his desk, "The Buck Stops Here." That says a lot.

Admiral Husband Kimmel, in command at Pearl Harbor when the attack occurred, immediately tore off the shoulder boards on his uniform, declaring that he would no longer have use for them. He was right. After absorbing blame for Japan's surprise assault most of his life he died with the stigma in 1986. In 1999 the full Senate voted to exonerate him, calling Kimmel the "last victim" of Pearl Harbor.

The Pearl Harbor attack was soon followed by a series of Congressional and other investigations into the responsibility of President Roosevelt. There was a conspirational theory that FDR, somehow, knew of Japanese plans and secretly kept quiet in order to bring the country into a war it never wanted. Over ten separate hearings, including a Joint Congressional Hearing, conducted years of testimony, tens of thousands of documents, hundreds of witnesses, but never found the "smoking gun." FDR remains "innocent until proven guilty," but the theory persists, to this day.

In February 1942 the Roosevelt Administration "interned" over 120,000 Japanese living in California to "camps" in the western interior on the pretense of national security. While almost all of them were US citizens, the Pearl Harbor attack sent the country into an anti-"Jap" frenzy supported by most of the media and population. While their families were later compensated (1988) the "blame" inflicted on them by national insecurity attests to the degree of political frenzy even democracies can muster when life is on-the-line.

In assessing blame, there are several degrees. The most popular, and the most damaging, is called "partisan," meaning "instinctive," or "by nature." In politics, partisanship is the normal, almost "second nature." All presidents, parties, officials etc. are subject to this, as unavoidable. With the current virus, Trump is no exception, as daily accusations from the print and TV media locate him, and him alone, as to blame for the global crisis that has killed in the hundreds of thousands. One reporter went so far as to call the virus "Trump's Vietnam."

Hyperbole aside, there is some merit in blaming the American president, as he most certainly did/did not do something that could have mitigated/erased the spread. That said, is this sufficient? When firefighters investigate a fire they go directly to the source. Maybe they didn't extinguish it fast enough, but to determine the cause they need the origin. When police investigate a crime, they need to inspect the "scene" to get "evidence." Then they investigate to find a "suspect." Who's to blame: the arsonist/suspect or the investigators?

Maybe a little of both, but the source/scene is always the location of "cause," and the investigators are helpless without evidence from there.

Partisan blame is frustrating, principally because of its nature. Anything so automatic, so instinctive has to be suspect if only due to its origin. Perhaps the accusations "jump" to conclusions; perhaps they "rush" to judgment. But any judgment does not enhance itself if there is no "jump," nor "rush." It means almost nothing if there was no need for either; if they were already "there" from the beginning.

Anyone who was plotting Trump's impeachment prior to inauguration cannot be taken seriously if they claim that he is to blame for this virus. The slogan "the duty of the opposition is to oppose" is true enough; it simply does not belong in any "true detective" work. In this respect politics is an artificial world, without responsibility or blame. It's a good thing that both police and firefighters are supposed to be "nonpolitical."

Partisan blame may even be correct, insofar as it goes, but *that* is the problem. It's also called "tunnel vision."

Now for "responsibility." What causes things? Take war, for example.

By 1898 Spain had controlled Cuba for about 400 years. On February 15, 1898 the *USS Maine* exploded in Havana Harbor, killing 250 sailors aboard. On April 21 the U.S. declared war on Spain, under the slogan "Remember the Maine, to Hell with Spain." The American media controlled opinion with its "yellow press," egging an aroused public to fever pitch. Publisher William Randolph Hearst allegedly told his reporters, "you furnish the stories, I'll furnish the war."

Official inquiries as to the cause of the explosion were inconclusive. In 1974 Admiral Hyman Rickover led a Navy inquiry that finally named an internal fire in the ship's engines. Immediate cause of the Spanish-American War: a complete fabrication. Yet all Americans blamed the government in Madrid, 3,000 miles away.

In 1919 the Versailles Treaty blamed Germany as being "solely responsible" for World War I (Article 231). That sentence alone was probably the most damaging single line ever incorporated into a human document, costing eventually hundreds of millions of lives and creating, effectively, the remainder of the Twentieth Century.

Article 231, once heralded a beginning of the "war to end war," has been amended and reversed many times since and is now generally regarded as the prime example of the tragic result of what now is known as the "blame game." Today, reflections now distribute the First World War as the result of a number of factors in the European system, of which Germany was primary but hardly alone.

Where does that leave us today? In assessing responsibility/blame for the virus where do we go? Where would Sherlock Holmes go? To the source!

Where did the virus originate, where is the "scene of the crime"? Peru? Indonesia? Hungary? Nigeria? The White House? All of the above?

The scientific verdict is unanimous: the virus came from Wuhan province, China. Being "unscientific," that is all, I for one, need to know. Thus we have a "scene," and that is where all investigations begin.

Any investigation of COVID 19 should be "constructive" in tone, not punitive. Yet, at the same time, there is a "responsibility" to locate and, as well, a degree of "blame." The virus is not a war; the origins were not deliberate. Still, there should be what might be called an "acknowledgement," or at best a "confession," a procedure that can lead to "case closed."

How do we get there? A responsible American president would lead the western allies, all 29 NATO plus others affected, and collectively announce to China: we know you did it, you know you did it, so let us help you help yourself so this doesn't happen again.

Case closed!

Strategic Doctrines, Then and Now

March 21, 2020

In its relatively short history (two and one quarter centuries) the United States of America has gone through several phases of foreign policies, each beginning with a form of strategic "doctrine" or outline of direction.

The first, and probably the greatest, came from the hand of the nation's "Father," George Washington. In his "Farewell Address," September 1796, the first president (with help from James Madison and Alexander Hamilton) published such an outline in a Philadelphia newspaper that charted a public, external course that was destined to last almost exactly a century and a half (or until 1947).

Washington's advice, later adopted as "isolationism," called upon the three million Americans then stretched in thirteen states along the Atlantic coast, to adopt a policy of strict "neutrality" against the continuous quarrels and wars of Old Europe.

Washington first stressed the unity that a sound policy required: "You have in a common sense fought and triumphed together, the independence and liberty you possess are the work of your counsels, and joint efforts of common dangers, sufferings and successes." Within a unified nation, he got to the heart of the matter, "It is our policy to steer clear of permanent alliances with any portion of the foreign world." With a series of questions the Founding Father provided the explanation:

"Why forego the advantages of so peculiar a situation? Why quit our own to stand upon foreign ground? Why, by interweaving our destiny with that of any part of Europe, entangle our peace and prosperity in the toils of European ambition, rivalship, interest, humor or caprice?"

The ultimate result saw the emergence of the American "sleeping giant," that conquered and developed a continent, fought within itself, eventually expanded into the seven seas, and managed to save the Old World from itself on two profound occasions. Within that history the wisdom of the Farewell Address steered the "ship of state" along a consistent, if wavering, line. When it was first abandoned, 1917, it almost immediately returned, with a vengeance, into a "normalcy" that only crashed with the attack on Pearl Harbor, Hawaii (1941), never to return again.

By the end of World War II, 1945, the US was too big to stay alone and Europe, conversely, too small to carry on. Between 1946 and 1947 came the "revolution" in foreign policy that at long last left the Farewell Address behind to take on the challenges of a "New World Order."

The second major Doctrine was regional in scope, originally a by-product of British foreign policy, was re-interpreted often to suit policies, was the longest in US history and can be considered as the most "strategic" in practice as it actually guided both defensive and offensive American actions. Of course this was the "Monroe Doctrine" of 1823, actually written by Secretary of State John Quincy Adams, in "collusion" with the British and was originally meant to keep Europe from interfering in the independence movements that had swept Latin America.

Originally a "shield" it soon became a "sword" to justify American interventions into Mexico, the Caribbean and to assist in protecting the Panama Canal. It was most recently used by John F. Kennedy during the Cuban Missile Crisis (1962) but was finally terminated by the Obama Administration (2013) for political reasons known only to them.

Then came "containment."

The origins of this dramatic and global change came from the mind of an otherwise obscure Foreign Service Officer, George F. Kennan, who, in February 1946, sent a memo back home from his post in Moscow that outlined the new departure in American foreign policy. It was called "containment" and urged a new and expansive policy that would, peacefully, save Europe from itself still a third time.

The essence of containment, which lasted to 1981, was to create a kind of "wall" behind which the US and western Europe would create such a position of strength that the Soviet Union, once an ally now an enemy, could not possibly overcome. In Kennan's original "Long Telegram," the brilliance of containment is crafted, wherein the "main elements" "must be a long-term, patient but firm and vigilant containment of Russian expensive tendencies ... by the adroit and vigilant application of counterforce at a series of constantly, shifting, geographical and political points, corresponding to the shifts and maneuvers of Soviet policy."

Kennan's advice was immediately adopted by the Truman Administration and incorporated into the historic announcement of the "Truman Doctrine," on March 12, 1947, with the president telling the world that American policy would, henceforth, support "free peoples everywhere" in their own wish for peace, independence and liberty. Then came the Marshall Plan (June 1947) which saved western Europe from both Soviet dominance and poverty, the Berlin Blockade (1948-49) saving West Berlin from the same and, of course, the North Atlantic Treaty (1949), which created the world order we still live under.

Containment was a huge success, for a while. In 1950 it expanded to Korea in the "forgotten" war that cost 38,000 American soldier's lives but made South Korea the prosperous democracy that it is today.

In that same year a State Department Planning Committee, chaired by Paul Nitze, drafted its own "strategic doctrine," called NSC-68, that gave the new American "worldview" a definitive identity. The heart of this historic document labeled the demise of the Soviet Union as the ultimate American design:

"we have no choice but to demonstrate the superiority of the idea of freedom by its constructive application, and to attempt to change the world situation by means short of war in such a way as to frustrate the Kremlin's design and hasten the decay of the Soviet system."

In the short run, this objective would not replace containment, which went through the trials of the Vietnam War and "Détente" (1960 through 1980). The net result was a "bipolar" world with two "superpowers" and an America still trying to escape the tragic aftermath of containment's shortcomings. With a Soviet military buildup, Watergate, Nixon's resignation and the failures of Jimmy Carter the stage was set for Ronald Reagan and the ultimate fulfillment of the designs of NSC-68.

On January 17, 1983 the Reagan Administration advanced "NSDD-75," a "national security directive" aimed at ending the Cold War, reducing the Soviet Union to a secondary position in the global hierarchy and elevating the US to "sole remaining superpower."

It did all three.

The beginnings of this historic paper laid out its results:

"... to reverse Soviet expansionism by competing effectively on a sustained basis with the Soviet Union in all international arenas ... to promote the process of change in the Soviet Union toward a more pluralistic political and economic system."

By 1991 the Cold War was history, Gorbachev and Reagan said goodbye, Bill Clinton came in on the slogan "it's the economy stupid" and both he and Boris Yeltsin were pictured together, arm-in-arm as though nothing ever happened.

Then we had foreign policies called "assertive multilateralism" and "leading from behind." That's nice.

The recent Democratic presidential debates targeted Harvey Weinstein, socialism and "white nationalism" as our biggest issues.

Where is Strategic Doctrine when we need it the most? What about China, the source of the virus?

The Balance of Power

ACTUALITÉS.   231.

L'Équilibre Européen.

March 24, 2020

In the realm of World Politics the term "Balance of Power" is the governing concept that controls the entire field, but it is rarely even mentioned in any popular media. The explanation, so far as can be seen, is that public opinion is so consumed with personality, domestic politics, self-indulgence, good or bad behaviors, and other topics related to circumstance that abstractions appear remote or so distant as to be irrelevant.

Yet, at any given time the Balance of Power (BoP) governs most, if not all, of the circumstances of daily life, including peace/war, powerful/weak, stability/chaos etc. as to be an all-consuming but invisible gear that drives life and death.

A possible reason as to why BoP receives such scant attention in America is that we are so accustomed to being on the top of the scales that being lower is inconceivable.

The closest comparison to the idea would be the historic definition of Capitalism given originally by the Scottish economist, Adam Smith, in his classic *The Wealth of Nations* (1776). Smith determined that national wealth/poverty was controlled by what he called an "invisible hand" that allocates sound versus bad investment and drives out poor competitors and rewards good ones. The final result is rich versus poor nations and a hierarchy of global life that controls both national and international realities.

In today's cultural *milieu*, Smith's conception has been challenged by quasi-Marxist ideologies that defines life as determined by a form of "dialectic" in which classes of "oppressed" versus "oppressors" compete endlessly for influence, power and wealth. In the American media and popular culture this concept has risen to a dominate position in the normal political "dialogue," usually defined as one or the other form of "ism."

Thus, blacks are "what" they are because of whites, women because of men, poor because of rich, "natives" because of "outsiders," "have- nots" because of "haves," etc. Only "men," the sole exception, are labeled for what they *really* are (as defined).

As shorthand, these competing conceptions can be divided between vertical against horizontal definitions of humanity, all "people" are either equal or "some are more equal than others" (Orwell). In terms of any analytical dimension, this can represent "reality" vs "utopian." The Marxist version is "utopian" since it has never existed.

But the global BoP has been around since time began but is totally ignored in American culture.

There are essentially two ways to approach this reality. The first is "descriptive." At any given time there exists a hierarchy of nations that can be divided into categories (as simple as 1, 2, 3). This is permanent and, indeed, essential, ie. it *always* has existed and "cannot-not" exist. Simply, these are a) multipolar, b) bipolar and c) unipolar. "Polar" simply describes the number of "poles" (peoples, nations countries, empires) that are involved at any given time. This can be seen by a quick description of historic BoP's.

Quickly (very), recorded history is about 6,000 years old. The vast majority of this time consisted of "unipolar" political structures, colloquially called "empires," wherein political power consisted of a single entity (king, emperor, party, dictator etc.) who governed usually by force, persuasion or some other form of control. There is no need to name these realities but Roman, British, Mongol, Byzantine, Chinese, Indian, Spanish, French, Dutch, Belgian, Russian, Austrian, Portugese, Japanese, German, Aztec, Inca, Zulu come to mind immediately.

Today there are 193 sovereign states in the United Nations. As speculation, probably 150 are "unipolar," in domestic governance, ie. tyrannical. The USA is the leading "multipolar" (democratic) country in world history, yet quasi-Marxism calls the US "imperialist."

America was founded precisely against empire and has been essentially that way since. True, the US had "territories" but they became either American states, (Hawaii, Alaska) or independent (The Philippines). The US has governed no "colonies" indefinitely against their popular demands.

The second category of BoP is "multipolar," consisting of three or more "poles," circulating among each other in a classic "balancing" mode. This is the heart of what modern historians mean by the BoP, wherein members compete in an endless series of maneuvers and where there is no overarching authority to govern. This means political "anarchy" and has been the basis of world politics since 1648, when the Peace of Westphalia ended the Thirty Years War, the Holy Roman Empire and inaugurated the "nation-state." Thus the "nation-state" world system is only about 350 years old, or approximately five percent of recorded history.

This is the model normally used in all BoP analysis. Essentially European, it consisted of at most twenty European nation-states who allied for or against one another in a chronic "game" of cat and mouse until it all crashed in the First World War (1918). Thus, the essential result of that war ended the classic BoP and brought on a totally new "bipolar" system that consisted of two dominate sovereigns, USA vs USSR, who played "Cold War" until one side fell (1991).

The result since then has been called "unipolar" since the only one left from all of this wreckage is America, the "sole remaining superpower" as the late Charles Krauthammer first put it in 1991. Whether America merits that title or not can be debated. Whether America even is aware of that is also debatable. (If one watched the recent Democratic Party debates the notion that BoP remains an unknown and alien concept can only be reinforced).

The second method to analyze BoP is "prescriptive," ie. to pursue an authentic "balance" in an anarchistic world. Historically, this was always British foreign policy, as a maritime power on the "flank" of a continent. Best described in 1907 by a British Foreign Office official, Eyre Crowe, his memorandum remains the best analysis of history's classic BoP.

From a British perspective the rise of a powerful Germany in 1907 threatened the independence of both Britain and the world. Therefore, it was necessary to create an "equilibrium":

"The equilibrium established by such a grouping of forces is technically known as the balance of power, and it has become almost an historic truism to identify England's secular policy with the maintenance of this balance by throwing her weight now on this scale and now in that, but ever on the side opposed to the political dictatorship of the strongest single state or group at any given time."

While such language may never reach the viewers of the next political debate, the question remains, how will American "weight" affect the Balance of Power that most assuredly will govern tomorrow's world?

Perhaps the answer will come from outside, as it always has in the past. The "sleeping giant" snores.

Geopolitics

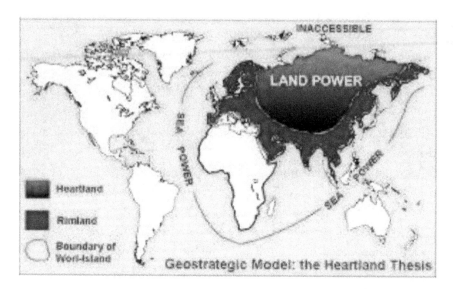

Map of Geopolitics Theory

March 28, 2020

For most of history geography represented an inescapable, deterministic phenomenon that controlled how, when and where nations and peoples lived out their short lives. Where you lived, the climate, access to outside, barriers *from* outside etc. were factors that pre-technology could not overcome. If you were born in a closet you lived in dark. If you were born in a field you ran. If you were born in the sea you swam.

I often asked my classes what are good examples of that reality in history. The answers often came in the form of questions:

Why doesn't Switzerland have a navy?

Why did England need a navy?

Why did Germany need an army?

Why did Japan expand into the Pacific Ocean?

How could the US afford isolationism?

Why was the Monroe Doctrine confined to the Western Hemisphere?

Why was Poland invaded so often and from every direction?

Why was the northern US industrial before the Civil War, the south agrarian?

Why did the northern US give up slavery voluntarily, the south only after defeat?

Why aren't Ecuador, Croatia or Indonesia great powers?

Why did German soldiers freeze inside Russia while Russian soldiers didn't (1941)?

Why did "General Winter" defeat Napoleon in 1812 Russia?

In 1962 why did Premier Khrushchev of the Soviet Union place ballistic missiles inside Cuba, a small island 90 miles south of Florida?

These samples illustrate the nature of a geopolitical assessment in history. At first glance they seem "deterministic," ie. as if no other cause could possibly explain. Yet, logic demands that there can be no one single causation of human reality, even if one cause clearly dominates. For example, one cannot "blame" geopolitics alone for the Civil War, there are human elements, sociology, psychology, political ("states rights") that have to be factored.

In today's cultural climate, single factors, mingled with a Marxist dialectic, offer single-factor "thought" (the expression may be pardoned): a host of "isms," placed arbitrarily into every situation, are sufficient as cause. Since "racism" is universal, it causes everything, from slavery to civil war, to segregation to prejudice, crime, disease, wealth and poverty.

Racism exists, so does land and water. Neither can cause everything.

If geography alone was decisive consider these questions:

Canada and Australia are both democratic and as large as the United States. Why aren't they "superpowers"?

China is larger than the US and has seven or more times the population. Why isn't China a superpower?

The Soviet Union (USSR) had more people than the US, had a larger military, a "blue water" navy, thousands of ballistic missiles, a larger area, a single party in control. Why did the USSR collapse almost overnight and without a single shot fired?

Brazil is larger than the rest of South America combined. Portugese is spoken more than Spanish in South America. Why doesn't Brazil control the rest of the continent?

How could Great Britain, an island in northern Europe with an average population and almost no resources, once control about twenty-five percent of the world?

With the same location, a larger army, navy and air force, the same people, why did the British Empire collapse almost overnight?

With the same size, population and effectively no military (1941) why did the United States go from an insignificant country to history's greatest super-power almost overnight (1945)?

By 1942 Germany had the greatest military in history, controlled Europe, bombed England and led a global "Axis." Four years later Germany was in total ruin, occupied, destitute with its leaders either dead or on trial. Compared to the great empires of history, that often lasted several centuries, what happened to Germany?

Why did the American superpower fail to win a war in tiny, backward Vietnam after more years than the Civil War, both world wars and Korea combined and after dropping more bomb tonnage than all sides in World War II combined?

These samples are not meant to deny geopolitical analysis but to put it into perspective. If one examines the main elements of geopolitical theories, however, it is difficult to deny the deterministic content of the subject.

The "subject" was European in origin and become important shortly before the First World War (1914). In 1904 Halford Mackinder gave the inaugural geopolitical sermon to the Royal Geographic Society. His lasting insight has remained a classic maxim of that century:

"Who controls eastern Europe controls the Heartland. Who controls the Heartland controls the World Island. Who controls the World Island controls the world."

In 1907 British civil servant, Eyre Crowe, gave the Foreign Office his classic memorandum on "The State of British Relations with France and Germany." This became the basis for British efforts in the war and subsequent British policy. It began as follows:

"The general character of England's foreign policy is determined by the immutable conditions of her geographical situation on the ocean flank of Europe as an island state with vast overseas colonies and dependencies ..."

During World War II the Dutch-transplanted geopolitician, Nicholas J. Spykman, teaching at Yale, answered Mackinder with a perspective on the nature of the war based upon American geopolitical realities:

"Who controls the rimlands controls Eurasia. Who controls Eurasia controls the world."

In effect the differences between these two competing forces are simply the same between continental and insular geopolitical perspectives. Mackinder was expressing the potential of "land" power from inside the European continent, ie. Russia or Germany. Spykman emphasized "rimland," ie. the maritime "edges" of vast continents, both Europe and Asia, ie. the US and Britain. Both have merit, to a degree.

Indeed, if one looks quickly at the Twentieth Century the realities of both viewpoints becomes clear. Essentially, both world wars and the Cold War bore strong resemblances to Mackinder, Spykman and world geopolitics.

All three involved conflicts between "Heartland" vs "Rimland" coalitions: either Germany alone or Russia/Soviet Bloc combinations against the maritime/airpower of America and Great Britain. NATO vs the Warsaw Pact became the essential rivals of the entire Cold War, from western Europe to the island allies in Asia.

The western alliance system even rhymed, NATO, SEATO, CENTO. Now there is only one left, but it has doubled in size.

With the Cold War itself long-gone (1991) how do we assess geopolitics in an air/space age? If missiles can fly in seconds over borders, if globalization ignores boundaries, if the world can talk and watch altogether, if a virus can cripple humanity, if man goes to the moon and Mars ... then why does ground, water or land matter?

The answer can also come with questions. Two, in fact.

1) What was the only real national security issue in the 2016 presidential race? Answer: the Rio Grande River and the southern border.

2) There are about 5,000 aircraft in the skies of the world at any given time. What about that? Answer: sooner or later, they all must land.

Stinson in Dayton News

Waking him up

April 2, 2020

Of all competing concepts in the political vocabulary, the term "national interest" remains both the most vital and simultaneously the most elusive. Barring outright treason, there can be no honest citizen in any sovereign nation that will deliberately advocate violation of a country's national interest.

Then the fun begins. Being vital is not enough. The phrase itself is so vague and compromising that it literally can coincide with the any particular "interest" that any particular individual, section, religion, race, nationality, political party etc. can muster with assertion. Moreover, it likewise is assumed that what is vital for one, by definition, must be vital for the whole as well.

Survival is the supreme national interest, shared by all. Security, essential for survival, is also universal. Others comprise a host of factors, economic, political, cultural etc., that vary from country to country. Many are unique to each individual arena. Central America, for example, has been considered "essential" to the US, especially the Panama Canal, as this 1927 State Department memo will attest:

"call it a sphere of interest, or what you will, we do control the destinies of Central America, and we do it for the simple reason that the national interest absolutely dictates such a course."

A further problem is time. What may seem mandatory in one time-period can be dismissed later. Between World War I and the Cold War, for example, US national security policies underwent six separate and fundamental changes of direction:

1914, neutrality.

1917, declaration of war.

1920, neutrality.

1941, declaration of war.

1947, containment of Soviet Union.

1983, elimination of Soviet Union.

(There has been nothing fundamental since)

The issue is compounded by the distinctions between morality and interest, ie. between principle and reality. This first arose at the beginning, when Alexander Hamilton addressed how the new American state should view revolutionary France, with admiration as a friend or neutrality as a hostile revolution:

"An individual may, on numerous occasions, meritoriously indulge the emotions of generosity and benevolence, but only without an eye to, but even at the expense of, his own interest. But a government can rarely, if at all, be justifiable in pursuing a similar course" (1791).

The issue was soon settled by George Washington himself when he advocated American distance and neutrality in Europe's raging revolutionary wars (Farewell Address, 1796).

But America was famously founded on principle, from the Declaration to the Bill of Rights. As the country developed and settled most internal scores, including Civil War, the issue of an objective national interest eventually collided with "exceptionalism."

"Wilsonanism" has become the personification of "American exceptionalism." Woodrow Wilson gave this identification a lasting cause in his historic reaction to the transgressions that Germany was inflicting on the world. "it is a very perilous thing," he once declared, "to determine the foreign policy of a nation in the terms of material interest. ... We dare not turn from the principle that morality and not expediency is the thing that must guide us ... We have no selfish ends to serve ... We are but one of the champions of the rights of mankind."

In his declaration of war Wilson gave idealism a permanent "interest" in how Americans would subsequently define foreign policy:

"right is more precious than peace, and we shall fight for the things which we have always carried nearest our hearts. ... for democracy, ... for the rights and liberties of small nations, [to] make the world itself at last free."

The interpretations of national interest failed to bother a people in diplomatic isolation or in Great Depression. The aftermath of World War II, however, confronted Americans with choices between principle and capability that would enter in a new "great debate" as to what the country was all about, once and for all.

The original "purpose," or "war aims" came with Franklin Roosevelt and the "Four Freedoms (from "hunger," "want" etc.) but soon gave way to geopolitical "containment" and political "realism" with the Truman Doctrine and a global alliance system.

While Truman promised to assist "free peoples everywhere" (1947) the realities and resources available proved too little to tackle the entire world. As the US looked on, the world's most populous country (China) went Communist in 1949 while the Eisenhower Administration tried to install another NATO into southeast Asia with SEATO in 1954.

Confounding reality and resource, President Eisenhower provided still another illusion in the same year, proclaiming that if Vietnam and southeast Asia went over to the enemy the rest of Asia, and beyond, would follow "like a row of dominos." The world rarely behaves automatically, Chess is a better analogy.

In his famous Inaugural Address, John F. Kennedy carried this "torch" to even newer heights,

"We shall pay any price, bear any burden, meet any hardship, support any friend, oppose any foe in order to assist the survival and success of liberty." (1961)

The subsequent war in Vietnam, carried on through five administrations, ended with an American retreat and a divided country, while Congress supported each and every request for funding each administration had requested. The tragedy, however, left any definition of "national interest" in shambles, a condition that no post-Cold War administration has even acknowledged, much-less resolved.

Clearly, America had come to assume that there was no or little distinction between our own values and those of all others. This was summarized famously by President W. Bush in 2003 when he announced that our invasion of Iraq required universal support, with the world "either with us or against us."

Clearly, the distinction between political principles ("ideals") versus resources ("realities") remains at the core of any understanding of "national" interest. The late German-born philosopher, Hans J. Morgenthau, first addressed this in 1949 with a distinctive European perspective. Definitely on the "realist" side, Morgenthau saw how "the intoxication with world embracing ideals which because of their vagueness and generality, can provide no rational guidance to concrete political action."

Two decades after the first Iraq War, the US remains "intoxicated" with ideals that have yet to challenge the realities of a tragic and troubled globe. Inside that vacuum the body politic is equally intoxicated with a completely domestic agenda driven by a set of sociological ideologies ("isms") that promise an equally volatile and divided future.

Is there an AA for countries?

Remembering The Blitz

April 4, 2020

As the world goes through another in history's life-and-death struggles it may be at least comfortable to acknowledge that today's crisis is neither new nor unsolvable. History has recorded the nature of most past events when it seemed that life itself was on-the-line. It may have seemed so but, looking back, it never was. Or, at least it didn't happen. It didn't happen either because the issue just dissolved, or "spent itself" or because the men and women of the time resolved it themselves.

Either way, humanity has tripled since the year of the Blitz, 1940, both the year of my birth and the year when it seemed to nearly everyone that civilization itself was about over. Or, as British Prime Minister Winston Churchill once put it, "...if we fail, then the whole world, including the United States, will sink into the abyss of a new dark age."

Few reading this remember the time, nor do I. But it was real and those involved felt it and believed it. The cause wasn't a virus nor an epidemic. It was an ideology, two countries, two peoples and, ultimately, two men. Technically it was bombs, airplanes, fires and, above all, willpower and the fight to live.

Churchill also called it the world's "darkest hour" and saluted the men who fought it over British skies as those to whom "... never was so much owed by so many to so few." The "few" were pilots of the Royal Air Force (RAF), numbering in the hundreds, who fought Hitler's "Luftwaffe" (Air Force), through 1940 into 1941 in what history has recorded as the "Blitz" (German for "lightening").

Operation "Sealion," as Hitler called the planned invasion of Great Britain, was to have been preceded by an airborne attack necessary to permit the German Navy to transit the Army to British shores, the first invasion attempt since 1066. With the confidence borne out by Germany's sudden conquest of France and most of western Europe (April through June) it appeared that western civilization was, in fact, "on the ropes."

Meanwhile, the United States remained under the constraints of a series of tight "neutrality" laws that both reflected the mood of the country and prohibited only "cash and carry" transport of any material to the British Isles. President Franklin D. Roosevelt did everything possible to circumvent these, intervening personally to veto legislation that would have restricted any US involvement in war except an outright Nazi invasion.

In March 1941 Roosevelt secured Senate passage of Lend Lease aid to Britain (with the help of his defeated Republican opponent Wendell Willkie) but by then the Blitz was over and the planned German invasion already cancelled "indefinitely."

Technically, the first day of the Blitz came shortly after the fall of France. While sporadic airborne raids ("nuisance") had occurred before, the first strategic German offensive began on July 10 and was concentrated on the convoys, ports, airfields and factories of southern England. These were intended to remove any obstacle to invasion but when RAF resistance proved too formidable the Luftwaffe began to attack the British "spirit," ie. morale.

On September 7 it began with London, first with daily then nightly raids. By the time the entire air assault was over (May 11, 1941) Londoners were hit on 71 occasions, most famously 56 nights in a row until the greatest hit, December 29. This was the worst assault on any city in human history, 136 bombers, hundreds more fighters, 100,000 bombs dropped in a few hours, 1,500 total fires. It was called the worst disaster since the "Great Fire of London" (1666). While it is beyond my talents to describe what it was like on that night alone, famous American war correspondent Ernie Pyle was there:

"Into the dark shadowed spaces below us, while we watched, whole batches of incendiary bombs fell. We saw two dozen go off in two seconds. They flashed terrifically, then quickly simmered down to pin points of dazzling white, burning ferociously ... The greatest of all fires was directly in front of us. Flames seemed to whip hundreds of feet into the air. Pinkish-white smoke ballooned upward in a great cloud, and out of this cloud there gradually took shape ... the gigantic dome of St. Paul's Cathedral. St. Paul's was surrounded by fire, but it came through. It stood there in enormous proportions, growing slowly clearer and clearer, the way objects take shape at dawn. It was like a picture of some miraculous figure that appears before peace-hungry soldiers on a battlefield."

Almost every major city was hit, many several times, as follows: Exeter (13), Liverpool (8), Birmingham (8), Plymouth (8), Bristol (6), Glasgow (5) while others (Coventry, Belfast, Portsmouth) were bombed at least one to three times. Total death toll was about 50,000 with whole cities demolished.

The COVIS 19 is horrible and tragic. But it is a month old (here). We still remember 9/11/01, which lasted several minutes. How would America survive nearly a full year of death and destruction all over, in New York, Washington, Boston, Miami, Chicago, Denver, Dallas, LA, San Francisco, Seattle etc.?

Months after the Blitz, America lost 2,400 lives and several ships and planes at Pearl Harbor, where two hours of bombing took place 2,000 miles away from the mainland, in the mid-Pacific, against a "territory." Nor did the enemy have the slightest intention, nor the capacity, to hit the continental US (although that was not apparent at the time). The result was a national unity seen neither before nor since. Together with Britain we won the war.

Where are we today? Does America have an RAF, a Churchill? What will the present crisis produce?

Where do the several "isms" that dominate the culture fit in? Will racism, sexism and white nationalism finally do us in?

Is the United States united?

Is Great Britain great?

"Dancin' in the Dark"

March 18, 2020

There are times when I wonder if I may have missed something, amidst the vitriol engaged between and among today's "populations." Or, to the contrary, am I all right while they keep talking "past one another" toward destinations unknown?

I finally take refuge in age: I'm simply too old to understand current interests (now that the Cold War is over).

Yet, even that won't do, since I've been teaching history since 1966, and they all seem to use history as argument, one way or another. Where have I been?

Americans are known as "ahistorical," which means that they care little and use it sparingly. Yet, the ones on TV, in the news, and on campus use history all the time. As the only known human "laboratory," this is unavoidable, but the history used in public controversies is almost completely channeled according to current events. Or, perhaps closer to intent, to future events, as wanted.

Thus, yesterday has value, but only for tomorrow.

This is not necessarily a contradiction in terms. "Those who do not remember the past are condemned to repeat it," (Santayana, 1931). But was this a warning or advice? If the first, it's meant to "avoid," if the second, it's meant to "apply."

Today's public "discourses," most obviously, have chosen number two. Nobody wants to re-start slavery, but many want us to pay for it.

The problem in this regard is the problem of "selection," i.e., we select that which conforms to our chosen desires, omitting that which does not.

In colloquial terms, this is called "cherry picking," a derisive term that denies the value of history altogether. Indeed, it turns it on its head and converts the subject to a rather low-level aspect of ideological ("emotional") and self-absorbed ambition.

If this kind of subject was included in any school curriculum, it would have to be identified as "Contemporary Ideologies." Which is fine, but it continues in "masquerade," which makes every day on campus Halloween.

"Application" in these cases requires two behaviors: forgetting and re-membering. Both are selective and, therefore, arbitrary ("ideological" by definition).

Remembering is the easy part, just look in a book. Forgetting takes deep attention. In fact, it should avoid looking in any book or recalling anything that may have occurred. For example, I remember Robert E. Lee as a Con-federate General, easy enough. But forgetting him takes intense devotion, both to the man (whom I never met) and even invention.

Invention requires attribution, i.e. to attribute Lee to an institution now gone but once universal. Whether or not this attribution is accurate, half-ac-curate, or even erroneous remains beside the point. The word itself, "attribu-tion," does not require support. In this regard, it then becomes reasonable, indeed necessary, to "attribute" behaviors to whole generations, whole coun-tries, whole peoples, religions, races, genders ...and the list goes on.

If General Lee, to continue, is to be "forgotten," then it would have to be the fact that he led (and nearly won) a rebellion. Yet this apparently bears little relevance to those who tear down his statues. He, thus, is to be discarded be-cause of slavery as opposed to secession.

Lee's statue, properly, does not belong on any public location, not because some of his people held slaves, but because he was in rebellion. If someone wants Lee's picture on their wall or his likeness in their yard, that is, and should remain, private. (My in-laws, RIP, had pictures of Benito Mussolini throughout their house in Maryland. I accepted that they were Italian).

Attribution, especially for a lost cause, is not only illogical and irrelevant but can be extremely disruptive. Immediately after the end of the Civil War, Appomattox, Union soldiers began cheering and shouting. General Grant hurried out and told them to be quiet, "The rebels are our countrymen now." In his Second Inaugural, Lincoln asked for "malice toward none, charity for all."

In today's "culture," we have nearly the opposite: malice toward all, charity toward none. The list goes well beyond the slavery issue, to include nearly all aspects of the human experience. To list the causes would be superfluous and to deny legitimacy of "cause" itself would be the same.

A critical component in contemporary beliefs is the separation of the particular from the universal. In the manner in which it is presented, the cause is identified as "American" and, as well, to be erased inside America. The problem: without exception, each cause is universal, observed from the Bible to ancient empires, and cannot be identified with any particular society or time period. The Founding Fathers provided liberty, not a change in humanity itself. (Ironically, America, despite today's grievances, has probably done more in each instance to rectify history's wrongs than any other large or diverse society.)

So where does this leave us? Nowhere, I fear. Ideology cannot be persuaded. No one could tell Hitler that Aryans would not rule the world. No one can tell a Communist that the proletariat will not rise. Professional Feminists will still insist that the only good males ever are now both "dead [and] white." And no one will convince me that modern medicine, prosperity, and technology comes from the Devil himself, "white supremacy."

Yet, these are widespread in our current culture.

Have I missed something? Here's "The Boss" (Bruce Springsteen):
You can't start a fire
Worrying about your little world fallin' apart
This gun's for hire
Even if you're just dancin' in the dark.

"Stayin' Alive"

February 27, 2020

Leaders who fail in their global missions are normally dismissed by history. What do we remember about Napoleon? Waterloo.

Woodrow Wilson, another case in point, is not remembered for his efforts to re-make the world but by his failure to do so. The League of Nations and Wilson's crusade to "make the world safe for democracy" in World War I remain today as lasting tributes to American "overreach" and disregard for the alleged "realities" of how tough it is to change things.

Wilson's efforts turned into "normalcy" in American foreign policies, intense isolationism, Pearl Harbor, and the greatest war in human history. He is remembered for those facts, the empty end of the First World War and his final stroke and quiet death in 1924. He is buried in the National Cathedral, and so is his mission. "Wilsonianism" is his lasting legacy, an expression of contempt for those who reach beyond the boundaries of normal play.

Other countries have tried to broaden their expanse by "missions," with similar results. At one point, England ("Great" Britain) owned one-fifth of the earth and its population. It's now all gone, and even Scotland and Northern

Ireland may revolt. Still, it remains the only nation on earth with an adjective in its name.

Others have created missions with both terrible reasons and disastrous ends. In 1917, Russia was taken by "Bolsheviks" who promised world proletariat-Marxist revolutions. Seventy-five years later (1991), the Soviet Union and communism collapsed, with nary a single "proletariat" revolution but a number of Soviet "republics," now independent oligarchies. Marx would not have recognized any part of the Twentieth Century.

In 1933, Hitler declared a "Thousand Year Reich." Twelve years later, Germany lay in ruins, Hitler a suicide, and the world's worst war finally over, 75 million dead. After bombing English cities, day and night, for over a year, he canceled the planned invasion. Failing to cross 26 miles of Channel waters, he then declared war on the U.S. (December 11, 1941), 3,000 miles away (Hitler was never in the Navy).

Missions can be horrible, given their single-minded purpose and all-out means. Normally, missions are ideologies, spelled ending with "ism," as today's political culture will attest. That means "worldview," which defines humanity under a single banner (race, religion, gender, economics, etc.) and tolerates no dissent. Missions are also "total," meaning nothing in-between and win/lose for the result.

Americans, by nature, are prone to mission-oriented purpose. Innocently, President W. Bush once declared that the Iraq War meant that the world was either "for or against us," no neutrality allowed. Secretary of State John Foster Dulles once famously declared that Cold War neutrals, like India, were "immoral" by not taking sides.

The origins of this lie in the original revolution for independence, with its historic impact upon political society. The idea "exceptionalism" is still used to define American political culture while the current Administration's "MAGA" campaign derives from the same source.

That does not imply universal acceptance, even within the same country. Americans have gone through periods of both expansive design and resolute isolation. Just compare John F. Kennedy's Inaugural Address (1961) with those of two other Democrats, Franklin D. Roosevelt (1933) and Bill Clinton (1993). The first had not a single word on domestic life, the other two barely anything on foreign policies. Kennedy challenged Americans to "bear any burden, pay any price." FDR famously said that the "only thing we have to fear is fear itself," while Clinton noted how "our mission is timeless" but completely within ourselves by: "helping troubled children ... reconnecting our torn communities ... [that] we must care for each other."

That's about where we are right now. Clinton's campaign slogan summarized the mood, "It's the economy, stupid." Foreign policies since then have been designed through near-meaningless and abstract slogans ("bumper stickers"). "Assertive Multilateralism" (Clinton), "Nation-building" (W. Bush) and "Leading From Behind" (Obama). President Trump wants to make the country "great" again, which, like today's Britain, remains an empty adjective.

There are 193 countries in the world today. How many are guided by "missions"? Probably one. But what is China's mission (that we hear so much about)? Control the South China Sea? All of Asia? The world? Do we fear Chinese soldiers patrolling downtown Boston?

In 1942, the government's *Why We Fight* series (shown everywhere) portrayed Japanese soldiers marching up Pennsylvania Avenue to take control of Congress. Apparently, they had just invaded California, marched across the Rockies, Great Plains, Midwest, and northern Virginia. In reality, the Japanese Army was in China since 1937 and was looking for ways out from their own version of "quagmire."

Hyperbole can be appreciated under stress, but exaggeration can be only short-term. In order to be functional, any mission must be "realistic." Which means that it must fit resources and design. Woodrow Wilson had a good idea but lacked the means and temper to succeed. The Bolsheviks were captured by fantasy, Hitler legally insane, and Japanese politicians failed to remember Admiral Yamamoto's warning: I can bomb Pearl Harbor, then what? (paraphrase) Al Qaeda destroyed the WTC. What for?

Does America have a mission today? If so, it is certainly not intended to go overseas. The Democratic debates, if nothing else, demonstrated this.

Which begs the question, does America need a foreign policy mission? The Australian singing group, Bee Gees, once recorded *Stayin' Alive*, meaning "to exist." We have been doing that since the end of the Cold War; it requires little effort.

The country can stay as it is, without foreign policy purpose, resolve, or goal. But are we satisfied with election debates that highlight exchanges such as "Pete are you calling me dumb" or "Mike did you once say 'fat broads'"?

Jefferson described the possibility of an *Empire of Liberty*. Monroe declared an entire hemisphere "American." Truman's Doctrine was aimed at "free people everywhere."

Reagan told the world that he was going to "leave Marxism-Leninism on the ash heap of history." He did. He then went to Berlin and told the Russians to "tear down this wall." They did.

If there is to be a "great" debate on foreign policy, it will have to address concepts such as those.

Otherwise, we will have to be content with *Stayin' Alive*:

"Life goin' nowhere,

somebody help me, yeah

I'm stayin' alive."

Unity in America

February 13, 2020

On our first day of practice, the football coach uttered these memorable words to his new team: "Remember men, there's no 'I' in team."

Such an admonition has remained a mainstay of human activity, sports included, since the dawn of time. The realization that human progress depends upon "teamwork" instead of "the individual" has descended through the ages as a first principle of the success and prosperity of the "species" (men and women together).

Despite this essential truism, the spectrum of American history has been dominated by division, interspersed by rare occasions of authentic unity. This is true even today. The divisions between parties, genders, races, religions, languages, sections, and sects is summarized by the colors "red" and "blue." Beneath this vague description lies deep and historical differences that have defined the American "experiment" from the beginning but have not, as yet, been able to break the "bonds that unite."

Time will tell, but division was dominant from the start.

As early as 1765, ten years before the first shot of the revolution, there were scarcely more than a handful of colonists who wanted to break from England.

Samuel Adams, his cousin John, James Otis, Ben Franklin, John Hancock, and several others led the origins of the rebellion. They formed the political squad "Sons of Liberty," formed the "Committees of Correspondence," and instigated the "Boston Massacre" largely on their own initiative. The Declaration of Independence was signed by only 52 co-conspirators, while the actual fighting itself was supported by less than one-third of the population. The remaining two-thirds were either neutral or "Loyalists," who favored the British.

The revolution was as much an internal war as against the Redcoats, where Loyalist and "Patriot" civilians waged a "civil" struggle more ferocious than the regular battles. A British Chaplin noted this hatred in his dairy:

"These Americans so soft, pacific and benevolent by nature, are here transformed into monsters, implacably bloody and ravenous; party rage has kindled the spirit of hatred within them, they attack and rob each other by turns, destroy dwelling houses, or establish themselves therein by driving out those who had before dispossessed others."

The divisions that separated the sides within the American Revolution left an indelible impression upon the political culture, one whose "aftershocks" can still be felt today. Professor Bernard Bailyn has summarized the nature of both sides of the American "cause" from the beginning:

"Committed to the moral as well as the political integrity of the Anglo-American system as it existed, the Loyalists were insensitive to the moral basis of the protests that arose against it ... They did not sense the constriction of the existing order, often because they lived so deeply within it ... They could find only persistent irrationality in the arguments of the discontented and hence wrote off all of their efforts as politically pathological."

A similar dysfunction was to plague the nation in the second consecutive British war. At the end of the War of 1812, the economic and political divisions between the South and New England provoked the most audacious wartime protest in U.S. history. The conduct of the war had devastated New England shipping with Europe, and the full area refused conscription, finances, and other support for "Mr. Madison's War."

The country was essentially divided into two, and talk of New England secession was rampant. A delegation of leading "dissidents" met in Hartford, Connecticut in December 1814 and sent a list of "demands" to Congress that amounted to a New England sectional veto over future declarations of war and other aspects of political and economic policies (such as restrictions on trade embargos and conduct of presidential elections).

The crisis quickly subsided after news of the U.S. victory at New Orleans and the conclusion of the war by the Treaty of Ghent (December 1814). But the repercussions of New England's divisive behavior only foreshadowed the deeper American sectional crisis that began when southern cannon batteries shelled the U.S. Fort Sumter outside Charleston, South Carolina (12 April 1861).

The Civil War represents the epitome of division that precluded any form of unification that the original revolution pretended. Whereas it is true that all societies have, in one form or another, divided themselves in half, the extent of the divisions in the aftermath of Appomattox will find few equals on the political earth.

The estimated death toll of the years 1861-1865 is now around 720,000, all male, almost all white, north and south. All this within a population of around 32 million. The psychological, political, and economic toll cannot ever be listed by any empirical standard. Suffice it to say that Vicksburg, Mississippi refused to honor July 4th until 1945.

The unity that eluded American society was finally closed, temporarily, on December 7, 1941, when the Japanese did what no domestic factor was able to do, namely, give Americans a singular cause. By and large, that semblance carried through both world wars and the Cold War (1991).

American unity is now under still another challenge, as "separatism" has taken on a number of forms, most ending with an "ism" and conducted under the banner "diversity." President Trump's impeachment trial may be the opening "shot" in this process, but "perspective" might offer some solace.

Imagine another "civil" struggle similar to the first. That war took the lives of about 2.5% of the population. Today, that would be around seven million, all white males ("dead"). How did the country conduct itself back then?

For one thing, it started with an impeachment trial. That failed, and, from that point until World War I, America expanded both on the continent and overseas. Republicans governed the country, and all presidents until 1900 were former Union Army officers (except Grover Cleveland), and the military, especially the Navy, became a global powerhouse. The Civil War had national repercussions that affected the entire world.

How would the present generation conduct itself if seven million American soldiers had been killed in war since 2016? Is a comparison possible?

Would the president ask NATO to increase spending by 2 %? How would "Black Lives" fit in, "Me Too," Harvey Weinstein, reparations, LGBTQ? What would the issues be? How would we approach the idea of "health care for all"? Would we "have a plan" for the body bags?

Would there even be a country left at all? To us, it is an imaginary world. To them, it was a daily reality.

Have we come a "long way"?

Half-People

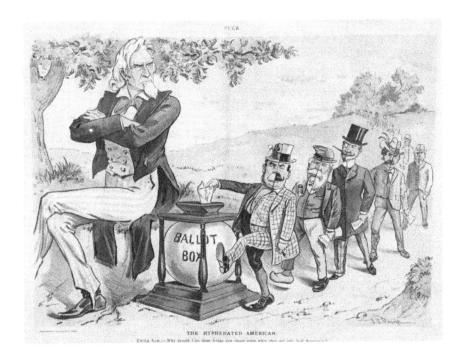

THE HYPHENATED AMERICAN.

February 13, 2020

The United States may be the only country on earth where most of its citizens represent themselves by halves. Hyphenated Americans appear to be the whole, with almost all of them identified first by their ancestry, and second by their citizenship. Not only does this mock the term "united," but it serves also to question the loyalty of the population. Are "African-Americans" loyal to this country or to the one of their racial origin? The same can be asked of all the others in the mix, from "Hispanic" to "Asian," to "Irish," "Italian," "German," "Jewish," "Native," etc. ad infinitum.

True, this is a "nation of immigrants," which makes it unique on the globe. True also, all the "halves" vote, serve in the military, and conduct themselves otherwise in patriotic manners. Yet, the very fact of a hyphenated citizenry carries with it, by definition, a question of both actual and potential divided loyalty. This fact has occupied American history from the beginning and has caused a number of deviations that have interrupted life to the national detriment.

Franklin D. Roosevelt is defined as the "savior" of democracy, both during the Great Depression and World War II. Yet, even he was forced to "intern" over 120,000 "Japanese-Americans" into camps for the duration of the war against Japan. The "necessity" of FDR's action is not at issue and can easily be challenged. The issue is that he did it without significant protest within the rest of the country. His actions, thus, reflect the contradictions of a hyphenated people, not disloyalty *per se*.

During World War I, both Irish- and German-Americans, for obvious ancestral reasons, protested the Wilson government's favoritism toward the Allies, especially the declaration of war against Germany. Both groups served heroically in the war, but the tensions between "civic duty" and the "old country" plagued the war effort, both during and afterward.

With Germany an enemy, German-Americans, the largest "minority," became the new target. With the sinking of the Lusitania in 1915 by a German submarine, causing 128 American deaths, and the increasing image of the German soldier as a barbarous "Hun," the American people began a national campaign against anything remotely "Germanic." This came with official sanction after the declaration of war, April 6, 1917.

President Wilson immediately declared all Germans in America as "alien enemies" and banned them all from seaports, airports, military facilities, and Washington, D.C. German-Americans had to disclose their bank accounts to an "Alien Property Custodian;" they had to register personal affidavits and undergo official fingerprinting. "Concentration Camps" were established in places like North Carolina, Georgia, and Utah, where thousands of suspect Germans were held. Localities, school systems, libraries, German place-names of towns, parks, buildings, theaters, etc. were changed to English.

Throughout the culture, nearly all remnants of "German" were closed or harassed. Thousands of "Schmidts" became "Smiths." German churches were painted yellow. Libraries banned books on Germany. German-language newspapers were closed. Beethoven and Mozart were banned. German food was banned. "Sauerkraut" became "liberty cabbage." "German measles" became "liberty measles."

The effect on Irish-Americans, all anti-British, was similar but not as virulent. Irish nationalists held an anti-war rally in Madison Square Garden in

June 1915, and the government closed all Irish-nationalist newspapers. *Irish Rebel*, an anti-war book of the time, declared the truism that "Ireland's liberty would best be served by a German victory."

Yet, Irish-Americans overwhelmingly served valiantly in the war, including the famous "Fighting 69th" of New York and "Wild Bill" Donavan, who went on to become America's first head of a spy organization (OSS). The famous wartime song, *Over There*, was written by Irish-American George M. Cohan.

But the Wilson Administration, super-alert to the possibility of subversion within the public, passed two major anti-immigrant laws meant to prevent "hyphenated" Americans from interrupting the war effort. In announcing the legislation, the President stated that, "There are citizens of the United States, I blush to admit, born under other flags but welcomed under our generous naturalization laws to the full freedom of America, who have poured the poison of disloyalty into the very arteries of our natural life ... and to debase our politics to the uses of foreign intrigues."

Both the Espionage Act (1917) and the Sedition Act (1918) were passed by Congress and severely curtailed the speech, writing, and other demonstrations that may have undermined the war effort against Germany.

The heritage of World War I and, indeed, the anti-foreign legislation of the 1920s, remain as a cultural heritage of the American "melting pot" as we debate the influx of "foreigners" across the southern border in the Twenty-first century.

The issue is the same, and the question still dominates public discourse. What is the significance of a "hyphenated" personality?

Take "Native-American," for example. It has two meanings: "my land," and acceptance of a political culture. All other hyphens contain an identical contradiction: different and the same.

In conclusion, note this comparison. There is no such thing as an "English-American;" it is not used. Why? Because that reality began a revolution, and they fought to eliminate the first. They distinctly became only the second and have remained the same since.

That's the model we should all pursue.

(Full disclosure: I sometimes have referred to myself as an "Irish-American," but I meant it only on March 17th.)

What Difference Does it Make?

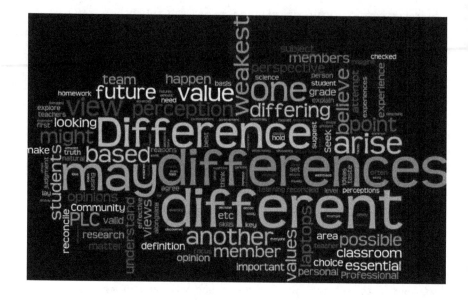

January 27, 2020

The key assumption behind this most-asked question states that any final solution is irrelevant and that any one of a series of solutions will suffice. In other words, the issue/problem is either too difficult to solve and would make little difference in any case. So, why bother? Better to leave it alone and let "nature take its course."

This kind of logic supports the long-held theory, "if it's not broken, don't fix it." Or, "let well-enough alone."

Should such an interpretation of life guide humanity? What would be the result? Would it lead to a general apathy that might stop any progress before it begins? Or, would it divide the serious from the quaint and select only those areas that need repair or improvement?

There is no definitive answer to those questions, but the philosophic quandary behind the question has plagued mankind from the beginning, with no end in sight. For one, it may just be the problem separating conservative from progressive, of those who are prepared to allow "natural" conditions to prevail from those who demand intervention in shaping "destiny." Beneath even that are those who believe in the notion of "destiny" in the first place versus those who deny it as a conceptual design.

In the animal kingdom, destiny rules. It's called "biology." There is nothing that will permit a fish to fly or a bird to swim. Lions eat zebras, elephants are big, giraffes have long necks, and cats kill mice.

In the human kingdom, destiny, "biology," must compete with psychology. Humans have "intellects," which permit "reason." Thus, the human brain has both an "emotional" and an "intellectual" content, that vie against one another for result. This combination eliminates the absolute predictability for animals and makes the "human condition" dependent upon which of the two parts of the brain prevail.

There is room enough for both. Animals act on "instinct;" they cannot "reason." Humans do both, which introduces the notion "rational" into their behavior. It also introduces "irrational," both terms derived from intellect and both observable but difficult to define.

If strict and consistent, "logic" evades definition; observation has to do. This equates with another old truism, "you will know it when you see it." Terrorism, for example, has multiple definitions and applications but has become the *reason d' état* for modern world politics. Yet, what distinguishes this "Age of Terror" from earlier ages, and, if it cannot be defined, why is it so pervasive?

Does a civilian beheaded by ISIS know the difference between himself and a soldier killed at Iwo Jima?

Getting back to the original question, does a definition make any difference? Even if we have a clear distinction between terror and war, what consequence ("difference") does it make? If the consequences are deaths and weapons, there is little fundamental difference. If the consequences are fundamental, it makes all the difference in the world. Which means it *changes* the world.

This perspective only begs the question: Has the world changed since human intervention, about 6,000 years ago? Not technology, not medicine, humanity.

What's the real answer, and does it "make a difference"? How is that judged? There is a "superficial" explanation and a "fundamental" one.

Superficial: The American Civil War started in 1861 within the United States and was confined to North America. The US entered World War II in 1941 and fought all over the world. Judgment: These are two separate events without any relationship.

Fundamental: Both wars were started when one side bombed an island of the other. Judgment: They are the same with marginal and thus irrelevant circumstances and conduct.

These examples are isolated and arbitrary and could easily be expanded to include the whole of human history. Hitler invaded Poland in 1939; the U.S. invaded Mexico in 1847. France invaded Russia in 1812. Germany did the same in 1941. Is a list necessary?

If one studies history to learn the differences, why bother? To learn patterns has meaning.

What's the difference? In the long run, philosophically and for posterity, very little. For the moment and for expediency, war or peace.

For the past three years, this country has been paralyzed by notions that the American President and foreign governments behaved "injudiciously" with each other, so badly that the President must leave. Not only must he go, but this must occur without an election, thus "interfering" with normal discourse (impeachment).

Thus we have "collusion" between two governments and "abuse" of authority. If these are new and unique, intervention is necessary. If they are "SOP" or characteristic, lesser action is best (or none at all).

There is no possibility that the actions taken by both sides in the U.S. political system since 2016 are new or unique. "*There is nothing new under the sun*," says Ecclesiastes.

Certainly, the overwhelming and most lasting "images" of the politics since then are not the nuances and misjudgments of the players (from both sides) but the sheer persistence, tenacity, and moral outrage exhibited from day one. One can easily forget or dismiss the daily and endless legalisms and argumentation that goes on ad infinitum. But the memories of the name-calling, the media, and theatric reactions, the use of descriptions as "hysteria" and "derangement" will last a lifetime.

This is "human behavior" from the "emotional" brain. It is also as old as history and has been described as "fundamental" by those who have experienced it.

In his classic 1796 Farewell Address, George Washington, who had suffered through this himself, labeled it "...the channels of party passion... this spirit, unfortunately, is inseparable from our nature, having its root in the strongest passions of the human mind."

Washington further noted that this side of the brain creates "ill-founded jealousies and false alarms" and "has perpetrated the most horrid enormities."

Now, more than two centuries later, we are doing the same thing, aided by modern technology. Who knows if we will do it again, regardless of who wins this round.

Many have compared today's political passions to the pre–Civil War era. How are such perspectives to be considered? If we view them as warned by the first President, restraint, foreboding, and caution. If we dismiss the comparisons altogether, we can go to "war."

I once had a cut on my hand. Someone asked if it was serious, I replied, "it depends on how much I scratch."

That's the difference.

January 21, 2020

The "nation-state" system is widely believed to have begun in 1648, after the *Thirty Years War* ended the Holy Roman Empire and created mankind's belief in the centrality of being part of something, "nation" (*Peace of Westphalia*). Henceforth, the division of the world's political existence has derived from two separate but equal conceptual designs. The first is geographic (territory) and the other is legal (sovereignty).

The "Westphalian" system still defines the political globe, although it is comparatively "recent" in the longer run. Prior to 1648, the vast majority of political systems comprised "imperial" designs, "empires," that stretched across regional land boundaries or, more recently, maritime "colonial" regimes tied together by navies.

The largest land empire was the Mongol regime begun by Genghis Kahn in the thirteenth century, which stretched from Mongolia and China, through India and Persia to eastern Europe.

The largest maritime empire was British and governed about one-fifth of the world in the late nineteenth century.

Today, all the empires have vanished, while almost 200 "nation-states," most of them former imperial subjects, exist more-or-less united by their differences.

These differences comprise the meaning of the word "nation." The underlying meaning of the "nation-state" term collects both words and joins one people to one political association. Whether the association is democratic, tyrannical, authoritarian, or other makes little difference. They are "one" by definition and define each other by that criteria.

The Communist Soviet Union fought World War II as "nationalist" Russia and both Imperial and Fascist Germany fought both world wars united by their common heritage as "volk." This is characteristic and shared universally, whether by Ecuador, Indonesia, or Latvia.

"Nationalism," therefore, has become the most important sociological definition in modern history. Hans Kohn, the great historian of nationalism, has characterized the idea as the only one that humanity "will die for." This implies that the same concept lies behind all the major secular, religious, or political movements, whether communist, fascist, democratic, or theocratic. Communist can mean Russian or Chinese, Fascism can be Italian or German, Democratic can be American or British, Jewish can be Israel, and Muslim can be Iraq or Iran.

"Colors" often define nationality. Communists were "red," Nazi's were "brownshirts," the SS wore "black," today's America is either "red" or "blue," the Chinese were "yellow," Indians were "red" also. There are people "of color" by any variation: American nationalists are "white," as is some form of "supremacy." Irish-Catholics are "green," as opposed to the "orange" or Protestant.

Even the services wear distinctive colors. Navies are attractive shades of "blue" and "bright white;" armies are drab, "khaki," "field grey."

The proper definition of nationalism, at its base level, is "a sense of national consciousness ... and placing primary emphasis on promotion of its culture and interests." Within itself, nationalism represents unity; among others, it represents division. Synonyms of the term may represent both forms, including patriotism, sectionalism, and jingoism. Like the term "human nature," nationalism can be held responsible for all phases of behavior, from war and violence to stability and peace.

Professor Kohn, in his many books on the subject, recognized all aspects of the phenomenon. In *The Idea of Nationalism* (1944), he distinguished between a European, or German, brand that rested its authority on ethnic, geographic, or racial definitions. Thus, we have concepts such as "Motherland," "Fatherland," and other manifestations of aggressive or hostile peoples who were housed next to one another with tight borderlands and armed against each by armed cultures. These nations, he wrote, found their "justification in the natural fact of a community, held together not by the will of its members nor by any obligation of contract, but by traditional ties of kinship and status" (p. 331).

By contrast, English and American nationalism was bound by conceptual definitions of law and social contract and organized around theological and political definitions based upon human liberty. Thus, he wrote, "America became the vanguard of mankind, full of a proud and blissful faith in its mission. This faith of the American people in itself and its mission made it a nation" (p. 308).

The English/American brand of nationalism was tied to their geopolitical separation from continental boundaries that provided for capitalist economies, maritime dominance, and the growth at home of democracy and political liberty.

Although Hans Kohn is long gone (d. 1971), he would undoubtedly revise his original definition of how the American "experiment" has survived the test of time. Instead of a country that had suffered the attacks of both Fascist and Communist ideological and nationalist challenges, while managing to survive both economic depression and political turmoil, he would find a citizenry in a condition of self-doubt and profound confusion.

The unity that survived Pearl Harbor, Adolf Hitler, Stalin, Khrushchev, Mao, and a Cold War for global survival now suffers through partisan divisions, historic revision, and an indifference to world order that promise to undermine the very fabric of what was once "a city upon a hill."

There is still nationalism in America, but it is on the defensive against a "post-modern" cultural attack that dominates opinion circles. From the academy, media, theater, "millennials," and parts of the political class, the symbolic nationalism of today's America would be fictitious: Simon Legree (from *Uncle Tom's Cabin*).

"Blame-game" dominates most conversations, the media, and even sports. Talk shows are largely political, comedy has become dark, and award ceremonies are judged by their advocacies. There is little left of any concept that can come close to the idea "nation," and instead we see a set of divisive "isms," illegal immigrants and "sanctuary" cities, divisions defined by colors, and historic symbols removed from public view.

If there is anything left of a "people," it is well-hidden.

Kohn recognized this phenomenon in other cultures in his history lessons many years ago. As such: "we do not know ourselves any longer, we are estranged from one another. Our spirit has departed from us" (p. 374).

Rather than a nation, we have become a "collection of sociologies." "Me" (too), "Black" (lives), "White" (supremacy), "Color" (people), "Gender" (alphabet).

A true smorgasbord of *homo sapiens*, each obsessed with self.

Why Is There War?

January 13, 2020

This question addresses the most tragic and recurring human event throughout history and, to this day, defies an answer. At bottom, the recurrence of war is nearly an illogical and irrational behavior.

Consider a fictitious occasion where boys 16 and older are dressed in uniforms and sent to a neighboring village to kill other boys dressed in different colors. The immediate adult reaction would be outrage and an immediate stop. Yet, when the age limit is moved up to 18, the same phenomenon is accompanied with garlands of flowers, downtown parades, and cheering adults in full jubilation. "Home By Christmas," "V for Victory," "The War To End War."

Why is two years so critical?

Such, plus or minus the theatrics, has been occurring for the 6,000 years of recorded history, with no substantial pause. What is the classic "definition" of "insanity? If the word "war" was substituted with another acronym, we might just reconsider our acceptance. Something like "mass slaughter," "organized killing," "murder incorporated," etc.

There is no human comparison to war, not random violence, murder, betrayal, deceit, belligerence, rape, dishonesty, hate, fear, plus all other expressions known to the human condition. Not the Mafia, Hells Angels, MS-13, or a bar fight.

Animals kill, but all for the same reason. Each war throughout history has been announced by separate causes, yet there must be a repeating cause that produces the identical phenomenon, minus local and individual circumstance. The Confederacy bombed Fort Sumter in 1861, and Japan did the same thing at Pearl Harbor in 1941. Were these different events or the same?

To be sure, wars have been universally defined as "necessary," and, indeed, have shaped the maps of all civilizations. But is that a justification or an excuse? Nor does it even try to identify "why," thus producing a mass and subconscious acceptance. They can all be defended as coherent, but the net effect is somewhat irrelevant. As in childhood, "he started it." In the longer run, so what?

Throughout the same expanse of humanity, there have been multiple efforts to end the cycle or at least explain it rationally. There have been pacifists and protesters throughout. Willian Penn founded both the pacifist Quakers and an American state. Jeanette Rankin was the first woman in Congress (R-Montana) and voted against U.S. involvement in both world wars (the only dissent in 1941). Today, there is a statue of her in the Capitol Dome. Both were great individuals, but neither made a tiny dent in organized warfare.

After World War II, the greatest war in human history, the U.S. quickly allied with defeated Germany and Japan in the Cold War. We are still allied with both of them. In 1968, anti-Vietnam protesters closed over 250 universities (including my own) to stop the war. It ended in 1975, and, today, the U.S. has normal relations with Communist Vietnam.

The best book to find general causes of war is (in my view) *Man, the State, and War* (1959) by the late Kenneth Waltz. He identifies three broad categories ("images") to allocate lasting causation. First is human nature, mankind itself. This is undoubtedly true but also irrelevant. Human nature, like "air," can be responsible for everything, including life and death, peace and war. In explaining everything, we explain nothing.

Feminists sometimes narrow this search to only half of human nature, men. Since all (most) wars are started and waged by men, they must be removed and replaced by "nurturing" people, women. Since this remains an empty hypothesis, we must suspend judgment. But journalist Kathleen Parker was once adamant on this: "Because territoriality is primarily a male trait, it seems that war will always be with us. Or, as it seems just as obvious, women could rule the world" (*Washington Post*, January 8, 2020).

Interesting thesis but poor timing, about 6,000 years too late.

Golda Meir (Israel) and Margaret Thatcher (Britain) might have trouble explaining this point to the Arabs and Argentina. This is the same problem as above: since men invented automobiles, it is not helpful to blame them for all accidents.

Waltz's second category is the "state," i.e. the political system that declares war. Here is the "democratic" theory of war, that democracies are passive and have not waged war upon themselves. This is self-satisfying but denied in history.

Britain and America were the only true democracies in the world, both in 1776 and 1812. Nor was the Confederate political system radically less democratic than the Union's, given circumstances in 1860 or before (Jefferson Davis was President Franklin Pierce's Secretary of War). To put an end to this theory, one need only trace the actions of President James K. Polk prior to the invasion of Mexico (1847). Also consult the government of Colombia, when U.S. warships took the province of Panama away (1903). The list goes on.

Finally, Waltz identifies the political "anarchy" that defines the nature of world politics. True enough, there has never been a world government, but that fact has not prevented almost every sovereignty, including the USA, from waging official war upon one another. That does not explain war at all; it just separates "internal" from "external."

So, what are we left with? Medicine holds out a possible cure for cancer and the common cold. At least they are working on it. How is war doing? Take a look at tomorrow's newspaper or examine what five straight U.S. political administrations have done in several places overseas. Examine how a varied mix of countries, regimes, sects, movements, religions, tribes, races, ideological "isms," and political ambitions have created the divisions that dominated history and, now, the present.

Even today, twenty-one centuries after Christ, there is still a vast and widespread acceptance of war, violence, and terror as the first and only solution to humanity's burdens of living together.

There is a renewed need for "statecraft" at the highest levels. This requires an appreciation of the "otherness" of other cultures, the need for patience and creativity in diplomacy, a search for lasting solutions, and a balance between military and pacific solutions to differences.

This has been the mission of The Institute of World Politics for thirty years.

A journey of a thousand miles begins with one step.

Peace Needs Policies, Not Wishes

January 12, 2020

In my many terms as a member of the U.S. delegation at the 40¬ nation Conference on Disarmament (CD), held annually in Geneva, we grew accustomed to a favorite accusation on the failure to achieve a lasting peace. If a resolution failed to achieve a majority, the sponsors would invariably decry the incapacity of "some member-states" to acquire "the requisite political will." This slogan became so common among the membership that it grew into a symbolic reference to the very nature and essence of world politics. A lack of willpower is what interfered with the work of peace.

That interpretation, on its face, says little more than "we disagree," but it became so pervasive that it represented the heart of every issue that came before the Conference. Rather than address the causes of disagreement and come to a result, the membership of the CD, professional diplomats, simply dismissed each other as lacking in mental capacity.

The result, year after dreary year, was a set of resolutions so compromised that they meant practically nothing and had little relevance to world realities. The package was then sent to the United Nations for approval, after which the CD adjourned to prepare for its next annual session.

Today, years afterward, the CD has expanded to 65 countries who debate the same issues with, presumably, the same context and nature and the same effect on the world, i.e., "nothing."

Yet the CD continues and represents something that keeps it alive and, simultaneously, continues to reflect an emotion that has become commonplace throughout the "peace" community, namely that "peace" is a dividend that can arrive through wish, thought, and resolve. The fact that this notion contradicts all history and reality apparently does not offer resistance to fervent (and well-paid) professionals who have full-time employment in the "peace business."

But they should be understood (and forgiven), as they only represent the same emotional assertions of a humanity that, from the beginning, has used wish, music, and sentiment in the illusion that the result, sometime, somewhere, will be a "lasting peace on earth."

That goal is humanity's hope, and, thus far, little reality has blocked its appeal. The global expression "give peace a chance," like the above CD quotation, implies that the problem is a certain stubborn mental trait that, arbitrarily and deliberately, refuses obvious and universal desires.

The same set of illusions pervades both the intellectual and theatrical world. This mindset is invariably underpinned by a quasi-Marxist ideology that humanity is essentially equal ("one") and that "diversity" is an arbitrary condition to be adjusted by sentiment, legislation, and "political will" ("requisite"). If the Equal Rights Amendment cannot do it, then "#MeToo" will. Pass bills and protest (again and again).

Both the slogan "politically correct" and the musical expression "We Are The World" exemplify a similar worldview that has dominated the Conference on Disarmament for generations. This is also an "elitist" outpouring. Like the "Climate Change" delegates who travel to conventions on luxury liners and private jets, hypocrisy is a virtue when we work for humanity.

For the global convention that produced "We Are The World" in 1985, peace is defined as a theatrical production engineered by a talented and sentimental elite. The fact that they are tiny in numbers and wealthy only enhances the message. Like diplomats in the CD, global leadership goes to the gifted and needs no intrusions from the "common man" or historic reality.

The anthem itself, like others before and since, betrays this illusion. Its hopeless references to pious and cherished wishes at the same time tragically dismisses the realities that mankind has faced from time immemorial: "the world must come together as one," "love is all we need," "we are the ones who make a brighter day," "we're all God's great big family."

These are all equally believed and noble ... and equally irrelevant.

To understand anything, one must first study it. This is universally true and universally applicable. "Why is there war" is a question for the ages and remains unanswered. "Why is there peace" is somewhat easier. Study it.

For example: neighbors throughout history have invaded each other, but why has the American-Canadian border remained free and open from the beginning (minus a disaster led by Benedict Arnold)? Why hasn't Switzerland fought a war since the fourteenth century? Why hasn't England been invaded since 1066? Why have Germany and Japan been essentially pacifist after years of aggressive militarism? Why was Europe essentially peaceful throughout the nineteenth century (minus a few quick local wars) then exploded into horrible, globe-shattering wars in the twentieth? Why does Islam declare war on most everything while Quakers are pacifists?

This is not to answer these questions but to pose them. They, at least, are far more realistic and relevant than chanting a few lyrics and passing a few senseless and repetitive UN resolutions.

Peace is obtainable but, like most worthwhile endeavors, it takes study, attention, diligence, and, above all, realism.

Which begs the question, what is "reality"?

It might just be the study of warfare within a pattern of history, circumstance, geography, and culture. But at least one thing is certain: it is neither songs nor slogans.

One World

January 12, 2020

The election of Donald Trump in 2016 and the recent election of Boris Johnson as Prime Minister of Great Britain has emphasized a fact which many have thought was either outdated or irrelevant in an age of mass communication and "globalization."

The resurgence of nationalism that has been promoted by Trump's "MAGA" campaign and by Johnson's "Brexit" has lifted the thin veil off the unity movements that have dominated elite opinion since at least the Second World War.

The notion of global unification, however, is as old as mankind itself. All the great religions have advanced a form of unification under God that, in retrospect, was considered His intention in the first place.

The very word "Catholic" itself means "universal," "undivided," "unqualified," while the Islamic word "Caliphate" is translated as land ruled over by a Caliph, or Muslim territorial authority.

Today, the world is witnessing a global "jihad" between a resurgent Islam for an expanded Caliphate versus Judeo-Christianity within its political authority. In this manner, the globe is facing an ancient conflict between two definitions of "unity," each based upon its own definition of theology. In effect, the medieval "crusades" have been renewed.

"Conversion" is endemic to religion, meaning "transformation," or "change-over," which, in effect, defines the nature of politics since there were religions.

Nor should a clash between hostile "unities" be considered remote or unique. Distinctions between the religious and the secular are often very fragile. Protestantism is widely alleged to be the origin of Capitalism (Max Weber's famous thesis) by its emphasis upon self-initiative. The Cold War, which ended in 1991, was itself a conflict between two competing "worldviews," either the Marxism of a global "proletariat" or the American view ("Wilsonian") of a world made "safe for democracy."

Yet, despite six thousand years of conflict, war, religious, and national rivalry, there has never been anything even close to a true, authentic world government. Most of world history has been comprised of "empires" that stretched over regional land masses but were never very distant from their home origins.

The largest land empire was the Mongol regime begun by Genghis Kahn into the 13th and 14th centuries. At its height, the Mongols ruled from Mongolia to east-central Europe, to the Sea of Japan, Siberia, parts of India, Southeast Asia, and the Iranian Plateau. The largest maritime empire, the British, reached its extent in the late-nineteenth century when it governed about one-fifth of humanity.

Modern "nationalism" is, in reality, a latecomer to the world scene. The Peace of Westphalia (1648) is generally considered the beginning of the "nation-state," making this form of polity occupy approximately five percent of world history. This makes both The Donald and Boris "newcomers" to world politics. This means little, however, to the notion that man's ultimate fate still resides in some form of unification. The idea just will not go away and remains to this day the lasting symbol for the future of the political earth.

In our times, perhaps the notion was first revived after World War I when President Wilson stunned the other allies by introducing a "League of Nations," the first formal effort to enroll the entire globe to keep peace and order. Nationalism defeated the weakened League without much effort (minus the U.S.), but its replacement was revived by Wilson's successor, Franklin D. Roosevelt, at the end of the Second World War.

By comparison to the League, the United Nations is a huge success, having lasted nearly four times longer with a large bureaucracy and a string of social/economic accomplishments unprecedented in history. While membership is nearly universal, the UN has failed miserably to convert into a truly international body. It remains dominated by nationalism, with 193 member-states, each clinging to the twin pillars of statehood: territory and sovereignty.

At the same time, the political globe is beset with the same internal and international conflicts that have endured from the beginning of time. Only the circumstances and locales have changed. One wonders why we even occupy ourselves with the particulars, unique maybe for the first few times, but tiresome after the next hundred thousand.

Yet the mystique of unity still persists as ultimate salvation. Theater and sentiment keep demanding "one" world, with the anthem "We Are The World" still in vogue. Regional unities, especially the European Union, are said to be the future, while "globalization" remains the definition favored by academics and politicians.

But beneath the ideology, reality dominates. Donald and Boris are mere symbols, beneath which lie competing sovereignties, religions, ethnic and racial groupings, tribes, languages, cultures, and the stubborn nationalism of nearly 200 states.

In Great Britain itself, both Scotland and Northern Ireland threaten independence movements. In the U.S., the political system is so divided that red-blue colors describe the sectional landscape, while a set of ideological "isms" (race, gender, white nationalism) have been introduced for deeper schisms. The future is so precarious that some compare it to the Civil War era, when "blue-gray" were the colors.

During World War II, the 1940 Republican presidential candidate, Wendell Willkie, published his seminal book, One World, calling for "peace on a world basis ... quite literally that it must embrace the earth. Continents and oceans are plainly only parts of a whole." One World was described by one reviewer as "the greatest nonfiction bestseller to date in U.S. publishing history."

Willkie died in 1944, but One World remains a legacy that continues to govern the thinking of much of the political and intellectual globe, bedeviled almost daily by uncomfortable doses of reality.

To quote the folk-song, "When will they ever learn?"

Trump Needs a Doctrine

January 3, 2020

Few presidents, if any, have been so vilified in the mass media and by the political opposition as Donald Trump. To be sure, much of this is self-inflicted, what with his incessant "tweets," poor language, rude behavior, "business"-type personality and overall demeanor. While this may seem to some as superficial and personalist, to his opponents, it typifies the worst in character and behavior that makes the man himself "unfit" for the office.

Thus, the impeachment process, openly and without apology, actually began before he even took office. The result was a verdict based upon overall and generalist behavior, "abuse," and "contempt," minus the judicial criteria of a criminal case. The verdict also remains completely symbolic, as there is no possibility of Trump being removed and every indication that it may even help his re-election.

History is, again, instructive. Many presidents in history have behaved both in "contempt" and with "abuse" of Congress and the opposition in general. Lincoln suspended Habeas Corpus and arrested thousands without charge, Franklin Roosevelt blatantly tried to "pack" the Supreme Court, many (including W Bush) went to war without authorization, and many as well, especially Wilson and Obama, circumvented the Constitution on a regular basis.

Trump has also been called the "liar-in-chief," and "fact checkers" from the media have tabled over 10,000 lies from his lips. But whether it is one, ten, or 10,000, the history of politics is, in a way, a history of lies. It also depends upon the magnitude and extent of the lie. For *Obamacare*, the Administration promised that patients need not replace their physicians, an untruth that affected millions.

In World War I, the U.S. declared "neutrality," while, simultaneously, billions of dollars of aid and assistance went to the western allies and practically zero to Germany. This was one great lie and led to the U.S. declaration of war and subsequent American involvement in all facets of world politics.

The Washington Post, the chief accuser of Trump lies, has just released the *Afghanistan Papers*, showing a history of official falsehoods stretching back decades on the American war in that country. Earlier, *The New York Times*, a "lie co-conspirator," published the infamous Pentagon Papers (1971), that revealed the history of official distortions which enabled the Vietnam War and all the tragedies surrounding its millions of deaths.

But perspective cannot help the Trump presidency; it is almost unsalvageable. Nor do many care. Even if he wins in 2020, his personality and that of the "nevers" will stubbornly remain. His "unpopularity" will be a constant, but this, too, is not without precedent. Lincoln won in 1860 with 39% of the vote, while his name did not even appear on the ballots of 15 states. He was reconciled to defeat in 1864 until the "soldier vote" turned the tide.

What saved Lincoln was Grant and the Union cause, and what gave the Union a "cause" was the Emancipation Proclamation, a form of "doctrine" that gave Lincoln a moral, rather than a purely political cause.

Neither army in the Civil War fought for or against slavery. They fought for "country," as each defined it. What elevated the American cause was Lincoln's announcement of the end of slavery, the "proclamation."

What Trump needs is something equally dramatic and equally appealing: a cause that is both morally right and universal.

Presidents are remembered by what is called "legacy," a term that means "transmitted from the past." James Monroe has been memorialized by his "doctrine" of 1823, not "officially" terminated until 2013 by Secretary of State John Kerry. Nearly 200 years, that's quite a legacy for an otherwise obscure president.

Nor does "doctrine" need, necessarily, to be effective. Monroe warned Europe to stay away from the Western Hemisphere, a few years after the British

Army burned the Capitol City (1814). If we couldn't save Washington, how on earth could we save Rio? The Monroe Doctrine, furthermore, was both ignored in Europe and misused by subsequent presidents. James K. Polk used it as an excuse for the annexation of Mexican land, while Theodore Roosevelt used it to intervene throughout Latin America, especially in Panama. Woodrow Wilson did the same against Mexico, 1914, 1916.

Yet the "legacy" of an "American hemisphere" became a key factor in the U.S. worldview, even employed by Franklin Roosevelt throughout World War II and by John Kennedy in the Cuban missile crisis (1962).

Other doctrines have had their own legacies, effective or not. In 1899, the U.S. announced the "Open Door" doctrine ("notes") warning against further aggressions against China. Most of the world went into China anyway, especially Japan, but the American stand remained – right up to Pearl Harbor itself.

In 1947, President Harry Truman declared probably the greatest doctrine of all, his own "Truman Doctrine," that outlined an American role in the world that stands to this very day. And it is precisely this doctrine that Trump opponents have charged him with either endangering or ending.

Here is where the President must (should) make his peculiar contribution to history. Making America "Great Again" remains an open and empty proposition with neither direction nor purpose. Bumper Stickers and hats do not a doctrine make. There has to be substance to Trump's rhetoric, and it has already become *passé*.

Trump, and America, needs a doctrine, the time for political debates over personalities and the weather should come to an end.

The particulars of the occasion cannot engage us here, suffice that it should be sufficiently broad to satisfy those who think that the world is ending and that freedom is finished with those who think that the American Revolution is still vibrant.

That means that it must be American at its core. As with past doctrines, positive, enduring, and appealing.

What Trump needs is something equally dramatic and equally appealing: a cause that is both morally right and universal.

If nothing else, at least a legacy.

Can the U.S. Get Back a Foreign Policy?

THE CHILD WHO WANTED TO PLAY BY HIMSELF.

President Wilson. "NOW COME ALONG AND ENJOY YOURSELF WITH THE OTHER NICE CHILDREN. I PROMISED THAT YOU'D BE THE LIFE AND SOUL OF THE PARTY."

January 3, 2020

The first response will probably be "what do you mean, we already have one"? Fine, what is it? Name it.

In describing U.S. foreign policy, what verbal description would you use? Is it "aggressive"? Not really, Hitler showed how that works. Is it defensive? Against what/whom? Well, perhaps the tariff walls on China correspond, but is that the sum total? There are 192 more countries in the world, so tariff walls on one are not really appropriate for a "foreign policy."

First, we must explore what the expression actually means. Obviously, it is "external," for or against something outside the shoreline. Then, it is a "policy," which can be defined as "a high-level plan embracing the general goals and acceptable procedures..." (of the institution).

What, then is U.S. foreign policy under Donald Trump? Is "Make America Great Again" a "policy"? To be sure, it's a goal, but what are the "procedures"? Are they "acceptable"? To whom?

In December, President Trump was impeached by the House of Representatives, while immediately afterward the same House overwhelmingly endorsed his legislation on North American Trade. If the right hand does one thing and the left the other, what remains of "policy"?

Does that imply that democracies cannot have policies or anything coherent toward the rest of the world? Can the U.S. even have a "foreign policy"?

Once again, history is our guide.

One of the great legacies of the first president was his foreign policy, a legacy that lasted for exactly a century and a half. In his Farewell Address (1796), George Washington outlined why and how the U.S. needed to avoid "entangling alliances" (Jefferson's phrase) with the constantly-warring European countries. This advice became an American "gospel" until 1947, when President Harry Truman formally abandoned it with his call for a "Truman Doctrine" to help "free peoples everywhere." This led to the Marshall Plan, the Berlin Airlift, and NATO, indications of a "world order" still in effect today.

Washington's foreign policy subsequently led to what has been called "isolationism," while Truman's led to what we now call "interventionism." Thus, within 150 years, the U.S. went from a near-complete strategic abstention with the rest of the world to a near-total involvement that reversed the policy of the American people by 180 degrees.

Within these vast parameters, a set of subordinate policies came to reflect the condition and nature of U.S. foreign policy. They go by different names and circumstances but belong within the parameters.

For example, after World War II, the U.S. developed over 800 military "presences" (many were actually bases). Before the war, we had almost none! Before the war, we had no peacetime alliances. Afterward, we had over 40. Before the war, "America First" identified the isolationism of the public. After the war, the entire country and the Congress voted time and again for intervention, in Europe, Asia, Africa, the Middle East, and in the Hemisphere. Everywhere! Before the war, we had only draft calls during combat; afterward, we had a continuous peacetime draft.

Was the U.S. schizophrenic or just responding to human growth in history? How could the most powerful/prosperous nation in world history let the globe come apart at the seams?

From the beginning, the American Revolution was much more than a mere colonial revolt. Jefferson called for an "Empire of Liberty," while the Founding Fathers were united that the event meant a watershed in human history. At first, the country was content to set an example, as Pastor John Winthrop said, as a "city upon a hill" (1630). But when American power rose to world status, President Woodrow Wilson elevated the mission to "make the world safe for democracy" (1918).

The clash between goals and strategy was shown clearly after World War I, when the Senate refused the League of Nations and President Warren G. Harding led the country "back to normalcy" (1920). "Normalcy" meant isolation, a policy shattered by Pearl Harbor (1941) and the Cold War.

The Cold War was over by 1991, which allowed the U.S. to return to normalcy again. Since then, various administrations have tried (not so hard) to create a new post-Cold War set of foreign policies. They had imaginative names but were hard to explain, much less implement: "Assertive Multilateralism" (Clinton)," Nation-building" (W Bush) and "Leading From Behind" (Obama).

Today, we have "Make America Great Again" as a goal but a glaring lack of "procedures ("policies") to do it. The net result is an impeached President, a divided electorate, and a Democratic Party debating socialism and the weather.

Time Magazine's "Person of the Year," is a 16 year-old girl who did nothing for 2019 (perhaps for 2050). Even Joan of Arc led battles.

Movie producer Harvey Weinstein is far more notorious than China and Russia together. Russia is accused of "meddling" and "collusion," while the meaning of those terms is still unclear. The memory of Soviet missiles in Cuba (1962) might as well recall Genghis Kahn. During the months of primary debates, twenty Democrats showed more attention to Kamala Harris' schooldays than to the phrase "national security" itself.

The word "world" in "world politics" has been effectively eliminated for "as usual," and "drift" is a generous description of America in the world-place.

Will somebody, please, give a foreign policy speech. Anything will do!

Boris and Donald:

Blondes Have More Fun

December 18, 2019

The recent electoral victory of Boris Johnson in Britain ensures that, with some certainty, both countries will be led by men who share more in common than a similar and unique investment in political democracy ("never Trumpers" notwithstanding). Not only do they share some common personality traits, plus similar impulses toward nationalistic isolation but, more importantly, they look like twins.

While it's possible that George III and George Washington might be mistaken for Anglo-Saxon brothers, the common traits shared by The Donald and Boris goes beyond any similarity that eighteenth century wigs might reveal. While it is probable that a blonde man has never held the highest political office in either country, it remains near-certain that blondes have never shared the same office in either country at the same time.

Nor does it even seem possible that two blondes have ever been involved as close allies, served together through history, or even gone to war against each other. This is truly a unique moment, even if it all comes out of a bottle (in Donald's case for sure).

Nazis eat your hearts out. Even a slight glance at Hitler or his vanguard would reveal that not a single "blue-eyed-blonde," the Aryan symbol, could be found anywhere near the Fuhrer or within his bunker (except for Eva Braun, his wife of a few hours).

But does this mean anything? If thirty seconds of a phone conversation could lead to impeachment, then it is equally plausible that two blonde heads could have the gravest consequences given purpose and intent.

Statements attributed to both President Trump, his aides, and enemies have often been emphasized in the press as "bombshells" throughout the impeachment hearings. That's called a "metaphor," like "you're a peach," or "smooth as silk," but metaphors are critical in political reference. It doesn't have to be intelligent or even coherent, attributes that would probably detract from the intent in any case.

What's to prevent politicians from either side of the ocean to appraise any dealings from either men as another example of those blonde "bombshells" from "meddling" together.

"Meddle" is a verb with several meanings and used to identify Trump with Vladimir Putin. They were tied together, according to the press, because Trump "liked" dictators. "Bombshell" is a metaphor used often to describe the personalities of blonde people. In its "sexist" form it means only girls. It is supposed to represent a form of "explosive" quality, as if Trump would be more demonstrative than, say, Bernie Sanders or Johnson than Jeremy Corbyn. Like "mad dog," it is not meant as a compliment.

The phrase "heads of state" now has a definitive meaning, another historic first. This expression, too, is a metaphor but rarely meant figuratively. Margaret Thatcher and Ronald Reagan shared this metaphor, as did FDR and Churchill, but the new relationship of The Donald and Boris is literal.

To the extent that they share policies, this could be attributed to their hair. Get ready for the press and "hair- brained" foreign policies.

The two leaders, indeed, have more than hair between them. Their respective electoral victories were shocks to one-and-all. Trump was not taken seriously from the beginning, while Johnson's recent victory gave Labour its worst defeat since 1935. One district went Tory for the first time since 1885! As in Trump's triumph, historic British working districts voted Conservative for the first time in generations.

Despite being entrenched in power for the moment, the future for both could be very uncertain. Trump's issues need no introduction. His blonde ally, however, has troubles that most on this side of the ocean can appreciate.

Like Trump, Johnson must pursue a balancing act to survive. While most Tories, like Republicans, share Johnson's social conservatism, like Trump, his party has serious economic differences. The gap between more or less taxes and more or less government haunts the ruling parties in both countries.

While these differences may be traditional, Johnson faces problems not seen in the U.S. since the time of Abe Lincoln and the Civil War. Secession may "invade" the British Isles as separatist parties in both Scotland and Northern Ireland threaten referendums that could well mean independence for both and an end to the "UK." At the same time "remainers" in Britain will do their best to interfere in Johnson's path to departure with even closer trade deals with the EU.

But the trade issue may well save the day for both blondes. Impending for some years, a new U.S.-British Free Trade Treaty is scheduled for early next year and will be even more critical with the new Johnson government. President Trump has called the Treaty "a very, very big deal, a powerful deal great for both countries."

Should both parties sign this treaty, it will mean a significant boost for the longest and most important bilateral relationship in the history of the world. It will also mean a much greater international status for the leaders of both countries, a status each could sorely use.

Move over Marilyn and Jayne. Boris and The Donald can still prove that "blondes have more fun."

A Tale of Two Countries:

American History 101, 102

December 10, 2019

If one wonders why there is so much division today, one need look no further than the two most popular textbooks in American history to discover why. The first, Thomas A. Bailey's *The American Pageant*, 1956, interprets the country along traditional lines that emphasized a fairly benign approach to the "grand experiment." The second, Howard Zinn's *A People's History of the United States*, 1980, interprets the growth of the country along distinctly critical lines, offering the most negative explanation for practically the existence of the U.S. in the first place.

Together, they both represent the critical influence of education on public attitudes. The first book represents an older, "traditional" generation, the second that of the more recent "millennial," youth generation. Philosophically, they offer distinct divides as well, something similar to Jefferson versus Marx. In political terms, Bailey is "Republican," Zinn "Democrat," with the first representing Lincoln and Reagan, the second domestic socialists, protesters in general, and, more recently, Bernie Sanders, "AOC," and the "squad."

No single President has ever reflected Zinn, but the great popularity of his book is shaping the current and possibly future generations. Whether or not the country exists as it is and was or becomes a completely different entity may well turn on the sharply radical distinctions between Tom Bailey and Howard Zinn and how they viewed the American story.

Just a brief review of how each interpreted the same events will demonstrate how generations have come to judge the country in such extreme lights. It may show equally why/how the future will unfold.

First, the nature of the people themselves. As expected, Bailey is enthusiastic and positive. Admitting that from the beginning, "social inequalities existed in all the colonies," Bailey quickly noted how "democratic forces were working significant changes. The most remarkable feature of the social ladder was the rags-to-riches ease with which an ambitious person might rise from a lower rung to a higher one" (p. 68).

Exactly the opposite, Zinn begins his book by overtly drawing American history from the worst possible aspects of societal range, highlighting only the "bad" and "ugly" while deliberately ignoring any real or potential "good" within the entire enterprise: "I prefer to tell the story of the discovery of America from the viewpoint of the Arawaks, of the Constitution from the standpoint of the slaves, of Andrew Jackson as seen by the Cherokees, the Civil War as seen by the New York Irish..." (p. 10).

As might be expected, the two stories go downhill (or uphill) from there, "as the twig is bent, so goes the tree."

On the Founding Fathers, Bailey: "These were the dedicated souls who bore the burden of battle and the risks of defeat; these were the freedom-loving patriots who deserved the gratitude and approbation of generations yet unborn. Seldom have so few done so much for so many" (p. 103). Zinn: "They created the most effective system of national control devised in modern times, and showed future generations of leaders the advantages of combining paternalism with command" (p. 59).

On the Civil War, Bailey: "The Civil War was the supreme test of American democracy. ...The preservation of democratic ideals ... was subconsciously one of the major objectives of the North" (p. 457). Zinn: "The American government had set out to fight the slave states in 1861, not to end slavery, but retain the enormous national territory and market and resources" (p. 198).

On World War I, Bailey: "... the conflict, above all, was a vindication of American democracy. The German militarists had sneered at our ability to gird ourselves for battle while there was yet time. We astonished them – and to some extent ourselves – when we joined as one people in a mighty crusade for victory. Democracy, after all, did not seem so spineless" (p. 747). Zinn: "American capitalism needed international rivalry – and periodic war – to create an artificial community of interest between rich and poor, supplanting the genuine community of interest among the poor that showed itself in sporadic movements" (pp. 363-364).

On the Great Depression, Bailey: "Roosevelt, like Jefferson, provided reform without revolution. ...Choosing the middle road, he has been called the greatest American conservative since Hamilton. He demonstrated anew the value of powerful presidential leadership. ... He helped preserve democracy in America when democracies abroad were disappearing down the dictatorial drain" (p. 856). Zinn: "When the New Deal was over, capitalism remained intact. The rich still controlled the nation's wealth, as well as its laws, courts, police, newspapers, churches, colleges. ...the same system that had brought depression and crisis – the system of waste, of inequality, of concern for profit over human need – remained" (pp. 403-404).

It may be superfluous to note that the above symbolic examples serve to demonstrate the clash between the two major opposing images of human society that still define the continuing crisis of our times. Howard Zinn is obviously a Marxist and Thomas Bailey a Jeffersonian; one a revolutionist in a Leninist mold, the other a revolutionist in a mold stemming from British thinkers Thomas Paine and John Locke.

As we view the ongoing struggles within contemporary society, it might be well to reflect that the actual origins of what may appear as recent events and personalities are, in reality, only "breaking news" in a life-and-death struggle between two opposite visions of humanity.

Both have been here for centuries. Both stem from historic and intellectual definitions. And both also stem from revolution, one from America (1776), the other from Russia (1917).

And we thought the Cold War was over!

As a descendant of the "New York Irish" who rioted against the draft in 1863, I object to Howard Zinn's portrayal of the Irish as victims in the greater drama of the Civil War. Yes, they protested the draft, but most of the police and soldiers that ended those riots were Irish as well. So were the men that re-elected Lincoln the following year, thus guaranteeing that America would remain one people. We Irish did not escape one tyranny to enter into another. To us, America meant freedom, and still does.

Why Commemorate Pearl Harbor?

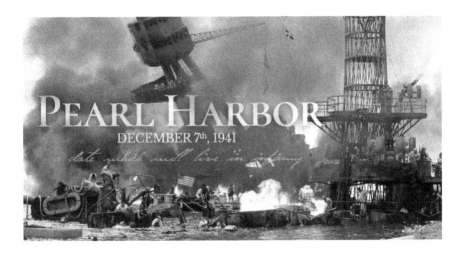

December 6, 2019

Nearly eighty years ago, the United States suffered one of the most disastrous moments in its history when Japan decimated the naval and air fleet sitting in Pearl Harbor, Hawaii. As President Roosevelt told it to Congress the next day, the attack by hundreds of carrier-based planes was "a day which will live in infamy" due to what he called "an unprovoked and dastardly" attack that took 2,400 American lives.

In addition to Pearl Harbor, Roosevelt also listed other targets that Japan had attacked on the same day: Malaya, Hong Kong, Guam, The Philippines, Wake, Midway. In declaring war, he noted that the U.S. was in "grave danger" but predicted eventual victory "so help us God."

So why do we still commemorate this occasion, December 7, 1941, as nearly sacred as Thanksgiving or July 4? What's so memorable about a disaster? What's so great about "infamy"?

The immediate answer is "unification." Despite the recent sociological emphasis on "diversity," there is little virtue in a quarreling and separated populace, tolerable in peace but suicidal in war.

America has been, from the beginning, a separated people united only by the constitutional bond of liberty. Fort Sumter produced Civil War. The immediate impact of Pearl Harbor was to unify the public as never before – a unification that carried through to victory in the war and eventual "superpower" status after a subsequent victory in the Cold War.

Today, all that is eroded, and not even the 9/11 attacks have been able to unify the country. Since then, an endemic war against terrorism, "red-blue" political divisions, impeachment, and a series of divisive "isms" have continued to unhinge the public consensus.

But unification was a temporary phenomenon, lasting only so long as there was danger. After the last summit between them (of five), Premier Gorbachev told President Reagan that one of the effects of the end of the Cold War was that you (the U.S.) "have been deprived of an enemy" (as attributed).

Even if this is apocryphal, the lasting truth of the observation is self-evident. Left to themselves, a population becomes very susceptible to isolation, political division, and social envy, as the current American spectacle has witnessed.

But the greatest and more lasting effect of Pearl Harbor has been the revelation of the deep and lasting qualities that unification brought forth, all qualities dormant both before and now: tenacity, patriotism, cohesion, engineering, entrepreneurship, diligence, dedication, courage, sacrifice, plus the three great virtues, faith (in victory), hope (in the future) and charity (toward enemies).

In his classic text *The American Pageant* (1956), Thomas A. Bailey summarized the importance of the event on the American *psyche*: "The Japanese fanatics forgot that when one stabs a king, one must stab to kill. A wounded but still potent American giant pulled himself out of the mud of Pearl Harbor, grimly determined to avenge the bloody treachery."

There are several metaphors in that summary which characterize Pearl Harbor as a lasting tribute: "stab," "wounded," "potent," "giant," "mud," "determined," "avenge." These express a sense of spirit, energy, and dedication, which, in retrospect, seemed to arrive overnight. Such qualities do not happen overnight, but were both latent and potent.

In the last analysis, that is the true meaning of Pearl Harbor: it brought to the surface lasting qualities that were either overlooked or not required. There may not be an event in all history that produced such an emergence of a people's true colors, virtues that seemingly appeared out-of-nowhere but were just below the surface all along.

But the question remains, where are those same virtues today? Have they disappeared or, as some profess, they were never there anyway?

The second answer can be thrown out: just ask Hitler, Tojo, or Gorbachev himself. Or read Tom Brokaw's best-seller, *The Greatest Generation* (1998).

As to the first answer, we should distinguish between "disappear," and "submerge." The first means "cease," or "dissolve," the second "suppress" or "obscure." There's a big difference; there is no hope in "disappear." Is today's America "hopeless"?

Can a nation's qualities be so tentative that they "disappear" forever, or can they "submerge" for the moment?

There is a big move on in the country to erase the past and replace it with symbolism more in accord with the current "culture." The destruction of statues and place-names is one example. A more prominent example is the effort by the *New York Times* and allied media to replace July 4 with August 20, 1619 as the nation's birthday (the date of the first slave ship). This move would make the spirit of Pearl Harbor actually "disappear."

We do not want another Pearl Harbor to save ourselves from ourselves. But what do we want?

After the end of the Constitutional Convention in 1787, Benjamin Franklin was asked what was made. "A Republic," he replied, "if you can keep it."

Over two centuries later, long after Pearl Harbor, the question remains.

History:

The "Dead" Science Comes Alive

November 19, 2019

Americans are supposed to be "ahistorical" by nature, meaning that the subject has not preoccupied them as opposed to the more dynamic topics that fit in better with the momentum and optimism of the so-called American "dream." Henry Ford, one of the architects of this dream, once called history "bunk," as it had little to do with his assembly line that produced the automobiles that helped make America an industrial and populist superpower.

One explanation of this country's distance from history may be its "exceptionalism," a phenomenon derived in part from the geopolitical isolation that developed over time. This was almost guaranteed by the thousands of miles of oceanic barriers that permitted America to prosper safely without major interference from powerful neighbors.

This was a luxury that few countries in the world would ever enjoy, a luxury that encouraged isolation and idealism. In this context, history can easily be distorted.

Ironically, the National Archives Building in Washington, D.C. has inscribed on its exterior Shakespeare's famous quote that "what is past is prologue," (*The Tempest*) meaning that history is responsible for what we are about to do.

Obviously, history is humanity's only "laboratory," without which we would have absolutely no criteria or reflection with which to judge the present. The great Spanish philosopher, Jorge Santayana, summarized this reality famously with his line that "those who do not remember the past are condemned to repeat it" (1931).

This leaves Americans in a "conundrum" regarding themselves, i.e. a riddle seemingly necessary but unsolvable (like applying for a job without experience). How can we reconcile our past with our present responsibilities and hopes? Or, to put it another way, how can there be a future without a history?

Thus far, this conundrum has been overcome by unchallenged acceptance. "Ahistorical" does not entirely eliminate the past but instead accepts it as given through generations. This "acceptance" does not involve facts alone, but interpretations of the same.

In historical reflection, there are five questions, all beginning with the letter "W." The first four – who, what, where, when – can be answered in a sentence. The last — why — may never be answered. That's because it requires interpretation, a word that means "subjective," involving thought, opinion, reflection, comparison, analysis, circumstance and other intangibles that go far beyond factual or "objective" conditions.

The Civil War began on April 12, 1861, when Southern batteries fired upon Ft. Sumter. Fact. Why? After more than a century and one-half, we can still say "that's a good question. I think..."

To challenge accepted versions, historians include "revisionists" that interpret the past differently than commonly understood. In a sense, revisionists are "rebels" who deliberately offer ideas that "debunk" orthodox (believed) interpretations. Like "party-crashers," they are usually not too welcomed.

But revisionists are necessary. Not only do they keep the subject alive and dynamic but they also just may — "may" — uncover some unknown truth thus far hidden from view.

That is a revisionist's merit, and a good merit it is. Yet it also contains a built-in danger: of exaggerating the discovery so as to dismiss central truths. In colloquial terms, this is known as "throwing the baby out with the bathwater."

A new interpretation or, even more telling, a new emphasis may well shift the importance of events and their significance into areas of thought and action that become truly "revolutionary." This has consequences that contain severe repercussions if accepted fully and used as agents of change. In America today, this is exactly what is happening to history.

It is here when "dead" history comes "alive" and when the subject truly takes on a "life of its own."

Consider: in 1919, the Western allies adopted Article 231 into the Versailles Treaty, labeling Germany as "solely responsible" for World War I. Most Germans reluctantly accepted this and soon joined the Allies in the League of Nations. Except for Adolph Hitler, who was a "revisionist."

Consider: Capitalism was universally accepted as the economic theory that allowed for progress... until 1858. Karl Marx had another interpretation.

Consider: By 1804, slavery had ended in the North but remained in the fifteen southern states. In 1833, William Lloyd Garrison began modern "abolitionism" with the Anti-Slavery Society, calling for an immediate end of slavery in the South. In 1852, Harriet Beecher Stowe published *Uncle Tom's Cabin*, an anti-slavery novel with great influence. Garrison and Stowe were revisionists. The Civil War began soon afterward, not by coincidence.

(After the war, former abolitionists, including Oliver Wendell Holmes and Henry James, formed "The Metaphysical Club" at Harvard in order to understand how they had unwittingly fostered one of history's worst calamities upon the country. Thus was born the idea of "pragmatism," America's only original contribution to philosophy.)

A related issue has returned to twenty-first century America, holding prospects of similar, but not identical, results. Under the ideological title "racism," American history is being re-written. The subject has enveloped influential portions of the media and political/theatrical elite and is challenging the interpretation of the country as a civilization.

As the most influential example, *The New York Times* has begun "Project 1619" to "reframe" slavery as the center of the American universe and the chief explanation of what the country stands for. As a beginning, the *Times* has proposed eliminating July 4, 1776 as the nation's birth and changing it to August 20, 1619, the date when the first slave ship landed (alleged).

Disney Studios is now considering revising its landmark films as outdated by current standards, showing animated crows in *Dumbo* (1941), for example, as "racist."

As so often in history, this attempt at historical revision contains profound consequences for society, and indeed the world. The great problem is that if a single item of the past is erased, then the entire subject, "history," needs to go as well. All or nothing. Consider the Crucifixion, for example, with Christ executed by lethal injection.

This is revisionism, with a vengeance, aimed at the very heart of rational or coherent thought: Simon Legree to replace George Washington as symbolic "father of the country." Snow White erased as "supremacist."

Cam these "Lemmings" be stopped before they reach the cliff?

How New Will the Better World Be?

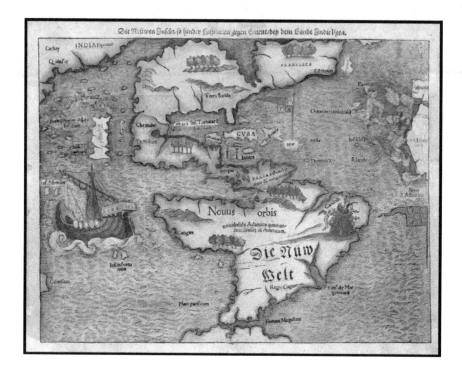

November 17, 2019

In 1943, historian Carl Becker ended his long and distinguished career at Cornell with a little book with this title. Becker's purpose was to dispel any postwar sentiment that the end of Hitler and Tojo would magically bring forth a new "world order" resplendent with peace, prosperity, and "justice for all."

The high hopes at the end of the last war in 1919 came to a sudden and depressing close with the Senate rejection of the League of Nations, President Wilson's monumental failure in Paris, isolationism, and Pearl Harbor. Becker hoped to avoid another repetition of history.

As a renowned historian, Becker understood how dashed hopes, particularly after a series of shocks and tragedies, could lead to even deeper feelings of despair and rejection. The First World War was often called Europe's "suicide," and Becker was making an effort to prevent another suicide, either of the West as a whole or of America itself.

Becker also wanted to inject a bit of "realism" into the American psyche.

Despite being conceived in revolution, the United States was born and raised on a steady diet of optimism and hope. Any "band of brothers" that could take on and defeat the world's ranking "superpower" and forge a "new beginning" based upon the twin pillars of liberty and equality had to have some hope in itself.

The circumstances of the late eighteenth century, while not exactly propitious for greatness, contained sufficient reason to keep it alive. Pinned against the Atlantic seaboard, surrounded by European colonial boundaries, and with a tiny population (about 3 million), the young America still felt no reason to fear either its circumstance or its potential.

From the beginning, George Washington offered a path to survival for the young Republic. In his Farewell Address (1796), Washington foresaw the time when the country would be able to stand alone against the ambitions of others: "the period is not far off, when we may defy material injury from external annoyance... when belligerent nations will not lightly hazard the giving us of provocation."

Typical of this "pioneer" spirit was the young Abraham Lincoln who reassured Americans of their invulnerability (1838):

"Shall we expect some transatlantic military giant to step the ocean and crush us at a blow? Never! All the armies of Europe, Asia and Africa combined, with all the treasure of the earth in their military chest, with a Bonaparte for a commander, could not by force take a drink from the Ohio or make a track on the Blue Ridge in a trial of a thousand years."

In his 1917 address declaring war on Germany, Woodrow Wilson gave this security a political and global purpose: "for democracy, for the right of those who submit to authority to have a voice in their own governments, for the rights and liberties of small nations ...and make the world itself at last free."

In 1961, John F. Kennedy reinforced this optimism within a Cold War struggle for the future of civilization:

"The energy, the faith, the devotion which we bring to this endeavor will light our country and all who serve it – and the glow from that fire can truly light the world. And so, my fellow Americans: ask not what your country can do for you, ask what you can do for your country."

In 1981, Ronald Reagan declared that it was "morning in America" and went on to dispose of the Communist Bloc, culminating with the stirring words in front of the Berlin Wall, "Mr. Gorbachev tear down this wall" (1987).

Today, Americans seem preoccupied with skepticism and despair of their own history and culture. With a singular and almost totally negative impression of the past and pessimistic on the present and future, the public and its attendant media "orchestra" focus on the "bad and the ugly" without reflection on what has been the "good."

Naysayers of our current generation will point to disparities and gaps in the full picture (slavery, partial suffrage, inequalities), but such drawbacks did not deter the momentum of American greatness. Nor were such critiques necessarily American, in either location or conception, but conditions of humanity since time began.

Our culture now seems to be torn by the twin vices of skepticism that sees only the dark combined with illusions that glorify the imagined.

When Carl Becker wrote in 1943, there was danger that the national mood could well turn ugly if the post-war settlement did not live up to pre-ordained expectations. The optimism that overcame the depression and Pearl Harbor hid the danger of reversing into contempt if it should turn out to be another 1919 all over again, *déjà vu*.

Becker tried to remind Americans that healthy cultural/political expectations have to be grounded in reality. Optimism is a virtue that should not be replaced, but it needs to be balanced by a healthy dose of historical perspective and political realism.

In his time, the enemy was nationalism, militarism, and imperialism, all exemplified by Nazi Germany and Imperial Japan. They are long-gone but have been replaced by ideological enemies that have simply picked up where they left off: racism, "white" nationalism, and sexism. Today's "war" is cultural rather than military but reflects the same vices and virtues that have occupied humanity from the beginning.

In recognizing these realities Becker observed that,

"Fortunately, there are at times a good number of people ... who are more or less actively, more or less passionately, concerned with the better world of tomorrow. ... That is their merit, and a great merit it is. Their chief weakness is that, living too much in the ideal world of tomorrow, they are prone to forget or ignore how inert and toughly resistant the world of today really is; so that as other men look back to a Golden Age that never existed, they too often look forward to a Golden Age that cannot in fact be created."

In the eulogy to his slain brother, Senator Edward Kennedy reminded us of Robert's private expression to these twin qualities inside human nature: "Some men see things as they are and say why; I dream of things that never were and say why not." (1968).

At War with the World

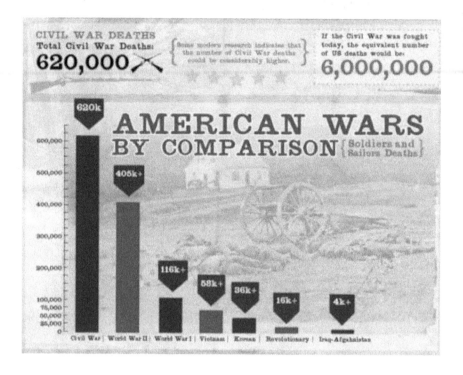

CIVIL WAR DEATHS
Total Civil War Deaths:
620,000

[Some modern research indicates that the number of Civil War deaths would be considerably higher.]

If the Civil War was fought today, the equivalent number of US deaths would be:
6,000,000

AMERICAN WARS BY COMPARISON [Soldiers and Sailors Deaths]

620k — Civil War
405k+ — World War II
116k+ — World War I
58k+ — Vietnam
36k+ — Korean
16k+ — Revolutionary
4k+ — Iraq-Afghanistan

October 29, 2019

The current crisis over Syria against Turkey on behalf of the Kurds may be a bit distant to most Americans. That, however, does not prevent many of them to view the situation with the utmost intensity and dire warnings, either opposed to the administration or in favor. But it really makes little difference.

How many of us retire at night or wake up wondering how U.S. foreign policies are keeping the country happy, free and safe? Just a guess, but probably very few. Often, parts of the country are unhappy, some lack freedom (or did), and safety from invasion is taken for granted. But such circumstances are rarely attributed to foreign policies, per se. They are, just "attributed," that's enough.

Currently, threats to the Republic seem entirely political and divorced from any strategic experience or geopolitical history. It's almost as though the entire polity has been gripped with emotion divorced from any aspect of reality. Some call it "hysteria," but it's quite understandable. Few people are historians or area specialists, and most "attribute" all issues to the politics that they see and hear every day.

Russia is now cited as a "threat," but not for what Russia has typically done, i.e. invade/conquer, but for what democracies typically do: interfere with the other party, "meddle." Would that big-city mayors be so devious as Vladimir Putin, 12,000 miles away in the Kremlin. Is Putin more of a threat in Kalamazoo than he is in Ukraine? Perhaps we should first read Ukrainian history or ask some of them.

Regarding Ukraine, the latest issue is whether either President Trump or former Vice President Biden used the Ukrainian president to influence American politics. While not exactly a Pearl Harbor nor a Cuban Missile Crisis, the issue has been used to determine the fitness of each to be president.

Indiscretions are universal and expected. There are few certainties in life, but one of them is that any alleged Ukrainian-Trump-Biden conspiracy will not topple the American democratic system. That does not deny the effort, just the significance.

By itself, Ukraine is one of 193 countries in the world but can be a very handy electoral "tool" if the situation warrants. Ukraine happens to be the focus because of the primacy of domestic politics and excessive personality behaviors. Who knows whatever "collusion" might we uncover with the remaining 192 countries, should the issue arise?

Which brings up the dichotomy between foreign/security policies and electoral politics. For most candidates and voters, foreign policy issues are important only insofar as they relate to home security and/or prosperity. Foreign affairs, by definition, are distant, remote, and indecipherable as either to causation or resolution. Threats are obscure and hidden, only to explode suddenly, such as Pearl Harbor or the World Trade Centers.

Thus, one's position on a foreign affairs issue nearly always coincides with the position of either the party or candidate one supports. Rare is the voter who breaks with party leaders on things such as Ukraine, the Kurds, Turkey, Syria, Korea, or some other distant trouble spot neither understood nor appreciated.

"Foreign" is always far away, "domestic" is always home. Foreign policy/national security is universal and timeless, but it has definite patterns. Circumstances, parties, personalities, weapons, locations, threats, alliances, etc. will differ time and again, but history "repeats." Never exactly, but always generally.

There was once a professor of World Politics who asked what one, single book would students take with them to an island. His answer was Thucydides, *The Peloponnesian War*, a war between two Greek city-states, Athens vs. Sparta, around 400 BC.

Why was such a far-off event relevant to modern times? The answer: because it was similar to the Cold War between the USA and USSR. Both wars were "bipolar" in character, total, used alliance systems, and were between insular and continental powers. Athens was the seapower and democratic, Sparta a military tribunal run by the army.

Thus began the theory of democracy as peaceful by definition, dictatorships as "warmongers." Does American history support the theory?

Today, in 2019, the U.S. is ending its second decade in its war against global terrorism. By comparison, the Civil War lasted four years, American combat in World War I about six months, and, in World War II, about three and one-half years. Yet the recent past, too, is quite characteristic, as any fast review of American wars will reveal.

For the U.S., these countries were once wartime enemies: Britain (twice), Germany (same), Russia/Soviet Union, Italy, Austria/Hungary, Spain, Turkey, Japan, China, Korea, The Philippines, Vietnam, Mexico (three times). These were the most well-known foreign wars, but the greatest war was between ourselves (called "civil"), plus four centuries of continuous conflict with native Indian tribes.

Throughout the nineteenth century, U.S. Marines and Navy forces intervened overseas on about one hundred occasions, at least one a year.

Beyond these, the U.S. fought original "terrorists" and Barbary pirates as early as 1783, contested both French and British seizure of shipping before the War of 1812, and intervened over twenty-five times in the Caribbean and Central America after the War with Spain (1898). We occupied Haiti for nineteen years, The Dominican Republic for eight, and Nicaragua twelve times since 1850. In 1929, one journalist noted that the U.S. governed Nicaragua "more completely than the American Federal Government rules any state in the Union."

The U.S. took or bought vast landscapes from Britain, France, Mexico, Spain, dozens of Indian tribes, invaded all over the world from Saipan to Normandy, took Panama from Columbia, occupied Greenland (a Danish colony), "meddled" in the internal governments of every country we recognized, and had 400 to 800 military bases around the world (depending on the definition of a "base").

Now we are in what has been called an "endless" war against what is actually a tactical employ: terrorism. The enemy is scattered, amorphous, domestic and foreign. There are no signs of closing. This week, on October 27th, the leader of ISIS was killed, and ISIS vowed vengeance. The war goes on ...and on.

Still, party passion dominates.

Advice and explanations of 2001 are repeated in 2019, *ad infinitum*. The Democratic Party is holding a series of debates, and national security is less significant than some Hollywood producer. At the same time, local headlines and reporters scream of words exchanged over a telephone call between Kiev and the White House. Biden's son has resigned from employment in both China and Ukraine.

All of this history took place before Donald Trump took the oath of office. So far, he hasn't entered a new war, but if he should, he will fit in quite well. If he should turn out to be a "dictator," which his critics foresee, he will be the first and only.

Can America survive its own success?

October 28, 2019

The possibility of being too "successful," or too "good," at what you do might just drive yourself out of the market. "Too much of a good thing" is an old phrase, but relevant when/if there comes a time when the enterprise simply goes overboard by its own ambitions.

If your team has won 52 consecutive games, why worry about # 53? See the movie, *Will Success Spoil Rock Hunter?* (1957).

"Downsize" is the business expression when a company is forced to reduce due to overproduction. Not only can the government stop monopolies, but overproduction can, and repeatedly has, led to unreliable products, cost-over-runs, and lay-offs. The history of American business is replete with stories of initial success turned to failure due to expansive and aggressive momentum. In the early Twentieth Century, there were over 300 automobile companies, eventually reduced to the so-called "Big Three" (Ford, GM, Chrysler).

The same applies to countries. There is not a single empire still around, from ancient Rome to the British. Where are the great imperial, militaristic conquerors of the last century? The Third Reich lasted twelve years, Mussolini was hung upside-down, Imperial Japan went down four years after Pearl Harbor, while the Soviet Union collapsed after seventy-five.

There is an old, apocryphal phrase, as to the "lasting" effect of the American Revolution: "it's too soon to tell." Can the experience begun in 1776 still expect to have an impact upon the world commissariat with its importance in the eighteenth century?

After the Constitution Convention of 1787, Benjamin Franklin addressed this point by stating that they had created a "Republic, if you can keep it." This question is still relevant, but a definitive answer remains as elusive as ever.

In 1940, the population of the United States was 120 million, it is now nearly three times that figure. Can unity continue without disruption, possibly fatal?

What is the prognosis today, having won both world wars, achieved historic prosperity, and ended the Communist threat?

Most experienced commentators will testify that never in their lives have they witnessed such vitriol, animosity, and political hatred as in recent America. It takes little more than a flick of the TV switch to appreciate this reality. With estimates of over 90% of the media intensively opposed to the Trump Administration, and the President daily attacking on twitter, the experience of a "red-blue" division has absorbed the culture for several years. This coincides with Trump, but he is symptomatic, not a causation.

How could the American people live through two British invasions, one civil war, millions of immigrants, a great depression, two world wars, and a cold war and still survive? The democratic system of the Founding Fathers has not missed a beat since day one: no canceled elections, no *coups*, no occupations (excuse Reconstruction), and no economic collapses. All this despite rumors and attempts from many quarters, imaginary scenarios (*Seven Days in May*, *The Manchurian Candidate*), failed excursions, and threats of "Armageddon" since Benedict Arnold tried to sell West Point.

To be sure, "vigilance is the price of liberty," which might explain *The Washington Post* repeating "democracy dies in darkness" every day for three years on page one. Within the above perspective, is this hyperbole, self-serving propaganda, or dire warning? Is the Post Paul Revere or Joe McCarthy?

At this stage of national life, is American democracy in danger? If so, what is the root cause: internal/external, a Chinese Army crossing the Rockies, Vladimir Putin disabling democracy from the Kremlin, President Trump, the media, the universities, immigration, liberal bias, conservative bias, all biases, racism, sexism, white nationalism, all nationalisms, all isms, China's economy, Islam, all terrorism, North Korea, Iran, Syria, Turkey, the Kurds, Iraq, Afghanistan, nuclear weapons, militarism, nineteen years occupying the same place, impeachment, Republicans, Democrats, millennials, climate change, "white privilege," apathy, hysteria?

This list, not exhaustive, could be shortened to just "people," doing the things they have been doing since the Garden of Eden.

The problem with this answer is that too much shows too little, everything means nothing. True, but what do we do? Eliminating the above list only will lead to substitutions. Back to Square One.

A tentative conclusion regarding "people": If any fault is ascribed to the "end" of anything, prosperity, democracy, survival, by definition, it cannot be individual. No single personality or movement is capable of erasing what so far has been history's most exemplary democratic experiment.

Trump is considered bad (we know), the media hates him (we know), the country had slavery (we know), women have been abused (we know), incomes vary (we know), etc., etc. When the perfect becomes the enemy of the good is when times *really* teeter on edge.

None of the above "faults" (plus dozens of others) are caused by single factors, all are collective and symptomatic of a larger whole. They are also reflective of general fields of human "anatomy": Trump-psychology, abuse-biology, inequality-sociology, war/slavery-history. Finding them unacceptable, we can simply erase them (We are trying, still another symptom).

Thus, when searching for causation, be aware of symptoms as causes. These reflect, as in lakes and mirrors, but cannot cause and cannot stand alone.

Demographics is people. As mentioned, the population of the country has tripled in seventy years. What if a family of four tripled to twelve over time? How would this affect its demeanor, its mode of existence; indeed, its very existence?

This scenario is strictly quantitative, not qualitative. We assume all are essentially the same. But what if they were different, in appearance, language, loyalty, religion, interests, dress, background, etc.?

What if the population continued with the same trend since 1940? How would the country function with 900 million, even if they all shared the same values?

How would democracy fare, having to accommodate nearly ten times the people of 1940? Imagine the "squad," four congresswomen contemptuous of American values. Double, quadruple them, factor in a sympathetic media. Illogical? Then dismiss it. Demographic math? Then pay attention.

Can one imagine a population disinterested or hostile to its own country, only to a utopia or to an imaginary place, a darkened history devoid of human component: a country with no virtue, where all should not just be equal but identical? A country where the architects of achievement came from "privilege," where invention and ambition came only at the expense of all others, and where the narrative was a myth created by national apologists?

Do you watch TV or read the papers?

Another symptom of our times is the existence of nearly eighty cities where illegal immigrants can find "sanction" from the law. If democracy is to survive, it needs a population, including politicians and voters alike, that will respect its institutions and culture. Amidst a ballooning population, such attributes are becoming less and less common.

Lacking that, as Franklin, again, said, "We must hang together or assuredly we will all hang separately."

The Most Important Battle in History

October 20, 2019

What is the most important battle in history?

Many claim that the answer is too complicated, as it "depends" on what one defines as "important" and as "history." Fair enough.

All this, however, only begs the question: what was the most important war in history? A significant battle in an obscure war has to be omitted. As does an obscure battle in a significant war. Thus, the first task is to identify the war and the battle will logically follow.

It is a consensus that World War I shaped modern history more than any other event. Not only did it cause its immediate successor, World War II, but it has directly or indirectly served as a background for practically everything that has occurred since: atomic/nuclear weapons, colonial wars (including Vietnam), the Cold War, the War on Terror and, for what's it's worth, all that can even be seen on the horizon.

The next question: why does the recent/present qualify as more "important" than previous wars? How about the Peloponnesian War (400 BC), the Battle of Hastings (1066), Spanish Armada (1588), Trafalgar (1805), Waterloo (1815), or even Gettysburg (1863)? They certainly influenced their own time periods, but we have no reason to insist that those times can be defined as more important than our times.

Here, we have to be somewhat "arbitrary," i.e. modern times, with seven billion people and with global issues, rather than local/regional, must take precedence.

Next question: what battle shaped that war more than any other? The one that started and defined it (Marne), the most horrific (Somme, Verdun tied), or the last (German Spring Offensive, 1918)?

Both the Somme and Verdun (1916) saw unprecedented casualties. On the first day of the Somme, July 1, the British Expeditionary Force, BEF, suffered 60,000 casualties, 20,000 dead. Until the battle's end, the BEF charged into German lines a total of 93 more times. The Battle of the Somme ended on November 18! Verdun began on February 21 and lasted nearly the entire year, December 18, with over 200,000 dead and about 800,000 total casualties, French and German.

Losses in each of these tragedies were unprecedented in all history, but neither stopped the war, which went on for two more years.

The German Spring Offensive was expected to end the war, despite the presence of millions of American soldiers. It was not to be. Beginning on March 21, 1918, the offensive effectively ended with an Allied counterattack on August 8, declared a "black day" in German military history.

The American presence, after four years, was certainly decisive but occurred only at the end, June to November. That ended the war, but the great tragedy of the event, and its ultimate importance, began in 1914, and it is to the beginning that we seek an answer to the question.

The Battle of the Marne, September 5 to September 13, 1914, is the most important battle in world history.

The selection of the first, rather than the last, battle of history's greatest war lies in the implications of the occasion. Neither the duration nor the casualties are historic by themselves.

To appreciate this, we must go back somewhat to 1870, the Franco-Prussian War. An upstart Prussia, led by Otto von Bismarck, maneuvered France, led by Napoleon's nephew Charles Louis Bonaparte, into a short but disastrous war that subsequently replaced France with Germany as Europe's foremost military power. This conflict was settled almost immediately when the Prussian Army routed the French at Sedan, September 2, 1870 and after a long siege of Paris the French surrendered and the modern German nation-state was formed.

In 1914, the two were again at war, with both prepared for another "Sedan" to decide the end. By early September, German Commander Helmut von Moltke had his armies poised to invade Paris again, but another counterattack, led by the Military Governor of Paris, General Joseph Gallieni, opened up a gap in the German line. French and BEF troops began entering that gap on September 6, creating a wide divide in the German lines, and thus ending any threat to the French Capitol. The possibility of another "Sedan" had disappeared.

As the Battle of the Marne (the 314-mile-long river east and southeast of Paris) progressed, German armies began a retreat west and northwest of Paris. With both French and British armies in pursuit, the Germans headed toward the North Sea, a retreat that saw them trying to affect an envelopment of the Allied armies toward a possible encirclement of Paris. Each effort was repulsed, a march that came known as "the race to the sea."

By the time both sides had reached the Sea, they had nowhere else to go and began replacing their rifles with shovels. As they dug deeper and longer, outlines of what soon would be called the "Western Front" began to emerge, a stretch of trench-lines that would eventually encompass the 500 miles between the North Sea and the Swiss border.

In his effort to strengthen his armies, General Gallieni initially "commandeered" the Paris taxi fleet, which he charged to transport the Paris Garrison to the front lines. With their meters still running, over 6,000 men were sent to the front, a fairly insignificant number, but a maneuver that became enshrined in French history as symbolic of national resolve (taxi companies were duly compensated for their service).

By September 13, General von Moltke (who suffered a breakdown and was relieved) is said to have told the Kaiser, "Your Majesty. We have lost the war."

But Moltke was only half-right. The Battle of the Marne guaranteed that neither army could either win or lose. "Home by Christmas" had now been replaced by a four-year-long strategic stalemate of defensive, barbwire and trench warfare, where millions of men would die in mud for a mile of territory. Where neither Paris nor Berlin would face occupation, but where a generation of Europe's elite young men would disappear for a contest without a clear winner, only to do it all over again, with a new generation and newer, even more terrible weapons.

The Twentieth Century is the significance of the Battle of the Marne.

Democracy Doesn't "Die" in Darkness:

By Then, It's Already Dead

October 16, 2019

For years, *The Washington Post* has printed the epitaph "Democracy Dies in Darkness" at the top of page one, every day, week, month, and year. We read the message, but what is the point?

All this has been done without official explanation or even suggestion; we are free to determine the intention. That makes the reader, more than democracy, in the "dark."

The timing provides one clue. The slogan began the day after President Donald Trump's inauguration, when he claimed to have the largest inaugural crowd in history and when his spokeswoman, Kellyanne Conway, suggested that "alternate facts" guide the administration.

Thus, clearly, the idea is meant to remind readers that the Trump presidency may often disregard the truth ("shock and scandal"). A related explanation, almost logically, is that the country needs free and independent sources of truth to keep the administration "honest." Those sources, also logical, come from journalists who, against the self-serving ambitions of politicians, can be relied upon to disregard falsehoods and present the electorate with the "truth" (apparently, journalists take an oath).

Enter the *Post*, only interested in "fair play" and integrity in shaping the future of society (alleged). Thus far, the slogan does little more than to remind Americans that "freedom of the press" is integral to a functioning democracy, going back to colonial times and John Peter Zender.

Zender, the original American free press advocate, was sued by the government for exposing hypocrisy and lies. In his famous response, printed in the *New York Weekly Journal* under "Cato," Zender reminded the young country that "...states have suffered or perished for not having or for neglecting the power to accuse great men who were criminals or thought to be so" (1721).

Under this grand tradition, the *Post* has *carte blanche* to define its purpose as conforming to that noble cause and to drum it in day-and-night for all to absorb.

And so it does. But there's a bit more. What is the relationship between "democracy" and "darkness"? Are they integral?

Journalism, by definition, needs a short perspective: "breaking news," "this just in, "stayed tuned," "don't go away." Otherwise, the attention- span of the reader is lost, almost immediately. Great issues, war/peace, crime/punishment, democracy/dictatorship, involve complexities and personalities that, also by definition, require deep and long attention spans and equally profound interpretations and investigations. Often, even these efforts are inadequate to resolve complications.

Who is to blame for the Civil War? Should all memories of the Confederacy be erased? Should there be reparations for slavery? These are just a few of the still unresolved issues of that time period. Here, slogans are worse than useless and can even lead to greater dissension.

Why is "darkness" necessary for an end to democracy? The scholastic method would be to compare and analyze how a set of democratic countries fell to tyranny and then to compare the results. Within that comparison, there would be room for the "darkness" theory and what role, if any, it played in the end.

Definitions would be needed. What is "political darkness"? When it comes, will we know it? Within this description, is there a "dusk" period, "moonlight," "twilight zone," "stormy weather"?

Perhaps the most famous expression of the phenomenon was Arthur Koestler's *Darkness at Noon* (1940), which showed how massive political "persuasion" can convert society into acceptance of realities previously unknown. "Every jump of technical progress," Koestler concluded, "leaves the relative intellectual development of the masses a step behind and thus causes a fall in the political-maturity thermometer." To recover from such shocks, he noted, would take "tens of years, sometimes generations" to overcome.

Koestler was referring to Josef Stalin and the infamous "purge" trials of the 1930s, and we can wonder if Russia has ever survived. Most analogies to political "darkness" refer to the totalitarian giants that stripped the Twentieth Century of its civility, taking the lives of hundreds of millions in the process. Given Koestler's projections and the state of American democracy, where in that perspective do we lie?

What is the "political-maturity thermometer" of today's American public?

How does *The Washington Post* describe the same in today's America? The answer is left to conjecture, but the newspaper has, for all to see, taken on leadership of the contest ("obsession" puts it mildly). For all practical purposes, the media has become an *agent provocateur* within the political process, precisely opposite of Zender's original vision.

American democracy has survived centuries against existential threats from both without and from within, including civil and world wars, economic depression, and vast social differences. Does it reflect faith in the durability of this civilization to defend it today, or do we need to adopt drastic methods against threats so severe that they cannot wait for another election?

The answer will lie in the result of the current impeachment process. *The Post*, *The New York Times*, and the Democratic Party target the Trump Administration as extinguishing the lights of democracy. The Administration and its supporters in Fox News and within the Republicans target the media and its national allies as the cause.

In another expression on the "darkness" analogy, British Foreign Secretary Edward Grey said on the eve of World War I that "The lamps are going out all over Europe, we shall not see them lit again in our lifetime."

Many consider Grey's reflection the most prophetic of modern times. It may equally apply to the current U.S. imbroglio. The several countries that were about to commit mass suicide on the European continent went to war eyes wide open and committed to the very end. When "darkness" came, it was way too late.

Europe didn't "die" because one side was wrong, the other right. Nor were they both enshrouded in "darkness." Europe died because neither side was able to adjust to the other, and both believed in the infallibility and the inevitably of their own cause. The summer of 1914 was very "bright," indeed.

The American democracy will probably not "die" tomorrow, the media notwithstanding. But if it does die, death will occur in the full and bright glare of its people and their instruments, guns or words. And not just one side will be the instrument of death, it takes two.

Finally, as Koester wrote, death will come not after nightfall, but at noon.

The Nonpolitical Country

October 15, 2019

It may be widely assumed that the millions of immigrants who have flocked to this country, legally or not, flee their own homes because of oppression there and freedom here. That's probably a safe assumption and certainly the one promoted now and throughout history. But everything is not politics, and there are many more advantages that others seek in leaving their places of origin.

Historically, and even now, they come in families, waves of related people who plan and devise their excursions together. Minus statistical analysis, it seems reasonable to assume that individuals rarely journey alone thousands of miles in squalid conditions to plant themselves, again alone, in some dark and damp tenement. The current tensions on the Mexican border invariably involve the treatment of families, children especially, and the fate of mothers and fathers as heads of large households.

Families invariably do things together, and politics is not exactly what keeps them growing and content in new environments. In this context, there are cultural and non-political explanations that not only inspire long and arduous journeys but also keep the new citizens satisfied in their new surroundings.

Is there anything attractive in America that might interest such large numbers of newcomers, who lack language, educational, vocational, and other skills that citizens take for granted?

Fortunately, the journal *National Review*, founded in 1955 by the late William F. Buckley Jr., has published a remarkable edition recently (September 9) that explores this important, but largely ignored, advantage of coming here. Entitled "What We Love About America," this edition contains 31 short essays by columnists of the journal on the varied nonpolitical, geographic, social, sports, and otherwise cultural components of the country that has the world's only subtitle "nation of immigrants."

One votes every few years, and most newcomers are not addicted to party politics. What do they do in their spare time? The answer: the same as you do, as I do, and as is available to every individual, whether their people came on the Mayflower or just arrived from Guatemala.

They have fun. So what's "so funny" about America. Answer: everything.

One of the delights of this issue allows the reader to judge his/her favorite pastimes against the ones chosen by the authors. The expanse is wide, which, incidentally, reveals the unique and unrivaled cultural attributes that give life, literally, to the expression, "from sea to shining sea."

If there is an emphasis, it is, as explained in the opening essay by Jonah Goldberg, in the geography, the "bigness" as he puts it. To be sure, there are countries that are bigger or equivalent, Canada, China, Russia, Brazil, India but, sorry about that, nobody wants to go there. While it is now fashionable to critique the past for its treatment of native Indians (and this can be justified), there is little doubt that the settlers who came west built a "colossus" that would have never happened if nomadic tribes remained in control. One of the greatest dates in American history is May 10, 1869 when the transcontinental railroad united with a golden spike at Promontory, Utah.

The expanse of America continues to attract followers by the millions. Having the freedom to go is essential, but once there can be unforgettable, from the towering Rockies, the national parks, sunny Florida, Hollywood,

New England autumns, rural Alabama, noisy Manhattan. This is also contagious, affecting the "American spirit" in the process. Goldberg puts it well, "America is also large of spirit. Foreigners know this and will often tell you this. ... What Texans and Californians are to other Americans, Americans are to much of the world."

The issue is littered with other essays on this theme: connecting highways (Wilhelm), parks and historic sites (DeSanctis), preserved homes (Magnet), the Capitol (Charen), Maine (Dougherty), New York (Lopez), Las Vegas (Williamson).

Music, entertainment, sports, and recreation occupy many of the others. One, in particular, caught my attention. Perhaps there is nothing more revealing about the country than its movies and the "stars" (think John Wayne, "The Duke"). Westerns were especially popular from the beginning, both in the theater and, later, on TV. Terry Teachout's piece on these, like the essay on geography, tells why western movies lifted an American "spirit" beyond myth and into accepted "reality," whether it was "real" or not. "But if it isn't all true," he notes, "neither is it all false, and there is something both beautiful and vitally important in the perfect simplicity of the story that these films collectively tell."

Sports is another connection between the land and the people. When I was a boy, the NBA (basketball) had six teams, all east of the Mississippi. One was my hometown, Syracuse, NY; another was our neighbor, Rochester. Now the NBA has 32 teams, from coast to coast. I saw the first black player ever to integrate the league, Earl Lloyd, a name unknown to almost everyone. Now the NBA has around 80% black players, most of whom make in the millions annually. Their games, including playoffs, are viewed nationally by millions as well.

There are several articles on sports in the issue. One, by Richard Lowry, also reminded me of my youth. Before televised games, baseball was broadcast everywhere by radio (Ronald Reagan began this way). I remember listening at night with my tiny radio in bed as Mel Allen did the Yankees play-by-play. Lowry did too: "Baseball on the radio remains an iconic American sound. One hopes that if ... archaeologists generations from now ever have to strain to recover what American civilization was like, they will stumble upon a recording of at least a couple of innings called by Mel Allen or Jon Miller."

Next time, you watch the news about how politicians always lie, turn it off and click on the radio. That's where the real country is.

Upside Down

Cornwallis' Surrender at Yorktown: "*The World Turned Upside Down*"

Painted by John Trumbull, 1797

October 10, 2019

After the British defeat at Yorktown (1781), their marching band played an old favorite, "The World Turned Upside Down," signifying the loss of the American colonies, a "first" in British history. There are signs in the modern American culture indicating that history has come "full circle," it's now our time.

Having studied and taught history for over fifty years, I remain astonished, bewildered, and confused ("abc") by the rush of events that have occurred over the past several years. President Trump has become the focus of this cultural clash, but no single man, even the President, can be fully responsible for the behavior of 330 million. Out front is seemingly the whole social "orchestra," the media outlets, politicians, entertainers, pundits, not to mention the multiplicity of races, nationalities, religions, and locales that comprise the whole?

America, the "melting pot," seems about to explode.

In 1858, Lincoln famously said that "a house divided against itself cannot stand," and many compare our current "red-blue" divide similar to civil war. But the comparison doesn't even matter. Any country totally preoccupied with intrinsic, self-identity issues, "me too," "black lives," "white supremacy," "people of color," racism, sexism, gender, diversity, inequality etc., etc. cannot possibly stay together long enough to even know what it is. When half the electorate is committed to removing the Chief Executive and the other half committed to keeping him, we can no longer even discuss the word "one." Our numbers won't even begin until at least we can overcome the first ten domestic divides.

As in the Civil War itself, the only existential threat to America's future is within itself. Any expressions of national unity will be decades gone before the first Chinese soldier crosses the Rockies. In the meantime, we fool ourselves that English will keep the pretense, as historic symbols, patriotic fashions, place-names and even the language itself, including pronouns and designations, are completely erased from the national memory.

Any society that does not like what it was cannot defend what it is.

Such an "Orwellian" culture (after George Orwell, British novelist), of course, has roots far deeper than "The Donald." The Trump "MAGA" movement has little in common with "Code Pink" or the "mainstream" media, any more than Thomas Jefferson has with Rachel Maddow.

Yet, the "movement" coincides with Donald Trump. Is this coincidental or deliberate? Searching for causations, one can reach as far back as Karl Marx himself, to "cultural Marxists" of the Frankfurt (Germany) school of "critical thought," to protests against the Vietnam War or to the socialist/progressive shift in American educational "institutions." It can also be identified with the "millennial" generation who has both time and ambition to reform humanity their way, no longer bothered with such incidentals as economic depression or war.

Should President Trump actually be removed, and can we expect a decline or increase in all this? An increase is more likely, particularly with the momentum that will undoubtedly fill the political vacuum. Any administration that advances the new agendas will, in effect, sanction them into law, as surely as Roosevelt's New Deal has been inherited from the Great Depression.

Against such a social "tsunami," one either rides the "wave" or resists. The phrase "resistance is futile" is often associated with the "Star Trek" series, but it has a long pedigree meaning that to combat is pointless, with the outcome irreversible. Ideologues, Nazis, and Communists, often applied the expression against any opposition to either the Gulag or the gas chamber.

Is America's "culture war" over, with the country transfixed to a "new beginning" based upon the new ideologies, in league against a series of "isms" that are identified with the "old order"? The past, progressives insist, has been based on such "deplorable" human cultures as "racism," "sexism," and "white nationalism" (adjective required). Some have referred to this as the "Cold Civil War," meaning that the stakes are no less existential, minus Grant and Lee (but especially Lincoln).

What is there left to hold onto against new and bold ideas that, seemingly, will lift humanity out of its centuries-old slumber? We have been down that road before.

"Workers of the world unite, you have nothing to lose but your chains" inspired world Communism, but nothing even remotely close has ever happened. There were many "Leninist" revolutions, not a single Marxist one.

"We hold these truths to be self-evident, that all men are created equal," "similarly," defined the Declaration of Independence, a proposition so idealistic in conception that it remains exactly opposite from "self-evident." (Jefferson was referring to under God and Law.)

Despite the metaphysical property of each slogan, together they have inspired more human beings to do more both for and against each other than any other expressions in the history of life. In short, they symbolize mankind's eternal quest for both equality and liberty, drives that have been at the core of human existence since time began.

In the Declaration of Independence, Jefferson's next sentence is the clincher. Expressing these ideas in logical order, he wrote that there are "certain unalienable rights, among them, life, liberty and the pursuit of happiness." Thus, for all mankind and for all time, the Declaration of Independence expresses life's priorities in perfect harmony and sequence. First, life itself, the creation. Second, liberty, the indispensable virtue. Third, a "pursuit," not a result. "Happiness" is undefined, appropriately, since accomplishment is individual and not determined.

The British band at Yorktown thought that the world went "upside down." Britain went on to cover the globe with history's greatest navy. They enlisted America in two world wars and won them both. At Gettysburg, 1863, the Confederates came within hours of going on to Washington and winning independence. The Great Depression eventually ended, and the U.S. had the greatest standard of living in history. After years of bitter war and protest, the U.S. evacuated South Vietnam to the Communists. A few years afterward, we formally recognized Vietnam and became the world's "sole remaining superpower."

During the German air "blitz," including 76 consecutive days of intense bombing, Churchill told the people to "keep calm and carry on."

Inspired by the wisdom of America's founding document and by Churchill's fortitude, Americans should know that things are never "upside down" forever. Sooner or later, we find this out.

The British marching band has since played to a "different tune."

"To Hell in a Handbasket":

The continual cycle of war in history

October 9, 2019

"Going to hell in a handbasket" is a phrase of frustration going back centuries to describe conditions so unsettling as to be irreversible. Today, it is commonly used as an everyday expression in situations that defy origin or cure, within which all must persevere.

The phrase is used universally from home to factory, nation to world, and current to past occasions to which there seemingly is no explanation. "Theirs not to reason why / theirs but to do and die," applies the same in "The Charge of the Light Brigade," Tennyson 1854.

From time immemorial, the same expression could justify the inherent condition of world politics, at any given time or circumstance. In her classic book, *Politics and Culture in International History* (1960, '94), Ada Bozeman chronicled the details of all the international political systems from the beginning of recorded history to the Napoleonic Wars (1815). In this massive chronology, she reconstructs the main currents of war, peace, diplomacy, and security from the earliest stirrings of Middle Eastern Empires, Chinese and

Indian political systems, Mongol invasions, Alexander the Great, Persian, Roman, Islamic and Turkish Empires, the Greek city-states, and the Westphalian nation-state (1648).

When reviewing this survey, I ask students to compare history with today, ignoring technology and location and strictly noting similarities between then and now. Differences are both easy and irrelevant, but comparisons expose patterns and, thus, have value.

The first and most striking comparison is the frequency and importance of war as the definitive method of settling differences. Diplomacy, to be sure, had importance but almost always was either a short-term solution or a process that led directly to war. Nor did it matter whether the system was "open" (democratic, libertarian) or "closed" (imperial, dictatorial), nor city-state or nation-state: the ultimate end was nearly always organized warfare.

In his equally classic study on the historic causes of war, *Man, the State and War* (1954), Kenneth Waltz has organized the three most common references to the causes of war in history: human nature, nature of the political system ("state"), and the nature of the international system ("anarchistic"). All three have been, off and on, attributed as the single causation, and there is sufficient evidence to "indict" all three.

But this leaves a remaining vacuum in any consensus on the subject. An honest answer to the question of war's single cause, like cancer, we still don't know, but we're working on it. This is not good news for either cancer patients or humanity.

A second and related reply to the question is the near-impossibility of fully appreciating the generic causes of human conflict and war and the parallel frustration in trying to understand these. There was a general confusion in even the attempt. Just as the far-off and lost historic names and places of forgotten wars are nearly impossible to comprehend, so, too, are the hurdles in even trying to appreciate the same in current wars of distant origin.

There is an expression that one should "understand the otherness of other cultures" before making rash judgments on their conduct and origins. This is nearly universal. After both world wars of the last century, Germany was considered inherently evil. The Allies made attempts to reduce Germany to a pastoral status, thus depriving them of any possible tools of war. The most (in)famous of these was the 1944 Morgenthau Plan developed by Secretary of the Treasury, Henry Morgenthau. These efforts failed, but Germany has on its own given up any military pretensions and has grown as a semi-pacifist economic powerhouse and ally for over half a century.

The same is true of Japan, once an implacable military monster turned into an economic and tranquil pillar of democracy.

Similarly, we are still trying to appreciate the cultural origins of terrorism. Is it religious, economic, psychological (envy, hate) or some combination? Most consider the roots as the religion, "Islamic," but President Obama refused to even invoke the word.

The list is endless. What motivates North Korea or Iran, why are these an "axis of evil" whose behavior threatens America's existence? If history is any guide, they will be reliable allies given time and patience.

A third observation on the impact of forgotten history is the failed efforts over time to replace world anarchy with a secure and reliable political system able to control violence and warfare. This list, as well, is nearly endless: empires all over the globe, world communism/ socialism, "world peace through world law," a "Thousand Year Reich," collective security, United Nations, "make the world safe for democracy."

President Woodrow Wilson viewed World War I as the "war to end war," not quite. but at least he was looking beyond tomorrow.

If we try to "connect the dots" between secure peace versus some relatively obscure incursion by some primitive oligarchy led by faceless and nameless creatures from a dark past, we will again be "spinning our wheels." Be aware that, unless we have answers to the key questions suggested by history, we will continue mankind's endless political "revolving door," circular, not linear, progression.

There is a theory of conflict entitled "crisis management" that posits some form of supervision that will turn hostilities or "crisis" situations into accommodation and stable peace. Maybe so, but the last six thousand years suggest that we somehow cannot stop our generic plunge toward "hell in a handbasket."

The ashes of one war contain the seeds of the next, eternally. Can anybody "break the chain"?

"Happy Days Are Here Again"

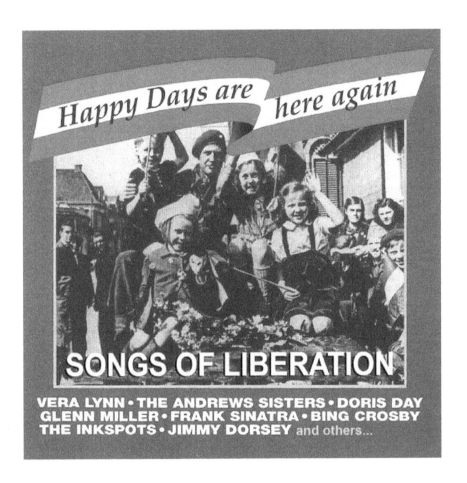

October 1, 2019

Certainly the greatest political campaign song ever, "Happy Days Are Here Again" was the theme of Franklin D. Roosevelt's 1932 victory, the first of four. The time was the Great Depression, and America was in the doldrums. Unemployment was everywhere, bread lines appeared in every city, banks closed, farms foreclosed, and there was no hope on the horizon. "Happy Days" provided just that, a hope that somehow, sometime, the good life would return. Written in 1929 by songwriters Milton Ager (music) and Jack Yellen (lyrics), "Happy Days" would be repeated in 76 future recorded albums and featured in 80 movies.

Waiting all day in line for a job opening, the words and melody of the song gave at least some inspiration to men who felt ignored and let down by the country itself:

Happy days are here again
The skies above are clear again
Let us sing a song of cheer again

Songs do not prosperity bring, but they do give hope that troubles are not permanent and that there will be a future. Today, 2019, the economy and lifestyles have never been better but, somehow, this matters little to the political class and our "public intellectuals." "Democracy dies in darkness" is the daily reminder, page one, day-after-day, in The *Washington Post*. For its part, *The New York Times* has begun "Project 1619" to "reframe" the birthday of the country to August 20 of that year, when the first slave ship landed. Thus, the current profile of America by these criteria is, 1) a political culture fast-disappearing into dictatorship (Hitler) and, 2) a civilization based upon slavery and inequality (Marx).

The political divisions of red-blue, the challenges to the integrity of elections, calls for "transformative" changes in all levels of society, accusations of ethnic ("white privilege"), racial ("black lives") divisions, and even hostility between the genders ("Me Too") has left the entire American civilization reeling into cultural depression.

Rather than a unified public, it is fast becoming a fragmented society driven by self-absorptions on a vast scale. Inside each layer there is "us-them."

The potential end of the democratic American "experiment" is normally blamed solely on President Trump, but often the full society is held accountable. In one single issue, on a single page of *The Washington Post*, there appeared two separate essays on this very theme. One, by Catherine Rampell, called "The death of democracy: a whodunit," begins with this cheery note: "R.I.P. American democracy. You still had so much left to give! Whom should we blame for your untimely demise?" She concludes Trump, of course. but, eventually, the whole country, the Democrats, media, and ultimately the public: "Yes, Trump has repeatedly, egregiously abused his power. He fired an arrow at the heart of our most cherished norms and institutions. But it took the rest of us to ensure that he hit his target."

Across the page is the same, by Michael Gerson, who blames Trump but also all other politicians who tolerate his regime: "Their tolerance for corruption seems limitless – and frightening. By what firm political principle would they condemn Trump if he closed down *The New York Times*... or arrested a few whistleblowers? None of this seems possible. But too many possibilities have recently become realities."

These are not out-of-character examples; they represent a widespread view of the current national political condition. If accurate, the United States is as Russia was in 1917, Italy in 1922, Germany in 1932, China in 1949, and Cuba in 1958. Again, if they are correct, we can expect the following to occur under Trump: elimination of the Democratic Party, purge of dissident Republicans, closing of all print, electronic and social media, concentration camps throughout the country, elimination of all dissident local and state legislators, creation of single political party, "MAGA," segregation of all stores, restaurants, and other facilities for MAGA party members, total ban on immigration, and withdrawal from the UN, NATO, and other globalist bodies.

While a partial list, the above is what we should mean when we say "death" of democracy. Whether or not today's "resist" members actually have such in mind is questionable, but that, historically, is the logic of their positions. But do they even know the basis of their opposition?

One point: the list above involved regimes that executed opponents at will, by the millions. President Trump is many things, but a mass murderer?

Still, in all, the society is on edge, and shows no signs of recovery. If it either transforms into something unrecognizable or holds fast to tradition, it will, in any case, be scarred permanently from the ordeal. But the country survived the Great Depression and put "Happy Days" to use during and even after the ordeal.

What do we have to laugh at today? The pending impeachment hearings, threatened since November 9, 2016, will not be funny.

There is no song today, no relief in sight. America's greatest comedian was Bob Hope, who entertained during the Great Depression and in five wars. Where is our "hope" today?

Gone With The Wind

Searching for America

September 27, 2019

Is anybody in America happy? The economy is doing just fine (so far), but it doesn't get much play. Doom and gloom dominates the public "discourse." There are two distinct entities, red and blue (as opposed to blue and gray), that are contesting for the soul and future of the country. One recognizes the past and political liberty; the other would discard the past, deny liberty, and start over. In between is the people and, like all wars, this one is also ugly.

Even football is angry, with the social agendas of players now prominent. Many kneel at the national anthem to attract attention and protest police "brutality." Definitely, police can be brutal, as are street criminals, Hells Angels, Bloods and Cripps, the Mafia, the Westies, terrorists, dictators, bosses (it's a human trait). Has anyone reminded these athletes that their profession just happens to be the most brutal pastime short of war on the planet? Thousands of ex-NFL players are suffering from concussions and are suing the league for redress. Since 80% of the players are black, the issue of slavery hovers over the sport. The men who pay the huge salaries, stadiums, uniforms, concessions, and all else important now have to rename themselves, from "owner" (as in "slaveowner") to something else. "Governor" is the favorite so far, as in Faubus, Wallace, Maddox and all other southern politicians who controlled slavery and segregation with a tight rein.

Perhaps the ex-owners should go un-named since there is no word in the language that fits.

The negative side of life inhabits nearly all else today. Most of it is derived from the new American ideologies, racism, sexism, and "white" nationalism. History, biology, and language are being transformed to accommodate the "cultural warriors." Pronouns, like "he" and "she," are suspect since to "misgender" another is insulting. Gender-free institutions, such as bathrooms, are now in vogue, while the campus culture is transforming from intellect to social adjustment. "Diversity" is adopted to accommodate "marginalized" personalities, people "of color," and disaffected youth seeking "safe" places to recover from something (yet to be clarified).

"White" people ("Caucasians") are accused, usually by themselves, of having "privilege" or of "supremacy." Thus, most Americans, including those who founded the country and discovered many of our conveniences, from pencils to airplanes, are now defensive, having to explain their existence or at least what it means to have "supremacy" or "privilege" (definitions of these expressions still being sorted out). One white presidential candidate explained that targeting white supremacy will "strengthen our communities."

American political culture has been called "deranged" or "hysterical." Wonder why?

Society is being transformed, promoted by political and media elites who maintain control by manipulation, invention, and exaggerated propaganda. Few speak against the wholesale dismissal of American history from a benign record derived from political virtues to a grotesque engine of oppression, imperialism, privilege, and hate. A brief "neo-Nazi" encounter in Charlottesville, Virginia in 2017 has been elevated to a symbolic reminder that Nazi-style hatred dominates society. Comparisons with the Third Reich and Adolph Hitler are supposed to represent the true nature of "white nationalism" in both Nazi Germany and today's America. The former Governor of Virginia, Terry McAuliffe, has a new book, *Beyond Charlottesville: Taking a Stand Against White Nationalism*.

Would this include George Washington, who looked white and was a nationalist, (at least the British thought so)?

Even a slight review of Adolph Hitler's twelve years in power would expose the gross and deliberate comparison of American society with the Third Reich: systematic attempt in genocide, especially the murder of six million Jews, total elimination of domestic protest, invasion of practically every surrounding country, occupation of them all plus Norway, forced labor throughout Europe, dozens of concentration camps, daily and nightly bombing of most European target cities, but especially Great Britain, including 76 consecutive days and nights over London. Not to mention history's greatest war and the deaths of an estimated 70 to 80 million individuals.

There are two types of Americans who would presume to make this comparison: those who believe it and those who think that's what they are. Swastikas and tattoos do not necessarily make Nazis.

But ignorance is a necessity to disparage what was once history's "last, best hope." Consider the effort, begun by the *New York Times*, to "reframe" the interpretation of American society from a "land of liberty" to a "land of oppression" requiring a total and definitive makeover. Focusing on slavery, the movement (which includes the *Washington Post* and certain presidential candidates) will revise July 4, 1776 as the national birthday to August 20, 1619, when the first slaves arrived (allegedly).

From that point on, it only gets worse. Like the Nazi symbol, the comparison can be sincere, but so was Hitler. The effect, tragically, will mislead millions, as did Hitler. On the surface, it can be argued, as can any case with an articulate prosecutor and a trusting jury. It is not difficult to emphasize faults, with both individuals and countries. But why does one choose the bad against the good? What is the ultimate purpose? In the final analysis, it is the tension between tradition and progressivism, i.e. to preserve what we have or to start over.

But are the two mutually exclusive? The past is not really "prologue," but is a guide, and the future is not completely unknown but can be designed. We can accommodate both Lincoln and Martin Luther King.

Reparations

September 22, 2019

America is the only country in the world that is exploring the idea of compensation to a portion of its people for behavior in history by another portion. The innocent people make up around twelve percent and are all African-American; the guilty percentage was minuscule at the time and has disappeared. These are called "reparations" and hold the potential to split an already-divided people to nearly the breaking point. Why does anybody want to do that?

The issue is always presented as slavery, but that is not real. The issue is culpability, and why should there be compensation for behavior already over? Slavery is but one of dozens (hundreds) that can be cited in the long tragic history of the human race. To put it personally: if my great uncle murdered his neighbor, why should I pay the neighbor's children?

The real issue is human responsibility or logic vs. emotion. The argument for reparations is almost always couched in emotional terms, and that is why it may win out.

A major item on the current agenda is reparations to African Americans for the centuries of slavery they endured in this country. It is a legitimate issue of interest but, to say the least, popular only in certain circles. The notion goes beyond race and, at bottom, defines the oft-neglected subject, history. The idea of reparations, unintentionally, brings history alive more than any classroom, TV show, textbook, seminar, or library section could possibly do.

In effect, reparations introduces history to modern society and includes all (repeat "all") as participants in its momentum by defining them as responsible for what occurred, without restrictions on time, place, or circumstance. This represents a revolution in the long odyssey of human conduct: people are held responsible for behavior that actually precedes their own birth, whether they are even aware of this behavior or not. Quite the opposite, their existence alone is sufficient for culpability, a definition of "group identity" in its vast extreme. If something bad happened in 1750 and you were born in 1950, any association automatically renders guilt. Pay up!

At first, this may seem to the unaware as both irrational and incoherent. Not only will it not "solve" ancient realities but it may just as well renew them. Nor is it even slightly reasonable to hold one responsible for conduct committed by someone else, especially those long-since deceased. Placed in an individual context, it seems ludicrous, absurd. My grandfather robbed a bank, should I go on trial?

On the surface, one wonders why the subject even exists. Is it only here or is it universal? Neither, it is rare indeed but not without precedent. Almost always in history, reparations followed war ("indemnities") but rarely settled anything. After World War I, reparations almost assured World War II.

In 1919, the allied victors of World War I included the "war guilt" clause in the Versailles Treaty, holding Germany as "solely responsible" for the origins of the war. It is fair to say that never before, or since, has a single sentence condemned so many to such a record of death and destruction as that single line. The line, Article 231, not only guaranteed the rise of Nazism, bitter revenge of an entire people, but the greatest scale of human destruction in the annals of history, an estimated 76 million dead twenty years later in the Second World War.

Not only were the reparations, as they came to be called, almost impossible to enforce, they condemned subsequent generations to the futility, year after year, of efforts to make them pay, regardless. The whole affair remains a living testimony to the folly of "human nature" in its self-contained craze to "draw blood from a stone."

The motivation was not financial (that was the "Roaring Twenties"), it was revenge, pure and simple! During the Great Depression of the 1930's, temporary moratoriums were announced. No matter, Adolph Hitler cancelled all German debts and tore the Versailles Treaty to pieces. German historian Bernadotte Schmitt wrote that reparations "poisoned the post war world for so many years," while British historian AJP Taylor wrote that "reparations ... kept the passions of war alive."

The U.S. itself, was instrumental. A delegate on the U.S. team, one John Foster Dulles, helped draft the treaty language. The U.S. also demanded the same from the allies. Both Britain and France had compiled huge "war debts" from American banks and industry, to the tune of $33 billion ($439 billion in today's currency). President Calvin Coolidge was as adamant that they pay as Hitler was that Germany would not. "They hired the money" he famously (or infamously) declared. During and after World War II, the U.S. came around to reality: both Lend Lease during the war and the Marshall Plan afterward were offered without debt obligations.

While reparations between countries are common, reparations within countries are rare. The current American debate on reparations for slavery represents a near-unique case when one generation of a people ask compensation for behavior done long ago by previous generations of the same people. This makes slavery reparations more symbolic and theatrical, divorced from any experience either suffered or initiated. Nor is it expected to improve current or future generations; there is no supervision on spending.

Some former colonies have recently brought up the reparations issue against "Mother" countries. As colonialism is a form of "political servitude," they would have a justification equal to historic American slavery. This would make the list of "slaveholders" practically the whole European continent: Britain, France, Germany, Russia, The Netherlands, Austria, Italy, Ottoman Turkey, Spain, Portugal. Then there is Belgium's King Leopold, who personally owned the Congo Free State in the nineteenth century and reportedly killed fifteen million natives while extracting diamonds.

In Asia, Japan once ruled almost the entire continent, from Vietnam, China to Korea. Just recently, South Korea demanded that Japan compensate for its long occupation, history of atrocities, and forced labor. Japan reacted indignantly, refused to either apologize or compensate and restricted exports to Korea. Now, relations are severely strained between these two U.S. allies.

In the American slavery case, the "plaintiff" is asking that 330 million citizens pay for the behavior of a small percentage of dead people in the old South. Relatively few southerners owned slaves. Accurate statistics are difficult, but "slaveholders" in the 1860 south numbered around 300,000, in a population of seven million. True, slavery was a shared institution, but it was on "death row" and could not possibly have lasted into the Twentieth Century.

A related question is the "selectivity" of proposed reparations. This presumes that the near obsession of the issue declares that slavery was the only institution on earth that can be targeted. Such an assumption is not only presumptuous but masks a deliberate and flagrant insult to the people, of all colors, religions, origins, and cultures who found life on American soil to be harsh, bitter and, with soldiers, deadly in the hundreds of thousands. The Civil War ended slavery and killed 720,000 white soldiers from both sides, nearly 3% of the population (three percent today is about nine million). What's the price tag for that reparation?

Is there compensation for child labor, twelve-hour work-days, slums, and tenements? Indeed, the nineteenth century was a hard one for most people. Who are the "deciders"?

A final question is the time period. Is there a cut-off, or is everything fair game? And if not, why not? If current Americans are to pay for slavery, why shouldn't they pay for the Indian Wars (four centuries), imported diseases, inequalities and atrocities of all kinds? Why shouldn't today's France pay for Napoleon, Italians for Mussolini, Germans for Hitler, Russians for Stalin, and Chinese for Mao? These regimes killed in the tens of millions and enslaved in the hundreds of millions. "... and Justice for all."

We might be living in a land of shared fantasies, but a tiny glance at the notion of reparations for old wrongs will show that reparations are not really history. *Au contraire*, they guarantee that history never ends.

The Age of Ideology

September 18, 2019
The Twentieth Century has been declared the "Age of Ideology," apparently to distinguish it from prior centuries, especially the nineteenth, when rationality, *raison d' etat*, balance of power, "white man's burden," geopolitics, evolution, industry, hierarchy, monarchy, stability, "cabinet diplomacy," "national interest," etc. were governing factors of common life. By contrast, the last century was governed by a set of "isms," Communism, Fascism, Liberalism, that held sway and dominated the evolution of mankind until now (maybe).

Yet, these concepts, "isms" all, contributed to what many consider the worst age in humanity: two world wars, a Cold War and a spiraling excess of violence, nationhood and deprivation that made earlier times seem tame and parochial. The Second World War alone, against Fascism and Militarism, took an estimated 75 million lives and ended abruptly with atomic blasts that murdered over a hundred thousand civilians in seconds. The Cold War, Communism versus Liberalism, saw tens of thousands of such bombs stockpiled within a global contest between "superpowers" for world supremacy.

In previous centuries, Europe controlled the world. Now there are almost 200 countries competing, most with their own version of some "ism," while global anarchy has replaced a rational "balance," and a semi-controlled "community" of interests has been replaced by endless chaos. The "War on Terror," begun in 2001, is now eighteen years old, a time that exceeds the total combat-years of the American military from the Revolution through the Korean War. In the Fourteenth and Fifteenth Centuries there was a "Hundred Years War" (actually 116) but it was both intermittent and between only England and France. Casualties, also, were limited and contained (arrows, not airplanes).

While the last century is history, the notion that ideology is over is, at best, suspect. Hitler, Stalin, Mao, and Castro are all gone, true, but "isms" still abound. An "ism," briefly, takes an innocent noun and turns it into a mass-movement, a comprehensive worldview that allows no interference, hesitation, qualification, or even explanation. As opposed to "intellectual," quiet, patient, tentative, inquiring, relatively non-judgmental, ideology is emotional, fiery, accusatory, judgmental, and often violent.

Sex, race, nation are, by themselves, benign and innocent, nouns that describe different kinds of people. In theology, God created them. In ideology, they becomes "isms," created by people themselves and applied against each other. "Nationalism" was the ideology of the "Westphalian" state system, "proletariat" was the ideology of Communism ("Marxism"), "Aryan" of Nazism and "democracy" of Liberalism. Their heyday was the Twentieth Century, but they have replacements in the new century.

Nationalism and Patriotism are in "holding patterns," at war with the influx of personalist ideologies based upon gender ("sexism") and ethnicity ("racism"). Both of these personify most of humanity, in any case, and they are posited as the "wave of the future" ("progressive") against "tradition." Thus, we have President Trump and MAGA in a cultural war against ideology, racism, and sexism. The global Cold War is now replaced by the new American "Civil Cold War," a war without the military, but a war nonetheless.

The stakes, as before, are defined in characteristic apocalyptical ways. Whole new meanings are being attributed to human conduct and outcome. History is being re-written or simply erased. Stalin did this in Russia by destroying old art, books, and memories of the Czarist past. Similarly, vestiges of the past are being torn down in the U.S., names are being changed to suit new ideologies, and definitions of any and all reminders of what was once part of a shared life is now defined as "institutional" vice. To remove the vice, re-move the institutions first.

Examples abound. *Washington and Lee High School* in Virginia is now Washington and Liberty; hundreds of street names and statues have been re-moved with new names and new definitions of civil acceptance. *The New York Times*, arguably our leading newspaper, has begun "Project 1619," to "reframe" America's birthdate to August 20, 1619, the date of the arrival of the first slave ship (alleged). That proposition was actually promoted in a recent Democratic primary debate, with that day to replace July 4, 1776. A prominent columnist in the *Washington Post* recently advised that we judge the Founding Fathers by their acceptance of slavery against any political or cultural virtues they may have brought forth. Thus, the country that brought liberty into the modern world will henceforth be defined by an institution that was both timeless and universal throughout history. Rather than being unique, America should now be regarded as both reprobate and "deplorable."

This is a tiny sample but, characteristically, is only the beginning. Ideo-logies are comprehensive and lack definition or conclusion. From an ideological perspective, the answer to the question "what is the lasting effect of the American Revolution?" is "it's too soon to tell." Race and gender are now ideologies, de-fined through slavery, "white privilege" and men as primal "predators."

The key dictionary definition of "ideology" is that it "may or not may" be factual and that it is not "epistemic." Thus, ideologues pose "analytical" or "historic" pretensions, but this masks deeper and hidden designs. Americans who challenge traditional values for alleged altruistic explorations are, realis-tically, "revolutionaries" themselves, seeking substantive transformation. When *The New York Times* claims that it seeks only the "unvarnished truth" about slavery and America, it actually behaves as an agent of societal change, history as enemy. Innocent inquiry hides aggressive and ambitious agendas.

But for most, it doesn't even matter. There was never a "proletariat" rev-olution in history, but millions of people and many countries still call them-selves "Marxist." Germany could never control the world, but Hitler took them to war under that pretension. Democracy will not fit everywhere, but that didn't stop Woodrow Wilson and "Wilsonians" since him, including "na-tion-building" nearly everywhere.

In 1951, the "longshoreman-philosopher" Eric Hoffer wrote *The True Believer, Thoughts on the Nature of Mass Movements*. His many conclusions are appropriate, for example: "A mass movement attracts and holds a following not because it can satisfy the desire for self-advancement, but because it can satisfy the passion for self-renunication."

Half-a-century later, we see that his message has still to reach the American people and the "elites" who continue to pledge the age-old ideological slogan, "we tear down to build up."

"Beware of Greeks bearing gifts."

Crossroads America

September 18, 2019

While there may be a number of metaphors to define our times in history, one certainly might be "an age of doubt." For even the casual observer of modern opinion, through the media, politics, entertainment, and even sport, the notion of doubt, uncertainty, and even refusal is both universal and comprehensive in the primary culture. Reasons are difficult to specify. There is the usual: Democrats blame Republicans, vice-versa, President Trump blames the "mainstream" (self-defined) media, "fake news," and many of his own staff ("ex" staff). But there are alleged deeper, more sinister, and foreign-born causes advanced. Russian "meddling," Marxist influence on campus, the "Frankfurt" (Germany) school of "critical theory," illegal immigrants, Hollywood, liberal "bias" everywhere.

Causes are, of course, important, but reality is more so, and pervasive. Historians still argue about the causes of war, but nothing brings back the millions who can't come back. The reality of today's America is a land of self-doubt, intense questioning, reflections on basic histories, virtues now turned into vices, and a complete reversal of many values that once were untouchable.

For better or worse, that's the reality, and it appears permanent, or at least enduring.

There is no need for examples; "pervasive" will suffice, and one would have to be blind and deaf to be unaware.

So what do we do about it? There are options. One is to accept, either "blindly" or willingly. Either way, a mass acceptance fixes the future. "Progressivism" defines the future, and history, to quote Henry Ford, is "bunk." All history is challenged, and the present will turn into a future nearly unrecognizable to the past. If, as many want, the country's birthday becomes the day of the first slave-ship (August 20, 1619), and Jefferson is defined by the slave Sally Hemmings, and "white privilege" erases Washington, Lincoln and Thomas Edison... then we have something brand new. So be it.

The second option offers a more "balanced" future. Accept critiques of history as "constructive" and work within them for a future combining both past and present. That takes prudence and restraint, rare commodities, both needed: "keep our eyes on the horizon, our feet on the ground." In his eulogy to his slain brother, Senator Edward Kennedy reminded us of the benefits of each approach from Robert, "there are those who saw things that were and asked why, my brother saw things that never were and asked why not" (1968).

That is one reason why America still survives today, the world's "sole surviving superpower." But not without fault. How have others dealt with our "faults"? Are they as horrible as slavery, "white privilege," or Harvey Weinstein?

In four years, 1861 to 1865, 720,000 white soldiers died in a population of 32 million. They (both sides) preserved the Union, and slavery was abolished. Not too bad (for "privileged" men), but at quite a cost. Could today's society go on after 2.5% of its people were killed in four years, say, 2015 to now? That would be around seven million! All male.

All that appears completely irrelevant to the enthusiasm that will erase any and all symbols of whatever happened before "modern times." But not to President Abraham Lincoln. A month before his murder, he told the country to build a future from our shared history. Many consider Lincoln's Second Inaugural to be the greatest speech in U.S. history (or the Gettysburg Address). "With malice toward none, with charity for all, ...let us strive on to finish the work we are in, to bind the nation's wounds."

Would "Honest Abe" turn over in his grave today? "Malice toward none" or "all"? "Charity for all" or "none"? "Bind the nation's wounds" or "open them up"? Today's cultural environment has to be the lowest in American history, and momentum is on the losing side.

If our definition of national life is slavery and privilege, I would advise moving (there has to be a place without either).

Fast forward to the Twentieth Century, the Great Depression of the 1930s. Franklin D. Roosevelt offered hope in a land where millions (mostly men) waited in lines for work, sold pencils and apples on street corners, or moved west in truck caravans. Farms and factories were closed, and it seemed that all hope was lost. FDR began with perhaps our second best Inaugural Address, proclaiming that "all we have to fear is fear itself." The New Deal put millions to work; Social Security and dozens of other programs continued to offer solace until the crisis ended.

History's greatest war established America the world over as the "land of the free," but 75 million died fighting it. That's about 35,000 each day for six years! But millions still flocked into this country (legally) to become a part. Billboards on roadsides proclaimed "world's highest standard of living," a "world order" of free peoples was created, enemies were helped, and fear was replaced with "faith, hope and charity."

Steinbeck's great novel, *The Grapes of Wrath*, became a historic movie, closing with Tom Joad (Henry Fonda) observing that "I left in love, laughter and in truth, and wherever truth, love and laughter abide, I am there in spirit" (1939).

Perhaps that's the issue: the spirit is broken. The "truth" is elusive; there is little love and absolutely no laughter. Comedy is serious, sport is politics, and, in today's "crossroads," you "can't tell the players without a scorecard."

The Eighteen-Year Wound

September 11, 2019

Today marks the eighteenth anniversary of the 9/11/01 attacks, probably the most significant event to "hit" this country in the new century. Most citizens old enough will compare it to Pearl Harbor, and those who don't, should. President Franklin D. Roosevelt called that day, December 7, 1941, as one that "will live in infamy," and indeed it has in the collective American memory. But what comparisons can we make to that historic event, which made the next day, December 8, certainly the most unified moment in U.S. history? Can anyone say that 9/11 has lived in "infamy"? Are we still unified as we were 78 years ago?

The answer to those questions is both obvious and easy. Yesterday, September 10, 2019, the *Washington Times* ran a headline that said, "Taliban militants fight way back to strength of 9/11." The story began by noting how the Afghan terrorists "are now stronger than at any other point in the post- 9/11 era, say military observers..." President Trump immediately canceled any future talks with the Taliban, declaring all communications "dead." Turn the page, and we get an essay by respected columnist Cal Thomas that begins by stating that "a premature pullout from Afghanistan will fulfill bin Laden's prophesy."

Premature?? Eighteen years later and ... "premature"?? Don't blame Thomas, as we all have been used to the ups and downs of a "war" that already is longer than any other single contest in American history. The Revolution took five years of combat, the War of 1812 two, the Civil War four, the Spanish War a few months, World War I a half-year (May to November 1918), World War II four, Korea three, and Vietnam, that we once thought much too long, thirteen (1959 to 1972).

Just imagine: post-Pearl Harbor, 1960, a headline screams "Japanese continue to bomb the Philippines." FDR would have died fifteen years ago and the American people go on as usual? Don't think so!

Fiction may be stranger than truth, but comparisons can be relevant. What else can we do? Apparently, the enemy terrorists are not bothered by long wars. A Taliban spokesman is quoted as saying, "We will fight. We have fought for 18 years and we will fight for a hundred years. We will continue our jihad."

In 2002, Derek Leebaert published his seminal book, *The Fifty-Year Wound*, an account of how the United States waged and won the near-half century Cold War and how that experience changed the composition of the culture and worldview of the country, its leadership, and people. Leebaert was not sparring in his use of the word "wound," noting how the U.S. went, nearly overnight, from a tranquil and isolated nation of the Western Hemisphere to a global "superpower," with about 800 military facilities overseas (many of them "bases") and a domestic society dependent upon what President Eisenhower termed the "military-industrial complex."

But we prevailed, and then 9/11 happened. What has been the experience since? Is that date one that has lived "in infamy"?

One measure of its impact can be attributed to one of the most bizarre statements ever attributed to a Member of Congress. In March of this year, Representative Ilhan Omar (D-MN) gave a speech to a Muslim group (Center for Arab Islamic Relations, CAIR) referring to 9/11 as "some people did something." Of course, she was roundly condemned for one of the most flippant statements imaginable for the deaths of nearly 3,000 innocents. But the sheer audacity of the statement, and coming from an elected official, is testimony to the long-term aftermath of this century's most flagrant violation of American life. Could one ever imagine a similar comment on Pearl Harbor? Would any American make the same reference to any tragedy, anywhere, against anyone? Would any sane person call John Kennedy's assassination "someone did something"? This comment is representative of the distance this country has gone from the 9/11 attacks.

Viewing the recent Democratic primary debates, one is immediately struck by the near-total lack of interest in any national security issues. The composition of the issues brought up are almost completely personalities, age, or whether the economy should remain capitalist or become socialist. One searches in vain for any comment at all on the legacy of 9/11, terrorism in general, or any issues relating to America's position in the world order. Indeed, the last statement on "world order" came with H. W. Bush in 1990, but seems to have been (characteristically) forgotten the next day.

It's been downhill since, with or without 9/11. Compare this to the apparent resolve of the global "Jihadists."

It's painful to write this, but the outlook for America in the world is not positive. We need a Churchill or a Roosevelt (either Roosevelt will do). The "tunnel" is long and dark and the glimmer of light is indeed faint.

But I would love to be proven wrong.

The American Campus:

Thought Police

September 9, 2019

In 1949, the British novelist George Orwell wrote *1984*, a mythical vision of totalitarianism based upon the Soviet Union and employing the continuous use of "thought police." It has turned into reality.

The recent American college campus has been overcome by a sociological "attack" that threatens to reverse the traditional character of a "school," from an "academy" of learning and scholarship to an "institution" of cultural rules and regulations. This has been a recent, completely unprecedented, phenomenon that attempts to remake in its entirety the American social character in revolutionary and transformative ways. Indeed, the movement has taken on the aspects of a cultural civil war that may well remake the very core and political/social fabric of what the term "American" has come to mean. In its fullest extent, the objective of the "revolutionaries" would, at the least, transform the word itself from an admirable and uplifting iconic noun to a damaging and regretful adjective symbolic of "institutional" vice, oppression, and degradation.

"Attack" is an appropriate term, meaning "to begin hostilities against; start an offensive against." It can have both a military and a social context; either will do, as the aim is to overwhelm or defeat. In this case, the concept is fully sociological but can overwhelm just as surely as a battle defeat or a military occupation. "Occupation" is also appropriate, since the objective is both comprehensive and final: no retreat, "total" war.

Leaders of this "attack" are few and generally "far between," but enforcing a revolution in behavior makes them, in effect, the "thought police" of the system. Nor does it take mobs to start revolutions. In 1765, only a handful of Americans wanted separation from England. In 1903, Lenin and his Bolsheviks could fit within a Swiss hotel room. In World War I, Corporal Adolf Hitler was a messenger boy in the Kaiser's army. When he came to power, there were 800 other Nazis in his regime, in a population of 80 million!

Examples of this brand-new transformation abound, both within the American scholastic system and "allies" throughout the culture, especially the media, political class, and "public intellectuals." The movement began primarily in the "academy" and is, thus, "academic" to the larger population, which seems blissfully ignorant. But, as in education generally, elites eventually define the manner in which generations view their own cultural past, present, and future. Indeed, the "attack" is fast-determining all three dimensions of public life.

In history, the American past is being "reframed" against the collective wisdom. Statues, relics, place-names, paintings, etc. are torn down according to current ideologies. The *New York Times* (allied by the *Washington Post*) has declared "Project 1619" to highlight slavery (the year of the first slave ship) as the "definitive" definition of America, against 1776 (do not be shocked if the Statue of Liberty undergoes a name-change). "Identity" politics target favored and "repressed" populations. People "of color" are declared "marginalized" and are provided "safe" havens on campus. White "supremacy" and "privilege" are defined as "oppressors," and campus administrators have declared "zero tolerance" against any vestiges of European ancestry in the Halls of Academe.

The rush to meet the new "standards" has poured millions of dollars and thousands of administrators to the nation's schools, from the Ivy League to the California system. To cite only a few examples of the nationwide shift in campus priorities: UCLA's Vice Chancellor for Equity, Diversity and Inclusion has a staff of over one hundred and a salary of $400,000. A similar position at UCal Berkeley has a staff of 150. Yale has spent $50 million, Brown $100 million for new faculty and diversity departments, while Princeton has pledged 20 new faculty for the same reason. Rather than a "trend," the race toward identity culture has become an "epidemic." Core curricula now emphasize the same: racial theories, gender and women's studies, LGBTQ. History, Biology, Philosophy, and other scholastic majors have given way to the new sociology. Dormitories have been segregated by race, as have graduation exercises.

Two metaphors, one a book title, express what has been occurring in the American academy. Daniel Patrick Moynihan, Senator, Professor, Diplomat has called it "the leakage of reality from American life," while Alan Bloom, Professor, entitled his seminal book *The Closing of the American Mind* (1987). "Transgressions" on campus are closely guarded, with the result that "micro-aggressions" are punishable as are "misgender" ID's and any and all speech idioms that can be labeled "racist." "Safe" havens are deliberately sought out by "victims" of any "politically incorrect" behavior.

Heather Mac Donald of the Manhattan Institute has noted that, in the California system, tenured professors had grown 25% in ten years, while diversity administrators had grown 125% in the same time frame. Her book, *The Diversity Delusion* (2018) notes that typical examples of "insensitive" speech on campus would be, "I believe that the most qualified person should get the job," and "Everyone can succeed in this society if they work hard enough."

She also describes the new administrators who supervise this revolution in thought and manner as "determined to preserve in many of their students the thin skin and solipsism of adolescence."

Tom Brokaw's book, *The Greatest Generation* (1998) chronicled Americans who survived the Great Depression and history's greatest world war. Then, the unemployment line or years in a Nazi POW camp might be an "unsafe" environment. Now, "unsafe" would be the campus green at Yale.

The origins of this movement would take several essays, but, briefly, it is both deep and long. The divisions during the Vietnam War and the civil rights "revolution" are often cited, but Marxist ideologies, especially "cultural" Marxism have come to dominate campus curriculums. Popular but critical texts on American history, such as Howard Zinn's *A People's History of the United States* (1980) have also served to influence opinion.

Orwell's novel, *1984*, remains a classic. He was prophetic, but his timing was a bit off.

REPUBLICAN PRINCIPLES.

SPEECH OF HON. ABRAHAM LINCOLN,

OF ILLINOIS,

At the Republican State Convention, June 16, 1858.

If we could first know *where* we are, and *whither* we are tending, we could then better judge *what* to do, and *how* to do it.

We are now far into the *fifth* year, since a policy was initiated, with the *avowed* object and *confident* promise of putting an end to Slavery agitation.

Under the operation of that policy, that agitation has not only *not ceased*, but has *constantly augmented*.

In *my* opinion, it *will* not cease, until a *crisis* shall have been reached, and passed. "A house divided against itself cannot stand." I believe this Government cannot endure permanently half *slave* and half *free*. I do not expect the Union to be *dissolved*—I don't expect the house to *fall*—but *I do* expect it will cease to be divivided. It will become *all* one thing, or *all* the other. Either the *opponents* of Slavery will arrest the further spread of it, and place it where the public mind shall rest in the belief that it is in course of ultimate extinction; or its *advocates* will push it forward till it shall become alike lawful in *all* the States, *old* as well as *new—North* as well as *South*. Have we no *tendency* to the latter condition?

Let any one who doubts, carefully contemplate that now almost complete legal combination—piece of *machinery* so to speak—compounded of the Nebraska doctrine, and the Dred Scott decision. Let him consider not only *what work* the machinery is adopted to do, and *how well adapted*; but also, let him study

In 1858, Abraham Lincoln declared for posterity that "a house divided against itself cannot stand." This reflection, now iconic, is actually both innocent and wrong. Innocent since anything truly divided will collapse, be it a "house" or a nation. Wrong since the American "house" had slavery from the beginning, while slavery was nearly a universal reality for thousands of years. All (or most) had ended the practice peacefully or legally, and that is exactly what would have occurred here had Lincoln not been elected president.

Slavery, the institution, cannot "cause" war; events that occurred in 1860-61 caused both secession and Civil War (there is no recorded war to free someone else's slaves, including the American Civil War). The abolitionist movement, which immediately preceded the war, "lit" the spark that turned 1861 into an inferno. The analogy is a "cut" on your arm: treated well, it will disappear; scratched repeatedly, it will cause infection. If, say, Stephen Douglas had been elected in 1860, there would have been no war and, eventually, as in all other societies, no slavery.

Lincoln's follow-up expression in the same speech was much more important. Here he made a prediction that the United States could not "remain half-slave and half-free": the U.S. would either adopt slavery without condition or it would abandon it altogether. In effect, Lincoln threw down the "gauntlet," certainly as the South saw it. The prediction was partly accurate: slavery could not possibly endure forever. But the U.S. was not "half-slave," as the white confederacy occupied only about one-fifth of the total white population (5.5 million out of 28 million). But the remark was interpreted as a dire warning, that one or the other side would prevail, and sooner rather than later. Subsequently, Lincoln's election to the presidency (with 39%) meant civil war, as the southern slave states seceded and fired the first shot.

But the Civil War was both the most avoidable and most tragic event in American history, by far. Lincoln was not an abolitionist, and secession was unnecessary. Afterward, abolitionist veterans, such as Oliver Wendell Holmes, William James, and Charles Peirce, formed "The Metaphysical Club" at Harvard. Horrified by the human and material destruction that they had helped bring about, they founded "Pragmatism," an effort to avoid fanaticism and dogmatism and use measured reason, legislation, patience, and restraint in solving problems. Pragmatism became America's single contribution to philosophy and served to promote the emphasis of ideas upon experience, which fostered "progressivism," public administration, and empiricism into American culture (Louis Menand, *The Metaphysical Club*, 2002).

But war takes two sides: neither Lincoln nor South Carolina (the first to secede) can singularly be blamed. The firing on Fort Sumter was the opening, but it didn't come from the blue. Such is the universal case, as the victors in World War I discovered when they blamed Germany alone. Likewise, Pearl Harbor is best remembered as naked aggression. True, but what preceded it: decades of tension, mistakes on both sides, and opportunities lost.

There is an analogy to today's America in the "House Divided" metaphor. The political/cultural divisions that have dominated recent society remind many of the period right before 1861. Fanaticism and "identity" politics have infected the polity. Divisions of states into "red, blue," seemingly "hysterical" reactions from both the President and the "nevers," existence of a "derangement syndrome," accusations from both of "existential" issues, the notion of a "cold civil war," the media as a political operative, and the search for impeachment reasons have all come to play a decisive role in public discourse.

On the one hand, today's division is overrated, without perspective. The USA has always, repeat always, been a divided house. From the beginning, the Revolution was supported by only about one-third of the people (the guerrilla war between "Tories" and "Loyalists" was, by some accounts, worse than even the Civil War). Probably the only true unity in American history came right after Pearl Harbor but slowly disintegrated and exploded around the 1960s (Vietnam War, civil rights movement).

Today's divisions on the surface seem self-provoked. They are difficult to explain, as they seem to arrive from no origin in particular but from a form of self-examination engineered by a new generation of cultural "watchdogs" and "revisionists." As in the past, these are frequently associated with foreign "agents," now identified as "meddling" or in "collusion" with "fellow travelers" inside (including the President, the Clintons, and assorted "operatives" from Washington to Australia to England).

Internal divisions before have usually been identified as coming from elsewhere as well. Immigration, now issue number one, has origins in the "nativist" movement of the mid-nineteenth century. Foreign ideologies dominated internal dissent in the twentieth century. The infamous "Red Scare" of the 1920s re-appeared in the 1950s in the form of "McCarthyism." Prominent figures in the 1930s, Joe Kennedy, Charles Lindbergh, identified with Nazi Germany.

In the current unrest, Communism has been replaced by Fascism, with frequent reminders of Hitler and the Gestapo and bringing the "Reich" to these shores. Much of the dissension, to remind of Lincoln's warning, predict no choice, either democracy or Fascism. The issue is almost always "existential." *The Washington Post*, on page one, every issue, declares that "democracy dies in darkness" (an implied warning) while political candidates frequently claim President Trump as an "existential" threat (an explicit warning). "White Nationalists" have swastika flags and are, thus, "Neo-Nazis" (but George Washington was a "White Nationalist" also).

There is also a theory that the cultural unrest, especially in the academy, is derived from overseas. "Cultural Marxism" has dominated the American academic landscape for decades, especially from the "Frankfurt (Germany) School of Critical Thought" and its expatriate Herbert Marcuse. Such origins were famously introduced by the late Alan Bloom in *The Closing of the American Mind* (1987) and later by Michael Walsh, *The Devil's Pleasure Palace*, (2018).

In my classes at The Institute of World Politics, since 1998, I have often asked the question: is the existential threat to the U.S. internal or external? Without hesitation, almost 100% (of maybe 1,000) have said "internal." The country has not been invaded since 1812, and, since then, the only real existential threat came within, 1861.

No one foresees a Chinese army occupying Washington, nor is a Russian-controlled political system credible ("meddling" notwithstanding). But the threat from within the culture threatens to tear the country apart if it continues. The obsession to re-discover history by highlighting "institutional" sins or by erasing unpleasant symbols are tactical maneuvers in this new "war." *The New York Times* has just begun "Project 1619" to "reframe" American history around slavery as the definitive national identification.

Harvard Professor Randall Kennedy has summarized this re-interpretation of American society as consisting of "all forms of social oppression ... suffused with white supremacy, capitalist exploitation, misogyny and the repression of unconventional sexuality" (*Washington Post*, August 25, 2019).

He did write "all forms": races, classes, economies, genders, sexualities. Is anything left?

Lincoln had it easy; he only had one problem: how to win a war.

Liberty vs. Equality

FREEDOM VS. LIBERTY
HOW SUBTLE DIFFERENCES
BETWEEN THESE TWO BIG IDEAS
CHANGED OUR WORLD

September 22, 2019

One hates to quarrel with, perhaps, the greatest political document in history, but it is not "self-evident" that "all men are created equal." Indeed, precisely the opposite is true. Why, then, did the Founders (i.e. Jefferson) put that clause in? At face value, it is ridiculous.

No doubt, Jefferson was referring to a much higher definition of the word "equal," one that appeals to both the theological and legal status of humanity. In this regard, he is correct, that all mankind is created with equal status by the Creator and by democratic law. By any other meaning, as is obvious, equality is but a fantasy dream of ideologues.

Yet, the tension between the two conceptions of socio/political virtues, liberty and equality, has dominated the political globe at least since the American Revolution, if not before. The year 1776 offers a good starting point since it represents history's first successful revolt for liberty against imperial authority.

Immediately after the equality clause, the Declaration gets to the heart of the matter, that "all men are endowed by their Creator with certain inalienable

Rights, that among these are Life, Liberty and the pursuit of Happiness." This sentence defines the purpose of the Revolution. It also expresses the human sequence in perfect harmony. First, life itself, the creation. Second, liberty, the goal. Third, the pursuit of happiness, the opportunity. Note on the third, a "pursuit" is not a goal, but an opportunity, which is all the document seeks. Unlike political movements (socialism, communism, equalities of race, gender, income, education, health, etc.) the Declaration does not (and cannot) promise results. Similarly, if a man is six feet tall and another five feet, both cannot be made to be five and one half. If one is lazy and another ambitious, they cannot split the difference. If China has a dictator and America a president, neither can be half-elected, half-imposed.

Today in the American political culture, equality has taken a decided lead in the tension, at least in the "popular" culture. It has also threatened to overcome the Democratic Party. The popularity of the youngest female representative in history, Alexandria Ocasio-Cortez (AOC for short) symbolically represents the culmination of this historic shift. Her "Green New Deal," a hybrid from the Great Depression and FDR, has excited the polity as nothing in memory.

True, this may be a passing phenomenon, but it is also a natural trend with momentum, including democracies throughout Europe and within U.S. society as well. Liberty is easy to take for granted; it is pervasive. But inequality is also evident and the two are often seen as mutually exclusive.

Can we have equality without liberty? Of course. Most societies on earth have an imposed equality: equally impoverished, equally oppressed, equally restrained, equally obedient, and, more recently, equally anxious to get the hell out. Examine the citizens of the old Soviet Union, Nazi Germany, Russia, China, most of the Middle East, Africa, Venezuela, etc.

Can we have liberty without equality? Of course (again). Freedom does not guarantee sociological results; it doesn't endow natural talents but only a better opportunity to achieve results.

Is equality even a desired product? If one starts a business, does he want equality with a competitor, or does he want to be better? In a game, do we seek a tie score? I am a professor and do not have the salary of GM's president. But I could have worked at GM if I wanted to (my father did). I have liberty.

Liberty, not equality, is the meaning of "American." It has always been that way, and, if it changes, it is no longer America, it is something else. Professor Paul Seabury once (1976, *Orbis*) summarized this reality, as follows: "For better or worse, since the beginning of the republic Americans have displayed strong sentiments about their country's role in world affairs. Liberty occupies a central thematic place among them. Emblazoned on monuments, sung about in anthems, stamped on coinage and expressed on placards, it still dominates our civic thought and language."

That sentiment is currently under assault. Some maintain that it amounts to a cultural "civil war," without arms. Perhaps liberty has been taken for granted, been around too long. Perhaps it needs reminders.

During World War II, posters were made for display, to be changed every few months, in stores, homes, factories as reminders of what the war was all about. One famous poster showed a group of 1943 GI's joining with 1776 Continentals on a mountain. The inscription read "Americans will always fight for liberty." Notice equality was not selected. Soldiers would not die for that.

Imagine a fictitious equality dominate in U.S. society. What did Patrick Henry say, "Give me equality or give me death"? Arriving in New York Harbor, what does the newcomer first see, the Statue of Equality?

To bring socialism into the country would makeover American political culture as much as any foreign enemy might have imagined. It would erode liberty into an afterthought in pursuit of an impossible, elusive equality for all. This is a pipedream but so was Communism, Fascism and all other makeovers imposed upon mankind.

After the 1789 Constitutional Convention was over, someone asked Benjamin Franklin what they had made. "A republic," he responded, "if you can keep it."

The jury is still out.

The Idea of White Privilege

August 22, 2019

In a recent political debate, one participant discussed how to make "our communities stronger." But after two hundred-plus years of American communities, why are they now in need of "strength"? Her answer: acknowledge "white privilege." What is she talking about?

By the dictionary, "privilege" is "special rights or immunities." That, however, begs the question: from whence do these "rights" and "immunities" derive? Which brings up another, competing, notion: to "earn." To earn is to "receive as return for effort." If there is privilege in the world, does it come from heaven, is it "bestowed," or is it derived from "effort"?

Recently, a major U.S. university announced "zero tolerance" for "white privilege." A critic then suggested that the school "shut off the electricity." Apparently, the school administrators were not amused by the irony.

The notion of a unique "privilege" or special position ("supremacy") has become a novel feature of the evolving political culture. The idea is both new and ideological i.e., it does not require analysis or reflection. It is, as well, meant for applause or political approval. Like "faith" in theology, the concept simply asserts belief without evidence. At bottom, it is simply "ideology," and ideologies do not seek evidence, i.e., the "Aryan" race, the "proletariat," "war to save the world for democracy," "nation building."

If one group is privileged, then all the others are, by definition, "underprivileged." How, again, did they get that way? Was it biology (God) or humanity (war/oppression)?

The concept "Nationalism," perhaps the most dominant sociological expression in human history, has also become "Americanized" in today's society/culture. Properly, the notion is now prefaced by the adjective "white." Whether this is a description or an accusation remains unclear.

Like "privilege," the idea "white nationalism" has now become a political movement. The former Virginia Governor, Terry McAuliffe, (not exactly a historian of the idea) now heads this initiative with his book, *Beyond Charlottesville: Taking a Stand Against White Nationalism*. McAuliffe's understanding of the sub-title is restricted to Neo-Nazis who rioted in Charlottesville in 2017. Essentially, this negates the expression altogether.

There is no societal connection between rioting and nationhood. But, to repeat, thought/analysis are unnecessary so long as the expression is accepted. Like "beauty," such beliefs are "in the eye of the beholder." To their descendants, the Founding Fathers were also "white nationalists," but, to the British, they were "terrorists."

Nevertheless, the issue of white nationalism is a daily read and is considered relevant and serious by many. But history does not acknowledge the subject in such a condescending way, nor has reality been bothered by the notion (until now). Consider a single case.

July 1, 1916: the Somme River, east bank, France. The BEF (British Expeditionary Force) begins its charge at 7:00 AM across "No Man's Land" toward the German trench-line, about a mile away. Although the enemy has absorbed about two million shells the previous week, they are still safe and secure in their own trenches. Machine guns in place, they begin strafing the "Tommies," killing around eight per second according to one eyewitness. By 4 PM, the day is done. British casualties are 60,000 total, 20,000 killed.

That's what happened on the first day of the Battle of the Somme. There was no "privilege" on that day. The Battle of the Somme went on until November 18th, one of hundreds of battles that absorbed white soldiers in the First World War. The British Commander at the Somme, Douglas Haig, ordered 92 more offensives like the first one. That's right, 92. By the end the British had "conquered" about five miles of ground, a long way off from Berlin. General Haig remains a respected figure in British military lore.

But perhaps "privilege" is a civilian notion, while the millions of Caucasian soldiers who returned in body bags throughout history are discounted. In the American Civil War, about 720,000 white soldiers died (within a 32 million population) in a cause that ended slavery but has since been erased amidst "white supremacy" ideological beliefs.

Behind the word "privilege" is the incessant quest for "equality." If, goes the idea, one is privileged within millions, there is "inequality." But here is another criteria for authentic "equality": soldiers going home in body bags accurately reflect the population. Has warfare been historically "sexist"?

Indeed, ideology has seemed to replace history and thought in modern America. People seem to be "chasing rainbows." Replicas of the past, designs, statues, place-names, writing, are seen as objects of destruction rather than reminders of actual historic people and events. Contemporary incidents are held up as symbolic of wider and deeper "institutional" societal attributes. Single issues are representative. The deaths of individuals – Trayvon Martin in Florida (2012) and Freddie Gray in Baltimore (2015) – nearly brought the country into an apoplectic fit over "racism" that is alleged as defining society. The millions of men killed in battle are accepted as ordained ("privileged"), while a single civilian death can be represented as a profound national crime.

Slavery may ask for "reparations." How do we "repair" damage from deaths at age 18 for nothing in "no-man's land"?

To anguish over someone's murder is appropriate and necessary. But to inflate singular and episodic events into belief-systems or societal convictions is fraudulent. This is also, tragically, evident in warfare: if a soldier was shot by a civilian, often, in war, the entire town was torched.

George Orwell caught this human disconnect years ago in 1984 and *Animal Farm*, in which "thought police" replaced reason and sanity with the irrational and ideological. Orwell was referring to Josef Stalin's Russia, his political "purges," and his removal of any vestiges of the country's Czarist history. If one does not like history, one simply erases it. Barring that, convenient adjectives are invented, and, most remarkably, accepted.

Today's America is fast approaching this public acceptance, and a favorite subject is historic and national "sins." It has become nearly an obsession. We search for what's wrong (and there's enough) rather than what's right (same). Some of the ideas prevalent today are as close to "Stalinist" thought that we have seen in some time.

Trump wants to buy Greenland:

What else is new?

August 20, 2019

Speculation that President Trump has expressed interest in purchasing Greenland from Denmark has inspired gossip in the media as to how "serious" he is. In history, countries either expand by conquest or by purchase, the former being the most common. Should Trump announce that the U.S. will occupy and seize the island, speculation would undoubtedly be far more severe (especially in Denmark). Yet Trump's (alleged) interest should not shock anyone with the slightest understanding of history – and human nature.

First, the President is, first and foremost (as has been apparent) a realtor. He spent most of his life buying and selling things, especially buildings and property. Greenland has both.

Second, countries have frequently bought land from proprietors, whether they wanted to sell or not. This is called "an offer they can't refuse." The President even wrote a book on this, *The Art of the Deal*.

Third, American history is replete with such exchanges. Alaska, purchased from Russia (1867), was once called "Seward's Folly." President Thomas Jefferson made perhaps history's greatest real estate deal in 1803 with the Louisiana Purchase from Napoleon. The area, about one-third of the continent, later became home to fifteen states.

Fourth, purchase is better than conquest. President James K. Polk invaded Mexico and in return obtained the rest of the continent left over from the Louisiana Purchase. This amounted to about one-third of old Mexico (and Spain), including Texas and the American southwest, California, parts of Colorado, Nevada, and Utah. Still, the legacy of land-by-conquest has since been a stain on the American record, beginning with opposition against Polk's war by both Abraham Lincoln (as a Congressman) and Ulysses Grant (as a soldier in the war and in his *Memoirs*).

Greenland is the world's largest island but is 85% ice and has only about 56,000 inhabitants, almost half in the Capitol, Nuuk. It does, however, have resource potential, energy, minerals, gemstones, and has geopolitical use, particularly with the U.S. airbase at Thule (home of a missile warning system since 1951).

Yet, there is no apparent U.S. urge or demand for Greenland as a possession, and Denmark has refused to sell. In 1947, President Harry Truman expressed a similar interest but quickly dropped it after a Danish refusal.

Denmark has owned Greenland since 1814, after sharing it with Norway before. Apparently, they want to keep it, to quote the original Panama Canal Treaty, "in perpetuity." But, in 1978, President Jimmy Carter gave the Canal Zone back to Panama, despite severe opposition from such as Ronald Reagan, John Wayne, and most Republicans. So much for "in perpetuity."

Why does President Trump (again, allegedly) want Greenland? He will visit Denmark soon and may well make an offer. By the same token, why does Denmark want to keep it? One way or the other, the island will be owned since there is no drive for independence from the native Inuit tribe.

Should the U.S. press the case for American ownership? Can a case can be made that western security and interests would benefit from such a transfer? If so, then why not?

If Danish ownership of Greenland may be defined as harmful for overall security of the NATO region, then why should an outdated colonial relationship be continued and supported? But if there is no case, or a weak one, then Trump should do what Truman did and drop the ball immediately. Surely his administration has enough problems without interfering in an ally's territorial imperatives.

But, as usual, there is precedent. If America wants something bad, enough America gets it. And Denmark knows it (or should).

It is 1916, the world war is in its third year, the U.S. is neutral but concerned about being dragged in. Denmark owns the West Indies, but they would go to Germany should Denmark be invaded. The American Secretary of State, Robert Lansing, approaches the Danish Ambassador with an offer he can't refuse. Should Denmark cede the islands to Germany, Lansing wrote, "the United States would be under the necessity of seizing and annexing them ...as we would never permit the group to become German." Shortly thereafter, the Ambassador reported back that under "the pressure of necessity [Denmark] would be unable to refuse to consider a proposition of the sale of the islands to the United States."

In his report to President Woodrow Wilson, the president expressed his "gratification" that the Secretary had been "so frank with the Danish Minister." Frank indeed! It was pure great-power extortion and today, for $25 million, the islands are known as the American Virgin Islands, now a vacation hotspot but once a critical issue of national security.

In his reluctant report to the Danish Parliament, the Ambassador, Edward Brandes, reminded them that they lived in a "world where justice is abolished or enforced by might, yes, where might not so seldom forms and moulds justice."

American opinion, naturally, was not quite so downcast. As Senator Henry Cabot Lodge, Chairman of the Senate Foreign Relations Committee, said, it was a vital interest: "The European power which attempts to establish itself in new possessions in the Americas, whether in a little island or a continental state, from Patagonia to the Rio Grande, is our enemy."

This all stems from a principle derived from nature itself, the doctrine of "self-defense." Yet it remains a doctrine of "possibilities," thereby very tangential. In the West Indies case, the U.S. acted against a possible danger of a possible consequence of a possible action from a possible enemy. Yet, to take no action at all would fall into the same category.

In 1941, with Denmark occupied by Hitler's Germany, the Roosevelt Administration, indeed, took action and occupied Greenland (and Iceland). Secretary of State Cordell Hull, in defending the occupation, gave a definitive and enduring explanation:

"As a result of Greenland's geographical location in the Western Hemisphere and inclusion within the general scope of the Monroe Doctrine, ... the

United States has a certain dominant interest in Greenland arising out of considerations of national and hemispheric defense. ... the United States could not tolerate an attack upon Greenland by any non-American power or an attempt by such a power to alter the present political status of the island."

The US evacuated Greenland in 1945 and Denmark, technically, never lost sovereignty.

National security, however, is always a game of chance and risk, be it Vietnam, West Berlin, Taiwan, Israel, even Greenland. As before, there is nothing too remote or too small, nothing to disparage.

Ask Denmark.

The Twentieth Century

August 7, 2019

I frequently ask my history class "what is the most significant enduring fact of the twentieth century"? In explaining, I emphasized "enduring" rather than single event. In most cases, the most significant fact was the beginning of something/someone. For America, it was July 4, 1776, for the airplane, the Kitty Hawk event, for the telephone, Alexander Graham Bell's invention, for the Civil War, the firing on Fort Sumter, etc. etc. Equally, everyone celebrates their birthday each year, whether they're 90 or 10.

Single events begin a process, so it is only natural that a conception is more important than a middle or an ending. For the century, it means that the answer must lie in the early part, so answers like the Great Depression, World War II, the Cold War etc. are invalid. What presupposed these events that explains the entirety, rather than its subsequent parts?

Explaining further, I note that consensus on the century targets World War I as the catalyst for most events that followed, including both World War

II, the Cold War, and most recent events, including Islamic terror. But World War I ended in 1918, so what continued its legacy from then until now? It's fairly easy to identify June 28, 1914 (assassination of the Austrian Archduke) as the single most important moment, but what carried this momentum into the unknown future?

Pause for your own answer....

The idea was to connect 1914 to 1939, to 1945 to 1991, to 2001. What single fact was common to all of these periods that, one way or another, either beginning or ending, was significant and consistent throughout? Answers varied, but not by much. Most students identified the great societal/ideological movements, Fascism, Communism, Socialism, etc. Fascism died in Hitler's bunker, the Soviet Union collapsed in 1991, while there never was, not once, a true "Marxist" government, i.e. a "proletariat" revolution. For Socialism, remember that Nazi Germany was the "National Socialist German Worker's Party," while the Soviet Union was the "Union of Soviet Socialist Republics" (USSR). Partly Socialist countries, such as Sweden, cannot make up the legions of failures, portrayed long ago in the classic book *The God that Failed* (1949).

That leaves Democracy as the only alternative. But students had trouble with this as a political movement, since Woodrow Wilson failed so badly with the League of Nations (the U.S. never joined) and governments that could truly call themselves "democratic" in the last century were few and far between (and still are).

So what is the answer, what defines the Twentieth Century? The answer is not precisely the political concept of democracy but, perhaps, is better understood as a "precursor" or "pre-condition" of Democratic Capitalism. The answer lies more within the word "civilization" than any single political concept. Democracy, furthermore, is a system of government that controls domestic behavior, while the Twentieth Century involved literally hundreds of movements, regimes, ideologies, and continuous warfare that cannot possibly be supervised by an electorate or an Assembly. The result may produce a number of democracies, but isn't responsible for the behavior of billions in a span of 100 years.

So what was? The answer (finally): the solidarity and cultural/strategic direction of the "English Speaking Peoples." That was, and is, my own answer, and, while no one student ever got it right, I always reminded them of the subjectivity of the viewpoint and then opened it up to discussion. I must confess, very little dissent, over many years (the course was taught by me 48 consecutive times).

What, then, supports this answer? Its origins go back as far as the Monroe Doctrine (1823), when Secretary of State John Quincy Adams (who wrote it) "colluded" with the British Navy to keep the Western Hemisphere free from attempts to re-introduce colonialism back into the region. By century's end, with a rising Germany, Great Britain began to cultivate the possibility of bringing the U.S. into its orbit should the need arise. British concessions on territorial claims helped alleviate American insecurities, particularly British acquiescence on U.S. control over any future interoceanic canal.

In effect, the "New World" was brought back to redress the imbalance of the "Old World." As Professor Samuel Flagg Bemis wrote, Britain:

"... left the New World to the American system, and henceforth she tried to bring the United States, thus strengthened, to cast its balance on her side in the world politics of the twentieth century."

The decision may have been the most momentous in British (and U.S.) history. The die, in effect, was cast for the remainder of the century. Through the trials of history's greatest wars, American strength, despite being neutral at the beginnings, eventually rescued Britain (and the western world) from the grips of despotism and Fascism, both in 1918 and in 1941. So secure was Churchill in his close relationship with Roosevelt and American power that he wrote in his diary the day after Pearl Harbor that, "I knew the United States was in the war up to the neck, so we had won after all."

The beginning of the Cold War saw Britain again acquiesce to the reality of American power. In February 1947, Whitehall sent Washington notes that Britain could no longer supervise the post-war world. The result was the Truman Doctrine (March), the Marshall Plan (June), the Berlin Airlift (1948) and NATO (1949). The following years of containment saw a continuation of this "special relationship" until President Ronald Reagan, aided closely by Prime Minister Margaret Thatcher, put an end to the Cold War and the USSR as well. Nor was it coincidental that Prime Minister Tony Blair was first to support and aid the U.S. War on Terror after 9/11, despite severe criticism at home.

The relationship has declined since then. Now we have Boris Johnson and Donald Trump, with Johnson occupied with BREXIT and Trump with MAGA. A free trade bill is pending between the two countries, an item that might just salvage a historic partnership. If this fails, we just have memories.

In a front pew in the Foundry Methodist Church, eight blocks from the White House, is a plaque that reads: "Here on Christmas Morning, 1941, sat President Franklin D. Roosevelt and Prime Minister Winston S. Churchill." The plaque is still there. Where are Roosevelt and Churchill?

What Foreign Policy Shall We Have?

July 29, 2019

The above question, attributed to Leon Trotsky after the Bolshevik revolution in 1917, was an ideological admission that world Communism would soon remove the need for any "bourgeois" remnants of history that might survive Marxism's final triumph. Assuming the inevitable, "scientific" victory of worldwide Communist-Socialism, the Bolsheviks of that time had complete faith that their revolution was final and irreversible and meant the end of nation-states and global Capitalism. Trotsky also is said to have answered his question with a dismissal that the foreign office was no longer needed and that the new regime had only to issue a "few pronouncements and close-up shop."

Obviously, Trotsky put way too much faith in Marxist doctrine and was soon driven out of Russia by Stalin, who believed that further, spontaneous revolutions elsewhere were "nonsense." Now in control, Stalin was forced to follow strict and nationalistic policies to survive both German Nazism and American Capitalism. He had Trotsky killed in Mexico in 1940 while he had to ally with the Capitalists to barely survive Hitler.

The above reflection on Trotsky highlights the faith that history's ideologues have had in denying reality. Trotsky was hardly alone, as the nature of ideological thought throughout history has, time and again, distorted reality and turned normal behavior into tragedy. There has never been a truly "Marxist" revolution, despite the durability of the idea and the existence of multiple countries calling themselves "Communist."

Where, on earth, has someone's "proletariat" risen and taken over a government?

Similarly, Hitler rallied eighty million people into following an "Aryan" racial doctrine toward an imagined world order that saw the utter destruction of Germany and 76 million dead in six years.

American efforts to convert foreign, entrenched cultural tyrannies into functioning democracies has been tried since Woodrow Wilson's time. It is still going on in Iraq, Afghanistan and elsewhere, apparently without end.

Today's American political culture has faint but dangerous similarities to ideological movements that both deny reality and supplant national security for domestic utopias. The United States is, without doubt, the most "liberal" country ever created. This is its greatest strength, but this characteristic, like most other qualities, can also lead into unchartered territory if allowed to go undisciplined and/or unsupervised. Political liberty has been supplanted by a host of ideological "isms," which distort reality and advance self-absorbed "causes."

Liberalism has meant "equality" from the very beginning. "We hold these truths..." is the declaration that began America and the endless search for an equalitarian social order. "That all men are created equal," however, was not meant to be taken literally. This is apparent from the expression itself: it excludes half of humanity, ignores any kind of social reality, including slavery and class, ethnic, religious and other human distinctions. The word "all" had nothing to do with the rest of the world, and the word "equal" was only theoretical, as meaning before the law and God.

Yet, it was a revolution and, by definition, cannot reach a finality. The proper answer (metaphorically) to the question "what is the lasting result of the American Revolution"? has always been: "it's too soon to tell."

The United States never really created its own "foreign" policy until the end of World War II. Before that, the country was absorbed by "isolationism," and, after both world wars, immediately headed back into "normalcy" (the 1920s expression) until isolation became untenable. A "policy" is a set of tactics, goals, and "high" strategies geared toward concrete ends, timetables and supported by an electorate. Both world wars are over, as is the Cold War. Since the early 1990s, the U.S. has veered, almost aimlessly, from one set of goals to another, but with a domestic agenda that, progressively, has left national security realities in the dust. That is both normal and understandable. But it has a potential to "repeat" history. The late UN Ambassador under Reagan, Jeanne Kirkpatrick, best identified this trend in an article urging the U.S. to be "a normal country in a normal time." For the most part, we have done just that. But for how long will "normalcy" prevail?

Judging from the current political climate, we are again asking the Trotsky question, "what foreign policy shall we have?" The recent twenty-person Democratic debates ignored foreign policy/national security altogether. The 2016 election did practically the same, with "name calling" taking over. The only concession to "security" was the immigration question, which has been misnamed as an "emergency." It is certainly serious, but the 1962 Cuban Missile Crisis was an emergency. In the 2012 election, the national security issue was the murders in Benghazi, but this was a tragic episode, hardly a foreign policy.

As so often before in human history, domestic beliefs have subsumed questions of national security. In the past, either a Pearl Harbor or a 9/11 was needed to arouse the "sleeping giant." Nor is the Trump Administration any closer to a serious look at the issue, with MAGA an empty political slogan (and hat).

The United States needs a foreign policy, but for or against what or whom? Every conversation, every "issue," almost all reporting reflects the American ideology, equality. It has infected not only the political process but the entire culture. This includes theater, the "news" (the word itself is an ideology), comedy, "talk" shows (once jocular, now serious). Sports has become a target. American women won the soccer cup; the biggest news is the team's political beliefs. Kate Smith once sang a "racist" song (1931); the Philadelphia Flyers tore down her statue. The Yankees banished her "God Bless America." NFL "owners" cannot use the term. Most champions will not go to the White House.

History and biology are questioned by ideology. Nike won't make a shoe that reflects slavery in America. If only one item from history is removed, logically, they all should be removed. Historically, that was once called "Stalinist." Females and "people of color" occupy most of humanity. Any and all references to them by "Caucasians," comprehensively, often reflects either "racism" or "sexism." Any and all past behavior toward either is the same. Ideologues do not split hairs.

History is eliminated, genders are no longer biology, and an Orwellian "newspeak" has banished pronouns. National security awaits the next attack.

Is this the lasting result of the American Revolution?

Political Hysteria:

As American as Cherry Pie

July 29, 2019

While most readers do not recall political history back to "I Like Ike," I certainly do, and I am, thus, appalled (but not surprised) by the fever-pitch of "hysteria" that has been ongoing for at least three years. Hysteria is defined as "...overwhelming or unmanageable fear or emotional excess." Synonyms are "frenzy, rage, fury, rampage, uproar." The term is extreme but appropriate. One feminist book entitled *Rage Becomes Her* shows why women should ignore biology and history.

All political/cultural wars are two-way events, and this one is no exception. It began even before the 2016 election and escalated when the new President began insulting nearly everyone in sight and then indicated that the world order we all know and love is finished. He then lied 10,000 times, according to "fact checkers" (who cannot lie). Many lies were told throughout the Vietnam War, also; the difference being around three million deaths, mostly Vietnamese (1955-1975). Politicians and diplomats lie, but some lies have greater consequence than others. W Bush lied about Iraq's WMD; sixteen years and about 300,000 deaths later (mostly Iraqi), we're still there.

The backlash against Trump came from nearly all the print and TV media (Fox excepted) in what can only be described as an all-out, to-the-finish assault meant to remove him ASAP. Trump may as well be a foreign agent with few distinctions drawn between himself and Vladimir Putin. Trump has even been identified with Adolf Hitler (despite a Jewish son-in-law and converted daughter, with no "Gestapo" to execute reporters).

Hysteria fits. Of all the tens of thousands of examples of this "assault," perhaps my favorite is one from a nationally-known reporter (anonymous) who confessed that "...once I'm awake, a gravitational pull takes hold and I am once more bedeviled by our preposterous president." That's hysteria!

I can remember disliking many of our Presidents, but when I awoke I first brushed my teeth (I controlled my rage until lunch). Would "preposterous" apply to the Vietnam War, Iraq, or having sex in the Oval Office with an intern (and then lying)? Politics in the recent past has been, to be sure, acrimonious, but "level heads" usually prevailed.

Today, reason seems to be missing, on both sides. Nixon broke the law and went quietly. Ford said that "Poland was free," but it wasn't, and Jimmy Carter warned against "malaise." Reagan was often labeled a "cowboy" but is now sorely missed. Bush forgot to remember his script ("read my lips ..."); Clinton was impeached, and his ratings soared. Bush II won thanks to Florida's Secretary of State, Katherine Harris, while Obama got a "free ride" from the media.

In the Trump presidency (so far), his personality and character are the only real issues. Emotions dominate. Tariffs and NATO rarely invoke emotions, but the emotional discharges about children in "cages" (like Rachel Maddow crying on-air) is directed against Trump alone, not the root cause of such mass migration itself (tyrannical regimes).

By and large, America is at peace, and there are no national protests against war (unlike Vietnam). By most indications, Trump wants to remove American soldiers from war zones. The economy is getting better every day (unlike the recession). On the surface, things seem tranquil. Malls are crowded, highways are jammed, factories are working, the press is free (extremely free), and any "emergency" is beyond the border.

Still, in some quarters, any emergency is outright denied. Denial has also infected the political campaign. The recent Democratic primary debates came off as "Econ 101," Capitalism vs. Socialism. The country's more important policies, national security, tariffs, for example, were simply left alone. The most critical issues involved what happened half-a-century ago: Senator Harris was bused to kindergarten and Senator Joe Biden "colluded" with long-dead southern Democrats (he should have hit them over the head with a cane, as one did in 1860).

Question: What is it about politics that arouses such seemingly irrational behavior? Athletes fight each other then embrace. Soldiers honor enemies who just tried to kill them. Germany and Japan have been American allies going back after World War II. We are now on good relations with Vietnam. Nixon was a hero for aligning with Communist China (a regime that killed sixty million of its own, the most in history). Trump is accosted by the press for cordial behavior toward North Korea, Russia and other world tyrannies. Should he ignore or threaten them (he's put sanctions on Russia)? Should we break relations with the over 175 dictatorships in the world? Franklin D. Roosevelt called Josef Stalin "Uncle Joe," and was revered while Mikhail Gorbachev had twelve (yes twelve) summits with Reagan/Bush. Everybody laughed when Clinton was photographed arm around a drunken Boris Yeltsin.

Is there something in the character of politics that makes it illogical, a "blood sport"? Is that why it is called an "arena"? Perhaps a brief look at early American history might give a clue.

From the beginning, Americans were fiercely independent, passionate, but deeply divided. Only about one-third supported the revolution; the majority were either neutral or remained loyal to the British ("Tories"). A fierce internal terrorist campaign raged throughout the war between these two groups of Americans. So intense was the divide that a British Chaplin was moved to write that,

"These Americans, so soft, pacific and benevolent by nature, are here transformed into monsters, implacably bloody and ravenous; party rage has kindled the spirit of hatred between them, they attack and rob each other by turns, destroy dwelling houses, or establish themselves therein by driving out those who had before dispossessed others. [Note the word "rage."]"

With the revolution over, the country settled down, but the acrimony went on. No one was spared, not even the "father of the country." In 1795, President Washington signed a treaty with Britain ("Jay Treaty") that gave concessions to Britain on the high seas in return for the British withdrawal from certain forts in North America. The treaty was so divisive that another war seemed likely. Washington himself became an overnight villain in many quarters.

There were calls for impeachment, charges of treason. Newspaper cartoons showed Washington being marched to a guillotine. Revolutionary war veterans infamously "toasted" Washington, "A speedy death to General Washington." A slogan by anti-treaty partisans declared "George Washington – down to the year 1787. And no farther."

Secretary of State Thomas Jefferson resigned in protest, and his followers demanded that all private papers of the treaty be made public. Several newspaper columnists claimed that Washington had been bribed by the British. A pro-treaty paper lamented that, "Washington has been classed with tyrants, and calumniated as the enemy of his country. Weep for the national character of America, for, in ingratitude to her Washington, it is sullied and debased throughout the globe." Privately, Washington noted that "infamous scribblers" were calling him "a common pickpocket, in such exaggerated and indecent terms as could scarcely be applied to a Nero." Washington's wife, Martha, claimed later that the hatred hastened his death.

The treaty passed and America survived.

If this all sounds familiar, it may be that it is generic, as the comment, above, noted to the "national character of America."

The Russians Are (Always) Here

Nobody Showed You the History Of Russia Like This!

July 17, 2019

Recently, I wrote that evidence demonstrating Russian involvement in the 2016 election was fragmentary, ambiguous, and certainly not "public knowledge." The testimonies of both Special Counsel Robert Mueller and Attorney General William Barr did little to dispel this conclusion, but Mueller is scheduled to testify to Congress next week.

One can hope that this, his second attempt, will dispel any confusion that his earlier efforts only amplified. Even a cursory review of the 448 page Mueller Report will reveal that a great deal of damaging evidence of "collusion" between Trump personnel and Russian operatives, while not technically "criminal," was sufficient to question the integrity of Trump explanations. Many of these actions were also sufficient to charge the administration with "obstruction of justice," justifying impeachment and possible removal from office. The Report identified over 150 sanctioned Trump official staff contacts with Russian operatives. Over 1,000 former government prosecutors, from both political parties, have formally declared that such actions justify "obstruction."

Such evidence, largely unknown to the public, is too serious to ignore. Politically, this testimony, fully vented, could give rise within the Republican Party, of serious efforts to replace the President in 2020.

Although evidence of involvement is real and threatening, it still remains impossible to ascertain its ultimate consequence. As has been charged, openly by Hillary Clinton and many Democrats, did Vladimir Putin actually "steal" the election for Trump? The result is a "contested" election, not unique in history (1876, 1888, 1960, 2000). We are left to speculate.

From the vantage of hindsight and perspective, what do we make of Russian behavior, overall? Is it like warfare and spying, universal and timeless? Or were the Russians of 2016 one-of-a-kind?

The answer to the question need not delay us. There has rarely been a time in history, when a country, a city-state, an empire has not, either once or always, attempted either to infiltrate or to persuade the political behavior of both rivals and allies. It is an essential of world politics, as endemic as the need for money and security and just as demonstrable. Churchill did it to Roosevelt and Roosevelt did it to Churchill (for a history of espionage, see Christopher Andrew, *The Secret World*, 2018).

The Mueller Report, like everything else, could use context. There is *Witness*, the memoir of Whitaker Chambers (1951) who recorded his years as a Communist agent spying on American political secrets and transferring these back to Moscow. A whole generation, in the 1940s, was glued to the Hiss-Chambers Hearings when Chambers detailed how Alger Hiss and (alleged) Communists in the four Roosevelt Administrations advised FDR, influencing the Yalta meeting and all of Eastern Europe going over to the Soviets. The Truman Administration was later accused by Republicans of "losing" China to Communism, an accusation that tied the Truman Administration to the Communists over the Nationalists in the Chinese Civil War. This allegation (vastly exaggerated) also played a major role behind the U.S. entry into Vietnam.

These remain only accusations, but the politics behind such "collusion" began the Cold War and determined much of the Twentieth Century.

Then there is the *Venona Secrets* (1995), containing hundreds of pages of testimony of the decades of Soviet and global Communist spy networks inside most western democracies. The Soviet Union tested their atomic bomb years earlier than expected (1949) due principally to the vast network of spies inside this country and even within the top-secret Manhattan Project (Stalin actually knew about the first U.S. test before President Truman).

The Russians, as a people, have had to be suspicious of foreigners from the earliest days, including centuries of spy networks by agents of the Czar's secret police. Putin is a Russian; that's "what they do" (see Hoover Institution, editors, *Double Exposure: Russia's Secret Police Under the Last Tsars*, 1957).

Modern Russia, the Soviet Union, was an ideological movement and escalated historic Russian fears with a global mission. Almost immediately after the 1917 Bolshevik Revolution, Leninist agents infiltrated the capitalist world in an avalanche of espionage, disruption, and violent incidents. Nearly the entire 1920s was taken up with the infamous "Red Scare," wherein Attorney General Mitchell Palmer (his house was actually bombed) and his FBI Director, J. Edgar Hoover, arrested around 10,000 "anarchists, socialists and communists" and deported 556 back to, mainly, Russia, Italy, and eastern Europe. The 1930s saw more of the same, culminating in the formation of the House Un-American Activities Committee (HUAC) in 1938.

The end of World War II (with the Soviet Union as an ally) saw the Cold War begin a new, but familiar, scenario of Russian infiltration attempts, widespread espionage activities, and a phenomenon now known as "McCarthyism." The whole country (myself included) watched the "Army-McCarthy Hearings" attempt to indict the American military as infiltrated by Communists. Having already claimed that the State Department was, essentially, ruled by Reds, McCarthy was censored by the Senate in 1954 and died in 1957, a lonely and isolated alcoholic. (His daughter, born 1957, is named "Tierney," my last name. Well, he can't be all bad.)

The end of McCarthy has not ended history or reality. During the Cold War, the United States Government had an intelligence component in every single nation that had an American embassy. When necessary, these interfered, infiltrated, and intervened to affect the politics of the home regime to align with U.S. needs. The CIA spent millions and sent agents to ensure the anti-communist election victories in France and Italy (1948). New governments elsewhere, the Shah of Iran and Guatemala in particular (1950s), were essentially "made in America."

Is McCarthy's "ghost" back, and do we exaggerate Russian influence, as he did? Or do we diminish it, as Cold War opponents of U.S. policies did?

Politicians rarely become national security specialists overnight. They "live and breathe" re-election and use available assets to win. The "Red Scare" of the 1920s was not ideological; it was directed against the influx of immigrants from Eastern Europe and Italy (leading to the 1924 restrictive immigration laws) and the growth of labor unions. "McCarthyism" was essentially a "witch hunt" for the Senator's political ambitions.

Who is the target today, Trump or Russia? Trump can be removed, and "Never Trumpers" have been on this since day one. The Republicans, for their part, are now "investigating the investigators." Russia won't go away, unless we do what all countries under attack do: close the embassy and send all agents home. That won't happen, with little left but "party passion."

Political parties and their interests can be decisive, even with national security the issue (alleged).

As one "insider" noticed, party allegiance:

"Serves always to distract the public councils and enfeeble the public administration. It agitates the community with ill-founded jealousies and false alarms, kindles the animosity of one part versus another, and foments occasionally riot and insurrection. It opens the door to foreign influence and corruption, which finds a facilitated access to the government itself through the channels of party passions. Thus the policy and the will of one country are subjected to the policy and will of another." – George Washington, 1796

Over two centuries later, have we come a long way?

Remembering Pat Derian, human rights activist

July 12, 2019

Undoubtedly, few readers will remember this name, yet she was the chief architect of American foreign policy during the Carter Administration, 1977 – 1981. She was neither Secretary of State, nor a member of the National Security Council. Her background was exclusively domestic, as an activist for civil and voting rights for blacks in Mississippi and the deep south. Carter appointed her as Assistant Secretary for Human Rights and Humanitarian Affairs, and, after her death in 2016, noted how she was responsible for the fact that

"...countless human rights and democratic activists survived that period, going on to plant the seeds of freedom in Latin America, Asia and beyond."

Derian (née Murphy) was controversial from the beginning of her tenure and came under fire often as opposed by the Reagan Administration and the views of Henry Kissinger and other "realists," who advocated ties with violators of human rights and the priorities of Cold War survival. As a member of the Reagan Administration, I fully understood the need for global allies against the spread of Soviet Communism. Under the tensions of that time period, it was appropriate to appreciate the necessity for strong and dependable allies against the notion of a crusade to punish them for their culture and history. Argentina came under special scrutiny for its notorious "dirty war" against dissidents, including dropping them to their death from airplanes. Argentina was a reliable and needed ally in Latin America against the spread of Castro-Communism, and national security took priority over "foreign policy as social work."

This was appreciated, and Derian remains a controversial personality, especially after the demise of the Soviet Union and the emergence of the American "superpower." Yet, that was long ago and it might just be possible to re-examine the role of human rights in a post-Cold War world and the legacy of Patricia Derian. It could be more lasting than previously believed.

It would be hard, indeed, to demonstrate how Pat Derian changed the fundamental nature of oppressive regimes around the world. To the extent that she, and the Carter Administration, did it was decidedly short-lived. Nor should we expect a single official in a one-term political regime to have had any lasting impact upon either human nature or political science. The lasting effect of the Reagan Administration in ending the Soviet Union and the world Communist threat was, by comparison, much more significant. Nevertheless, Pat Derian may still be looked upon as a symbolic figure reflecting the nature and character of the American political faith and the eternal virtues of a foreign policy based primarily on these qualities.

In his seminal study of the nature of American values in foreign affairs, Walter McDougal (University of Pennsylvania) separated the American approach into two essential parts. His book, *Promised Land, Crusader State* (1997) noted that the original approach was "a city upon a hill," when American values were confined to represent political virtue without the need for overseas conversion. The second approach, associated with Woodrow Wilson and World

War I, emphasized a more vigorous and aggressive mandate to export these values wherever they were lacking, whether they were welcomed or not. Given "superpower" status, a "city upon a hill" is no longer a position for American values in foreign policy.

There is something admirable about policies advanced by virtue, as opposed to the "Old World" emphasis on political "realism" or *reason d'etat*. Yet, at the same time, there is also something onerous about one set of values being imposed against a foreign culture that, by definition and history, has never known nor desired to be converted into another's image. As repetition and practice has demonstrated, the effort has, more often than not, led to long-term failure and bitter and lasting legacies.

But those are tactical failures, not strategic. Like Wilson himself, his vision was admirable; his politics were abysmal.

Since the end of the Cold War, 1991, it is fair to say that U.S. foreign policy has — overall — lacked an essential purpose or demonstrative vision that, in the past, has captured the imagination and political appeal that goes beyond the borders of North America. Calls for a "new world order," "nation-building," "globalization," "leading from behind" and other catch-phrases have failed to dent a society fully absorbed by domestic priorities and a variety of home-grown "isms." President Trump's call to make America "great again" sounds mighty but implies the decline of purpose ("again") and implies equally a return to self-absorption (isolation).

So where does Patricia Derian fit in? By the same token, where does the Universal Declaration on Human Rights fit in? Signed by all countries in 1948, the document spells out, in thirty articles, the basic "rights" that all societies, and all their citizens, have by birthright. In philosophy, this is "Natural Law." The Declaration is the embodiment of the ultimate purpose behind the Second World War and, essentially, the reason for the United Nations in the first place.

It also happens to reflect the liberty and justice that formed the United States of America and the basic reason why American soldiers fought and died, from Saratoga, to Gettysburg, to Normandy Beach.

Two American women stand out in this regard: Eleanor Roosevelt, the U.S. delegate who shaped the document in 1948 and Pat Derian, who represented the same principles during the Cold War. Today, in a period of great confusion, dissension, and division, it would be prudent for an American President to dedicate the country behind principles that reflect the heritage, not only of the country but of the two women that kept the "fire" alive.

President Trump has been criticized for his harsh attitude toward foreign populations and leaders alike. He has even been taken to task for demanding that NATO allies honor their financial commitments. It would be a welcome diversion if this same behavior could be directed against the near-universal violations of "basic human rights" that visit the planet every waking moment. In this respect, his instinctive personality would, at last, serve a purpose worthy of the country he leads, including the human rights pioneers who represented it when he was out selling buildings.

It matters less that tyrannies are not converted overnight; and it matters more that we keep trying. In this time of crisis and confusion, America needs to stand up — and be counted!

Isolationism:

The People's Choice

July 11, 2019

George Washington's 1796 Farewell Address set the stage for more than 150 years of "isolationism" for American foreign policies. While the advice was challenged prior to both world wars and brought the U.S. into each, the idea of abstention from external political affairs became a near-sacred political "theology" for most American history. Even after it was "violated" by both Woodrow Wilson (1917) and Franklin D. Roosevelt (1930s), the idea that foreign "entanglements" were taboo grew into a political article of faith for most Americans. Washington's advice was finally laid to rest by Harry Truman and the Cold War in 1947, but the idea has had such a profound impact upon the culture that it never permanently disappeared.

Today, Donald Trump, with his slogan to "Make America Great Again" recalls the isolationist past, and he has been roundly accused of destroying the "world order" established by Truman. But foreign policy is rarely an election issue, and the 2016 campaign, like all those since the end of the Cold War, proves the point.

If President Trump really wants to return to an isolationist past (which is uncertain), he is only "preaching to the choir." America was "conceived" in isolationism, and the culture that held to that strategic wisdom throughout its early and mid-history is unlikely to discard the notion. Today, after historic achievements through two world wars and a Cold War, the American public has evidenced little or no tolerance for either world leadership or the "superpower" status that history and war seemed to have bestowed.

Nor should they, either by nature or geopolitics. Why would a factory worker in Ohio, a nurse in Seattle, a farmer in Nebraska, an inner-city waitress, a housewife in Scranton, a bus driver in Alabama, a ski bum in Colorado take the slightest interest in the background issues of Islamic history that produced 9/11? By the same token, Americans were shocked by Pearl Harbor, but they were still out of work from the Great Depression. Why would an Asian island country matter in the unemployment line?

Through self-interest and geopolitics, Americans have never, not once, voted to change foreign policies. The issues are historically remote, geographically distant, and equally impossible to relate to "Main Street" and the issues that impact the voting public.

In the 1916 campaign, Woodrow Wilson won re-election with the promise "he kept us out of war." Five months later, he declared war on Germany, and both the Congress and its public endorsed the war (enthusiastically). Either way, peace or war, the public aligns its security with the President, his diplomats, and the military. During the entire Cold War period, nearly half a century, no Congress, no public, no protest movement ever seriously challenged any administration's adherence to the foreign policy of "containment," no matter where on earth it was pursued (Vietnam included). Nor was Ronald Reagan's policy of ending the Cold War through intrusive policies against the Soviet Union ever challenged by the Democrats or the public (those few who knew of it).

The best the opposition could do was to ridicule the Strategic Defense Initiative (SDI) as "Star Wars." Well into the new century, SDI was still critical in ending the Cold War (and the USSR).

After historic achievements in peace and war, the public has always, repeat, always, reverted to Washington's original advice. After World War I, the Republicans retreated into "normalcy." After World War II, the military was reduced from 16 to 1 million personnel within two years. Likewise, the public ignored the Cold War until Truman adopted his "Doctrine," and the Marshall Plan (1947), the Berlin Airlift (1948), and NATO (1949).

In 1990, President George H. W. Bush promised a "new world order" after the invasion of Iraq. Iraq was invaded, but the new order was quickly forgotten. Bush also forgot his pledge to "Read my lips: no new taxes." The electorate cared little about any "world order" but couldn't forgive Bush for new taxes.

The Cold War ended in 1991, and, the following year, the Governor of Arkansas became president on the slogan "It's the economy, stupid." Clinton's first Inaugural Address was an inspiration to renew "ourselves, our families, our communities, our country" but revealed nothing on either the Cold War or a new foreign policy. He then adopted something called "assertive multilateralism," which later was re-named by Barack Obama to "leading from behind." Neither slogan indicates the slightest interest to forge a world order based upon the political qualities of Western civilization or the American founding.

Going into the 2020 election, Americans have seemed to completely "isolate" themselves from the rest of the world. As before, foreign policy will arrive only after another attack like the 2012 murder of U.S. diplomats in Benghazi. But these are not "policies" but "incidents," derived from a history that few in the public were even aware of.

After four televised hours, in the June 2019 primary debate among the twenty Democratic candidates, the subject "foreign policy" never surfaced. Race and capitalism vs. socialism (Econ 101) dominated, while seven billion people in the other 192 countries heard nothing from us about them. Economist Robert Samuelson noticed this disparity: "The campaign's attention is focused heavily — almost exclusively — on domestic problems and programs, but the most pressing issues that await the next president will probably involve foreign policy." (*The Washington Post, July 1*).

Unlike most of the rest of the world, the American political culture has rarely had to prepare for high tension or war from a powerful neighbor. Even England, a country that practiced a "splendid isolation" from the continent, is just twenty-six miles across the channel. The United States is 3,000 miles away. In an air and space age, with instantaneous communications from hemisphere to hemisphere, this simple geopolitical fact can explain why twenty Democratic Presidential aspirants can still talk as if no one else was listening.

Kamala Harris advertised her qualifications for President because she was once "bused" to grade school ("that little girl was me"). Joe Biden once "colluded" with southern Senators on issues of the day. These are emotional and contrived arguments, called the "race card." These things also occurred in another generation and in another century. Bernie Sanders wants a socialist culture, and most of the others want free things taken from the rich, who were unanimously ruled out of the culture as if they were an "enemy within." The whole episode appeared theatrical, seemingly right out of a "Me Too" stage-play.

If these "issues" (such as they are) appear surreal, unworldly, or a bit "dipsy," there is still a silver lining: at least the candidates are not talking national security.

But, by nature and definition, foreign policy issues cannot be argued coherently by an electorate. The analogy is baseball: one does not analyze the game by what happened in the bottom of the ninth. For the general public, the issue is generic and instinctive, ie. leave us alone.

Recall the Gadsden Flag rattlesnake: "Don't tread on me."

The Second Civil War

July 2, 2019

There's an old political adage, "the job of the opposition is to oppose." Makes sense, and what would a democracy be without opposition? Kings, dictators, and military officers are not known for their patience with political dissent. But when the job of the opposition is to "remove, replace," we have an altogether different situation.

When the opposition wants to change policy, it is doing its job, win, lose, or draw. But when the opposition wants to change the government and the people in it and become, in effect, a "power broker," we have "a whole new ball game." Then they become the "enemy," not working together *for* a better place but *against* for a completely new place. Then the opposition becomes a revolutionary "movement;" in the true sense, they become "rebels," against not only the state but the political culture itself. Normally, they go into hiding, but, in a democracy, they can remain both open and announced. Here, the institution itself either encourages or allows its own extinction, whether it knows it or not. In effect, the result is suicide, not murder. In a democracy, elections are supposed to change regimes, but conspiracies, apparently, cannot wait.

Page one of *The Washington Post*, every issue, asserts "democracy dies in darkness." But who is shutting the lights?

There are two levels on which the current political climate is revolutionary. The first is a growing and widespread cultural shift to view the nation in primarily, if not only, its worst side. The spectacle of removing visible symbols of the Confederacy only highlights this historical emphasis. While the tactic can, by definition, be only symbolic the symbol is sufficient to emphasize the point. There are an estimated 1,500 Confederate monuments and memorials in the U.S. distributed over 31 states. In addition, there are countless more schools, roads, libraries, historic sites, place-names, and other manifestations of the country's most perilous moment.

Since 2015, there have been about 60 statues and monuments removed from locations in the south. Obviously, the job "to replace" or "remove" can never be finished. If only one, or even a handful, of these symbols remain, it will continue to haunt generations until there are no vestiges left, not one. This is probably impossible and, if possible, would require generations of committed "rebels" to finish. Would future generations remain committed to destroying remnants of a nineteenth century event?

The symbolic destruction of "things" also reverses the purpose of the Civil War, and the character of the country itself. "Reconstruction" began immediately after the war was over. After the surrender at Appomattox, Union troops began cheering. General Grant went out and stopped it, telling the men that "The Confederates are our countrymen now." This corresponded also with Lincoln's Second Inaugural Address, where he told the country that the need was "malice toward none, with charity for all ... to bind the nation's wounds." Todays "revisionists" know malice when they see it, with no room for charity.

Detractors against the USA never stop reminding us of slavery. Yet slavery was both a universal and historic reality, present in all or most countries and since Biblical times. Are they against the country or history? The first seven Presidents at one time owned slaves. Already, statues of George Washington are being removed from college campuses. "White supremacy" is now representative of American character, where one college promised "zero tolerance." Dissenters remember the existence of slavery and lynchings that killed over 3,000 blacks. Others remember 720,000 white soldiers, blue and grey, whose deaths ended slavery. The phrase has taken on a universal quality, to include the whole world. One U.S. college has dropped the campus "Churchill Club." Was Christ white? Is Christianity "white supremacy"?

The list of grievances knows no bounds, nor can it. The nature of all time periods, personalities, injustices, poverties, discriminations, inequalities, inequities and all sorts of behavior "oppressions" dominate popular assessments of the people and their character. "White Supremacy" condemns the Caucasian male, while the fruits of their labor (such as electricity, cars, houses) are used subconsciously, without complaint. Language is ideology, right out of Orwell. Is "supremacy" a description or an accusation (*J'Accuse*)?

Lonnie G. Bunch, the new CEO ("Secretary") of the Smithsonian, the country's revered cultural museum, has called America's history "... all about white supremacy and racism." That fairly well summarizes our new cultural "elite." Apparently, the millions who flock to get inside have not been told the news (outsiders seem to like us more than even we do).

This is a cultural "war," but it has recently been joined by a political one. The ascension of Donald J. Trump, by itself, has occasioned the second revolution against the "order." The expression "by itself" does not indicate that Trump as an individual is singularly responsible, only that his presence alone has sparked a rebellion that challenges the nature of the political system in ways unprecedented. The opposition is not content with opposition; it has been, from the start, intent on removal. That's revolution.

Space does not allow evidence, but just a casual review of both print and electronic media, even for an hour, is sufficient that what we have here is more than mere dissent. It has increasingly become a national obsession, sometimes a hysteria, against not the public policies, but the very psychological composition of the President of the United States. "Unfit" puts it mildly but is the "code-word" most often used. It's almost as though Trump is on a couch and dozens of reporters swarm in, asking probing questions of his mental stability and all personal relationships, going back to childhood. Somewhere along the line he just had to "cheat," on his taxes, wife, family, business, country ... anything. Even when the President had a physical, they were disappointed that he was OK and wanted the doctor removed.

No mistake, the President is his own worst enemy, but the "blame ratio" is seldom 100 to 0 percent. The "revolt," however, began well before the election and has only intensified. The intention is total, neutrals not invited, removal with or without cause, guilty until proven innocent. No Mueller Report, no "exoneration," no "collusions," no "meddles," no dictators, no scandals, no firings, no leaks, no nothing is enough. It goes way deep, psychological.

A single confession from a prominent commentator (anonymous) will suffice: "... once I'm completely awake, a gravitational pull takes hold and I am once more bedeviled by our preposterous president." Perhaps I am not sufficiently "political," but, when I awake, I first try to see if the bathroom is empty.

In a recent essay on an "insider" anti-Trump book, the reviewer noted that "The author is mostly interested in Trump's psychology. He is adept at documenting the president's lunacy." Precisely!

In today's America, unlike many times before, there are no great foreign or domestic issues at stake. No one is threatening war (unlike Franklin Roosevelt), no Great Depression (unlike Hoover), no great terror strike (unlike W) no recession (unlike Obama). The economy is actually great, but that is unwelcome news. Power, personality, and influence: those are what's "at stake."

But unlike the original, this war is "uncivil." As the losing candidate herself confessed, "if we are fortunate enough to win back the House and/or the Senate, that's when civility can start again."

Trump may be impeached, but it won't be over tariffs or the border.

Do Elections Shape Foreign Policies?

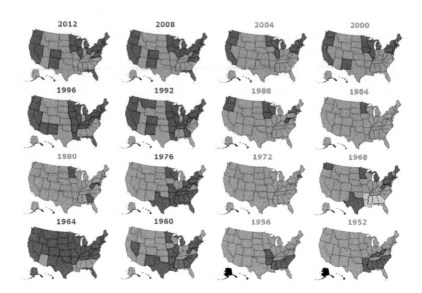

June 28, 2019

Readers may know the immediate answer to this question by thinking about their motivations in the last presidential election. Was foreign policy the determinate factor between Trump, a realtor and media personality, and Hillary Clinton, a former Senator and Secretary of State? The same may be done for other, previous contests since the end of the Cold War. Obama's foreign policy was self-described as "leading from behind," W Bush's was to wage the war on terror and invade Iraq under the slogan "nation-building," while President Clinton's was called "assertive multilateralism." Do voters remember casting their ballot on these or any related issues even remotely connected to them?

While this is decidedly "guesswork," the immediate conclusion is a decisive No Way! Transcripts/videos of the various presidential debates, however, reinforce this view. During political campaigns, foreign policies were either addressed in separate, incident-derived, and episodic adventures or ignored altogether in favor of home issues, economy, healthcare, race, gender etc., that transferred directly to votes and living conditions.

In the 2012 campaign, the death of the U.S. ambassador to Libya and three others in Benghazi created a furor against the foreign policies of President Obama and Secretary of State Clinton. Her answer as to the cause of the attack to a Senate Committee, "what difference does it make," only created more confusion for the electorate on foreign policy directions. Benghazi was not a "foreign policy" but an incident reflective of deeper and distinct issues of policy and history that could not possibly be debated openly in any political campaign. The Ambassador's father himself probably reflected the irritation of the public when he asked the candidates to cease "politicizing" his son's death. But that, precisely, is the problem: they are "politicians," and politicians "politicize."

Which brings up a larger issue: what, if any, quality does a democracy have in the process of any country's foreign policies? Is the subject itself even amenable to any form of intelligent discussion to an electorate several times removed from issues that were created centuries ago and reside thousands of miles from Main Street USA?

Perhaps Ronald Reagan, who created a historic and decisive foreign policy, knew this all along when he campaigned on a slogan close to home: are you "better off" than you were before?

The classic "model" in history has always reflected the European style of "Cabinet diplomacy," wherein the national leadership steers the "ship of state" through the dangerous waters of international intrigue and deception. The public's role, by definition, was to accept and support the security of the state and to serve obediently in war should this be threatened. Who wants, for example, to defend the complexities of the "balance of power" to a public only concerned with neighborhood safety and job security?

In practice, is this model the one, by necessity, that has to be followed by democracies, as it was by the old regimes of continental Europe? What does American history reveal?

Our first, and most lasting, foreign policy came in George Washington's Farewell Address (1796) and urged a benevolent abstention from the intrigues of Europe until the U.S. could be powerful enough to participate in world affairs. This was entirely the brainchild of Washington himself and his Secretary of the Treasury, Alexander Hamilton. This subsequently turned into "isolationism" and expansionist "Manifest Destiny" but served as the near-sacred epistle of U.S. foreign policy until world events forced an abandonment after the

Second World War. During this long expanse of time, foreign policy was rarely invoked as an explanation or defense of either incumbency or election to the presidency. When it was, the public invariably supported the particular policies then in-force. Never, ever, was the public an engineer of change. When change occurred, it was subsequently endorsed by the electorate, but only after the fact.

The twentieth century was the most relevant period to judge this question, beginning with the first election, 1900. In this campaign, the public had a chance to endorse or repudiate the McKinley Administration's overseas expansion after the Spanish-American War.

McKinley's overwhelming victory against Democrat William Jennings Bryan and the "Anti-imperialist League" inaugurated the country's first major leap into both the new century and American global expansionism. The next test came during World War I when Woodrow Wilson's 1916 campaign appeal "he kept us out of war" was heartily endorsed. Five months later, we were at war with Germany with both Houses of Congress fully behind Wilson. So much for the election. In the 1920s, the Republicans' return to "normalcy" was supported throughout, as was Franklin D. Roosevelt, both during the Great Depression and World War II.

During the long Cold War, neither isolationists like Robert Taft nor dissenters such as Henry Wallace or Adlai Stevenson were able to challenge the dominant policy of "containment," despite the Republicans' 1952 platform against it. Containment continued through the 1950s, '60s and '70s, while the Nixon Administration's "détente" policy, led by Secretary of State Kissinger, was tacitly supported despite conservative-Republican dissent. The era of anti-war protest during the Vietnam War challenged the political culture but failed to prevent each and every Congress (until 1972) to support the billions of public expenditures necessary to wage the war. Nor was a major Vietnam era political protester able to capture either party's nomination, to the bitter end.

Ronald Reagan promised to increase defense spending in the 1980 campaign against President Carter, but not a word was said on the historic foreign policies that he used later to undermine the Soviet Union. Nor was any of this challenged by his 1984 opponent, Walter Mondale, who went down to a landslide defeat. In 1992, Arkansas Governor Bill Clinton expressed little or no foreign policy and campaigned that "it's the economy, stupid." He won twice on something like this, while surviving removal over sex with an intern.

Fast forward to two years ago: foreign policy was left in disarray, without direction or interest. The loser called the winner's supporters "deplorables," while the winner rallied his support under the cry "lock her up."

Conclusion: the role of the public in foreign policy issues has been little more than a "rubber stamp," while most important changes have been conducted in private. The European "model," apparently, applies to democracies as well. That, by definition, happens to be the "nature of the beast."

Related conclusion: American political discourse, the administration, the Congress, the media, and the public seem to have lost both the interest and the ambition to take national security and foreign policy seriously. Almost all concerns are self-serving, depending on what race, gender, class, age, party, or income one has.

P.S. June 28, 2019. The Democrats just finished four hours of debates with twenty candidates. Not a word on foreign policy. After all this, the greatest attention was on former Vice President Biden's role with southern Senators back in the 1970s.

For a "superpower," the electorate seems completely disinterested with anything outside its two coasts (until there's an attack).

The Russians Are Coming,
The Russians Are Coming

June 19, 2019

The classic comedy film (1966), of the same name, depicts the adventures of a Russian crew whose submarine goes aground off a New England beach. While essentially a theatrical farce, the movie tried to bring out some of the absurdities and misunderstandings between the two sides at the height of the Cold War. In a strange twist of irony, the film title could just as well be employed today to describe the near-hysteria that has consumed the nation over Russian "meddling" in the 2016 election. Although the long-awaited Mueller Report has exonerated any form of "collusion" between the two sides, the lingering menace of Russian threats to American democracy has continued to remain the chief focus of the anti-Trump opposition. Their ongoing vendetta has only escalated while Russia remains targeted as the single most critical threat to the U.S. political culture.

Still, at the same time, substantive evidence of exactly what, where, and when Russia changed the election results have yet to be disclosed to the public. Perhaps Hillary Clinton herself came closest when she assessed her loss in Florida to Russia: "...the Russians were in the county electoral system of every county in Florida." Unfortunately, being "In the ... system" is not exactly the epitome of empirical evidence, but, along with the term "hacking," it is probably the best we can get from the available evidence. If there's an enemy at the door, all within should know it.

Years ago, in the Watergate scandal, Senator Howard Baker issued a question that famously summarized the public's frustration with the Watergate scandal: "What did the President know, and when did he know it?" In a similar vein, we may be excused if we ask the following: "What did the Russians do, and where and when did it occur?" That means, for example, what did they do in Orlando, when, and how did they affect Florida's vote? Multiply that evidence with other precincts throughout Ohio, Wisconsin, Pennsylvania, Michigan, etc., and we just might begin to appreciate the accusation that has kept this country on hold for over two years. Instead, we get words that remain undefined and ambiguous, "meddle," "collusion," etc. The first should mean "involvement," the second, technically, means "price fixing" in business. Neither satisfies even the slightest curiosity, much less threatens a country with centuries of democratic political life.

In the current volatile political histrionics, both President Donald Trump (USA) and Vladimir Putin (Russia) are widely accused as being out to destroy the American democratic "experiment." Some even accuse both of "collusion" toward that exact end. Trump is endlessly accused of favoring Putin over all other tyrants for some business or ideological motivation. Again, the proper accusation remains with the word "innuendo," meaning "a veiled or equivocal reflection on character or reputation." In a "nation of laws" there seems to be a plethora of loose and reckless talk strewn about, completely out of character in a legalistic society. Does the public buy this?

The United States has survived and prospered through dark periods of turbulence, warfare, and political "meddling" and has come out intact and even stronger each time. What can Putin's Russia, twelve thousand miles away, do that Jefferson Davis, Robert E. Lee, and the entire Confederate Army could not do in a trial of four years and over 700,000 dead soldiers (with 32 million people)? The greatest armed forces and the greatest world wars in human history left the U.S. not only stronger and more prosperous than before but also bestowed the "superpower" status on a reluctant nation. The Great Depression could have easily toppled the government, yet the aftermath saw the U.S. with the "highest standard of living" in human history (as highway signs of the

1940s proudly testified). The U.S. expended 58,000 lives in Vietnam, years of protest, and a near-revolution atmosphere, yet came home empty and failed. A few years later, the Soviet Union was gone, the Cold War over, and the country became the "sole remaining" superpower.

The Russian (or Soviet) political behavior over time does not need new evidence to render an understanding. There is no mincing words; it's there for all to see: the Bolshevik revolution, the massacre of millions at home, the purge trials, the alliance with Hitler's Germany, the Iron Curtain, espionage all over the world, Whitaker Chamber's *Witness* and the "Fifth Column" inside the U.S., thousands of nuclear weapons, missiles, nuclear submarines, the Cuban Missile Crisis (where the two nearly went to war), U2 flights over the USSR, the Brezhnev Doctrine (against eastern Europe), Solzhenitsyn and the Gulag. Finally, on the brighter side, we had Gorbachev, Glasnost, and Boris Yeltsin. Today, there is Putin, his throw-back to history, KGB background, the invasion of Ukraine, and miscellaneous threats and "meddling" in the Middle East. Now, of all places, Venezuela! In these cases, there is no confusion about "meddling." The Russians are there, for all to see.

Now they are held accountable for Trump and the 2016 election (accused). In the scenario of threats to existential United States, where does Russian interference (alleged) in the American democracy rate? Number one, two, four, ten? Where is it against China, terrorism, nuclear proliferation, illegal immigration, civic divisions, "Balkanization," the trillion-dollar debt (to mention a few)? How does it compare to Soviet espionage over time and against the entire Capitalist world? How does it compare to espionage by all other countries, including the U.S., Israel, Britain, China, and most of the rest of the world, starting with ancient Greece?

Yet if evidence on Russian interference is being withheld from the public, who is threatening democracy: Russian officials or American?

Until and unless we get intelligence on both the capabilities and intentions of the Russian state, we shall forever remain in "the dark." And, according to one source, isn't that where "democracy dies"?

Geopolitics in an Aerospace Age

June 19, 2019

To simplify, analysis can be either "traditional" or "progressive." The first views the past to reach the future, the second views the past as an impediment for the future. Alone, both are hazardous for serious analysis. Together, they both are needed for the same. There is an old expression, "Keep your eyes on the horizon, your feet on the ground."

As an analytical concept, Geopolitics should follow this rule. Yet, typically, there are approaches on both sides that continue to see the subject in only one dimension. The first views the subject as a hard and fast, semi-deterministic guide to state policy. At first glance, this is understandable. Switzerland will probably never have a navy. Ecuador will probably never be a great power. The logic and constraints of nature alone has permanently decided the issue.

But geopolitics is not deterministic. Other factors interrupt. The American continent and South America are both vast territories, rich in resources, people, and land. Yet, one is a world "superpower;" the other is not. Why? Because one united itself, the other divided itself, basically. In 1917, Russia was captured by a tiny group of fanatics, and for the rest of the century challenged the legitimacy of the rest of the world. In 1962, it put missiles into Cuba, making that tiny place a geopolitical threat to nuclear peace. Today, both Cuba and Russia are more "traditional," but Russia's alleged "meddling" in U.S. political campaigns goes far beyond its traditional and geopolitical foreign policy interests (Which brings up the question: is Vladimir Putin a "Commissar" or a "Czar"?)

For most of its history, American foreign policy was "isolationist." Since World War II, it has been involved everywhere, with something like 400 military "bases" worldwide. Why? The land stayed the same — what changed? The answer: circumstances, politics, ideologies, personalities, technology, sociology and other factors, both substantive and abstract. The geography, as always, stayed the same.

Now, in an "aerospace" age, nothing seems the same. This is a field-day for "progressives." They even have a new word for human history, "Anthropocene," roughly defining humanity's interactions with the earth. Generally speaking, Anthropocene asserts that, since the Industrial Revolution, mankind has been systematically destroying its geographic and human environment. Geographically, pollution and gaseous emissions threaten climatic life, while, sociologically, "racism," "sexism," "nationalism" and "imperialism" are simultaneously destroying human lives (progressives favor totalities, "isms"). The result concludes that the earth's problems rise far above tradition and require new and adventurous solutions. If not, life is doomed.

Beyond these scenarios, the global Communications Revolution, like the previous industrial one, have rendered any reference to tradition not only obsolete, but dangerous. If the earth is melting and people can communicate instantly while global institutions make boundaries ancient, why worry about rivers, borders or mountains? "Protect the environment" and "open borders" are communal slogans.

These dominant notions associate geopolitics with history. It reminds critics of railroads, of cavalry charges, of armies in uniform, the draft, sea battles, men in top-hats making colorful appeals to national virtue, territorial disputes, and all other vestiges of a by-gone age.

Inside this culture reside "enemies." The main targets, to use a "feminist" cliché, are "dead white males." The expression "white supremacy" has become both a global accusation and assertion for society's ills. The variety of "isms" that have dominated current cultural trends, needless to say, leave little room for geopolitics. It has, in this view, become, an intellectual relic, a "dinosaur."

For its part, historic geopolitical thought lived by strictly deterministic, and singular, rules. It was tied to the nation, control of the earth and water, and, later, the air. Both the famous syllogisms by pioneers such as Halford Mackinder and Nicholas J. Spykman tried to demonstrate that location, "Heartland," "Rimlands," "World Island," "pivot" state, and other territorial possessions determined life. Expressions such as "commands the world," "controls the destinies," etc. gave national strategies an "inevitable" scenario. Classic was President Eisenhower's theory (1954) that if Vietnam fell, other countries would surely follow, "like a row of dominos." Vietnam fell in 1975, nothing since.

Summarily, airpower advocates, like Guilio Douhet of Italy, argued that the airplane was the ultimate weapon against which there was no defense. British Prime Minister Stanley Baldwin used this idea in support of disarmament and appeasement in the 1930s, stating in one speech that "the bomber will always get through." In Vietnam, U.S. airpower exceeded the bombing tonnage from all air forces in World War II, but the jungle stayed impenetrable.

Mere location and size hold no promises. Geopolitics is geography with strategy. Britain is a stony island next to a continent, but once governed one-fifth of the world. China is a huge mainland, but suffered invasion and occupation throughout its history. Like Britain, Japan is an island, but once controlled the western Pacific and invaded China on multiple occasions. Today, Japan is peaceful and prosperous. France built the Maginot Line in the 1930s to stop the Germany army. The *Wehrmacht* went around it, and the *Luftwaffe* went above it. Nazi Germany had the greatest military forces in world history but couldn't cross 26 miles of water to invade England. The U.S. crossed 3,000 miles of ocean and occupied Germany. Canada, Brazil, and Australia are continents the size of the U.S. None has ever been a world power and in all likelihood never will.

In today's time period, both tradition and future can coexist. Since the last election, the border with Mexico has been (rightly or not) the chief security preoccupation of the American people. This is both natural and arbitrary. Natural since immigration is, and always has been, a security issue. Arbitrary since a "MAGA" is in office. Yet, even if an "open border" administration won, the same issue could very well return, meaning that it was postponed, not eliminated.

Still, a border is a geopolitical problem, even within a space age. In the last analysis, how do we reconcile geopolitics with the aerospace age?

Fact: At any given time, there are about 5,000 aircraft in the skies.

Answer: At any given time, each one will have to land.

Is China a Permanent Enemy?

June 16, 2019

If there is any word that should be removed from the world politics vocabulary, it is "permanent." The subject, i.e. foreign policy, international politics, has a history that almost makes a mockery of the adjective and testifies to a near-total lack of anything durable within its midst. The only thing, tragically, that seems to endure is the universal rivalry, enmity, and, ultimately, war that has existed within and between the separate units. Be they city-states, empires, or nation-states, they have invariably taken up the "sword" to resolve their differences in six millennia of history.

Since warfare is seemingly endemic to human nature, it has accompanied mankind throughout time regardless of the political environment or "system" involved. There is hardly a society on earth that has not undergone, in one manner or another, some form of "civil" or internal conflict. The greatest war in American history still remains the Civil War, despite U.S. involvement across the globe from the beginning. Total American casualties of both world wars, Korea, Vietnam, and the current War on Terror still would not surpass the figures of the Civil War. That, even more astonishing, in a population then of only 32 million.

Although the exact number of actual military conflicts in recorded history is nearly impossible to count, a general figure would number in a minimum of tens of thousands, a maximum of hundreds of thousands. The most useful estimate has recorded that approximately 90 to 95 percent of human societies have engaged in war at one time or another, many of them in endless and chronic war with bordering neighbors. As a single case, note that French armies crossed into Germanic regions on no less than thirty occasions long before the Prussian invasion of 1870.

The history of diplomatic relations shows a remarkably similar pattern, i.e. inconsistency, unpredictability. The U.S. fought two of history's greatest wars against Germany in the last century, but, after the second, Germany became the most important and reliable U.S. ally in continental Europe. Shortly after the atom bomb ended the war with Japan, that country became the same in Asia (both still are).

The first two major American wars were against Great Britain and they aided the Confederacy in the Civil War. Yet, for over a century the "Anglo-American" relationship has become "special" and has defined the nature of the twentieth century from beginning to end. After a near-quarter century of conflict/war against North Vietnam, the U.S. has now recognized the unified country and has normal and stable relations with them (so much for the "domino" theory).

An examination of US-China relations would reveal the same conflicting scenario. At the beginning, the U.S. was the only country on earth to support China when it was occupied by a host of foreigners from both Europe and Asia. In 1899, Secretary of State John Hay (who was Lincoln's personal aide) sent the so-called "Open Door" notes advocating that the others respect China's territorial integrity and sovereignty. From that point forward, the U.S. continued to defend the Chinese cause which, on reflection, became the chief issue separating the U.S. with imperial Japan. Pearl Harbor and the Pacific war was the result while the U.S. continued to support the Chinese Nationalist government, first against Japan and then against Mao Zedong and the Communists.

The Communist victory over the Nationalists in 1949 saw a reversal of policies between China and the U.S. Washington supported Chiang Kai-shek's government on Taiwan while the Communist mainland joined the Soviet Union and become an Asian Cold War enemy.

This went on during the early Cold War, and the two became bitter opponents, with the U.S. assuming that Beijing was firmly in line with Moscow in a common global and ideological front. But this was not the case at all, and, by the 1960s, it became apparent that China and the Soviets harbored profound historic, ideological, and strategic differences and that the "China-Soviet split" opened up still more opportunities for creative statecraft.

In 1972, the Nixon Administration, led by Secretary of State Henry Kissinger, made a series of overtures to China that ultimately led to the "Shanghai Communique" and an open diplomatic rupture between the two Communist giants. Into that breach was a new and positive American presence in Asia, particularly after the American withdrawal from Vietnam in 1975. Another "about face" began.

Eventually the U.S. recognized the mainland (1978), and Taiwan was downgraded to "representative" status. The Shanghai Communique forbade any one country to "seek hegemony in the Asian-Pacific region," thus marking an informal *rapprochement* between Beijing and Washington. The USSR, in the meantime, was left out of the picture, and began the eventual process leading to its own dissolution (1991).

There has been no major Asian war since while the U.S.-China relationship has been in flux. Taiwan's status remains ambiguous, as both countries formally recognized that Taiwan is technically part of "One China," while the U.S. continues to support the autonomy of the Taipei government. The Taiwan Strait remains one of the world's most dangerous "flashpoints," while China's assertive behavior in claiming the South China Sea still presents a volatile region for open war. But control of adjacent sea lanes has rarely been occasion for world war between great powers.

Trade has been the greatest obstacle to "normalcy" with China in the Trump Administration, but the ratio of imports to exports, as with sea lanes, is usually negotiable.

If there is one area of the world in which relationships between political units continue to fester, it is in East Asia. Practically every critical issue remains in a continuous but precarious flow of momentum. The past record gives profound testimony both to the dangers and opportunities that present themselves to the great powers. One can emphasize one or the other, but the decision to take advantage of opportunities offers the best hope that resolution of issues can be peacefully arranged.

Overall, East Asian strategic history demonstrates the temporal and fleeting nature of world politics. This, however, should encourage, rather than restrain, twenty-first century leaders to seek solutions that will avoid war and create stability. For American foreign policy, the opportunities are there for the taking, as before.

There's a difference between "permanent" and "final." The first can mean "perpetual," while the second has but one meaning, "the end." With the first, there is always hope, with the second there is none.

The Best Foreign Policy Presidents

June 9, 2019

Normally, U.S. presidents are ranked overall, without qualification. To date, there has (seemingly) been no ranking of "domestic" presidents, nor "commanders-in chief," nor best "environmental," etc. Yet "foreign policy" can be justified as vital to national life and, indeed, higher than any domestic issue that supports life.

National Security is life itself and rises above any and all parochial or self-centered domestic issues that may occupy national attention. "Black lives matter," "#MeToo" are important for their own constituents, but all of them require the capacity to advance their causes without outside interference. Without security from the beginning, there would not even be a social/political culture able to recognize opportunities for gains within. When security competes with society, invariably the first wins, without question. A country at war or threatened by it has little interest in "equality" back home.

Throughout history, most nations lived side-by-side, a situation that required the "national security state," a reliable military and a masculine social order where war was always just around the bend. By contrast, the U.S. grew up thousands of miles from this order and rarely (if ever) felt these demands. Democracy grew and flourished, and most historical attention focused on home issues (voting, labor, business, health, crime, economy, immigration, ethnic/racial movements, and equalities of all kinds). Even America's greatest and most tragic war was a domestic problem ("civil").

Within this context the ranking of "foreign policy," presidents becomes severely limited. The geopolitical realities of North America were diametrically opposite than those that confronted, say, Prussia under Bismarck, or Russia under the Czars, or France before (and after) World War I. Throughout history, most national leaders would have been ranked almost exclusively on how they advanced state security. To them, that's all that mattered.

Ranking of U.S. "foreign policy" presidents is constrained by these realities. Most U.S. national security problems have originated outside, where the U.S. reacted to circumstances not (mostly) of their doing. German U boats, Pearl Harbor, Hitler, the Cold War, the Korean War, Vietnam, 9/11, etc. all were either arbitrary or imposed from without, which makes "foreign policy presidents" an accident of history. Most American presidents took the oath of office expecting a country to run, not a war. To this day, the American political culture still defines "war" as an aberration, not consistent with political life. ("War is a continuation of politics by other means" comes from Carl von Clausewitz, not Thomas Jefferson).

What follows is more a "listing" than a "ranking." Since most presidents in history did not even have a "foreign" policy, the list is considerably reduced. While most overall rankings list Washington, Lincoln as 1-2, 2¬ 1, we will eliminate Lincoln right away. At one Cabinet meeting, some members wanted to declare war against Britain for supporting the Confederacy. Lincoln (allegedly) replied, "Gentlemen please, one war at a time." That was probably his entire foreign policy but, considering, it was quite timely and, perhaps, even historic.

Continental expansion will not be considered as "foreign" since Manifest Destiny was decidedly domestic. Otherwise, Jefferson and Polk, who were responsible for most expansion, would be the only ones on the list.

The list herein is not "analysis" *per se* but more critical reflection, subjective, based upon personality and politics. Expect error; response is welcome, actually encouraged. In chronological order:

Washington: Farewell Address (1796) may be the most important foreign policy statement in U.S. history, pledged neutrality and allowed for growth and was not actually abandoned until 1947 (with exceptions), which makes it a 150-year long foreign policy;

Madison: War of 1812 began American nationalism;

Monroe: "Doctrine" defined entire Western Hemisphere, invoked and expanded time and again, abrogated by Secretary of State John Kerry in 2013, making it 190 years old;

McKinley: began naval expansion into Caribbean and Philippines. (Qualification: McKinley was a figurehead, leaders were John Hay, Henry Cabot Lodge, Theodore Roosevelt, Albert Beveridge, Alfred Thayer Mahan, etc.);

Theodore Roosevelt: Panama Canal, Portsmouth Treaty (Japan, Russia), Great White Fleet, first serious imperial moves, prelude to "superpower" and modern nationalism;

Taft: business, "Dollar Diplomacy";

Wilson: American ideology as cornerstone of global identity, "Wilsonianism," "nation-building," father of international organizations, globalization, theory of the "democratic peace";

Republicans, 1920s: "normalcy," isolationism; "arms control" treaties (none of these lasted);

Franklin D. Roosevelt: Good Neighbor Policy, wartime diplomacy, height of "special relationship" with Britain, United Nations, end of isolationism, Yalta, atomic bomb;

Truman: Cold War alliances, Marshall Plan, NATO, Korean War, "New World Order";

Eisenhower: containment, stability, "domino theory";

Kennedy: Cuban Missile Crisis, oratory (Inauguration speech);

Nixon: "Vietnamization," Shanghai Communique (add Kissinger);

Reagan: peaceful end of Cold War, relaxation (summits with Gorbachev), "Iran-Contra";

Since Reagan, the U.S. has turned decidedly inward, taking Ambassador Jeanne Kirkpatrick's advice to be a "normal country in normal times." Clinton's foreign policy of "assertive multilateralism" and Obama's "leading from behind" were exactly what they seemed, or as Obama once defined foreign policy as "sometimes you hit home runs, sometimes you hit singles." Secretary of State Hillary's foreign policy memoir *Hard Choices* is a travelogue.

For what it's worth, here is a "ranking" in order, of all the foreign policy presidents who deserve any recognition at all. Criteria is: innovation, creativity, longevity, security.

Washington (surprise!), Monroe, Franklin D. Roosevelt, Wilson, Truman, Reagan, Theodore Roosevelt. Aside from the first, the others may be shuffled back and forth in ranking. Reagan and Truman, for example, are reversible: one began U.S. policy toward the Soviet Union, the other ended it (and the Soviet Union).

But at least all these men had one thing in common.

What was it?

The Most Dangerous Moment in History:

A Personal Account of the Cuban Missile Crisis

U.S. IMPOSES ARMS BLOCKADE ON CUBA ON FINDING OFFENSIVE-MISSILE SITES; KENNEDY READY FOR SOVIET SHOWDOWN

June 3, 2019

It was October 22, 1962, and President Kennedy would address the nation that night at 7 (EST). I was a new grad student at Penn and had class starting then. There were about 50 of us, seniors and first-year grads, and the class was "International Relations," taught by Robert Strausz-Hupe and James E. Dougherty. Both had co-authored (with others) *Protracted Conflict* (1959), a penetrating analysis of Soviet foreign policies (and the reason I was at Penn).

Strausz-Hupe was born in Vienna, founder of the Foreign Policy Research Institute (FPRI, 1955), and an author of classic texts on geopolitics who would become U.S. ambassador to five posts, including NATO and Turkey (1981-89). I attended his funeral in Philadelphia (2002). Dougherty (d. 2012) was at the FPRI and taught Political Philosophy for over a half-century at nearby St. Joseph's (where my daughter Lauren went). Dougherty, with Robert Pfaltzgraff, then a Penn Professor (later at The Fletcher School at Tufts University) co-authored *Contending Theories of International Relations*, a text still used by Dr. Lenczowski here at IWP.

During the day, there was great speculation on what Kennedy would address. Many thought that it was on U.S. Steel, where he had had some difficulties. At 7 promptly, Strausz-Hupe placed the small black and white TV on his desk, and we all sat and waited. The President began. "This government, as promised, has maintained the closest surveillance of the Soviet military build-up on the island of Cuba..." Most of us nearly fell out of our chairs. What Cuba, what "promise," what "buildup"? He then went on to describe in detail just what Premier Nikita Khrushchev had been doing since August. Unbeknownst but to a handful of Soviet and American officials, he had been slowly shipping medium and short-range ballistic missiles (1000 – 4000 miles range) into the island, that the Soviets had co-opted since Castro came to power in 1959. Cuba was, in effect, now a land-based Soviet "aircraft carrier," 90 miles from Miami. These sites, nine plus four air bases identified by U-2 (not the band) flight photos, could hit northern South America, Chicago, New York, and, of course, Washington itself.

Rationales for the next several days were on everybody's mind. What was Khrushchev trying to do? Destroy the U.S.? Use Cuba as a bargain to pressure NATO out of Germany? Since the Soviets were far behind in nuclear deployments, was he trying to avoid the northern defensive shields that we had in Canada and Greenland? Or was he just trying to strengthen his position at home?

Speculation was rampant. Normally we went to Smokey Joe's to meet girls; now all beer-talk was on the "crisis." Although no one knew it, "back-channel" diplomacy, especially by JFK's brother Robert, was working feverishly to avoid Armageddon. Cables went back and forth between Kennedy and Khrushchev, who was beginning to feel trapped and threatened by the possibility of an invasion of the island. The U.S. now had a naval blockade (called a "quarantine") around Cuba, and all shipping was searched for missile paraphernalia.

As tension gripped the nation, the crisis mounted, day-by-day. Kennedy met regularly with his "Executive Committee" (Ex-Com), divided on either side of the table. One side was led by General Curtis Le May, he of World War II fame for the bombings of Germany and Japan. They wanted an invasion, once and for all. On the other was UN Ambassador Adlai Stevenson, who lost twice to IKE. They wanted negotiations, what else? At one point, CIA Deputy Director Ray Cline, a friend of Kennedy's from Harvard, walked in. He asked, "Mr. President, where should I sit, with the hawks or the doves?" — thus defining the two sides of the Cold War from that point on. (Ray was father-in-law to IWP Professor Roger Fontaine. I attended Ray's memorial service at Murphy's Funeral Home, Falls Church, 19 March 1996. When I got home, the phone was ringing. My own father had died that hour.

The naval blockade and further U-2 flights demonstrated just how serious the crisis was. One flight alone brought back nearly 1,000 photos of various stages of deployments. Soon, the whole island would be ready for action; America was, for the first time in history, literally "under the gun."

In his speech, Kennedy warned the Soviets that any missile attack from Cuba against "any nation in the Western Hemisphere" would be met by a "full retaliatory response upon the Soviet Union." Nuclear war was now a reality.

Secretary of State Dean Rusk later described the final stage when Soviet ships carrying missiles continued closer to Cuba. As the nation watched on TV, the ships kept moving, then they stopped *en route*. The U.S. blockade was just ahead — what would they do? Suddenly, they made "a U," and headed back home. The crisis was over! As Rusk described it later, "we were eyeball to eyeball, then someone blinked" (I played rugby for several years with his son, David, who later served as Mayor of Albuquerque).

The crisis ended in late October. The U.S. promised not to invade and removed missiles from Turkey and Italy (which was overdue anyway), and Khrushchev was ousted two years later. He retired to a *dacha* in the suburbs while his son Sergei became a professor at Brown (quite liberal I hear).

Was this the "most dangerous moment" in history or is this just overkill? Speaking of "overkill," the nuclear weapons of 1962 were approximately 100 times more powerful than the ones dropped on Japan in 1945. Harvard Professor Graham Allison, who co-authored *Essence of Decision* on the crisis, speculated that over 200 million Soviet and American citizens would have died within minutes from any nuclear exchange. Had any exchange escalated either to Europe or Asia, figures go as high as one-third of humanity. An invasion scheduled for the third week was quickly cancelled.

Relieved, we began meeting girls again at Smokey's.

Did the Moon Landing Have Meaning?

May 27, 2019

On July 20, 1969, Astronaut Neil Armstrong left Apollo 11, stepped on the surface of the moon, and told the world that he was making history. His first step, he declared, was "one small step for a man, one giant leap for mankind." But what was the "giant" leap? Was the moon landing a singular event without implication or consequence, or was it a decisive moment in the evolution of "mankind" itself?

Many pundits judge the American Revolution of 1776 as having a meaning that is "too soon to tell." Translated into history, it bestows even greater significance to the event than its most enthusiastic admirers could know. A "timeless" occurrence, like the Crucifixion, has consequences that go far beyond the capacity of mortal man to digest. Events like that, few in history, take perhaps an eternity to fulfill, if that.

Can the moon landing be in that category? Some say that the fact that it hasn't been repeated nor expanded since 1972 (there were five more landings/returns since the first) demonstrates that it is of little consequence. Interesting. How many Declarations of Independence have we had? How many Civil Wars? How many Pearl Harbors? How many 9/11's?

Conversely, the singularity of an event, rather than endless repetition, may well define both its uniqueness and its significance.

A few say that the first landing never occurred, that it was an early example of "fake news." The only plausible explanation for such a deception is technological impossibility. Thus, it was beyond science to accomplish. The hundreds of rocket launches, returns, orbiting vehicles, satellites, GPS systems in outer space, both before and since, makes this explanation implausible if not impossible. Why hide something you already can do? It's equivalent to denying the "Space Age" itself. In any case, the conversation itself is probably irrelevant, since the event is embedded in recorded history.

Yet, there was ample notice that the Space Age was coming. Prior to 1969, both the Soviet Union and the U.S. had sent a number of unmanned "soft" landings on the moon: the Soviets had four, the U.S. eight. Those were the successes; both had a total of 39 crashed or malfunctioned failures. Since then, there has been a total of 325 global manned space flights launched, with three failures, most famously the Challenger. The Space Shuttle alone has made 135 flights, 198,000 man-hours, 29,000 orbits, and 1,300 man-days.

But July 20, 1969 remains enduring. The picture of American astronauts planting the stars and stripes on the surface of the moon fits in as one of the most decisive and profound images in the annals of mankind — something that every American school-child should have implanted in his or her memory. What is comparable: the signing of the Declaration of Independence, the "rockets' red glare" over Baltimore Harbor, the dead at Gettysburg, Lindbergh landing in Paris, the USS Arizona at Pearl Harbor, John Kennedy Jr. saluting his father's coffin, the collapse of the World Trade Center?

Regardless of time and circumstance, an event is measured by its impact upon its own generation and its legacy. The context of the moon landing and its impact on the world, especially in 1969, is the only meaningful standard with which to judge the event. There was no domestic reason, political, cultural, or economic, for the U.S. to attempt a successful landing on the moon at that time. It was conceived by a Democratic administration, executed in a Republican one, and took place in the middle of a protracted and frustrating insurgency war 12,000 miles from home. Landing on the moon could not help the U.S. in Vietnam, nor could it save Richard Nixon's doomed presidency.

President Kennedy made the purpose of the moon landing clear from the very start. In his Inaugural Address, he called upon Americans to reach high: "...let us explore the stars, conquer the deserts, eradicate disease, tap the ocean depths." The first of these missions was the moon. Just months into his administration, he told Congress that the top priority was, "...before this decade was out of landing a man on the moon and returning him safely to the earth." The following year, at Rice University in Houston, he told the world why. Summoning challenges imbedded in the pioneer spirit, he repeated three consecutive times the phrase, "we choose to go to the moon." Why? Because the challenge of outer space is "...one that we are willing to accept, one we are unwilling to postpone and one which we intend to win." Invoking history and nature, he rhetorically asked, "...why climb the highest mountain, why thirty-five years ago fly the Atlantic?"

At the time, the U.S. was behind the Soviet Union in space technology. The memory of the first space satellite, Sputnik, in 1957 circling the earth for all to see was still fresh in memory. The Soviet Union was also the first to plant a man-made object on the moon, September, 1959. The alleged "missile gap" that haunted the 1960 election was also a memory, as was the first man in space, cosmonaut Yuri Gagarin on April 12, 1961. If the Cold War was a war for the world, the "space race" was nothing less. And the U.S. was losing.

Yet the first moon landing had significance that defined the end of the Cold War. Kennedy never lived to see his greatest achievement, and the Cold War would end several years later. It is in this context that the "space race" should be judged. The Cold War was won, as they say, "without a shot being fired." But the "shot" to the moon played a significant, and peaceful, role in that historic endeavor. Like the Strategic Defense Initiative (SDI), a laboratory event rather than a "battle," the perception of ultimate failure that haunted the Soviet Union played the single most critical role in its eventual demise. This confession comes from the testimony of former Soviet officials, including Mikhail Gorbachev himself.

As the Soviets gradually lost ground in the space race, they had good reason to provoke conspirator theories. As a Pravda journalist once expressed it, "Secrecy was necessary so that no one would overtake us. But later, when they did overtake us, we had to maintain secrecy so that no one knew that we had been overtaken."

Today, when the Cold War is but a memory, outer space is still there while America debates the Mexican border. Last January, China landed its first spacecraft on the moon. Last year, President Trump announced plans for a new "Space Force." As we proceed into the new century, how will the picture of July 20, 1969 shape America's future on earth? Where is another JFK?

Why Do Americans Refuse History?

May 25, 2019

As a start, we need to understand the verb "refuse." Why not "ignore," "deny," or "hate"? On the other side of the issue, why not "embrace," "accept," or "heed"?

There are two opposite and colloquial definitions of history that serve to polarize the use we may make of the topic. First is the expression from Jorge Santayana, Spanish philosopher, who wrote: "those who do not remember the past are condemned to repeat it." The other comes from Henry Ford, who thought that "history is bunk." Synonyms for "bunk" are absurd, silly, inane. Ford, characteristically, was American.

There are at least two close definitions of "refuse" that might describe the American intellectual culture: "ahistorical" and "anti-historical." The first is indifference; the second is hostility. The first presupposes an innocent, casual dismissal, the second a deliberate, premeditated dismissal, but both "dismiss" the subject. Dismiss is a synonym of refuse.

The second meaning is more insidious, insofar as it implies a deliberate manipulation of the subject for personal advancement. In a colloquial definition, it is called "cherry picking," i.e., a selected use of evidence to endorse one's opinions. Such a preference is truly "anti," thus intellectually dishonest. Unfortunately, it happens also to be the dominant strain of American "Studies" as they have advanced in the academy. It is also dangerous, since it is a convenient and useful tool to undermine and/ or destroy the value of the country. But if that is exactly the purpose, substitute "dangerous" with "necessary" (if that is one's intention).

One can emphasize "faults" if the intention is to improve. But the intention becomes "dangerous" if it means to "replace" or "destroy." Two presidential slogans represent the difference. Trump wants to "Make America Great Again," which depends upon history. Obama declared that he wanted "Change We Can Believe In," which depends upon the future. One relies on the past and wants to renew it. The other, in effect, "refuses" history and wants to change the present for the future. That's the difference between "traditional" and "progressive."

From a larger perspective, that defines the differences between the two political parties, or, as it once was called "armed camps" (metaphorically). If the differences were just philosophical, the argument would be "civil," as some would cast it. The argument, however, is not philosophical when it enters the political arena, when it involves daily life, and when emotion enters. Then, it becomes hostile and, indeed, polemical.

And that's exactly where we are right now.

In the hands of politicians, argument becomes accusation, and life itself seems to depend upon the latest speech or conversation. There is a great deal of exaggeration also, but it appears needed to prevail. Perhaps that's why politics is called an "arena," or a "blood sport."

To demonstrate the manner in which the history/futuristic debate is cast in apoplectic terms, one need only to pick up a newspaper. In a single column in a recent *New York Times*, the issue was expressed in terms that might be considered as life or death for the entire country (presumably the world as well). The author viewed the future in excited and expectant terms. The author was also highly "political": "When Barack Obama was elected, it felt like we were moving to a bold, gleaming future with a young, appealing president..." On history, the same author had nothing but fear and loathing: "...Donald Trump got into the White House and began yanking us back to the '50s ... Trump always seems like someone who walked out of a Vegas steam bath in 1959. And now the whole country is starting to smell of moth balls."

One might be forgiven if the metaphors appear as "overkill," "gleaming future" against a "moth ball" country. But journalism, as opposed to analysis, should entertain.

Beyond the rhetoric, however, lies a profound issue: how to employ both past and present toward a favorable future?

Unfortunately, the temptation to express the twin preferences as life or death becomes too strong to resist. To progressives, history is only a repetition of a series of "isms," be they of race, sex, nation or other. The worst is singularly applied as definition of country, be it slavery, voting rights, sexual orientation etc. Traditionalists show the "gleaming" highlights: liberty, prosperity, democracy, "pursuit of happiness," etc.

The first chooses defects, the second chooses solutions. Take the great Civil War: the first says slavery existed, the second says it ended. Approximately 4,000 blacks were lynched from the end of the Civil War to about 1950. In the war itself, four years long, approximately 720,000 white soldiers died. What facts best describe the country?

A related problem involves separating reality from idealism. Are the defects of one country separate and unique or part of humanity itself? What does one oppose against slavery, for example, the country or society? Thomas Jefferson owned slaves. Are we against him or the eighteenth century?

To be fair to journalists, on the same page of the newspaper, above, another author related the dilemma for his own children. He neither wants them, in his own words, to be "trapped by nostalgia or tempted by the darker side of nationalism" or on the other hand "falling prey to the progressive tendency to remember the past only in order to hold it in contempt."

To Lose a Country, Part II

May 22, 2019 (photo, Paris June 1940)

As the title notes, countries can be "lost," but, in this context, what does "lost" mean? Where are the examples? One meaning, certainly, is the ultimate purpose of all national security policies and goals, i.e. to survive.

"Lost" is past tense, an adjective that is final; "lose" is present tense, a verb that is temporary. The conclusion is suspended until it becomes "lost." Scanning history, in the West we have examples of both. Britain "lost" its colonies, Germany "lost," the U.S. "won" in both world wars, etc. Many countries win battles and lose wars — ask Napoleon, Robert E. Lee, Adolph Hitler, Hadeki Tojo, Paul Reynaud, and many more. Others lose battles and win wars — ask the Soviet Union in World War II and the American North in the Civil War.

In this context, the concentration is on "lose" and what the intellectual classes do in anticipation of loss of country. That means the precipitate events, circumstances that created a "loss" in the first place, not the consequences. The consequence of "lost" is disappearance. It is far more consequential to discover why Rome fell than what took its place. If there are patterns or repetitions as to losing a country, then it is instructive. If it recovers from loss, that is also instructive. A disappearance may be tragic but empty unless we know "why."

The possibility of a loss, the ultimate conclusion, is fundamental, i.e. "existential." Avoidance of loss is the purpose of all national security strategies and goals. Without the specter of a final defeat, there would be little or no logic to the term "national security" itself. The word is "national" not "partial."

Take France, for one. In 1803, Napoleon sold nearly half of North America (Louisiana Purchase) without affecting the home front. In 1871, France surrendered Alsace-Lorraine and stayed intact (and later recovered them). Britain lost its American colonies in 1781 and still went on to build the world's largest empire. In April 1975, the U.S. evacuated Vietnam after years of war, and few on Main Street seemed to notice. Then the U.S. became the world's "sole remaining superpower" (alleged). The vast Soviet Empire collapsed in 1991; now, for years, the entire American public has been obsessed that Russia will take democracy away and create a Trump dynasty (alleged).

On it goes, *ad infinitum*.

The point of the endless quarrelling between Trump and the media appears existential. To pose it in less than apoplectic terms might reduce it to simple, rational issues of political power. Cynics might describe the infighting as between the world's richest man (Jeff Bezos, owner, *Washington Post*) vs. the world's most powerful (Trump). Instead, it is ideological, posed in moralistic, idealistic expressions between good and evil, democracy and despotism. A daily reminder of the terms are inscribed at the top of page one of the *Post*, every issue, every day and night. "Democracy dies in darkness" is not political philosophy, it is an incessant assertion that the stakes are nothing less than "win-lose." A Trump presidency, over and over, is "to lose a country" (alleged).

To be sure, there have been times when the threat was real and imminent. It could have been lost from the beginning, most certainly in the Civil War, possibly in the Great Depression. Military coups are frequently mentioned as possible, conspirator theories abound that distant, anonymous groups, families, bankers, and cliques mastermind the country and the world. Conspiratorial accounts of loss have entertained millions through time and circumstance, *Propaganda* (1928), *The Manchurian Candidate* (1959), *Seven Days in May* (1962), *None Dare Call It Conspiracy* (1972), *Critical Path* (1982), *The Unseen Hand* (1982), and *The Fourth Reich* (2008), to name a few.

Illusion, entertainment, and conspiracy may intrigue the public, but at the same time today's U.S. political culture hovers between lunacy, exaggeration, and hysteria. President Trump has his share of blame, but the "resistance" in the media, even in comedy and talk shows, appears, on surface, to have reached epidemic proportions. At the bottom of all of it is the ultimate specter, not of Republican gain, not of Hillary's defeat, but of "loss of country."

As a demonstration of the depth of intensity, consider how often the American president has been compared to Adolf Hitler. Adolf Hitler! As if Hitler would have a Jewish son-in-law and a Jewish (converted) daughter. As if Trump has announced "A Thousand Year America" and plans on invading Mexico and ending NATO. The U.S. has no concentration camps, no Gestapo, while the media remains free to openly provoke a change in government.

The idea that Trump was an existential threat came well before he even took office. The day after his nomination, *The Washington Post* ran an editorial that the new Republican nominee was "a unique threat to American democracy." It's been downhill since.

Shortly after Trump's election, *a New Yorker* column invoked history to indict the President-elect. The author, John Cassidy, announced that "Over Thanksgiving I read up on some history: Hitler, Mussolini, Franco, Berlusconi, Putin." After turkey and pumpkin pie, presumably, this quick study of selective tyrannies came up with a (foregone) conclusion that "Trump's victory heralds the imposition of Putinesque authoritarianism and maybe even full-blown Fascism." Soon afterward, New York Times columnist, Nicholas Kristof, drew upon ancient Rome to condemn the president. Comparing Trump to Caligula and Nero, the first who murdered his mother and the second who burned the city, he concluded that what "...was true two millennia ago ... remains true today." And that the whole lot, "...may not be, er, quite right in the head."

"Pundits" are allowed free rein to glance at history with imagination to arouse dissent. That may be a quality of equalitarian democracy, whether fault or virtue. But loss of country is decidedly not a subject to be taken lightly, or to serve as a polemical platform against domestic opponents. There is hardly a nation-state, empire, tribe, jurisdiction, or ethnic grouping that has not, somewhere in time, experienced the phenomenon of "loss." To some, it meant "lost," and we haven't seen them since. To others, it was "loss," and they are still here.

Consider Poland, for one. It was eliminated, "absorbed," by its three great neighbors, Russia, Prussia, and Austria in 1794. After World War I (1919), it came back to where it was, only to disappear again by two of the original team (Germany, Soviet Union) in 1939. In 1945, it was again "lost" to the one remaining (Soviet Union) but "arose" once more in 1991. How many losses can one nation take?

The subject "loss of country," be it political theater and polemical or real and historic, has always been dominant in human history and has, in fact, defined the political map of the globe, before and now.

The next time you see the slogan "democracy dies in darkness," consider the source. Compared to reality, it's a bumper sticker.

Us or Them? Inside vs. Outside Threats

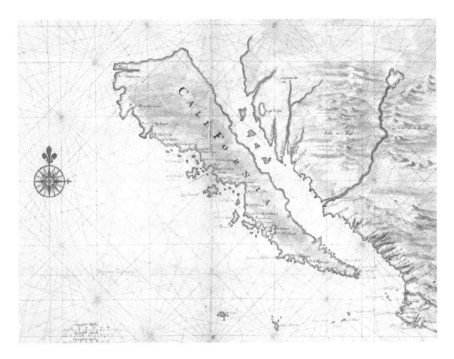

May 9, 2019

Throughout history, countries have come and gone, some by their own hand, some by others. There is no other way, either suicide or murder. In the final analysis, this issue hovers over any and all discussion and debate on the future. National Security is just that: "national" and not partial or selective.

Even implicitly, the current debate between President Trump and the "resistance," be it political or the media, involves the ultimate question: will the country survive this administration? In some ways, it amounts to "total" war, reminiscent by many of the period before the Civil War itself.

There is no need to bring up the evidence, it can be seen daily and nightly, in the press, on talk shows, in the annual Correspondents' Dinner (that Trump has boycotted), in sports, in theater, on the subway, on bumper stickers and, in short, everywhere people "congregate."

The issue is apocalyptic and is couched that way. In other words, it is "existential." The full story can be summarized by the daily reminder on the top of page one of *The Washington Post*, "democracy dies in darkness." That says it all, but it remains uncertain as to who is putting out the lights (the media thinks Trump is, while Trump thinks they are).

Many think that Europe itself committed "suicide" in World War I. One of the most prophetic statements in history was made by the British Foreign Secretary, Edward Grey, as he was drafting his war message in 1914. Turning to his staff, he proclaimed "The lamps are going out all over Europe, we shall not see them lit again in our lifetime." Grey was correct but probably didn't realize that he was one of those blowing out the candles.

By geopolitical definition, the threats to American sovereignty/integrity have generally arisen from within. The great Civil War was by far the worst time in U.S. history, where 2.5 percent (720,000) of the population died, almost all white, male soldiers (more from disease than bullets). The closest external threat came in World War II, but even this is fanciful. Japan had no intention or capacity to invade the west coast. Pearl Harbor itself was meant to force an armistice to allow them to occupy China and the south Pacific. While German bombing killed tens of thousands throughout continental Europe and England, Japan's efforts to "balloon bomb" America killed a grand total of six people (a family in Oregon).

Regarding Nazi Germany, the U.S. may have never declared war had not Hitler taken the initiative four days after Pearl Harbor. Even with the worst of intentions, Germany had neither the resources nor the ambitions to take over the Americas. The German threat to Atlantic shipping was largely gone by 1943, while "Operation Sea Lion," the invasion of England, was also gone by 1942. The English coast was 26 miles from Nazi air bases; the U.S. coast was 3,000 miles!

Good luck *Luftwaffe*.

In the Cold War, the Soviet Union, certainly, had the means to obliterate the American homeland, thousands of times over. So did the U.S., *vice versa*, leading to the horrible acronym, Mutual Secured Destruction, "MAD." Combined, both sides had approximately 100,000 nuclear bombs, most at least 100 times more lethal than the two actually used against Japan. It is one of the most amazing facts in human history that for such a long time (nearly a half-century) these two "superpowers" possessed such explosive power and never, not once, chose to use them against each other.

Of all the thousands atomic/nuclear weapons ever deployed, by all countries in the world, it remains a singular truth that only the first two were ever launched against a human target. The code-word for the Cold War, "deter-rence," meant that the purpose of a weapon was to remain in-place. If it went off, it lost its purpose, i.e. it "failed."

Against this background, what is the "existential" threat currently facing the United States? Is it external or internal?

Typically, the strategic threat, now and before, sees primarily the "enemy within." Since the 2016 election, the chief focus of the Trump Administration has been to build a wall on the Mexican border so as to "safeguard" the culture inside. Often, the "caravans" coming in, especially illegals, are defined as an "invasion." This stretches the term but acknowledges the origins of the prob-lem, i.e., Central American governments and people.

The American government and people have done nothing to solicit this immigration except to offer a safe haven. Many in the U.S. actually welcome the influx, and over 75 cities offer "sanctuaries" in defiance of federal law.

So, is the issue external or internal, existential or peripheral? It's external since it comes from outside, internal since it shapes the character of the culture. It's existential if it radically alters the internal culture, peripheral if the culture is able to absorb the influx.

Thus, as in earlier immigration waves, the answer hinges on the capacity of the newcomers to "assimilate" within. Thus far, the USA has benefitted from immigration since the focus has been on how they will help the culture, not how the culture will help them.

There are warning signs: illegal entry, scarce documentation, overwhel-ming numbers, crime, poverty, disease, and violence, plus allegiances to hostile legal or political systems. Historically, the existence of Ellis Island served to safeguard the country from the vices above and still serves as a symbol rep-resenting a "nation of immigrants" (President Kennedy's book title).

Now, as before, Americans still are afraid of how foreigners might shape their internal lives. Russia, once an existential nuclear threat, has been reduced to a computer hacker allegedly defining the outcome of local elections. "Cyber," a technology, is distant and complex, however lethal it may yet be. But the cyber threat also comes from outside. China remains the subject most mentioned as external, but few Americans, including the Trump Administration, see it as much more than a trade rival. North Korea has occupied most of public attention, but how existential can "rocket man" be?

Globalization has many consequences. Historically, threats were relatively easy to define. Nationalism was healthy, the Redcoats were from England, Teddy Roosevelt carried a "big stick," the Kaiser and Hitler were from Germany, Mussolini from Italy, Tojo from Japan and immigration was carefully controlled. Now, everything is interconnected, and one can scarcely tell friend from foe. Nationalism is now "white supremacy." History was horrible and needs to be erased. Immigration controls are "racist."

After the defeat at Yorktown, 1781, the British band played "The World Turned Upside Down." Now we know why.

Is America normal?

Isolationism and internationalism in American foreign policy

May 6, 2019

After the traumas of World War I, Warren G. Harding campaigned for president in 1920 to bring the U.S. back to "normalcy." Toward the end of the Cold War in 1989, former UN Ambassador Jeanne Kirkpatrick wrote a major article pleading that the U.S. return as "a normal country in a normal time." Basically, they both meant to "return home," to avoid the international obligations and policies that took America so far away from its original purpose and nature.

Technically, "normal" means conform to standards, patterns, not to deviate from principle. To Harding, it meant "...to steady down, to get squarely on our feet, to make use of the right path, [that] tranquility at home is more precious than peace abroad." Kirkpatrick expressed a similar theme toward century's end, to concentrate on "...pressing problems of education, family, industry and technology."

Americans have always claimed to be "exceptional," so how does this equate with being "normal"? For most of its history, certainly before Warren Harding, America's "normal" pursuit of foreign relations was "isolationism." From George Washington's Farewell Address through to Pearl Harbor, the dominant American purpose overseas was to trade and prosper but to avoid any and all "entangling" political relations with others. To the 1920 generation, the world war was a deviation from this and "normalcy" meant a return to isolation. World War II and the Cold War interrupted this again, and to Jeanne Kirkpatrick and others, it was time to renew the main purpose. In Harding's words, to "steady down."

America was an "exception" by itself and did not need to export home values elsewhere. President Donald Trump indicates this belief and wants America "great again," which may mean what Harding also wanted, "normalcy."

In his classic book, *Promised Land, Crusader State* (1997) University of Pennsylvania Professor Walter McDougall traced the historic tension between these two strains of home vs. foreign policies that have competed for the American purpose. A comparison of the Inaugural Addresses of John F. Kennedy (1961) and Bill Clinton (1993) will show the disparity between, not only two presidents, but between two time periods and two purposes. Both came from the exact same philosophical source and the same set of political values. By definition, they both are equally "exceptional" and, thereby, equally "normal."

Kennedy's speech, in the middle of the Cold War, had not a single word on domestic issues. His ringing declarations announced the renewal of a global commitment to the finish. "Let every nation know," he declared, "...that we shall pay any price, bear any burden, meet any hardship, support any friend, oppose any foe, in order to assure the survival and the success of liberty."

Clinton's oration, after the Cold War, contained oblique references to "change" in the world and "opportunities" but was largely a call for renewal at home. "We must do what no generation has had to do before," he announced. "We must invest more in our own people, in their jobs, in their future, and at the same time, cut our massive debt. And we must do so in a world in which we must compete for every opportunity."

Kennedy's call was for dramatic action on a global front; Clinton's was a renewal for continuity. Clinton's was the more "normal," especially if we just substitute "every" for "no" in Clinton's first line, above.

The difference between the two inaugurals reflects the difference between the two main American purposes. Throughout history, the American people have always identified their own security and well-being with safety at home. Dangers from outside have rarely occupied great or sustained attention while "internal" issues have, by comparison, consumed the gravest and most immediate "existential" threat.

As Lincoln famously stated it in 1858, "a house divided against itself cannot stand." The chief explanation for this phenomenon is geopolitical: unlike Europe and most of the world, the United States has not had to defend its external borders against powerful and aggressive enemies. It had the freedom to expand and prosper without too much interference (relatively). Also, while Britain is separated from Europe by 26 miles of water, the U.S. is separated by 3,000 miles.

If there is any central fact in this explanation, it might reside in the sacrifices that Americans have expended against internal threats. The Civil War, in a population of 32 million, took approximately 720,000 lives, more than in all other U.S. wars combined! That's about 2.5 percent of the population. What is 2.5 percent of 330 million, and what would it take for today's Americans to sacrifice that part of the population?

Certainly, more than 9/11 and individual terrorist attacks. The question hovers over the Republic but cannot even be addressed. But it is not abstract and has, in fact, happened before.

The two defining moments between the tensions within the American purpose are April 12, 1861 and December 7, 1941. The first ensured internal unity and saw a renewal of isolationism in foreign policy. The second ensured the world would be safe from Fascism, then Communism, and began internationalism in foreign policy.

Today, the country has been in strategic "limbo" since the "unipolar moment" came and went. This critical "intersection" has been approached but not crossed. Aside from political interests and personalities ("crooked" Hillary vs. "racist" Trump), the tensions between Trump and his critics center on the two competing worldviews.

Sooner or later, the country must decide which threats are "existential": the ones from within or from without. Unfortunately, history offers no clear guide as to the answer. The honest answer would be "both."

Unfortunately, again, it will probably be the pull of events that will decide. Lacking a long-term worldview and obsessed with self-identities and infinite, petty quarrelling, strategic "drift" seems likely to continue, until another dramatic alarm wakes the slumbering giant.

Is this "normal" or "schizophrenic"?

What Happened to World Order?

May 2, 2019

In August 1990, President George H. W. Bush promised a "New World Order" in his address to the UN General Assembly. Bush was seeking international support in his run-up to the invasion of Iraq. He got his support, but world order was soon lost in the shuffle. He probably didn't mean it anyway, given his often-claimed distaste for "that vision thing."

Since then, world order has taken a deep backslide to lesser priorities in the U.S. political culture. The Governor of Arkansas ran in 1992 on the idea that "it's the economy stupid;" Bush II tried "nation-building" in the Middle East and Afghanistan. Nearly two decades later, most of that area is either falling apart, fleeing to Europe, or hosting Islamic terrorists. The Obama Administration spent eight years "leading from behind," about where we are now. President Trump has promised nostalgic greatness but cannot even fund a border wall.

This should not (necessarily) be taken critically; it's "politics as usual," or as it was once called "normalcy." But war and peace are far above normalcy.

Since time began, mankind has tried to create order out of chaos. The record is, at best, mixed. The Peace of Westphalia, 1648, created the European nation-state system, now worldwide. But 1648 to now represents only five percent of recorded history (6,000 years). What happened during the earlier ninety-five percent?

Most of recorded political history has consisted of single-centered rule, i.e. empire, dynasty, monarchy, or tyranny. In her classic book, *Politics and Culture in International History* (1960, 1994), Adda Bozeman has traced government up until the Congress of Vienna, 1815. With the single exception of ancient Athens, the remainder of political rule has been imperial, one-party, one ruler. Most of these are familiar names, but lost to posterity. The empires of China, the Mongols, India, Persia, Greek city-states, Alexander the Great, Islamic, the Ottomans, Roman Empire, Byzantine, Holy Roman Empire, the colonial empires of Britain, France, Spain, Holland, Belgium, Germany, Italy, Russia, Austria, Portugal. In more modern times, to name names: Napoleon, the Kaiser, Lenin, Stalin and their protégés, Hitler, Mussolini, Hadeki Tojo, Fidel Castro, Pol Pot, Mao Tse-tung, Kim Jong-un, Saddam Hussein.

The efforts of modern totalitarian rulers have been based upon ideological fantasies that, from hindsight, have proven both tragic and ridiculous. Karl Marx may be the most famous philosopher since John Locke, but what country has been ruled by a "proletarian" revolt? There have been many "Communist" regimes, but not one remotely "Marxist." Hitler's prediction of a "Thousand Year Reich" lasted twelve years, while Mussolini wound up on the wrong end of a rope. Asian Communist governments are simply totalitarians under a false flag. What is left of Communism in Cuba: poverty and despotism.

The scarce efforts to organize the world democratically have been American-inspired but, like all the empires, have also failed. So far on earth, there has been no such thing as a "world government," but many have tried.

The first attempt to organize a democratic world came with Woodrow Wilson and the League of Nations in 1919. Not only was the League irrelevant in preventing World War II, but Wilson could not (or would not) even persuade the Senate to join. Franklin Roosevelt fared better with the United Nations in 1945, but the Cold War made the UN "stillborn" from the beginning. The end of the Cold War has seen an increasing anarchy envelop the globe, while the U.S. descends deeper into party and partisan bickering about who lies the most, what affidavit is accurate or not, and what a Supreme Court nominee did as a teenager.

Today's politicians quarrel over almost everything, while the "war on terror" approaches its third decade. World Order is about as far removed from the culture as a Mars landing, while the daily shouting matches between the media and the administration sounds like recess at St. James elementary.

Where's the light in this dark tunnel?

If U.S. politicians and media pundits find world order too distant for their intrigues, others find it compelling. Dr. Kissinger, in *World Order* (2014) traced the history of the idea and concluded that the Westphalian system was here to stay. Calling the need for order "the ultimate challenge … in our time," Kissinger described the American role as "philosophically and geopolitically imperative [toward] a modernization of the Westphalian system informed by contemporary realities."

Perhaps foreigners can inspire "normalcy." On April 3, last, NATO Secretary-General Jens Stoltenberg addressed a joint session of Congress and suggested an expanded unity: "Together, we represent almost one billion people. We are half of the world's economic might. And half of the world's military might. When we stand together, we are stronger than any potential challenger."

Spokesmen for the prodigious Atlantic Council have added specifics to this message. Mr. Damon Wilson of the Council told the House Foreign Affairs Committee recently that the United States "should lead a more concerted effort to thicken the political bonds between NATO and its global partners." These included U.S. partners in both Asia and Latin America.

Messages such as the above reveal a need for "statesmanship" at the highest level by U.S. politicians. It is past time that both the Trump Administration and serious Members in Congress enroll American human and material resources to things higher than someone's last conversation recoded on tape.

Erasing History

April 26, 2019

America has long been known as "ahistorical" (indifferent), but it also has demonstrated signs of being deliberately "anti-historical" (opposed).

Recently the iconic American singer, Kate Smith, has been "erased" from certain parts of U.S. history for recording a "racist" song ("That's Why Darkies Were Born") in 1931. Smith was probably the country's most famous songstress, issuing many uplifting titles during both the Depression and World War II. Her rendition of "God Bless America" (1937) may well be the most patriotic song ever released (excluding the National Anthem). This song was used both by the New York Yankees and the Philadelphia Flyers in their home games, and the Flyers erected a statue of Smith outside of their arena.

Now both the song and statue are gone, in keeping with the current American mania to eliminate memories of anything unsettling in human conduct. This fits in with the more-recent destruction of monuments and place names recalling the Confederacy.

History is replete with examples of political or ideological censorship. Totalitarian regimes, in particular, are famous for shutting out what contradicts their power and belief systems. Stalin in the Soviet Union made censorship and personal "disappearance" an obsession and used it to control the millions under his governance.

The Soviet Communists were both systematic and ruthless in the control of belief and memory. State organizations were used to stop any and all independent thought. The Goskomizdat censored all printed material. The Goskino was in charge of cinema, the Gosteleradio in charge of radio/television, and the Goskomstat controlled state secrets and sensitive information. Under Stalin all pre-Bolshevik books, journals and newspapers were removed from libraries and other public arenas, and those found in possession of such literature were arrested. All references to historic Russian art, music, literature, and culture were suppressed or destroyed. From the beginning, Lenin and Stalin used the phrase "Socialist Realism" to confiscate and destroy any references to Western culture, history, or beliefs and to promote the goals and methods of the government.

Nazi Germany, among many others, needed censorship to justify its movement. Like the Soviet Union, Hitler's regime was comprehensive and ruthless. Under the guidance of Joseph Goebbels, Reich Minister of Public Enlightenment and Propaganda, all forms of communication were controlled or banned, including newspapers, music, literature, radio, and film. The Ministry employed 1,500 people with seventeen departments. On May 10, 1933 alone, Goebbels ordered the destruction of one-third of Germany's library holdings. The infamous "book burnings" that continued throughout the Third Reich characterized the Nazi's contempt for independent thought. Needless to say, all references to Jewish existence were destroyed.

While these two are, admittedly, extreme examples, they nonetheless demonstrate the lengths that humanity can go toward restricting access to thoughts or examples that contradict any and all social mores. But like war itself, violence, persecution, prejudice, and other myriad forms of human behavior, censorship is both universal and pervasive. What matters is the degree and the patterns.

No country or nation is exempt. In its periodic ratings of worldwide censorship, Freedom House recently proclaimed that, maximum, 30 countries were free, 60 partly free, and 99 not free at all. Although the U.S. is in group one, it also has its own history of speech, press, and political restrictions. Neither the degree nor the pattern, however, has altered the fundamental democratic nature of the country.

Most, but not all, American censorship came during wartime or periods of national stress. In 1798, when U.S. shipping was threatened by Britain and France, President John Adams proclaimed the Alien and Sedition Acts that severely restricted the rights of immigrants, non-citizens, and citizens who critiqued the government. During the Civil War, President Lincoln eliminated the writ of *habeas corpus* (unlawful detainment) and arrested some 14,000 northern dissidents against the Union. During World War I, Woodrow Wilson issued his own version of censorship (Espionage and Sedition Acts), while Franklin D. Roosevelt in World War II issued proclamations with Enemy Alien Acts and interned 120,000 Japanese- Americans.

Censorship against books, films, music, newspapers, and other forms of communication were also common in U.S. history. In Hollywood history, the Production Code Administration, headed by Joseph Breen, expunged "unacceptable" showings. A list of 25 such items were included and erased by fiat, including arson, cruelty, seduction, brutality, sedition, drugs, lust, etc. Books, such as *Ulysses*, *Tropic of Cancer* and *Lady Chatterley's Lover* were routinely banned from bookstores and mailings.

How can a democratic, modern, and "liberal" society grow so hostile to its own past, values, and culture? In reality, it amounts to an assault upon the intellect and the victory of emotion over thought. It actually denies life itself (if that's possible). It is also normally associated with either tyranny, self-doubt, or war.

History is comprehensive and not selective. It's intellectually dishonest to pick and choose what parts of society we want to keep. This does not mean sanction or any official endorsement, but it does require perspective and recognition that life is larger than our own current sympathies. At the same time as Kate Smith recorded her "Darkies ..." song, the Black actor and activist Paul Robeson did the same. No one has yet called for Robeson to be erased, and the distortion is barely acknowledged.

The Kate Smith case, as before, will not end democracy. But, again as before, it is not a healthy sign. As the course of history has shown, restrictions are universal and often necessary. But when they arise from ideology, emotion, or political designs, they become gratuitous, unnecessary, and dangerous.

In his classic book, *1984*, George Orwell reminded us that "Who controls the past controls the future. Who controls the present controls the past." In 1982, President Ronald Reagan awarded Kate Smith the Medal of Freedom, stating that she was "an undying reminder of the beauty, the courage and the heart of this great country of ours."

Now she is an outcast, a non-person, a bygone. Who "controls" the American present, the past? Who will control its future?

Some say "democracy dies in darkness." This is not a bright moment.

Irony: the New York Yankees banned her song of 1931.

1931. A year when the Yankees would not allow a Black man to wear their uniform or sit in their dugout.

Forget Kate. Ban the Yankees!

The Democratic Peace II:

War with Spain

THE LAST SUNSET OF THE "MAINE."

April 17, 2019

A previous essay tried to demonstrate the Mexican-American War as a contradiction to the assumptions and assertions of the "Democratic Peace" theory. This one will extend the point to the U.S. war against Spain, 1898 ("Spanish-American War").

From the beginning, the settlers in British-North America had landed in a hostile country, where war, violence, and constant vigilance were necessary for survival. Warfare was rampant on the frontier, both against native Indian tribes and French, British, and Spanish armies, who quarreled incessantly with each other. Both the Pequot War in Connecticut (1630s) and the French and Indian War in both Canada and the colonies (1754-1763) were just two of the most vicious, but they were characteristic.

The American experience and dominant culture did not just come to an end with the triumph of political democracy. Neither the Declaration of Independence nor the Constitution were dependent on pacifism, while the subsequent settlement of the continent relied on force or its threat.

A mere list of the belligerents that the U.S. has faced since the beginning will suffice to demonstrate how the people of the nation were asked to defend, or at times, to extend their influence or jurisdiction. These were all "wars" by any definition, although the formal "declaration" of war was rarely invoked. At the very least, they were all "combats."

They include, as follows (in no particular order): Great Britain (twice), Germany (twice), each other, Indian tribes (about four centuries), Austria, Hungary, Italy, China, Korea, Vietnam, Spain, Russia (intervention, 1918-20), Mexico (three times, 1847, 1914, 1916), Japan, Afghanistan, Iraq, Syria, Mediterranean pirates (early nineteenth century), The Philippines (1898-1902 and afterwards), interventions and occupations in the Caribbean and Central America (over 50 times), plus others since forgotten.

That's an impressive list, which could easily be shortened to, "most of the world plus ourselves." Not exactly an affirmation of the "democratic peace" theory. Even if most of them were foisted upon a reluctant democracy, there must be some in which the democracy was neither reluctant nor passive. Perhaps *none* of them were reluctant, a possibility that brings up another interpretation: the dangerous and aggressive democracy.

Without going into them all, given space and time, perhaps the Spanish-American War will do. Why did the U.S. declare war on Spain in 1898, a place 3,000 miles away with no particular ax to grind and long since kicked out of the area altogether (except Cuba)?

At first glance, "no particular reason" could be asserted. Within human conduct, it is not unknown for someone to "pick" a fight. The sociology or psychological cause of such behavior is beyond our task. Only the objective reality is needed (for now). Was the American culture ready to assert itself in 1898 to pick on a country that had to real means of defense? For the moment, we can leave the answer out and let the question alone. Instead, what were the reasons given?

The immediate cause was simple: the blowing up of the USS *Maine* in Havana Harbor, 15 February, killing 250 sailors. This, indeed, was a "Pearl Harbor" of its time, but, unlike Pearl Harbor, it wasn't obvious as to what happened.

A Court of Inquiry held in March concluded that a mine had caused the explosion but failed to indict whoever laid the mine. It didn't have to, as the "yellow" press centered in New York concluded, arbitrarily, that it was Spain who had detonated the mine. The press, led by Joseph Pulitzer and William Randolph Hearst, controlled opinion to such an extent that they created a war-fever hysteria to rally against Spain.

Spain had controlled Cuba for centuries but was facing an insurrection that found willing sympathy in America for the rebels. Spain's cruel and sweeping atrocities against the *insurrectos* aroused further condemnation in the U.S. and fed the movement to rid the area of colonialization once and for all.

Why would Spain, thousands of miles away and facing an insurrection, blow up an American warship? On its face, it is illogical. Pulitzer himself, responsible for much of the hysteria, privately noted that "nobody outside a lunatic asylum" would find Spain responsible. It was pure "theater," many times stronger than what we today observe in the media frenzy against President Trump. Hearst once told a reporter assigned to Cuba, "you furnish the pictures and I'll furnish the war."

Subsequent inquiries, as late as 1974 by the Navy and 1999, by *National Geographic*, concluded the mostly obvious: that an internal explosion blew up the *Maine*. No matter, the 1898 generation acted on emotion, reinforced by the national expression, "Remember the *Maine*, to hell with Spain."

Congress declared war on April 25. In his war message, President McKinley never mentioned the Maine, but demanded that Spain "...relinquish its authority and government in the island of Cuba."

The war lasted ten weeks, in Theodore Roosevelt's expression a "splendid, little war." At the same time that the U.S. was relieving Spain of its remaining possessions in the Caribbean, the American Navy was taking over Spain's authority in The Philippines, a country that had been Spain's since 1565.

The Spanish-American War was a watershed in U.S. history and saw the American flag begin its long trajectory into first, a two-ocean power and eventually, a world superpower. At home, democracy continued to flourish; overseas, it was a great idea, and an American mission, off and on, from the beginning.

Theory of the Democratic Peace:

The Mexican War

April 16, 2019

International Relations "theory" includes the idea that "democratic" nations are inherently "peaceful." The word "democratic" can be defined without too much trouble; "peaceful" is another issue altogether.

On one level, it is fairly easy. Within their jurisdictions, democracies are alone in their capacity to resolve differences between their people. The notion "rule of law" is sacrosanct in the democratic settlement of disputes and can even lead to accusations of a "litigious" society. Better litigious than how most of the world's one-party states resolve disputes. The Guillotine comes to mind, as a beginning. So does the Gulag and the Gestapo (the "three G's" theory).

But on an international level, it gets more complex. During the nineteenth century alone, a democratic United States sent military forces into foreign countries on some 100 occasions. That's one per year. Some stayed for hours, some for days, some for years. Maybe they were justified, maybe necessary, but they were hardly "peaceful."

This alone makes the definition highly qualified.

Democratic theory posits two separate but related principles. One, democracies do not fight each other; two, they are not aggressive or "militaristic."

On the first principle: somewhat suspect. In 1812, Britain and the U.S. were among the most advanced democracies in the world. So how does the theory explain that war?

Was the Civil War not fought by two sections of the same democracy? The President of the Confederacy, Jefferson Davis, was also an American, named for the author of the Declaration of Independence. He graduated from West Point, fought in the Mexican War, served as Congressman and Senator from Mississippi and Secretary of War under Franklin Pierce.

In World War II, the U.S. was allied with the Soviet Union, one of the worst totalitarian regimes in history. This was necessary for victory, but democracy had nothing to do with it.

On principle two, can a democracy plan an aggressive war? Again, somewhat suspect. The name James K. Polk is not exactly a household item today. Yet Polk's presidency, 1845 – 1849, saw the U.S. expand its frontiers throughout the southwest, California, the Rocky Mountain states, and the Pacific northwest. Unique among politicians, Polk kept his promises, and most of them meant force, war and expansion.

This was made plain from his Inaugural Address. While praising American democracy as the "... most admirable and wisest system of well-regulated self-government among men," he nevertheless urged a policy of limitless expansion. Under the idea of "Manifest Destiny," Polk brought Texas into the U.S. and promised that "... our system may be safely extended to the utmost bounds of our territorial limits."

First on the schedule was the Oregon territory that had been in dispute with Great Britain for many years. Calling the U.S. title to the "Oregon Country" (which included Washington State) as "clear and unquestionable," Polk and the Democratic Party put the U.S. on a war-footing to challenge British claims. Under the slogan "54-40 or fight" (the dividing line) Polk announced that "... the only way to treat John Bull is to look him straight in the eye." Declaring that he would give Great Britain one year to vacate, Polk pressed the issue until both sides settled on the boundary in the treaty of 1846.

In retrospect, neither side was prepared for or wanted a war over Oregon. Polk's "diplomacy" has subsequently been called "brinkmanship," but, in the end, he confronted the world's democratic superpower over territory they felt was too remote to contest.

The case with Mexico would be much different. Polk wanted to push the country to the Pacific Ocean, but, unlike the Louisiana Territory, it was not for sale. He settled on conquest.

The dividing line between Mexico and the U.S. had been disputed going back to Spain's colonial rule. The area was sparsely populated, but Mexico resented the annexation of Texas in 1845 and sent soldiers across the Rio Grande. The two sides clashed, resulting in several losses for the American Army. Polk sent General Zachery Taylor and 3,500 soldiers down to the disputed area across the Nueces River, about 150 miles north of the Rio Grande.

After the initial fighting, Polk declared war, and Congress approved it 174-14. The resultant conflict was decided in 1847 with the capture of Mexico City. The peace treaty of Guadalupe-Hidalgo the following year gave 55% of Mexican territory to the U.S., the states of Arizona, New Mexico, California, Nevada, Utah, and parts of Colorado and Wyoming, an area the size of Western Europe.

American continental expansion essentially ended there, while the doctrine of "Manifest Destiny" settled the territorial expanse for the remainder of the century.

James K. Polk was one of the most successful presidents in American history. He promised only one term and stepped down in 1849. He also kept his promise to expand U.S. sovereignty across North America. In doing so, he (unwittingly) contradicted any theory on the passive nature of democracies.

But democracy allows dissent — that is its virtue. Ulysses Grant was an officer in the war but thought it was contrary to democracy. In his Memoirs, Grant confessed that he thought the war "...unjust, an instance of a republic following the bad example of European monarchies." John Quincy Adams believed that it was "...a most unrighteous war," while, years later, a Republican Platform Committee called the war "...one of the darkest scenes in our history."

Protest, typically, also came from the intelligentsia. Henry David Thoreau wrote the pamphlet *Civil Disobedience* against the war, while Ralph Waldo Emerson wrote that it "...will be as a man who swallowed arsenic, which brings him down in turn."

In Congress, a Member from out-West challenged Polk, demanding several times exactly what "spot" on American soil did the Mexican Army occupy? He became so insistent that he developed the nickname "spotty."

His real name: Abraham Lincoln.

"Remember the Alamo,"
and Latin America too

April 11, 2019

Venezuela is falling apart, the Mexican border is a sieve, Brazil has been in a corruption crisis since 2014, and the U.S. Senate has rejected any "emergency" on the border.

There was once a time when *any* activity south of the border was some sort of emergency. Take the Alamo in 1836, when 250 Americans, including Davy Crockett, were slaughtered by the Mexican Army. Revenge was swift. A month later, the Mexicans were routed, Santa Anna caught, and Texas proclaimed independence (for nine years).

Almost all of early U.S. foreign policies were on or about Latin America. The first major "Doctrine" on foreign policy, James Monroe (1823), declared the entire hemisphere as under American jurisdiction. Rather bold indeed, considering that the British Army had just burned the Capitol (1814). In reality, however, the British Navy was instrumental in the Monroe Doctrine.

Still, since then, the Western Hemisphere, by stages, became a sort of strategic front-line for the United States. That was meant from the beginning. The Founding Fathers never intended the Revolution to stay inside the country.

The concept of a "New World" was behind the idea of a geopolitical departure from "old" Europe. In *The Federalist* (# 11) Alexander Hamilton urged Americans "to aim at an ascendant in the system of American affairs ... erecting one great American system, superior to the control of all trans-Atlantic force or influence, and able to dictate the terms of the connection between the old and the new world." In 1808, Thomas Jefferson supported the independence movements there: "We consider their interests and ours to be the same, and that the object of both must be to exclude all European influence from this hemisphere."

In 1820, Henry Clay urged the translation of this idea into a separate security system: "It is within our power to create a system of which we shall be the center and in which all South America will act with us ... let us become real and true Americans and place ourselves at the head of the American system."

It did not take long to turn these ideas into reality. Continental expansion ended basically with the Mexican War (1848), while the "China Trade" was bolstered by Commodore Perry's "opening" of Japan in 1853 and the establishment of bases in Fiji (1844), Samoa (1856), and the Marshall Islands (1881). The end of the Civil War saw the American "experiment" go overseas. Alaska was purchased in 1867, and, by the 1880s, U.S. interests in the entire hemisphere grew expeditiously. Secretary of State James G. Blaine called the first "International Union of American Republics" in 1890, while the Navy, guided by the writings of Captain Mahan, ascended as a world power.

A minor territorial dispute between England and Venezuela (1896) was settled by U.S. intervention, prompting Secretary of State Richard Olney to declare: "Today the United States is practically sovereign on this continent, and its fiat is law upon the subjects to which it confines its interposition."

This was a critical departure in world politics, when Britain, in the words of historian Samuel F. Bemis, "...left the New World to the American System, and henceforth she tried to bring the United States ... to cast its balance on her side in the world politics of the twentieth century."

That's exactly what happened and explains much of what transpired throughout that time period, from world wars to the Cold War.

The rest, as they say, is history.

Gradually, the original defensive nature of the Monroe Doctrine turned from shield to sword. Manifest Destiny controlled a continent; now the Navy would control the seas. By the turn of the twentieth century, the U.S. had engineered two strategic moves aimed at, in Hamilton's words, "as an ascendant" in the region. In 1898 came the war with Spain, and in 1903 came the independence of Panama from Columbia, arranged from Washington and assisted by the Navy. By 1914, the Panama Canal was completed, the U.S. flag flew over The Philippines, and America found herself as a two-ocean, global power.

Nor was Washington shy about exercising that power. In 1904, Theodore Roosevelt announced his "corollary" to the Monroe Doctrine, giving the U.S. "the exercise of an international police power."

Between 1890 and 1927, U.S. troops landed on the shores of Latin American countries at least 35 times. Some stayed for days, some for months, years, and sometimes even decades. But Franklin Roosevelt's "Good Neighbor" policies secured U.S. interests through diplomacy minus the military. During World War II, the U.S. even occupied Iceland and Greenland, thus pushing the Monroe Doctrine into the polar regions.

By war's end, the U.S. was the strategic master of the entire hemisphere, and the formation of the Organization of American States (OAS) in 1948 reflected that dominance.

The 1962 Cuban missile crisis was ended by John F. Kennedy by invoking U.S. hemispheric doctrines as a potential instrument of nuclear war. "It shall be the policy of this nation," he told a nationwide TV audience, "to regard any nuclear missile launched from Cuba against any nation in the Western Hemisphere as an attack by the Soviet Union on the United States requiring a full retaliatory response on the Soviet Union."

The missiles were withdrawn, and the U.S. went on to victory in the Cold War, while Islamic terrorism continues to shift focus away from Latin America. In 2013, Secretary of State John Kerry ended the American system altogether. "The era of the Monroe Doctrine is over," Kerry told the OAS, and henceforth the U.S. would treat regional countries as "equals."

This version of President Obama's "leading from behind" approach would elevate nations such as Haiti, Ecuador, Peru, and Chile, while deflating American power and historic responsibilities.

For the future, U.S. interests might somehow find common ground between Teddy Roosevelt's "corollary" and Barack Obama's global "equality." The U.S. can be both a "good neighbor" and "great again" in foreign policy. It takes vision and interest, and our own "backyard" is the place to start.

Surprise:

The Pearl Harbor Case

April 8, 2019

One of the most lasting mysteries in American history remains the Pearl Harbor case, not who did it but who was responsible. The planes were, to be sure, Japanese, but this is not the issue. Who made it possible, or how complicit was President Roosevelt? In a larger context, how complicit was the United States itself?

If this question was raised on December 8, 1941, it would probably be cause for treason. At no other time in U.S. history — before or since — was there so much national unity — a unity that carried throughout the war (only one Member of Congress voted against the declaration of war).

After the war, Congress held hearings to uncover any possibility that Roosevelt deliberately withheld advance intelligence of Japan's intentions. After years of testimony, the case remains controversial, but FDR is still "innocent until proven guilty." That case, for sure, is closed.

Beyond that, the larger question remains: what, if any, responsibility does American diplomacy have in the event? During the war, the answer, at least in the public's eye, was, none. That is perfectly understandable. The vast machinery of the American propaganda arm could not possibly raise even a scintilla of doubt as to who was guilty. National morale is hardly lifted by academic queries.

Undoubtedly, the shock of the sudden attack, seemingly out of the blue, contributed to much of the anger. That, too, is understandable. In his declaration of war, Roosevelt labeled the attack as "unprovoked and dastardly." The word "dastardly" is uncommon but means "treacherous" or "underhanded." Fair enough, that's what an unwelcomed surprise is meant to be. "Unprovoked" is much more difficult, i.e. Japan acted without reason. Do countries attack each other without motive?

Japan wanted to attack the United States in 1941. How is one question, why another. Both are within reason.

How? It was a "surprise." What on earth else might it be? Has there ever been an "announced" attack? Would Admiral Yamamoto cable Hawaii, "We'll be there on the 7th around 8 am, have a nice day"?

Did Jefferson Davis warn Lincoln that Ft. Sumter was about to be attacked on April 12, 1861? Did Hitler tell Stalin that 2 million soldiers were heading his way on June 22, 1941? Did North Korea warn the South that they were crossing the 38th parallel on June 25, 1950? Did the hijackers try to evacuate the World Trade Center before 9/11?

Surprises in war are common and deemed necessary, but never appreciated. Nor are they meant to be.

So Japan did what others have done since time began: they kept their intentions a secret.

This brings up the "why?" Roosevelt felt that Pearl Harbor was "unprovoked." To his listeners, the American people, that meant one side was 100% guilty, the other 100% innocent. Good for morale but more complicated than that.

Much of the hatred of Japan has roots in what is now called "racism," a term unknown until recently. Another reason is the notorious behavior of the Japanese army before and during the war. Reports of the "rape" of Nanking, the Bataan Death March, and countless Japanese atrocities throughout the Pacific theater made any appreciation of Japanese national ambitions totally irrelevant.

Yet Japan had needs and ambitions that fit in with other colonial powers, including both European and American. The U.S. declared jurisdiction over the Western Hemisphere in the Monroe Doctrine and intervened over 50 times in Latin America between 1890 and 1927. Japan announced the "Greater East Asia Co-prosperity Sphere" in the late 1930s, albeit with more of a "sword" in hand than a "shield." European countries had governed most of the rest of the globe for centuries, including most of Asia and China.

The sociological/racial antagonisms between the two peoples hardly helped understanding. In the 1880s, U.S. legislation excluded all Chinese from entering the country, and bans in California extended these to Japanese. In 1907, a "Gentleman's Agreement" between the two countries governed mutual immigration, but this was ended by the 1924 Act, which prohibited all Asians from entering.

But these were backgrounds. The diplomatic differences between the two over China served as a permanent and unbridgeable wedge that prevented any accommodation and led eventually to Pearl Harbor.

This began in 1899 with the so-called "Open Door" notes to the world from U.S. Secretary of State John Hay (once Lincoln's personal aide) asking to respect the territorial integrity of China. These notes collided directly with Japan's ambitions to expand in Asia, beginning with her war with China in 1895. With Taiwan and Korea now Japanese protectorates, the stage was set for a deep and permanent split that finally ended in open war.

With Japan expanding almost everywhere, the U.S. took the defensive. Japan defeated Russia in 1905, and Theodore Roosevelt mediated the peace negotiations, held in Portsmouth, New Hampshire. The Japanese Government and people considered the result an insult and began a national grievance that further separated the two societies.

Japanese incursions in China during World War I were rejected by the Allies after the war. The alliance (1902) between Britain and Japan was also ended then, mostly through U.S. pressure. In the disarmament treaties of 1922 held in Washington, Japan was forced to limit her battleship construction and was prohibited from constructing naval bases in the Pacific. Japan's occupation of Manchuria (1931) was refused recognition, and any further Japanese expansion was condemned by the U.S. ("Stimson Doctrine"). The U.S. refused recognition when Japan occupied China (again) in 1937 and when she took over Indochina from France in 1940.

Everywhere Japan went, she met American opposition. In July 1941, Roosevelt "froze" all Japanese financial holdings in the U.S. and stopped the export of oil, thus depriving Japan of most of her foreign trade and 80% of her oil.

Japan faced financial ruin and would soon have no petroleum. So she attacked. Yamamoto knew that he couldn't win but hoped for a quick victory and a free hand in the western Pacific. He was shot down by an Army Air Force fighter in 1943.

Before Pearl Harbor, for decades, Japan was too aggressive, while the U.S. was too defensive. Like ships in the night, they co-existed for years until FDR pulled the plug. Shortly afterward came the "day which will live in infamy."

America may have had the moral high-ground to protect China, but Hideki Tojo was not impressed. Pearl Harbor was "dastardly," but hardly "unprovoked."

It takes two to fight.

The Uncivil War

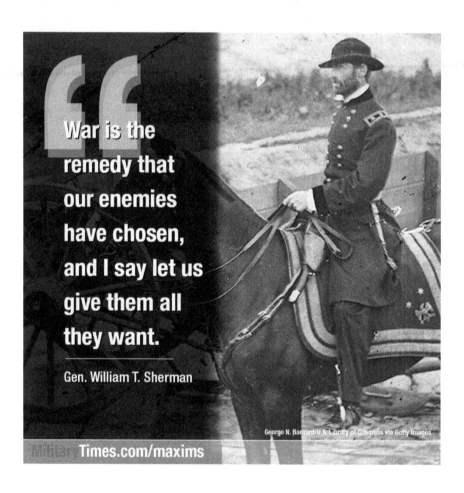

War is the remedy that our enemies have chosen, and I say let us give them all they want.

Gen. William T. Sherman

George N. Barnard/U.S. Library of Congress via Getty Images

Times.com/maxims

April 4, 2019

One of the best evidences of the horrors of war, especially to the innocent, are the photos of bombed out cities after the Second World War. The destruction of once-magnificent architectural marvels such as Berlin, Tokyo, Coventry, plus the atomic bombings of Hiroshima and Nagasaki, gives testimony to mankind's lasting capacity for horror on scales formerly unknown to rational minds.

Yet rational minds conducted such devastation, against civilians, in causes that were seen as fully justified and appropriate for the time. Years later, history has not in the least reversed that verdict. Bombing continues as a weapon of war, coming from all angles, the skies, trucks, cars, "suicide bombers," against crowded school buildings, malls or skyscrapers. It doesn't matter: war is war, and terror is terror. The two cannot be divorced and, indeed, are integral, whether as tactic or strategy.

Americans have not been spared the scars of such terror, but the reality is, nevertheless, considered new and novel. The 9/11 attacks are seen by most Americans as evidence of a new and totally horrific brand of warfare, suddenly invented by Islamic radicals from distant and unknown lands with reasons un-fathomable. That's understandable. The total number of Americans killed by bombs in World War II was six: a family that happened upon a Japanese bal-loon-bomb grounded in an Oregon picnic forest.

By contrast: in the air "blitz" of 1940, residents of London endured 76 consecutive days of German air attacks, at times with over 1,000 planes in the sky at a cost of over 50,000 dead. In American terms, that's 76 straight 9/11's, non-stop! That would have made a Churchill out of anybody, even including "W" Bush.

But has America really been spared? There have been four wars inside the country since independence: two against the British, one, long war against In-dians (now termed "Natives") and one among ourselves. By far, extremely far, the only one that cost the country any serious destruction was the last one, called "Civil." In terms of a war between two parts of the same country, it was civil (i.e. "within"). In terms of its impact upon the land and its people, it was anything but.

For casualties alone, the Civil War stands by itself. There were more com-bat deaths in the Civil War than all other foreign wars combined. In 1861, the population was 32 million; by 1865, an estimated 720,000 men from both sides were killed (more from disease than bullets). That's 2.3% of the population. In today's population of 330 million, the same percentage would yield 7.2 mil-lion dead. All within four years! The War on Terror began in 2001, eighteen years ago. By Civil War standards, that would result in approximately 30 mil-lion dead Americans fighting Islamic terror. How would the country react to that stat? How would Russian "collusion" equate?

Today, the two parties are waging political "war" against each other. Mostly, each accuses the other of always lying or being "unfit" for anything. Accusing a Supreme Court nominee of misbehaving at 17. Condemning a

Vice-President for acting giddy with women. When he was Vice-President, Aaron Burr shot and killed Alexander Hamilton, a Founding Father. Now, *that's* serious! Today's political culture seems theatrical, as if a Director is on set. In historical perspective, they also seem silly. Childlike. But perspective has rarely been a political virtue.

In history, the South, alone, is the only region to have memories of the horrors of war firsthand. The memory still lingers, but time is passing quickly. The last Civil War soldier died in 1958, the last Gettysburg reunion was in 1938, and Vicksburg refused to celebrate July 4 until 1945.

The past is prologue, but experience shapes behavior. It is no coincidence that South Carolina revolted first and still remains the most "militaristic" American state.

In her penetrating book, *War Upon the Land*, (2012) Professor Lisa Brady (Boise State) has reminded Americans how "a foreign troop" can wreak havoc upon the people and land they have invaded. Her study has relevance today.

For one thing, it explains the American "way" of war. Total and final. The devastation of the Confederacy in the mid-nineteenth century compares equally with the complete obliteration of European and Japanese cities that modern airpower of the twentieth century would produce. Like the missions of advanced B-17 "Flying Fortresses," it was also deliberate and systematic. Dr. Brady described in chilling detail the devastation of the land wrought by the Civil War:

"Across the South, and in a few places in the North, massive armies collided, leaving trenches and rifle pits gaping like open sores; pits from the explosions of underground mines pock marked the ground, and where thick woods once stood, little but broken trunks and shattered limbs remained. In the most heavily contested areas, the effects of the Civil War were akin to a natural disaster, a comparison often made by those who witnessed its destructive power."

General Grant, famous for "unconditional surrender," provided his top Generals, Sherman and Sheridan, *carte blanche* to wage what we now call "total" war. To Sheridan in western Virginia, he ordered: "... eat out Virginia clear and clean as far as they go, so that the crows flying over it will have to carry their own provisions with them." An eyewitness later recorded the result:

"I try to restrain my bitterness at the recollection of the dreadful scenes I witnessed. I rode down the Valley with the advance after Sheridan's retreating cavalry beneath great columns of smoke which almost shut out the sun by day, and in the red glare of bonfires, which all across that Valley poured out flames and sparks heavenward and cracked mockingly in the night air."

During his "march" through Georgia, Sherman cabled Grant, "...when the rich planters of the Oconee and Savanna [rivers] see their fences and corn and hogs and sheep vanish before their eyes they will have something more than a mean opinion of the Yanks."

William T. Sherman famously later called war as "all hell," a metaphor he helped create. But the description lasted. Today, it is commonplace to call the country "divided," often compared to the Civil War itself.

Where's the "hell", in the Mueller Report?

American Terrorists

April 1, 2019

Thus far, the bulk of attention in the twenty-first century on U.S. foreign policy has been the so-called "War on Terror" that began with the opening strike in 2001. Although few believe that American existence is at stake, the violence, death-toll, and societal disruption have made a lasting impression. Like Pearl Harbor, the 9/11 attacks still resonate in the body politic as symbolic of a "new age" in global politics.

There is a saying, "there is nothing new under the sun," and it applies to war as well, including terrorist warfare. As the new century began with a terrorism "bang," so too did the United States of America. Nor was it confined to the origins, as applied terrorism went to stamp aspects of the American "experiment" well past its national beginnings.

If this is surprising, and perhaps even shocking, one should repeat the slogan, above. The reality of guerrilla war, "unconventional," "irregular," and otherwise "asymmetrical" conflict has been with the world since time began. Movements and causes that lack tanks, infantry, and airplanes use what they have. That means stealth, deceit, mass-murder, torture, secrecy, and all the paraphernalia that we have come to identify with today's terrorist thugs.

That "partisan" war, including systematic terror, was once employed by patriotic Americans against each other may come as a shock. If so, the reason is the definition of warfare that Americans have come to accept as universal.

In his massive history, *The American Way of War*, Russell Weigley has identified the conception of war that has arisen in the U.S. since at least the Union victory in the Civil War. Based upon the strategies employed by General Ulysses S. Grant, Americans have since come to define the nature of war as essentially the massed annihilation of the enemy's armed forces and population. "The strategy of annihilation," Weigley wrote, "became characteristically the American way in war."

Grant's approach against civilians aiding the Confederacy reflects the mindset that Americans have developed against terrorists. In his instructions to General Philip Sheridan in rural Virginia, Grant defined war as total and final: "... Give the enemy no rest. Do all the damage to railroads and crops you can. Carry off stock of all descriptions, and negroes, so as to prevent further planting. If the war is to last another year, we want the Shenandoah Valley to remain a barren waste." Sheridan told his men, "I want you to be bold, enterprising, and at all times full of energy, when you begin, let it be a campaign of annihilation, obliteration and complete destruction."

General William T. Sherman and his "march to the sea" perhaps expresses this strategy best. "I will make the march and make Georgia Howl," he wrote Grant. Soon afterward, he promised to "smash South Carolina all to pieces." He did both and remains a legend.

Ironically, the original American campaigns for independence involved exactly that aspect of conflict that Grant and the Union Army destroyed when the army had the resources. It must be emphasized that the first Americans were revolutionaries, with all the attributes that term connotes. They were fighting the world's superpower at the time and used the weapons that they had, which included systematic terror.

The Revolution was not only a war against the British; it was also a civil war. Only about one-fifth of the total population (about 3 million) favored war; the rest favored the British (Loyalists) or were neutral. From the beginning, the Revolutionaries (Patriots) fought the British Redcoats simultaneously with the Loyalists in an internecine series of battles for control of the population. By definition, these battles were terror attacks, particularly for the civilians that got caught in the middle.

The South became the principal terrorist battleground in the war between Patriots and Loyalists (also called Tories). The southern campaigns were nearly all guerrilla in type where terrorism reached a gruesome peak. Lynchings, ambushes, and murders became a common feature of daily life. Between 1780 and 1781 in South Carolina alone, terrorist attacks claimed over 4,000 casualties. The names of guerrilla captains, Daniel Morgan, Andrew Pickens, and, most famously, Francis Marion, the "Swamp Fox," became notorious for both the British Army and the Loyalists. Marion's fame has since resulted in over 70 formal places — towns, schools, landmarks — named in his honor, second only to George Washington.

Historian John Shy wrote that "... neither side had the capacity of fully protecting its supporters among the civilian population, and a ferocious guerrilla war spread throughout South Carolina and into Georgia and North Carolina."

Professor North Callahan quoted the diary of a British chaplain in revealing his shock at early American warfare:

"These Americans, so soft, pacific and benevolent by nature, are here transformed into monsters, implacably bloody and ravenous; party rage has kindled the spirit of hatred between them, they attack and rob each other by turns, destroy dwelling houses, or establish themselves by driving out those who had before dispossessed others."

But terrorism was not confined to the South. In New Jersey, historian Robert Calhoon described Bergen County as "... a grim twilight zone of random violence and increasing insecurity." Patriot vigilantes, "Sons of Liberty," rounded up and deported suspected Tories in New York City, prompting historian Claude van Tyne to write that the times were "... months of terror for the Loyalists." He also described Pennsylvania as a place where "... Tories were cowed by a reign of terror." Historian Howard Swiggett described warfare in the Susquehanna Valley:

"The sinister terror and suspicion which so cruelly attends civil wars enveloped the valley. ...There was something fearful in every footfall. The lone valley, pictured by so many as an Arcadia, was in reality a cauldron in the hills, boiling with greed and violence and fear."

Professor Callahan described New Jersey:

"Much of the fighting done by the Jersey Tories was not orthodox, to say the least. They became so desperate, and often depraved, ...that they plundered friends as well as foes, warred upon aged persons and defenseless youths, ...butchered the wounded while they were begging for mercy, allowed prisoners to starve, and destroyed churches as well as public buildings."

History cannot absolve the present. But perspective helps understanding. War is war, whether it is a pistol shot that ended an empire or an atomic bomb that killed 100,000 civilians in about 30 seconds.

What's in a name?

Anatomy of Terrorism

March 27, 2019

The title of this essay may be somewhat confusing. This is unavoidable, as one should automatically assume that the subject is the current "War on Terror" with the U.S. as target. Not exactly. The title might just as well be "Warfare," as terror itself is a weapon of war, not an end in itself. Even today's terrorists have motivations, Islamic Caliphate in particular. They are "at war," but their weapons cannot include battleships, tanks, or infantry. They use what they have and target what is vulnerable. In both cases, this means primarily civilians.

The title "war on terror," thus, is a euphemism, a linguistic problem, as it identifies the enemy as a tactic, not a cause or a people. Just as there is no such thing as a "war on tanks," the vocabulary on the current (and seemingly endless) war is a strategic misnomer.

Names are not irrelevant. President Obama refused to identify Islam with terror, the Confederacy refused to fight a "civil" war, and World War II was named since it continued the first one. Most wars have place names: Korea, Vietnam, Afghanistan. There has never been a nameless war, and each name has a meaning.

Normally, the tactics of war have strategies. This is universal in conventional wars but obscure in terror wars. That's because terror as a weapon cannot, by definition, go any further than its particular locale. When soldiers capture a city, they intend to occupy the whole country. When the Allies stormed the Normandy beach, they wanted to take Germany, not just the French coast.

By killing civilians in buildings or blowing up a mall, what is the strategy of terrorists? What have they gained? Unlike "real" war, the answer is not obvious or even apparent.

In trying to uncover the purpose of terror, one runs into obstacles immediately. That may be why the subject infuriates so many: there seems to be no purpose. After 9/11, where over 3,000 innocents died, radical Islam gained nothing but notoriety. No space was occupied, no government toppled, no strategy recognized. Today, eighteen years later, there also has been no apparent gain. Even ISIS, spawned after 9/11, has had to yield back the sizable territory that it gained. So, what is the value of "back to square one"?

A related problem is the enemy himself. Wars are defined as large movements, huge countries, millions of men, crushing of material, profound conclusions. On 9/11/01, nineteen men, who couldn't even land an airplane, refocused the energy and direction of history's greatest superpower, forced it to spend billions of its dollars; all without tangible gain. On the positive side, it hasn't happened since.

That does not mean that terrorism has no consequences. But consequence without purpose is demonstrably irrational. Western lifestyles have been disrupted, buildings secured, lines at airports, new agencies and departments created, but for what? If terrorists wanted to murder and disrupt societies, they have been successful. But what is their ultimate purpose if it stops there?

Even something as basic as a definition remains elusive. The term itself is French, *terrorisme*, "great fear," "dread," related to the Latin verb, *terrere*, "to frighten." In 1793, The French National Commission declared that "terror is the order of the day." That period saw the first formal "reign" of terror, with Maximilien Robespierre proclaiming that "terror is nothing other than justice, prompt, severe, inflexible." The first recorded English definition appeared in 1798, to mean "systematic use of terror as a policy."

We haven't come much further since. Neither the international community nor scholarship has been able to draw a consensus definition. In 2003, the United States Army counted 109 different definitions, covering a total of 22 separate elements. Terrorism expert Walter Laqueur wrote that the "only general characteristic is that terrorism involves violence and the threat of violence [but] so does war, coercive diplomacy and bar room brawls."

Perhaps a larger perspective may shed light. Examined further, terror is as old as warfare itself. Even the Bible has its own references. In Paul's *2 Corinthians*, terror is employed much as it is used today: "Knowing, therefore, the terror of the Lord, we persuade men."

Terror has had a great impact on modern times beyond the French Revolution. Around the turn of the twentieth century, eleven heads of state were killed by terrorists, including President McKinley and Hapsburg Empire heir Archduke Franz Ferdinand. Ferdinand's murder caused the First World War and much of what has happened since. All by a young man with a pistol, a member of the Serbian terrorist gang, "Black Hand."

The rise of totalitarian regimes throughout the globe has given an equal rise to the so-called "age of terror." The "Red Terror," invented by Vladimir Lenin, and the "Gestapo," invented by Adolph Hitler, have perhaps done more than any other ideological movements to create the fear-psychosis now endemic in the American political culture.

But the past was much worse. In his book, *The Great Terror*, Robert Conquest has estimated that "the whole range of Soviet regime's terror can hardly be lower than fifteen million." One explanation of the use of terror came from former Soviet KGB General Aleksandr Sakharovsky, who wrote that, "In today's world, when nuclear arms have made military force obsolete, terrorism should be our main weapon." In 1969, when 82 airplanes were hijacked by the KGB-financed Palestine Liberation Organization (PLO), he boasted that "airplane hijacking is my own invention."

Finally, an "anatomy" of terrorism can go no further than a description of the "externals," the instruments and tactics. The "internals," motives, strategies, are beyond this scope. Perhaps St. Paul, above, was right: they either think that they're God or that they are acting for Him.

In 1949, *The God That Failed* revealed the "repentance" manifestos of former members of the Communist Party. One reviewer wrote that the book "promoted an American agenda [and] was immediately read as a volley from the American side of the Cold War."

Perhaps we need a new "volley."

Could/Should the U.S. Have Stayed Out of World War I?

Imaged by Heritage Auctions, HA.com

March 21, 2019

The answer to the first question is easy: of course. The U.S. could easily have avoided the war, if it chose to. That brings up the second question: why did the U.S. choose to enter the war, and did it matter? This is somewhat more complicated.

The first reaction might be, so what? That means that history is irrelevant. Well, then, what *is* relevant? Did World War I have any consequences for this country, for the world? The answer, just about everything: World War II, Hitler, Lenin, Stalin, the Cold War, NATO, Korean, Vietnam Wars, the end of colonialism, Israel, the rise of the Middle East, Islam, and the current war on terror (to mention a few).

To assess the consequences of the question, history needs to be re-examined. When the war began in 1914, President Woodrow Wilson immediately declared U.S. neutrality. In 1916, he won another term with the slogan "He Kept Us Out of War." Five months later, he declared war on Germany; Congress approved with 56 "No" votes. Were the opponents right? What happened?

Background will tell us something. How "neutral" was the U.S.? First, all the Cabinet members, except one, plus Wilson, were fervently pro-British. The exception was Secretary of State William Jennings Bryan, who resigned in protest in 1915. Second, the moment war began, the American industrial and financial system, then in a depression, began pouring arms, munitions, and bank loans to the Allies (primarily Britain and France). At the same time, the British Navy began a tight blockade of the Central Powers (Germany, Austria-Hungary), thus restricting any possibility of trade or aid getting through.

The blockade was so tight that trade with Germany fell to almost nothing by the middle of the war. In 1914, U.S. trade with Germany totaled 170 million dollars; by 1917 it had dropped to about one million, a 99.9% decline. Trade with the Allies in 1914 was about 825 million dollars; in 1917, it had risen to about three trillion, a 300% increase.

Beyond the blockade of the continent, Britain mined the North Sea, thus supervising all American cargo ships that needed sailing instructions. If the cargo was objectionable, the ship was seized and brought to a British port. The British Navy ruled the entire ocean. American merchant ships suspected of carrying contraband were seized, often boarded, and often brought to ports and held for periods of days or weeks. Official Washington sent diplomatic protest notes to the British Foreign Office, but they were either ignored or delayed for months at a time. Interior Secretary Franklin K. Lane summarized the U.S. attitude:

"There isn't a man in the Cabinet who has a drop of German blood in his veins, I guess. Two of us were born under the British flag. I have two cousins in the British army, and Mrs. Lane has three. ...Yet each day that we meet we boil over somewhat, at the foolish manner in which England acts. Can it be that she is trying to take advantage of the war to hamper our trade?"

The U.S. Ambassador, Walter Hines Page, was more pro-British than American. Historian Thomas A. Bailey wrote, "Instead of faithfully representing the United States in England, as was his duty, Page represented the British cause to the government in Washington. His bias finally became so blatant that President Wilson wrote him off as 'really an Englishman.'"

British behavior on the high seas was flagrantly illegal. In January 1917, Germany announced a resumption of "unlimited" submarine warfare, which was also illegal. In March, German subs began sinking unarmed American merchantmen, and, in April, the U.S. declared war. The world hasn't been the same since.

In order to assess the original question, we have to change the U.S. position entirely. President Donald Trump has been accused of lying, but politicians have been known to lie. Still, of all the presidential lies in American history, none may equate with the fabrication of American "neutrality" in World War I. In criminal cases, to "aid and abet" is to be liable. U.S. aid/trade kept the Allies afloat until American soldiers won the war (in six months).

But what if the U.S. had authentically stayed neutral? How would the century have unfolded? First, some sort of "Cold War" would have occurred anyway. The Bolsheviks declared war on the capitalist world in their 1917 revolution, and the U.S. was capitalist.

Second, the most that can be stated with confidence is that World War II could/should have been avoided. By 1918, after four years, both sides were exhausted and war-weary. There was mutiny in France, impatience in England, and revolution in Germany. The end was in sight. It would have been a negotiated armistice or a German victory. The Allies alone could not possibly have defeated Germany.

Without U.S. entry, there would have no Versailles Treaty, termed a "diktat" by Hitler, who used it to arouse Germany against the Weimar Republic and Wilson's League of Nations. Neither the U.S. nor Germany (nor Russia) joined the League initially, and the U.S. never joined. Both Weimar and the League became two of history's worst creations; both collapsed and made the Second World War a near certainty. Wilson's acquiescence to French demands for an occupation, reparations, and German acceptance of war guilt made the next war absolutely certain.

The other events of the century would have mostly still occurred, with time and circumstance different: the end of colonialism, birth of Israel, Communist China, Cold War, Islamic terrorism.

Should the U.S. still have stayed out? Only if you wanted to avoid World War II, the worst man-made calamity in history.

On the Versailles Treaty, French Marshall Foch stated, "This is not peace. It is an armistice for 20 years." As Prime Minister, Churchill wrote President Roosevelt that the Second World War was "The unnecessary war, there never was a war more easy to stop."

From hindsight, neither man knew how right he was.

AU or the EU?

March 15, 2019

Most people know that EU stands for European Union, begun in 1993. But nobody knows what AU means. That's because it doesn't exist (aside from American University).

The initials AU stand for Atlantic Union, an idea that goes way back but remains just that, an idea. While the notion of solidarity can be traced to colonial America, the first popular effort toward a reality came in 1939 by an American war correspondent/journalist, Clarence Streit. His book, *Union Now, A Proposal for an Atlantic Union of the Free*, urged that the democracies forge a single political unit against despotism (Nazis, Communists) while still maintaining sovereignty. He included the U.S., Britain and parts of the Empire, France, Scandinavia, Switzerland, The Netherlands and Belgium. Initial reactions were favorable. *The New York Times* wrote that "some day, in the kind of world we live in, with space annihilated and interdependence between nations complete, something like Mr. Streit suggests will have to come to pass."

None other than Winston Churchill himself suggested a variation on the same theme. His famous "Iron Curtain" speech, March 1946, may be the most important oration of modern times. But, buried within the speech was a hidden, but central message. Near the beginning, Churchill noted that "the crux of what I have travelled here to say" was not the Iron Curtain, but a unification of the Anglo-American political culture. He then proposed a "fraternal association of the English-speaking peoples ... a special relationship between the British Commonwealth and Empire and the United States." Churchill went even further: "Eventually there may come — I feel eventually there will come — the principle of common citizenship."

In 1949, the first, and only, trans-Atlantic unit was formed. NATO is a military alliance that includes Canada and the United States and was formed to thwart any possible invasion from Stalin and the Red Army. Article five of the treaty requires a collective front should an invasion be imminent. In the over seventy-year history of NATO, Article five has been invoked just once, on an issue that had nothing so do with either the Soviet Union or Russia (9/11 attacks).

Stalin died in 1953; the Red Army no longer exists. NATO now has twenty-nine members. What are the chances of Putin's Russian Army invading an alliance with twenty-nine members? What are the chances of France invading Belgium?

While NATO remains the only trans-Atlantic organization, Europe has formed unities of its own, primarily the Common Market (EEC), the Coal and Steel Community (ECSC), and the Atomic Energy Community (Euratom). The European Union (EU) has since absorbed the first two. Britain has since announced its withdrawal from the entire EU (Brexit).

Trans-Atlantic relations have served both parties well, despite the lack of a formal political/ cultural association. When President Trump publically asked fellow NATO members to pay their dues, the reaction was swift and hostile. One would think that he was withdrawing the U.S. from the treaty itself. Any "tampering" with the status quo, it appears, is seen as a betrayal.

Yet NATO is over seventy, past the time when most people retire. The year 1949 is a quaint memory: Harry Truman was president, Bill Clinton and Donald Trump were three, and Ronald Reagan had just met Nancy Davis, while Barack Obama's parents had yet to even meet.

In 1962, a team of scholars at the University of Pennsylvania's Foreign Policy Research Institute (FPRI) published *A Forward Strategy for America*, a book that outlined a spectrum of initiatives to take the offensive in the Cold War. The book had several contributors but was led by FPRI Director Robert Strausz-Hupe and his Deputy Director, William R. Kintner. *Forward Strategy* provided a background and guide for the subsequent Reagan strategies in the 1980s that eventually ended the Cold War and terminated the life-span of the Soviet Union.

A year later, the same team published *Building the Atlantic World*, which offered similar advice to develop an authentic unity that would embrace both sides of the ocean. That advice still remains on the table. The end of the Cold War has witnessed a reversal of American designs on the global stage. Both Clinton's "assertive multilateralism" and Obama's "leading from behind" confirmed this reverse.

It is never too late. American foreign policy has always needed a "cause" to promote its momentum. World War I was "to make the world safe for democracy." Then came FDR's "Four Freedoms," Kennedy's call to "ask not what America will do for you, but what together we can do for the freedom of man" to Reagan's "it's morning again in America."

Trump's call to "Make America Great Again," while inspirational rhetoric, is widely interpreted as either isolationist or overly nationalistic. In any case, it does not offer an expansive cause beyond the shorelines.

To be kind, President Trump's talents do not highlight diplomacy. Yet, with just a single reference or a major speech, any American President has the authority to put the world on notice. With a declaration toward a "cause greater than ourselves," he has the power to commit the country to a historic and global agenda, reminiscent of both Woodrow Wilson and Winston Churchill.

NATO doesn't need to just be ended; it needs to be expanded in creative and positive ways. It's time for America to "build the Atlantic world." It's time for an American "cause" greater than ourselves.

Predictions

March 14, 2019

At the end of his long-running talk show, the late John McLaughlin would ask the panel for "predictions." They would then offer insights on the latest political gossip regarding personalities or upcoming events. Often they were wrong, but nobody kept score; it was entertainment.

McLaughlin's panel, made up of columnists and "public intellectuals," reflects the problem involving prediction of things to come. They were usually the result of guesswork or "insider" information. It surely was not "science."

Perhaps the closest thing to scientific prediction is the weather. Each night, a trained "weatherman" predicts tomorrow's climate. But even these experts are famously wrong. On any given night, channel 4 might say, rain, channel 7, snow, and 9 "sunny skies." The public takes this for granted.

These specialists are often dead wrong, but we still depend on them. While predicting tomorrow's climate is precarious in itself, the so-called "environmentalists" have no doubt as to what the climate will be 100 years from now, or 50, or 12. Predictions can be inherently illogical (and "science" can be wrong).

Probably history's most famous predictor was the French 16th century physician and astrologer, Nostradamus, whose "Prophesies" contain over 900 "quatrains," or predictions of the future, including wars and invasions, natural disasters and, ultimately, the end of the world. His methods, never explained, were considered mystical and intuitive, but have long-since been dismissed by most serious historians.

But, on occasion, predictions regarding future human behavior have been made that, on the surface, seem to have been divinely inspired rather than scientific. Another Frenchman, Alexis de Tocqueville, made this observation on the "Russians and the Anglo Americans" in 1832: "each one of them seems called by a secret design of Providence to hold in its hands the destinies of half the world."

Tocqueville counselled demographics for this prediction, but did he have any insight into the twentieth century's Cold War, the world wars, the Great Depression, or any other event of the future? Of course not. He may have had some evidence based upon populations, but the rest had to be only guesswork.

As a field of inquiry, is prediction much else? History itself, the most "scientific" of inquiries, based upon observation, collection, and painstaking research, is still being debated as we speak. If things that happened are denied and contested, how can things that never happened be accepted?

That doesn't mean that we don't try. Almost everybody does, all the time. Example (fictitious): Joan and Harry just got married. One friend says, "it'll never work;" another says "made in heaven." Where's the science (in heaven)?

The fate of civilization is frequently predicted. The latest is the "decline" of some or the other nation or world order. By definition, it is always the "West." It cannot be either North, South, or East; one must "rise" before one can "decline."

The German historian/philosopher Oswald Spengler began modern "declinism" with his two-volume *Decline of the West* (1923). In Spengler's view, Western civilization would not end as a sudden catastrophe but rather a "protracted" fall, a "twilight" or "sunset." Spengler's word for the West, *Abenland*, is German for "evening land."

The British historian Arnold Toynbee (1889-1975) published a definitive ten-volume history of the rise and decline of civilizations, *A Study of History*, defining the fall of societies through a "challenge-response" scenario in which a minority rises to the top only to fall prey to forces from within ("suicide"). Both Spengler and Toynbee, while not without dissenters, have provided platforms for whole generations of historians to make predictions on the inevitable/probable downfall of their own or current world orders.

The following list, while certainly not exhaustive, will suffice to appreciate the range and extent of the predictors of Western decline (each theme in parentheses):

James Burnham, *Suicide of the West*, 1964, (liberalism will end Western dominance),

Paul Kennedy, *The Rise and Fall of the Great Powers*, 1987, ("imperial overstretch" has produced the decline of history's great powers),

Samuel P. Huntington, *The Clash of Civilizations and the Remaking of World Order*, 1996, (Western dominance will give-way to the rise of civilizations throughout the world),

Carroll Quigley, *The Evolution of Civilizations*, 1961, (Americans will "cop out of the system [and] ultimately prefer communities"),

Jeremy Griffith, *Freedom: The End of the Human Condition*, 2016, (humanity can end the "human condition" only by understanding its biological/psychological roots),

Martin Heidegger, *Being and Time*, 1927, (considered the West headed for total war, consumed by nihilism, a "wasteland, characterized by ignorance and barbarism. In which everything is permitted."),

Whittaker Chambers, *Witness*, 1952, (considered the West to be in a Spenglerian "twilight" in which Communism is a symptom rather than a cause).

More recently, it has become fashionable to predict the rise of Eastern culture, especially China, as a replacement of the West in the next world order. No timetable is given, no scenario, almost total conjecture, as though "it's time." A new book by Cambridge professor J.C. Sharman *Empires of the Weak* (2018) revives ancient history to demonstrate the point. Since, he reasons, Western dominance was comparatively short-lived compared to Eastern cultures, it should be inevitable that the cycle will eventually bend again eastward.

A bolder, more insistent, theory was recently presented by British Marxist/historian Martin Jacques, *When China Rules the World*, 2009. Here, he predicts that "in time" the sheer economic, technological, population, and cultural impact of China will be able to govern the entire globe, from Sweden to Indonesia to Nebraska, to Paris.

That's a tall order, never even close in world history. The closest was the British Empire, governing at its height about one-fifth of the globe.

Are Americans worried about all this? Doubtful. Any society whose attention was dominated by the behavior of a Supreme Court nominee when he was 17 doesn't appear concerned about world order. Any president who declared that U.S. foreign policy would "lead from behind" has a similar worldview (parochial).

But will America be "great again"? Not when the governor of a leading state replies that it "was never that great" anyway.

As for predictions, there is one certainty: "that remains to be seen."

Who/What Caused the Civil War?

March 4, 2019

The Civil War, America's worst experience, was caused by people, as are all wars. But which ones? The title of this essay implies that either certain people or their institutions caused this calamity. Who or what? Thus, the ultimate causation was "nature," either human or human-created.

Interesting, but not much else. Neither explanation separates the American Civil War from any other war. But can they be separated?

Kenneth Waltz, in his profound inquiry on war, *Man, the State and War* (1959) examines three "levels of analysis" — human beings, the nature of their political institutions, and the "international system" (anarchy).

But the American Civil War was within a shared political institution (democratic republic) and was, thus, "domestic" and not international. That leaves only the first cause, human, but, again, who?

Today, the legacy of the Civil War, more than a century and a half later, can still dominate public discourse. Daily reminders of slavery and "racism," erasing of memorials to both and to the Confederacy have become commonplace in the media, entertainment, politics, and most all aspects of contemporary culture. (I recently toured Monticello, Thomas Jefferson's home, and heard more of his slave/lover Sally Hemmings than of Jefferson).

Within this perspective, it is commonly held that slavery caused the Civil War. How can that be? The institution of slavery was present from the beginning and was still legal in all thirteen colonies in 1776. During the Civil War it existed only in the south and was not legally outlawed until after the war (thirteenth amendment). The United States was the only country in the world where a war was required to end slavery, but did the institution pull the trigger at Fort Sumter?

How can an institution that existed for centuries in a country, and was universal, cause a military conflict that nearly terminated its own existence? What took so long? Why didn't the Civil War begin in 1661 or 1761 or 1850? And if slavery was the reason, why wasn't it announced at the beginning of the war instead as a moral causation after the Battle of Antietam (Emancipation Proclamation).

The logical answer, of course, is that slavery was a "background" cause, not a precipitate one. But that relieves human decisions as causations and blames the institutions they created. That also means that only backgrounds cause wars.

The same can be said of democracy as inherently "peaceful," as opposed to dictatorships as inherently warlike. In American history ("Wilsonianism"), this has grown into an article of faith. So has the slavery myth.

In turn, slavery has its own background: cotton and the invention of the cotton gin (1792). Translated into human beings, this means that Eli Whitney (the inventor) was more responsible for the war than Jefferson Davis. It means that the British demand for cotton was more important than the 1000 (or less) men who owned plantations. And it might mean that the southern climate created both plantations and cotton, then slaves, and then war.

If this list is too conflated for reality, then a closer examination is needed. What is more important for the Civil War, slavery or its mortal enemy, abolitionism? Slavery was condoned in the Bible, both Old and New, and was present in North America before Columbus. The abolition movement began around 1830 and was confined to the North, especially New England. Secession started in December 1860 in South Carolina, and the war began four months later.

Do the math.

In his classic study of "pragmatism" in America, *The Metaphysical Club* (2001), Louis Menand (CCNY Professor) notes the impact that the Civil War had upon abolitionism and its philosophical supporters, principally Oliver Wendell Holmes, William James, Charles Peirce, and John Dewey. Holmes, in particular, was wounded three times and looked upon the war as an unnecessary and tragic calamity engineered in large part by the insistence of abolitionism as a total and final solution to slavery. They later formed a "Metaphysical Club" at Harvard that tried to reconcile their pre-war beliefs with the calamity that the war had inflicted on the whole society, especially the horrible death toll (over 700,000 in a population of 32 million).

Thus, "pragmatism" was born, the sole American contribution to historic philosophic thought. Pragmatism sought to relieve "ideas" from immediate, drastic, or ideological action and to seek solutions in orderly, moderate ("pragmatic") manners. This approach is often explained by a metaphor: if one tries to eat soup with a fork, he should not destroy soup or forks; he should simply invent spoons.

The impact upon Holmes, in particular, is described graphically by Menand: "The moment Holmes returned from the war he seems to have fast-frozen his experience, and to have sealed its meaning off from future revision. ... he could not bear to read histories of the Civil War. He rarely mentioned the issues that had been the reason for the fighting or expressed a political opinion about the outcome. The war had burned a hole, so to speak, in his life."

Thus, immediately after the war, the instigators knew full well who was responsible, and it wasn't the slaveholders. Yet, it takes two to make a fight. While abolitionism was the immediate spark (the "primary" cause), blame also goes to the heirs of John C. Calhoun and the "sovereignty" apostolates of South Carolina. They erroneously viewed Lincoln's election as a violation of "states' rights" and the end of their cultural life. But Lincoln was not an abolitionist and opposed only the westward extension of slavery.

South Carolina voted for secession, and the die was cast.

Thus, the Civil War, like most all others, was begun by normal people, "politicians," making terrible mistakes and not stopping long enough to see the consequences. Like it died almost everywhere else, and in the American North, slavery did not need a war to end it. It would have gone quietly (or "quieter").

What is the Most Important Moment in Modern History?

March 4, 2019

When I ask my History class this question for the first time, certain answers dominate. Many say "who cares"? Then comes sarcasm, "my birthday," and, more seriously, the 9/11 attacks.

By the last class, perspective has grown, with some actually acknowledging something important preceding them. That's progress.

Definitions are in order. First, who does care and why? Everybody should, because history is the only known human laboratory and it "repeats." If it didn't repeat, everything would be unique, i.e. a "first." Human events, of course, are never identical, but they do demonstrate patterns of behavior. This is demonstrably true on individual levels. Every human being knows his or her life story and, in turn, usually can point out the exact moment something "critical" happened. Actually, "my birthday," while meant jocularly, is appropriate. What is the most critical moment in U.S. history? Most would answer, July 4, the birthday.

Second, what is "important"? Does it affect persons, locales, regions, countries, or the world? By definition, the world has to be the answer; everything else is parochial, relatively.

Third, why "moment"? While this is admittedly arbitrary, it helps to narrow down an event by the most precise term. One of the greatest texts in the New Testament is the moment St. Paul was struck by lightning and converted to Christianity. The rest, so they say, is history.

Fourth, what is "modern"? Again, this is arbitrary, but I have chosen the beginning of the Twentieth Century. If one goes further back or forward, the answer could be much different. Either way, the answer is still important.

The first task is to identify "important." This is, perhaps, the most decisive, and subjective, decision. Although not entirely arbitrary, the identification of this event will dictate the moment. Here is where controversy can intrude, and elimination of every other occasion is almost certainly to bring about dissent.

Upon reflection, there aren't that many candidates, if one accepts the boundaries. Some prominent candidates:

- 9/11 (September 2001) began the War on Terror;
- Hiroshima, Nagasaki (August 1945) introduced the Atomic Age and ended World War II;
- Pearl Harbor (December 1941) brought the U.S. into world politics;
- Yalta Conference (February 1945) began the Cold War;
- Fall of the Berlin Wall (November 1989) ended the Cold War;
- German invasion of Poland (September 1939) began World War II;
- Communist victory in China (October 1949) began China as a global power.

While certainly not exhaustive, this list defines many of the decisive events of the time period. Yet, there is a problem. They all occurred around mid-century or afterwards, which begs the question: what prompted them?

Thus, if one wants a "critical" moment, one usually does not start in mid-life. Unlike people or countries, world events normally do not have "birthdays." But they do have beginnings. What preceded the above?

Thus, it's only logical that the first half of the century caused the second half. Similarly, most psychiatrists claim that the human personality is formed early, around ten years of age. So, by the defined timeframe, we must look at the beginning, rather than in the middle, and certainly not at the end.

It is a historic consensus that World War I remains a divide between modern and "pre-modern." The outcome of that conflict has haunted both the recent and present generations, from the beginning of the end of colonialism, the creation of Israel, the beginning of Communism, Fascism, Nazism, Democracy in world politics (America), the end of Europe as the main contender, and the rise of the Soviet Union and the United States as world "superpowers." The world's most recent wars, bloodbaths, and terror strikes stem indirectly from that war: the atrocities in the Balkans in the 1990s, the unending battles in the Middle East and Afghanistan, the terror attacks from a resurgent Islam itself.

So in seeking a "moment," it must be related to what they once called "The Great War." They were right, but didn't know it. World War II, while much worse in casualties and destruction (75 million dead by most accounts) was, in retrospect, a direct result of the first war. It was, in fact, the second part of a two-act "theater" begun in 1914 and not resolved until 1945. Same contestants, same issues, but a definitive ending. The First World War did not really have an "end," only an armistice, a pause (half-time).

Thus, in seeking a moment, we must look at the first critical event of the century; the one we are still living out. As in all events, there are background and immediate causes. For background, we have the nation-state, begun around 1648, nationalism, militarism, the European alliance system begun in the late nineteenth century, etc. That's accurate, but it doesn't say where and when.

World War I was declared by Germany on August 1, 1914, and within days Britain joined in. The U.S. waited until April 6, 1917 to join and didn't fight on the front until mid-1918. But what started the war?

On a summer excursion to Bosnia in 1914, the heir to the Hapsburg throne, Franz Ferdinand and his wife, were murdered in Sarajevo by Gabriel Princip, a member of the Serbian terror ring, the "Black Hand." The die was cast. A month of futile negotiations between the powers failed to stem the inevitable, and modern history began its reign.

Two people shot by an obscure teen eventually saw the destruction of a world order and the deaths of tens of millions. The "moment" was approximately 10 AM, June 28, 1914. Few saw ahead, but one may have. Noticing the lamplighter closing the streetlights below, British Foreign Secretary, Edward Grey, uttered this prophetic sentence, "The lamps are going out all over Europe, we shall not see them lit again in our lifetime."

That was August 4, 1914. But the moment had already come and gone.

Good Walls Make Good Neighbors

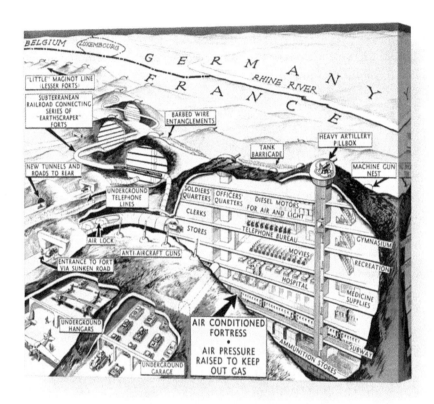

February 19, 2019

Paraphrasing poet Robert Frost ("good fences") is only symbolic since the words are interchangeable. They can also be used as "lines," "barriers," or any other obstacle to traffic, whether man or beast. The title is also erroneous; fences "make" nothing but serve only to separate otherwise "bad" neighbors.

Historically, human walls serve only two purposes, to either keep people in or out. The Berlin Wall during the Cold War served the first purpose; President Trump's project is meant for the second. Either way, walls are usually a last resort, short-term, awkward, ugly, and violent. Almost nobody likes them but sometimes they are necessary, at least in the minds of the builders.

Borders are "boundaries" that can be both human and geographic. Human boundaries are psychological and define codes of behavior that should be observed.

The Ten Commandments are God's "borders" for mankind. Similarly, nations, empires, cities, counties, jurisdictions have their own boundaries which are also meant to be observed. When they are not, barriers are erected to enforce the boundary line.

These are universal human realities, not invented by Trump or any other official. Borders have been essential for existence since the beginning of time, and no technology or global movement has yet dented this reality. Thus, no one should be surprised that in a nuclear-space age, the U.S. still clings to a border-wall as the top security issue. That includes both those opposed to it and those in favor.

Borders have defined history as much as warfare itself. U.S. borders were expanded by both purchase and conquest. The Louisiana Purchase (1803) bought land from France that expanded the American border from the Mississippi to the Rockies. The defeat of Mexico (1848) converted over half of Mexican territory into U.S. land to the Pacific Ocean.

The "nation-state" system began with the Peace of Westphalia (1648) and defined territoriality as definitive for existence. Today, there are 193 such entities in the United Nations, and each guards its frontiers with equal vigilance. Sometimes this hasn't worked.

In 1794, Poland ceased to exist, absorbed by its neighbors, Russia, Prussia, and Austria. Poland "resurrected" in 1919 (after World War I) only to disappear again in 1939 by the same culprits (without Austria). Then it was occupied by the USSR only to reappear again as a sovereign in 1991 (with the end of the Cold War). To the Poles, borders are critical for life.

Other examples abound. Using the same general region, Austria lost its entire empire in 1919 and became a tiny ski resort. In 1938, it lost even that ("Anschluss") to Hitler, only to re-emerge as a ski resort again in 1945.

Most countries are small and, thus, guard their borders jealously. The United States, being extremely large, has not usually had this problem. The northern border needs no mention as a security issue. Historically, the southern border was always just a nuisance; nobody feared a Mexican invasion. Today, the issue has grown to enormous heights and has defined American security since at least 2016. How ironic: an abstract, an idea, occupies chief national attention. This idea even shut down part of the government itself.

Throughout history, walls have defended existence ("existential") when territory was threatened. Thus, the U.S. today, after all, is no different. In his definitive book, *Walls: A History of Civilization in Blood and Brick* (2018), archaeologist David Frye notes that: "No invention in human history played a greater role in creating and shaping civilization than walls. Without walls, there could never have been ... Chinese scholars, Babylonian mathematicians, or Greek philosophers. Moreover, the impact of walls wasn't limited to the early phases for most of history, climaxing spectacularly during a 1,000 year period when three large empires – Rome, China, and Sassanid Persia – erected barriers that made the geopolitical divisions of the Old World all but permanent."

Most people are familiar with history's more famous walls, the "Great Wall" of China, Hadrian's (Britain), Jericho (Jerusalem), Trojan (Turkey), Ston (Croatia), Babylon (Iraq), Zimbabwe, Sacsayhuaman (Peru), Diyarbakir (Turkey), West Bank (Israel), "Iron Curtain" (Berlin).

But, as author Frye has emphasized, the net effect of walls in history was to preserve civilization against outside "barbarians." These included an assembly of structures around an astonishing number of countries: Syria, Egypt, Greece, Iraq, Bulgaria, Ukraine, Romania, Turkey, Russia, Britain, Peru, Afghanistan, Iran, Azerbaijan, Uzbekistan, Libya, China, Korea ("partial" list).

Now, in 2019, approximately 77 countries have some form of wall or structure to protect their frontiers, with a reported 45 planning same. In Europe itself, home of the EU, 800 miles of fencing has been built since 2015, including in Bulgaria, Hungary, Slovenia, Macedonia, Austria, and France.

Now the U.S. is contemplating one, but only the administration in power. Many Americans, especially Democrats, oppose "Trump's Wall," and have refused his budget. Much of this, of course, is pure American politics and will probably be compromised sooner or later.

In the long-term, a far better solution would be a *mutual* arrangement between the two governments, diplomacy being the "art of the possible." Barring that, a barrier, by any name, will certainly go up.

In summarizing internal debates that occupied the construction of walls before and now, author David Frye has noted: "For every person who sees a wall as an act of oppression, there is always another urging the construction of newer, higher, and longer barriers. The two sides hardly speak to each other."

Sound familiar?

The Mexican Border, Part II

February 11, 2019

A previous essay on the border (February 4) traced the early background of the region through the Eisenhower Administration (1953-61). Thus, the current turmoil on the issue, plus the government shutdown, has a 400 year legacy and is more a continuity than unique. While the caravans now challenging border security are new, they also have a background.

A modern beginning to the present crisis logically starts with the 1965 Immigration and Naturalization Act. This law (Hart-Celler Act) marked a radical break from immigration policies of the past. Historic preferences for northern and western Europe (especially Ireland, Germany, and Italy) had by now become "discriminatory" under the Lyndon Johnson administration's emphasis on civil rights. This eliminated national origin, race, and ancestry as criteria and gave priority to relatives of American citizens and legal residents as "special immigrants" not subject to numerical restrictions. Refugees were given a "category preference," including those seeking asylum. This began an immigrant shift from Europe to Mexico and Central America.

The Hart-Celler bill was widely supported in Congress, with 74% of Democrats (minus the "solid south") and 85% of Republicans voting in favor.

President Johnson signed the bill at the base of the Statue of Liberty. Supporters promised that the bill would not upset the demographic composition of the country; Johnson himself declared that it was "...not a revolutionary bill. It does not affect the lives of millions." Key supporter Senator Ted Kennedy stated that "our cities will not be flooded with a million immigrants annually ... the ethnic mix of this country will not be upset."

Of course, exactly the opposite happened.

Although the Western Hemisphere was numerically restricted, the net effect of the 1965 law reversed the source of historic immigration to these shores. Nor were they any longer "shores" (Ellis Island was closed in 1954). In the 1950s, for example, approximately 68% of immigration came from Europe or Canada. By 1991, Latin America constituted almost half (48%) of the total, with 24% of these from Mexico alone. Absolute numbers were also greatly increased. In 1970, immigrants constituted 11% of the population; by 1990, they had grown to 39%.

Nor did the 1965 law end border problems — it only shifted them geopolitically. One, somewhat bizarre, example of this was President Nixon's 1969 "Operation Intercept," intended to eliminate drug traffic from Mexico. Surprising everyone, including Mexico's president, Nixon imposed personal, three-minute, inspections of every vehicle and person crossing the border. After strong complaints from the Mexican government, these were reduced in ten days, abandoned in twenty. Few drugs were caught.

At the same time, the strong demand for immigrant workers by U.S. employers led to a dramatic rise of illegal immigrants who could not meet requirements or who exceeded existing quotas. The 1986 Immigration Reform and Control Act (Reagan Amnesty Act), criminalized hiring of illegals but legalized certain workers who were employed in agriculture. The Act also granted amnesty to 2 million of the 4 million illegals then residing. In 1987, President Reagan gave an Executive Order to legalize minor children of parents with amnesty, thus giving a blanket deferral of deportation to about 100,000 families.

In 1983, the U.S. Supreme Court forbade schools or hospitals to deny service to illegal immigrants. The country was slowly becoming accustomed to these newcomers who openly defied the law. Dozens of "sanctuary cities" provided physical protection despite federal law. Now, law-breaking became the norm on *both* sides, not just one.

For the first time since the mid-nineteenth century, with the "Know Nothing" nativists, the subject of immigration has become defined as an existential threat to American culture. The seemingly inevitable "white minority" threatens the fabric of society, leading now to racial accusations of "white privilege, white supremacy" as the definition of the American "way." Immigration is now challenging the very sociological composition of any national consciousness. Divisions have led to "uncivil" behavior, seemingly everywhere.

As time and exposure went on, several acts and laws attempted to reduce or soften the growing cultural divide. In 2006, Bush II passed the Secure Fence Act, which constructed 654 miles of new fence along the Mexican border, at a cost of $2.3 billion. Yet in 2017, the Government Accounting Office (GAO) documented 2,287 "breaches" of the line, noting that it "could not identify the cost effectiveness of border fencing compared to other assets."

At the time, however, President Bush said that "This bill will help protect the American people. This bill will make our borders more secure." Again, the opposite happened.

The border has been the top U.S. security issue for several years, including the recent U.S. Government shutdown. Now we have "caravans," which assumes the guise of organized armies. Security experts have identified a total of 43 such caravans recently, from a low of hundreds each to thousands.

In conclusion, is the issue "existential," especially in a globalization age? Recent Gallup Polls predict 42 million crossings within years, 5 million this year.

Consider a real possibility: half of the population can't/won't speak the language, they don't know/care who Jefferson was, they vote only for one party, their first formal decision was illegal, gangs and drugs accompany the influx, and they are protected by "sanctuary cities."

On a spectrum, what is the best response: alarm or acceptance? If it's the first, Trump is right, if the second, Pelosi is. Either way, it has to be existential. The issue approaches 1860 levels, but where is Lincoln?

The Mexican Border, A Short Background

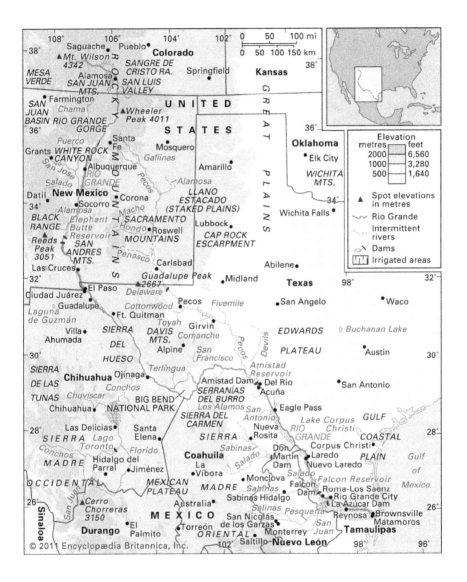

February 4, 2019

It is one of American history's greatest ironies that, since 2016, amidst the space age, with a generation of nuclear deterrence, instant global communications, and social media, that a border issue has dominated public attention. In an age of globalization, it is fashionable to dismiss geopolitics as "tribal," reminiscent of old Europe when armies crossed borders to start wars. The new phenomenon, "cyber" war, would come from computers and attack other communication targets.

Meanwhile, tens of thousands of unwelcomed (mostly) illegal "aliens" south of the border threaten to subvert the culture and change the existential nature of the country. Some refer to this as an "invasion," no-less-so than Lee's invasion of Pennsylvania.

Is this a sudden event, or an "emergency" as the President has called it? Or, more to the point, is it just another historical repetition like war and peace, nation/country and sovereignty /territory? Are the millennials right, that we can escape (or erase) the past?

First, the border itself is one of the most contentious places on earth. The total length, from the Pacific Ocean to the Gulf of Mexico, is almost 2,000 miles (1,954). It is the most human-transited site in the world, with approximately 350 million documented crossings annually. The area is characterized by diverse terrain, deserts, rugged hills, daily sunshine, and two main rivers – Rio Grande and Colorado. There are 48 designated crossings, in California, Arizona, New Mexico, and Texas, and 330 ports of entry. The largest port of entry, San Ysidro, transits about 50,000 vehicles and 25,000 pedestrians every day. Total population on both sides is 12 million.

The history pre-dates the Republic itself.

As early as the mid-16th century, with the discovery of silver, settlers from all over began to arrive, and, until the early 19th century, the area remained a kind of undefined "no-man's land." This changed with the Louisiana Purchase (1803) and Mexican independence from Spain (1821), when both independent Texas (1836-45) and Mexico vied for control of the region. Constant warfare without a defined border led to Texas statehood (1845), the Mexican War (1847-48), and the Treaty of Guadalupe-Hidalgo (1848), wherein Mexico ceded over half of its territory to the U.S. (nearly a million square miles). This treaty saw the states of California, Arizona, New Mexico, Utah, Nevada, and parts of Colorado, Wyoming, Kansas, and Oklahoma eventually join the Union.

Abraham Lincoln served only one term in Congress (1847-49) but left a fairly-unknown and curious border legacy during his term. President James K. Polk declared war due to Mexico's invasion north of the Rio Grande, an area that had been left disputed by both sides. Opposing the war, Lincoln repeatedly demanded from the floor of the House that Polk indicate the precise American "spot" that Mexico had occupied. Colleagues soon called Abe "spotty Lincoln" for his efforts in vain. Ironically, Lincoln began his public political career as a committed war resister.

A subsequent treaty (1884) officially declared the middle of the Rio Grande as the border, and an International Boundary and Water Commission (IBWC) was established in 1889. Further Immigration Acts (1891, 1917) provided supervisory procedures for legal immigrants, including literacy tests and a head tax. The 1924 Act established the U.S. Border Patrol (USBP).

The Mexican Revolution (1910-20) caused serious friction between the two countries, including a series of military raids into Arizona and New Mexico by rebel chieftain Pancho Villa and armed clashes between the American and Mexican armies. Woodrow Wilson sent the Army into Mexico both in 1914 and 1916, the latter led by General Pershing. Neither incursion produced any tangible result, and Pershing was brought home in January 1917. At the same time, Foreign Minister Arthur Zimmerman of Germany sent a dispatch to the Mexican government promising the return of lands taken in 1848 if Mexico would join the Kaiser in World War I. Mexico declined, but Wilson used this note as a *causus belli* to declare war on Germany, a decision that ultimately made the U.S. a superpower.

Thus, the Mexican border provoked perhaps the most decisive moment in U.S. foreign policy history.

During this time period, various fences and barriers were built as border towns were progressively turned into battlegrounds. Today, there are an estimated 654 miles of these impromptu barriers.

After World War I, the U.S. government encouraged legal immigration from Mexico as it was simultaneously issuing quotas against immigration from the rest of the world (1924 Immigration Act). Southwestern farmers were eager for cheap Mexican labor, while the Mexican government actually opposed this flow as their own crops were left rotting in the fields. Throughout the 1920s, an annual rate of 62,000 legal workers and 100,000 illegals crossed the border annually, with American farmers actually welcoming the illegals.

During World War II, the "Bracero" program, encouraged by Mexico, regulated the border, with over 5,000 Mexican soldiers helping supervise the region. By 1964, approximately 2 million Mexican laborers had crossed, with a peak of 445,000 in 1956.

By then, however, the Eisenhower Administration grew nervous on the border issue and promptly (1954) began "Operation Wetback," a program to round up and deport illegals. Using 700 military vehicles plus cars, buses, and airplanes, and doubling border agents (to 1700), approximately 1.7 million illegal aliens were deported, all with the cooperation of Mexican authorities, who loaded them up and transferred them deeper into the interior.

"Wetback," appropriately, ends this background (the name alone would be called "racist"). The nostalgic past ends here, and "current" history likewise begins. If nothing else, this brief glance back shows that the border issues we have now are hardly unique and that, through turmoil, chaos, congestion, and outright war, both countries have seemed to survive.

Who Goes There, Friend or Foe?

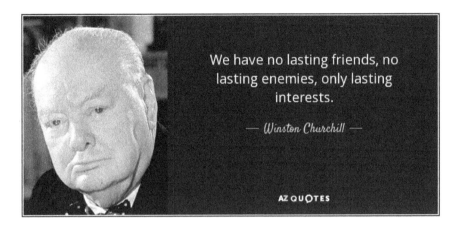

We have no lasting friends, no lasting enemies, only lasting interests.

— *Winston Churchill* —

AZ QUOTES

February 1, 2019

The above question seeks the identity of the figure and whether he is shot or let in by the sentry. It is purely symbolic but, in a larger context, represents one of the enduring dilemmas of foreign policies, whether they be ours or theirs. Who is our friend, who is an enemy?

It is not as easy as it may seem. Betrayal, deception, and disguise all combine to confuse our "sentries" in their inquiry as to the nature of the "figure" in front of us. What, for example, is China? Is anyone absolutely sure of the nature of that country and as to whether it represents a threat or just another competitor? The very fact that the subject elicits debate is proof sufficient that the answer is not only difficult but elusive.

What was Japan on December 6, 1941? For most Americans, it was at least a dangerous competitor to be addressed. The next day, it was a mortal and existential enemy that united the country as never before (or since).

These categories have a confusing and unpredictable lifeline. They go back and forth almost like the weather. Communist China was enemy number one in Asia during the early Cold War. We fought their army for three years in Korea. Suddenly, in 1972, Nixon/Kissinger made them an ally against the Soviet Union, a move that hastened the end of the Soviet Union and the Cold War itself. Who predicted that?

Friends and enemies change all the time. Most of today's American allies were once mortal enemies. We fought them all over the world and throughout our history: Great Britain (twice), Germany (twice), Russia (twice, in 1918-20 with an intervention and then the Cold War), China (twice, 1899 against the "Boxers," Korean War), Spain, Japan, Mexico (three times, 1847, 1914, 1916), North Korea, North Vietnam, ourselves (called "civil"), Italy (Mussolini), Turkey (World War I), Afghanistan, almost all the Middle East, and dozens of occupations in Central America and the Caribbean.

There may be others, but that list will do. Why did all of these wars occur? If we listen to our radical "resisters," it is due to a unique mindset, located perhaps in Kansas, the epicenter of "American imperialism." But, like slavery, discrimination, aggression, violence itself etc. etc., the issue is both timeless and universal.

Within that perspective, the very notion of friend/enemy takes on a fleeting and superfluous context. Why bother, since, as the saying goes, "today's friend is tomorrow's enemy" (and vice versa). That's exactly right, but there must be a hierarchy at least to distinguish a policy in the first place.

We get our news mostly from the media, whose perspective is limited to tomorrow's "story." For some time now, the headline story has centered on Russia, and Russia almost alone. What was the extent and nature of President Trump's "collusion" with President Putin, and, conversely, how did Putin "meddle" in the election?

Typically, this "journalism" (as it was once called) is centered on personality and personalist descriptions of great power behavior. Perhaps this is necessary. Perhaps world politics must be reduced to back-fence gossip to sell papers.

Trump's conversations with Putin are monitored by the press to see how much he "colluded." How does one "collude"? Collusion is actually defined as "price fixing," mostly between companies. Likewise, how does one "meddle"? The word sounds more like interference in a love affair.

Diplomacy as it goes now has become a public affair, whereas by definition it was always meant to be secret. Thus, at bottom, democracy is only conducting itself as it should. Fine, but this doesn't help the question at the start: who is a friend, an enemy? It just satisfies daily curiosity. But its policy reach is just as short and finite.

To help answer the question, perspective is imperative. For example, is Putin a Czar, a Stalin a Khrushchev or a Brezhnev? Or none of the above? If he interfered in Ohio's election, is he trying to overturn American democracy, or is he just "meddling" around? Does he want to absorb Ohio and take over the Cleveland Browns?

In 1942, the U.S. government put out propaganda films, directed by Frank Capra and supervised by General Marshall, to help keep morale high for the war effort. "Why We Fight" pictured Japanese soldiers marching up Pennsylvania Avenue about to occupy the Capitol. Right! The "Japs" (as they were called) invaded California, marched east across the Rockies, through Nebraska and the Midwest and camped out in Arlington Cemetery.

This was, as we call it now, "fake news." Not to say that neither Trump nor Putin are innocent of doing something, but after two years we have precious little. If Putin is an enemy, just how dangerous is he?

Could he be a "friend" or at least a neutral factor? How can we find out? Certainly not by reading the paper or turning on TV.

It's easy to be nice to friends and allies, and even to be critical (by asking them to honor their obligations). But it's hard trying to be pleasant to others, including potential enemies. That takes diplomacy and, to succeed, it has to be private. It's time to stop second-guessing those outside our orbit and begin to pursue alternative avenues. This is called a "professional" approach. These may fail, but "nothing ventured, nothing gained."

Nixon did it, why not Trump?

Can Closed Minds Govern?

January 27, 2019

There has been much attention recently about the state of American education and the mindset of today's "millennial" generation to appreciate the country they live in and the nature of the polity and culture. Polls indicate that much of current sentiment has become wholly critical of America and believes that its history and belief systems are either hypocritical or completely absent of virtue.

The two main critiques of the country focus on equality and justice, virtues that are supposedly synonymous with the term America, but, allegedly, absent from any reality. In fact, the critique goes, exactly the opposite is true, and the sum total of American culture is dominated by the twin ideological expressions, racism and sexism. This, in turn, makes the white male guilty of historical crimes against humanity to the point that the slogan "dead white males" is all that remains for identity. "White Privilege" is an equal charge against these people and any achievement in life that they may have brought to the world (such as television, vacuum cleaners, and airplanes).

The classic exposé of such notions came in 1987 with Allan Bloom's *The Closing of the American Mind*, which dissected the origins and direction of the modern "movement" with a cautious, but pessimistic warning against recovery. "It is difficult to imagine," Bloom concluded," that there is either the wherewithal or the energy within the university to reconstitute the idea of an educated human being and establish a liberal education again."

Bloom died in 1992, but should he reappear today he, undoubtedly, would be horrified as to how far his deepest fears have been realized. If the educational system represents the hopes and desires for the future, the current state of campus unrest and lack of civility overall attests to a very turbulent future for the nation, its core beliefs, and its supporters. These, all together, are in retreat ("stampede"?) and affect the entire polity as well.

The state of government today reflects this culture. The "blame game" has been ongoing for over two years but, after the longest government shutdown in history, it grows tired. It also leads nowhere, but at least acknowledging the problem as systemic and mutual is a beginning. And at the bottom of that human pyramid is education.

Instead of tranquil centers of reflection and learning, however, today's campus environment has become a hotbed of protest, intolerance, and social activism. "Identity" politics and class division have replaced traditional learning, while outdoor demonstrations substitute for the library. Throughout the country, the word "school" has been transformed from its original to a place for social movement, especially for identified sectors, races, genders (or none at all), and ethnicity. Many universities have inaugurated whole departments for "Diversity, Inclusion, and Identity" as the centerpiece of campus importance. The California system, as one example, began their centers in 2015, with millions of dollars in grants, hundreds of staff personnel and "Deans" making three to four hundred thousand dollars annually (almost as much as the average coach).

A new generation of "educators," children of the 1960's and preachers of "deconstruction" theory, seek to unmask Western civilization as the perpetrator of global injustice. Traditional values, "truth, justice, and the American way," are disparaged routinely as obstacles to progress and as barriers against "oppressed" minorities of all stripes, classes, races, and genders. Inside the Academy, "victims" of the three main "isms," colonialism, imperialism, and capitalism, has provoked counterattacks through a series of "identity" curricula, including Women's, Black, Queer, and Chicano Studies. This, too, has affected the political class, as, for example, when a California State Senate Committee recently outlawed the use of the pronouns "he or she."

Allan Bloom's book, above, became a best-seller, with over 200 worldwide reviews. And it was pathbreaking. As reviewer Camille Paglia wrote, the book was "the first shot in the culture wars." A quarter century later (2012) author Bruce Bawer wrote a sequel, *The Victims' Revolution, The Rise of Identity Studies and the Closing of the Liberal Mind*.

Bawer, an American living in Norway, notes how the educational revolution has affected the political culture en masse. "The ideas that have increasingly dominated American universities since the sixties," he noted, "have followed the graduates of those institutions into the larger society. The results are all around us, from workplaces where an innocuous statement can brand one as a bigot ... to election campaigns in which legitimate criticism of a black or a female candidate can be discounted as racist or sexist."

Yet, as Bawer also notes, these movements "remain an almost complete mystery" to the average citizen. The walls that hide the "ivory tower" remain intact, but they are destroying the fabric of society right under the nose of the general public.

As Aldous Huxley once put it, we are indeed in a "brave new world."

A World Restored

Europe, 1815
Treaty of Vienna

0   200 Miles
0   200 Kilometers

1. Kingdom of Sardinia
2. Lombardy (Aus.)
3. Venetia (Aus.)
4. Parma
5. Modena
6. Tuscany (Aus.)
7. Papal States
8. Kingdom of the
   Two Sicilies

January 23, 2019

Dr. Kissinger's first book was *A World Restored*, a history of the negotiations in Vienna (1815) that ended Europe's chronic wars going back to the French Revolution (1789). The theme, "restore," demonstrates how the "Holy Alliance" that fought Napoleon for decades managed to revive "legitimate" (monarchy) government throughout Europe, a movement that kept great-power peace for the next century (to 1914).

The restoration of traditional culture and government ended Europe's obsession with revolutionary politics that kept the "old regime" in continuous violence and turmoil. The names of those men (Metternich, Castlereagh, Talleyrand, Alexander) have since become synonymous with stability, legitimacy and restraint among the great powers of the world and still resonant when reflecting on today's unrest and chaos.

Of course, the world has "changed" since 1815. Kissinger knew that — we all do — but are there similarities? Since they lacked rockets, computers, and abortion (progress?), do we dismiss their minds and circumstances? Does bringing order out of chaos before either Trump or Pelosi were born preclude their contributions to logic, reason, and thought?

The Congress of Vienna produced the resultant "Concert" of Europe, minus musicians. The diplomatic meaning of the word attests to a natural harmony of interests among the units, an "accord" or a mutual agenda toward common ends. The actual machinery, meetings, of the powers came to an early end (1822), but the spirit of cooperation and commonality lasted right up until the disastrous World War I. This saw the end of the European system in world politics, which led to communism, fascism, the end of colonialism, the rise of American liberalism (democracy), World War II, and the Cold War. Now we are left with a blend of chaos, terror, fanaticism, crypto-fascism and a political globe unsure of itself or its future.

Within the U.S., the domestic agenda has taken hold of the public, in an arena where ideological "racisms," "sexisms," and personalities dominate. The biggest story of 2018 was the question of whether a Supreme Court nominee behaved himself as a teen. With its acclaimed "America First" slogan, the primary effort of the administration has been to fortify the southern border, perhaps overdue, but hardly sufficient to inspire global leadership. So far in 2019, the new year has been dominated by the spectacle of the President and the Speaker of the House cancelling each other's public appearances. Meanwhile, much of the government has stopped working.

Perhaps a higher calling might help the culture develop.

The world of 1815 also knew anarchy, but far more terrible and bloodier. They settled it with a concert that "restored" both stability and sanity to the terrible past and opened the way for a brighter, and more peaceful, future. They didn't outlaw violence or change human nature. Nor did they create a new and larger bureaucracy, rules, or institutions. What they did was restore values, community, and coordination into a system that had been wrecked by war and death.

The "Brexit" crisis highlights the contradictions of today's global paradox. What will the future bring: a new and larger set of unions or a restoration of the nation-state? Which values will predominate: sovereignty and territory or globalization? Great Britain, America's oldest ally through war and alliance, is torn in half by this very question. As before, the political globe calls out for answers and solutions, but this country, from both parties and the public, stands as if paralyzed by its own uncertainties and identities. When Woodrow Wilson fought a war to "make the world safe for democracy," he planted the seed, realized after his death, for a "world restored." When Harry Truman created the Marshall Plan and NATO, he created his "Doctrine" to aid "free peoples everywhere." These reflected sentiments and values that go deep within the American psyche, to the very roots of the Founding.

That is what is missing now. "America First" sounds great, but it's a bumper sticker, an emotion, harking back to a long-forgotten past.

At the beginning, Jefferson promised an "Empire for Liberty." As he wrote Madison, the idea has "never surveyed since the creation, and I am persuaded no constitution was ever before so well calculated as ours for extensive empire and self-government." The inherent contradiction aside, Jefferson's "empire" meant to him a vehicle for liberty and political freedom. His day never knew "concert," only empire, but his values and direction were true to the cause.

What cause do we have today? How can a cause overcome intractable and petty quarreling? Washington himself foresaw this problem in his Farewell Address, warning that party infighting "leads at length to a more formal and permanent despotism."

This is the "present danger," and the fault is mutual and systemic, but the "blame game" continues.

The future needs a higher calling. In world politics, a global "Concert of Liberty," like the original, would fill the vacuum. Led by this country, the new vehicle would be comprised of nations that meet the qualities of sustained freedom in all aspects. This makes it selective, which is its nature in the first place. Unlike other regional groups, the beauty of a concert is its ambition: nothing. It exists for what it *is*, not for what it does. Like the Concert of Europe, it should meet periodically, under alternate leadership, to discuss and review the "situation." New members are invited, if they qualify. Its growth depends on the strength of liberty worldwide.

This should not be difficult, but it will attract dissent. But dare any politician deny a U.S. official transit for their trip to the "Liberty Summit."

Latin America:

The Forgotten Neighbor

January 17, 2019

The recent national obsession with the Mexican border has obscured a fact of even greater significance for American public attention. Within a general *malaise* in foreign policies since the end of the Cold War, the overall neglect of Latin America as a central focus has obscured an area which, from the beginning, played a central role in American external relations. The neglect of Latin America, in fact, may well provide a critical background causation for the unrest which now threatens American cultural stability.

Over half-a-century ago (1962), Soviet missiles in Cuba presented an immediate challenge to America's existential survival. The missiles and their nuclear threat were quickly removed, while the subsequent preoccupation with Vietnam, the Soviet Union, the Cold War, and now Islam and the Middle East, has left attention south-of-the-border on the back burner. Today, the new threat is human and cultural and has, once again, focused public concerns back to where they used to be. Unlike weapons, however, this issue will not go away quickly, or quietly.

There was once a time, and a long one, when Latin America was the singular area of U.S. interests. The first major assertion of *any* U.S. foreign policy goes back to President Monroe's Doctrine (1823) which defined the entire hemisphere as under American strategic jurisdiction. Originally, Monroe made only a statement of interest against foreign "meddling" in the region. Subsequently, the shield became a sword, as subsequent presidents, from Polk to McKinley, used it as an excuse for expansion and conquest. Theodore Roosevelt's "corollary" (1904) justified U.S. "police power... in flagrant cases of wrongdoing or impotence." America had become, in effect, the arbiter of the foreign relations of the Western Hemisphere.

Between the Spanish-American War (1898) and the last intervention into Nicaragua (1926), the United States intervened militarily in Central America and the Caribbean on twenty-five occasions. By the end of this period, Washington had become frustrated with the overall lack of finality of these occupations and the unpopularity they had aroused both here and abroad. The Coolidge Administration began a tentative withdrawal from these places (including two expeditions into Mexico), while Herbert Hoover, even before his inauguration, made a historic "good will" tour of Latin America. But the cause was then taken up systematically by Franklin D. Roosevelt.

FDR's first Inaugural Address has been hailed as the greatest in history (or Lincoln's second inaugural). Devoted almost entirely to the Great Depression, it contained a single sentence on foreign affairs, "In the field of world policy, I would dedicate this nation to the policy of the good neighbor." What followed was a flurry of diplomatic activity that, upon reflection, should be recognized as one of the most successful and long-serving foreign policies in U.S. history.

By a series of military withdrawals and policy agreements, FDR enrolled the entirety of Latin America behind the U.S. for both the oncoming world war and subsequent Cold War. Moves were swift and timely. Troops were withdrawn from earlier occupations. A multilateral non-intervention pledge was signed in Buenos Aires (1936). The Declaration of Lima (1938) pledged hemispheric solidarity should a new war occur. The Act of Panama (1939) declared the Western Hemisphere a neutral zone in the world war. The Havana Declaration (1940) defined the security of all states in the region together as one unit and announced the "no transfer" principle against any foreign intrusion. In September 1940, the U.S. began occupying British possessions in Bermuda and the Caribbean in exchange for U.S. naval destroyers. During the war, the U.S. signed bilateral treaties with sixteen regional countries for base rights and provided "lend-lease" aid to nineteen. In 1942, Washington enrolled both Canada and Mexico into the North American Joint Defense Board.

By the war's end, the entire hemisphere (including pro-fascist Argentina) had been enrolled as a single strategic system unique to world political history. The Rio Treaty (1947) affirmed that an attack "upon one is an attack upon all" (followed by the NATO alliance in 1949) and led the next year to the formation of the Organization of American States, the most successful regional body in modern history.

The Cuban missile crisis (1962) was the greatest threat faced by the hemisphere in modern times. President Kennedy invoked the unity of the region by announcing that the U.S. would consider any missile from Cuba "against any nation in the Western Hemisphere as an attack by the Soviet Union against the United States, requiring a full retaliatory response on the Soviet Union."

The immigration crisis that has engulfed this country is not immediately existential, and certainly not nuclear. Whether it is long-term existential can be argued. Nevertheless, it is still a crisis and has provoked the longest government shutdown in history. The infamous wall that is in the center of the debate, while important, is hardly the real issue. Any wall, under any circumstance, is both decidedly short-term and last-resort. Something strategic, and long-term, is needed.

The immigration crisis from Mexico and Central America is not new; it goes back generations. President Eisenhower dispatched troops and armed vehicles to round up illegals and send them packing, a policy called "Operation Wetback." He had the full cooperation of the Mexican government (but they didn't pay).

Older solutions are outdated. The root cause of the crisis, in any case, resides in Mexico and Central America, not here. Still, the United States alone has the capacity and resources to arrive at imaginative and constructive answers to the current problems down south. We have a history. We need to be "good neighbors" again, and we need something on the scale of the Marshall Plan (1947) that saved western Europe (in a crisis may times greater than this).

Open up the government and go to work! This means both sides of the "aisle" and both sides of the "border."

Trump as Kaiser:

The Need for a Doctrine

January 14, 2019

President Trump's abrupt decision to relieve the 2,200 American soldiers from Syria is by-no-means life or death for global democracy, but the exaggerated reactions make it seem so. As for many of his behaviors, the style often destroys the substance. Even with adequate warning and planning, however, the decision comes within a strategic and substantive vacuum. So we leave a country — what's next, or, worse, so what?

Making decisions of magnitude without a context is both confusing and empty. That is why alliances are formed and why policies become "doctrines." A doctrine is simply a systematic application of principles toward a defined or strategic outcome, or goal. Doctrines, with or without the name, are standard operations for almost every serious venture. Businesses need "plans," armies need "strategies," and individuals need "goals" in life. Even football teams require "plays," each of which is designed for a touchdown. So someone misses a block, you just try another play.

Successful foreign policies are almost always planned out (disregarding the occasional lucky move). Otherwise, tragedy can occur. Take pre-World War I Germany, for example. The Kaiser went about intervening here and there, in Africa and Asia, threatening the British Navy with Dreadnaughts, violating Belgian neutrality.

After the World War, there was a cottage industry analyzing the Kaiser's mental state, many concluding that he was, shall we say, a bit "mad." German historian Thomas Nipperdey, for example, concluded that Kaiser "Bill" was "... superficial, hasty, restless, unable to relax, without any deeper sense of seriousness ... without balance or boundaries or even for reality or real problems. ... unsure and arrogant, with an immensely exaggerated self-confidence and desire to show off, a juvenile cadet ..."

American historian William Langer was equally alarmed about the Kaiser's effect on the world: "... he did lack stability, disguising his deep insecurities by swagger and tough talk ... vacillations in policy. [He] lacked guidance and therefore bewildered or infuriated public opinion ... This trait in the ruler of the leading Continental power was one of the main causes of the uneasiness prevailing in Europe at the turn of the century."

Sound familiar?

The result was general hysteria (a word used often today) and a tragically avoidable war, the worst in history at that time (1914).

There's a relevant line from the play *Jesus Christ Superstar*. Judas turns to Christ and says, "you'd done better if you had a plan." Judas, of course, had no idea.

Every bright spot in American foreign policy was preceded by a "plan." From the beginning, George Washington began a systematic plan for American survival based upon the avoidance of long-term ("entangling") associations with European power politics. This plan, later turned into "isolationism," served American national interests for exactly 150 years, 1797 to 1947. It was interrupted by a U.S. president once, in 1917 when Woodrow Wilson declared war on Germany. But this was followed immediately by a return to a deeprooted isolationism.

President Monroe's Doctrine (1823) defined the political nature of an entire hemisphere until it was unilaterally abrogated by Secretary of State John Kerry in 2013.

When Hitler declared war on December 11, 1941, American global isolation ended in a practical sense. After the war, a brief isolation interlude came and went, ending in 1947 with a brand new world ("Cold War") and a brand new American responsibility for world order.

This, too, had a plan: the Truman Doctrine. Harry Truman, himself a controversial and idiosyncratic personality, created a global structure still in effect today (Western solidarity, NATO) and the very one critics say Trump will destroy.

Like the Kaiser a century ago, appearances could dangerously lead to realities. That is, unless Trump "had a plan."

At this juncture, it seems evident that American foreign policy has gone long enough without either a structure or a strategic goal. Like a football team without a play, the whole game appears empty of content. This is not new; it began actually when the Cold War ended and the U.S. became the "sole remaining superpower." Absent any long-term history in this role, the team fumbled the ball right away.

As Colin Gray, the British strategist, wrote, "The Soviet Union was not all that died in December 1991. What also died was the centerpiece and the compass of U.S. foreign policy. ... a rapid loss of old, detailed definitions of U.S. interests."

The Governor of Arkansas was elected in 1992 with the slogan "it's the economy stupid," and he meant it. His "doctrine" (small "d") was called "Assertive Multilateralism." Figure that out! Strategist Michael Mandelbaum did (1996) and concluded that the U.S. was "pursuing the foreign policy of a big-city mayor ... without an overarching principle to guide the nation's foreign relations ... the promotion of domestic interests is the default strategy of American foreign policy."

Bush II tried "nation-building" in the Middle East. Eighteen years later, we are still at it, and no nations have been built. President Obama's contribution to strategic thought was called "leading from behind." That's what it was (highlighted by Secretary Kerry's decision, mentioned above. He ended a Doctrine).

Which brings us up-to-date. President Trump, and the country, needs a purpose, a strategy, or a Doctrine with which to pursue a coherent external policy. Making decisions in a vacuum will go nowhere. Whatever strategy is pursued must, of course, be consistent with his instincts and directions, and that's up to him. But he needs to consult, to negotiate, and to think, hard and long. We have been empty for nearly three decades, and it's high time, to quote John F. Kennedy, to "get this country moving again."

Should There Be a Term Limit on Interventions?

January 12, 2019

President Trump's abrupt decision to remove American forces from Syria produced a storm of critique from all quarters, left, right, and center. Defense Secretary James Mattis resigned almost immediately, while op-ed opinion from the "mainstream" media was almost universally opposed.

That last point can be discounted as political, but, more disturbingly, Trump's erstwhile political allies were equally opposed. Senator Lindsay Graham proclaimed that Trump's decision "has rattled the world," while Senator Marco Rubio predicted a dire future for U.S. foreign policy: "... this is a major mistake. And I hope they reverse it. Because if not, it will haunt this administration." Mattis agreed, stating that the move might disrupt the entire alliance system: "We cannot protect our interests or serve that role effectively without maintaining strong alliances or showing respect to those allies."

Mattis had a point, as Trump's idiosyncratic style is his own worst enemy.

But Trump still backed off a bit, telling reporters that, "I never said we're doing it that quickly."

Involved are a grand total of 2,200 soldiers. During the Vietnam War, the U.S., in three consecutive administrations, sent over two million troops and withdrew them all by 1975. A few years later, this country became heralded as the world's "sole remaining superpower."

Do the math.

What is the expiration date for America in someone else's country? (Is there a warning label?) There are 193 countries in the world, so how important is this one (Syria)?

These questions are deliberately rhetorical, only meant to open the imagination (mind). Maybe history can help.

Occupying other countries and then leaving is, as they say, "old hat." Which means that there is nothing new under the sun.

Every occupation in all history has ended, no exception. The only question is when. So, we are arguing about tactics and circumstances. Nobody wants to stay in Syria indefinitely, (I can't imagine) but when can we leave?

There is a profound difference between an intervention and an occupation. The first is almost always very popular or unnoticed. The other can tear societies apart (remember Vietnam?).

The less they are remembered, the better they were. In July 1958, President Eisenhower sent Marines into Lebanon to restore order after a pro-Islamic coup. Order restored, the Marines were gone by September. History has all but forgotten that episode, mainly because it worked. On October 25, 1983, President Reagan sent U.S. troops (Seals, Rangers, Marines) into Granada to restore order and protect American students. Four days later, they all left, and today, Granada celebrates October 25th as "Thanksgiving Day."

Three months in Lebanon, four days in Granada, and now seventeen years in Afghanistan and fifteen in Iraq. When President George W. Bush landed on the deck of the USS Abraham Lincoln on May 1, 2003, he declared "mission accomplished," and that the conflicts in the region "have ended." Unbeknownst to anybody, the real conflicts had just begun. This is hardly unique.

The U.S. has spent all of the current century trying to restore order in Afghanistan and in the Middle East. That's a considerable time period for one central mission. Compare this to American military history. Time in Afghanistan, for example, equals total combat time combined in major American wars to 1945: the Revolution, War of 1812, Mexican War, the Civil War, the Spanish-American War, World War's I and II.

Is something out of sync today? Trump signals removal of a couple thousand soldiers from Syria (after four years), and all hell breaks loose. This, too, is not unique.

Between 1898 and 1926, American troops intervened in Caribbean and Central American countries on twenty-five occasions, plus the Philippines. Some were long, nearly fifty years in The Philippines (a territory until 1946), nineteen years in Haiti, eight in the Dominican Republic, and "in perpetuity" in Panama (ended in 1978).

In Nicaragua, Marines intervened in 1926 (for the twelfth time since 1850), again, to restore order in a civil war. They stayed for seven years, without restoring order or even catching the guerrilla enemy, called "Sandinistas" after leader Augusto Sandino (today a latter-day Sandinista, Daniel Ortega, is president and there is another civil conflict).

After several years of frustrating occupation, President Hoover decided to evacuate, regardless of consequence. Criticisms from Congress and from overseas made the occupation generally unpopular. In the Senate, several resolutions called for an immediate withdrawal. At times, as now, debate grew emotional. Senator Clarence Dill (D-WA), for example, called the occupation, "one of the blackest and foulest crimes that has been committed against men." The "mainstream media," again, like now, joined the attack. The Scripps-Howard chain asked, "What is all this fighting about? Why are these young men in Marine uniforms being killed?" Governor Franklin D. Roosevelt of New York demanded that foreign occupations should end "for all time."

By the fourth year, even the Department of State had turned against the occupation. The Assistant Secretary for Latin America wrote Secretary Henry L. Stimson (who ordered in the Marines originally) that "Nicaragua should assume the obligation of policing its territory and that the United States should be relieved of this burden at the earliest possible moment." The Marine Corps Commandant told the State Department that to continue the occupation "would require many times the total available force of Marines and ... would produce no definite military results."

Stimson himself privately closed the door: "It is now over three years since I succeeded in bringing to a conclusion the war which was going on in Nicaragua. ... Yet apparently we are as far from pacifying those provinces as we were three years ago. In other words, there has already been consumed a longer period of time than we required to subdue the Philippine Insurrection in 1899 ... a longer time than was required for the British forces to quell the guerrilla fighting in all South Africa. Such a situation would seem to indicate that we are not on the right track."

Sound familiar?

Me First, America Too

December 30, 2018

The subtitle of this essay has reversed two main "movements" in the contemporary culture: "Me Too" and "America First." The result is a modern example of what George Orwell originally labeled as "doublethink" in his classic novel, *Nineteen Eighty-four*. In reality, the title confuses the priorities of social movements, beyond the current ones, insofar as it reverses the order, putting the source of all aspirations and liberties as an afterthought.

Liberty precedes aspirations, without which there would be none. Without an America, there would be no hope of opportunity or aspiration, and, like most of the world's people, equality would only be a dismal by-product of a dictatorial government. Most Russians, for example, share a blanket equality, equal in poverty, social status, and lack of opportunity (so do most all other 7 billion members of the earth).

Endemic in the current political culture is an instinctive repudiation of the sources of "Americanism," possibly even encouraged by President Trump's call to make the country "great again." This implies a loss of the virtue and the need for recovery (kind of like the Great Depression).

Typical of the anti-movement was the response recently given by none other than Governor Cuomo of New York, noting that in his view the country was "never that great." Examples dominate the media. A *New York Times* columnist recently typified the atmosphere by writing that the U.S. was conceived in "slavery, genocide and colonization." Feminist contempt for the other gender through the phrase "dead white males" (presumably to include Washington and Lincoln) has become a rallying cry, while the derision of a country embedded with a series of ideological "isms" (sexism, racism) has come to typify our dominant agendas. To erase the past, many have even sought to destroy landmarks, statues, and name-sites. And on it goes. (What, for example, can we do with Virginia's Washington and Lee University? Erase both names: they're males, dead and lived with slavery. That's enough).

Orwell used other phrases that now define American society. In a culture that tries to eliminate history and biology, where pronouns are prohibited and where an entire gender (men) is dismissed as tyrannical, the phraseology of George Orwell is catching up with us. "Politically Correct" (PC) characterizes what Orwell described when *Nineteen Eighty-four* was published (1949). For example, "Ingsoc" is English Socialism wherein language is supervised. "Newspeak" is similar, controlled language, simple terms of simplistic meaning. "Thoughtcrime" harbors dark ideas against contemporary beliefs ("hate" crimes). "Unperson" is what we are doing to history's "incorrect" personages (which condemns almost everybody). "Oldthink" is dated thoughts (which implies almost all of them). "Thinkpol" is thought police who control all of this (self-appointed, mostly residing in faculty lounges, Hollywood, and "mainstream" media). "Blackwhite" is not racial but implies that we should not distinguish between identities; all are the same.

And on it goes, again.

What is the root source of this cultural phenomenon? Some attribute it to the legacy of the Vietnam War era protesters and the beginnings of a movement that condemned the war as endemic to the society. Michael Walsh in his excellent book, *The Devil's Pleasure Palace* identifies the influence of the Frankfurt (Germany) school of "Critical Theory" and intellectuals such as Herbert Marcuse as the controlling campus culprits.

It seems fair to say, however, that, whatever the root cause, the phenomenon is a sociological one and, below that, essentially Marxist in origin. Sociology is group-study in any case, and Marxism is certainly the most powerful socio-logical movement in modern history. Nor need this accept Marx's "proletariat" as the source, since the phenomenon includes many other factors above eco-nomics. The Italian Marxist, Antonio Gramsci, who espoused cultural Marx-ism from one of Mussolini's prisons, probably represents a more relevant inspiration for what we are witnessing.

The bottom line: like most social phenomena (war-peace, progress-stag-nation, investment- spending), the cause resides in the intellect. The issue is, ultimately, intellectual, and can only be addressed in the same element, i.e. the mind. For those who embrace the movement and its implications, they should push harder: invest in the schools from grade one up, control the media, elect "progressives," and await the results. So far, they are ahead.

For those who fear the implications, they should do the same, only more and harder. While many may not recognize it, this war is a cultural conflict between two diverse and separate visions of both the past and future. From this writer's perspective, history is essential, not only because it explains what happened but also because it is the only social laboratory from which to guide the future. All others are products of the imagination and, as such, are dan-gerous and fleeting.

Orwell himself knew this. In *Nineteen Eighty-four* he emphasized it as the ex-planation of what was going on in totalitarian societies such as the Soviet Union: "He who control the past controls the future. He who controls the present controls the past."

What does this mean: a return to reality, to fundamentals, to a true intel-lectual curiosity and away from unproven and far-fetched ideologies. Back to basics (and let Washington and Lee alone).

The "S" Word: Secession

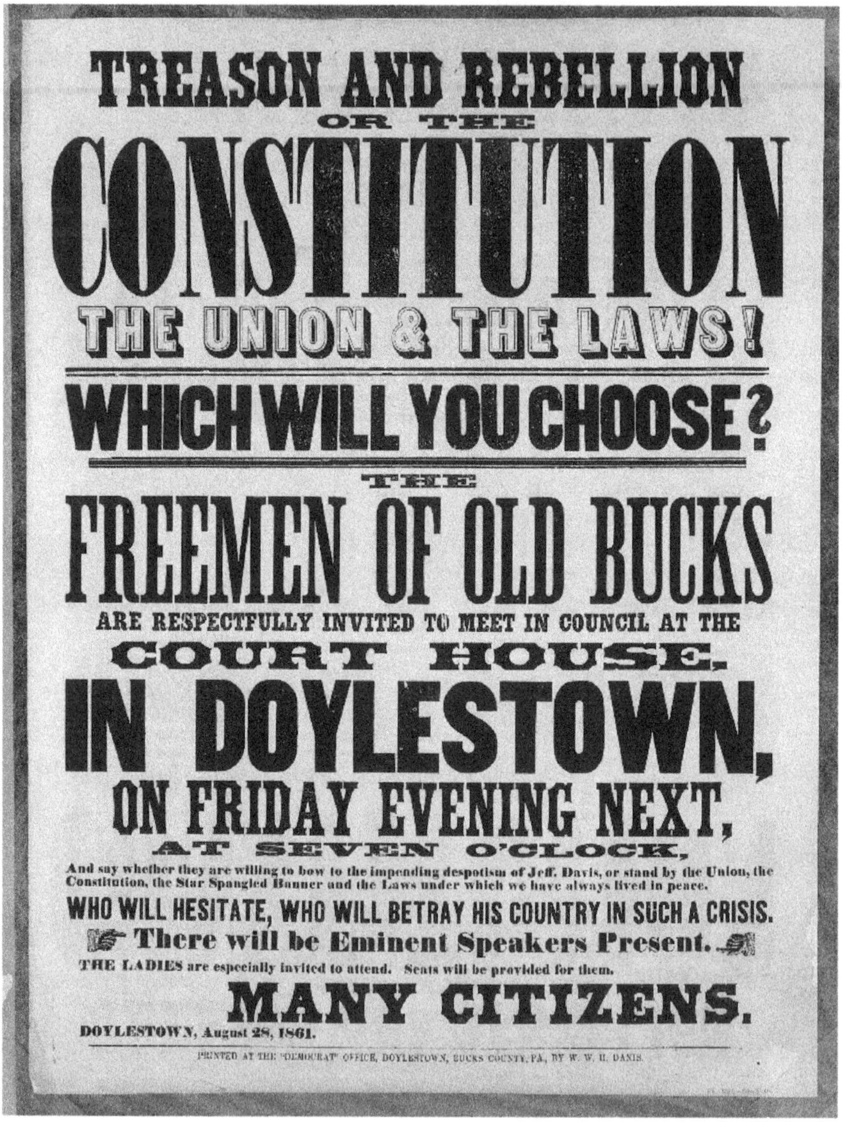

December 11, 2018

"When in the course of human events it becomes necessary for one people to dissolve the political bands which have connected them with another, and to assume among the powers of the earth, the separate and equal station to which the laws of Nature and of Nature's God entitle them, a decent respect to the opinions of mankind requires that they should declare the causes which impel them to the separation."

With that historic claim, the United States of America was conceived. The Declaration then listed 28 separate grievances that the colonies harbored against Great Britain. This was the first ever revolt against a European "Mother" country (an appropriate metaphor). The leadership of the revolt, from George Washington on down, had pledged loyalty to the Crown. They had now broken that pledge and thus were "traitors" by any definition. They also represented a fairly small percentage of the American colonists, with all the others remaining British, since condemned by history books as "Loyalists" (or "Tories," an even more diabolical symbol.)

Washington is the "Father" of the country (equally appropriate) and will always remain as the brave and noble "Patriot" that led the successful revolt to independence. The symbolism of expressions identifying the roles of each side in the conflict (mother, father) approximates a much-more familiar break in modern society: Divorce (the "D" word). On a far-higher level the break in political relations has forever been labeled as the "S" word, Secession. Essentially, they're the same.

Washington's legend depended upon a military victory. Without that (aided and abetted by France), Washington would probably hold no more sympathy in history than Benedict Arnold or Jefferson Davis. The equally noble reputation of Robert E. Lee is currently undergoing a metamorphosis, inside an ideological reversal that demands erasing the memories of any and all vestiges of southern secession.

But like divorce, secession has been a normal and often rightful break in association. We can erase concrete symbols and street signs but not the word nor the reality. The "S" word, in fact, is one of the most persistent and critical explanations for the geopolitical contour of the globe. When all is said and done, we have all seceded from something, at least once. In 1945, there were 51 countries in the United Nations; now there are 193. Where did the other 142 come from? Like the U.S., almost all were colonies. Whether they seceded violently (Vietnam, Kenya, Algeria, Indonesia, Malaya, all of the Middle East and Latin America, etc.) or peacefully like the British Caribbean spots (Jamaica, Barbados, Bermuda, The Bahamas) they all have one main experience in common: they valued independence over any benefits that a colonial association might bring.

While the United States is not responsible for the word or its many disciples, it was, in fact, the first to advance the notion to its fruition. It then went global. After World War I, President Woodrow Wilson shocked the victorious Allies (and the Germans) with his appeals for "national self-determination." Had this idea been applied comprehensively, the UN today might have hundreds of member-states. The U.S. is still now, 242 years after conception, the beacon for liberty and sovereignty throughout the political globe. The ultimate answer to the question as to the lasting effects of the American Revolution remains apocryphal: "it's too soon to tell."

Today, in a so-called "globalized" and advanced technical world, secessionist movements plague every quarter. Challenges to governance exist in practically every sovereign entity in the world; rare is the completely tranquil population. In Europe alone, the home of national sovereignty, 28 countries face ongoing and recognized independence movements (Spain with 17 and Italy with 11 head the list). The Brexit victory in 2017 has sent political shockwaves throughout the continent, with the lasting effects of this also still unknown (we may have to wait at least a couple of centuries).

In Africa, 35 countries face similar movements, 18 countries in Asia (Tibet against China probably the most recognized), 17 in North America. In the U.S. today, there are six main geographic independence movements (California, Texas, "Cascadia" (northwest), Vermont, Hawaii, and Puerto Rico). But these are minuscule groupings, nostalgic and cultural rather than substantive. The deeper challenge to American unity now is political, not geographic.

The Red-Blue divide that has taken shape lately threatens the very fabric and identity of any future American "nation." This divide also has a geopolitical core: rural middle (red), urban coastal (blue), the red twice the size but half the population. The very idea of secession may seem a fantasy to some, but secession still remains the worst event in American history. Like other shocks (Pearl Harbor, 9/11), secession can appear without adequate warning, but we are warned.

Having divisions in society is common; how to respond is the question. If one side finds society intolerable and needs transformation, that side will not be satisfied with anything less. Half-measures will avail us nothing.

Today's divisions threaten unity. "Nationalism" is now discredited, at the bottom of the several "isms" currently in vogue. The social movements now competing should, in reality, be reversed, as follows: "#Me First, America Too." The divide is real.

Be careful of what you want, you might just get it.

The Civil Cold War:

What's It All About?

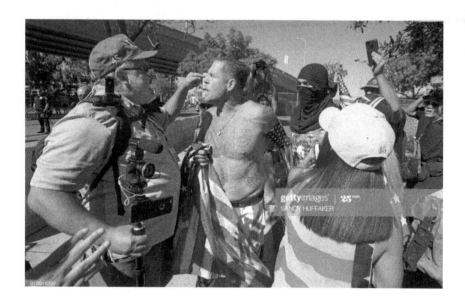

November 27, 2018

A new acronym has crept into the vocabulary to describe our societal situation. A "Civil Cold War" has been used to describe the rapidly-growing schism between what may be called the "progressive" wing of society versus the "traditionalists." Such expressions are hardly new, but the term "Cold War" both separates today against the real, "hot" Civil War that took 720,000 lives and saved the Union and the more recent "Cold" war with world communism that saved civilization. Thus, the stakes are profound but the conflict is mostly nonviolent. It is also local: only America's future is at stake, not the world's (yet).

Is this "war" credible, or is it just another journalistic word-game? Certainly the acrimony is there. Rarely since the "real" Civil War has society witnessed the cultural/societal divides that separate the Trump resisters against those who either voted him in — or Hillary out. Sometimes it appears near-theatrical: Hollywood vs. the "deplorables," Kanye West vs. all black pundits, CNN vs. Fox, *The New York Times/Washington Post vs. The Wall Street Journal.*

It is also consuming the culture, infecting sports, talk shows, and even comedy, where the president seems the butt of all humor. The annual correspondents dinner has now excluded humor altogether. The Post announces daily that the "end" is near: "democracy dies in darkness" at the top of page one, day after day, after day, after day... The next election is already being forecast as (per usual) the "most important" in all history.

Certainly, hyperbole is at play. Doomsday, after all, is newsworthy, but there is the absurd. Trump is regularly compared to Hitler as if we are about to invade France.

There is, however, a critical element absent, i.e. what's it all about? What are the stakes? Throughout history, there was purpose to impending doom; it was real. Hitler *did* invade France (and everybody else), but today's atmosphere seems almost invented, *surreal*. Perhaps the most damaging charge against the President is that he won due to Russian "meddling" in the 2016 campaign.

Any slightly positive Trump reference to Vladimir Putin is widely condemned as near-sacrilegious. This requires a lack of perspective so incredible as to defy thought. Josef Stalin massacred ten million Russian farmers who resisted collective farms. He also eliminated thousands of political opponents and put thousands more in concentration camps ("gulags"). His agents stole U.S. atomic secrets at will. Stalin was an American ally in World War II, was provided billions of aid dollars, and, at war's end, was given east and central Europe by Franklin D. Roosevelt, a Democratic icon. It is generally estimated that Mao Zedong eliminated about 60 million Chinese dissidents in the Great Leap Forward of the 1960s. President Nixon and advisor Henry Kissinger signed the Shanghai Accord with the same Mao in 1972. The policies of both Presidents were generally applauded and, now, stand as positive landmarks in U.S. history. Both Nixon and Kissinger began arms control talks with one of Stalin's successors, Leonid Brezhnev, another widely-approved initiative. Both Roosevelt and Nixon made many endearing remarks about their Russian opposites, Roosevelt's even embarrassing to his best supporters.

Can the "Civil Cold War" explain away such massive mental distortions that dominate this country's attention? Are local and party hatreds so embedded that all reason escapes? Or, to use Shakespeare, is this "much ado about nothing"?

Throughout history, progressives and dissenters against the *status quo* have announced some design, a purpose, and a vision for the future. It was never enough to just condemn; they had to build, to make a new and brighter future. They were revolutionaries. America was the first in history to start this. The French Revolution took it to a higher extreme, began The Great Terror, and ravaged Europe. Marx, himself, condemned Capitalism but provided hope for the "workers of the world" ("proletariat") to "break their chains." Even Hitler promised a "Thousand Year Reich," but he finished just 988 years short.

Marx gave the world a "Manifesto." Jefferson gave us a "Declaration." These are probably the two most influential documents in human history. Only one was right.

Ironically, America has never produced a lasting philosophy of its own. Even the thoughts behind the Revolution were English: Locke, Hobbes, Adam Smith. Marx is still the most influential thinker in modern history despite there never being a true "Marxist" revolution. Marx, himself, once declared, "I am not a Marxist," but there have been many Marxist "movements," including those occupying today's political culture. They are neo-Marxist hybrids, which have substituted the proletariat for group, racial, gender, and class identity. They reflect the thoughts of the Italian "cultural Marxist," Antonio Gramsci, and the Frankfurt School of Critical Theory and its campus spokesman, Herbert Marcuse. Their net effect is to divide and target, particularly male Caucasians ("dead white males"), held responsible for all deficiencies and the variety-garden of ideological "ism's" associated with them. These, as well, are foreign-born.

Racism:

Discrimination vs Ideology

November 7, 2018

Most of the American intellectual heritage is European, England (Locke, Hobbes, Adam Smith) and now Germany and Italy (Marx, Marcuse, Gramsci). Thus, it should not be surprising that the most recent American ideological movements, typically, are anti-intellectual: "racism" (color) and "sexism" (gender), are biological by scope and definition.

"Color" schemes have played an inordinate role in US history and continue into this century. The nineteenth century opposed a "yellow peril" (Chinese) as much as today's ideologues identify distinctions with colors: "supremacy, privilege" (white), life itself (black), colors themselves ("people of"), Bolsheviks and Chinese Communists and even athletic identities (red). Today's political distinctions are "colored" (red/blue states) while even social distinctions have their own "bluebloods."

Welcome to "Crayola" country.

There is a profound difference between the two nouns in the sub-title, above. The first is sociology and ancient. The second is political and relatively new. The first is universal in both time and space and can span a spectrum of behavior from societal outcast to slavery and murder. The second defines whole societies from cradle to grave, past, present and future. The first can be changed by legislation and social intervention. The second can only end through war or revolution (violent or political).

Hitler and former-Alabama Governor George Wallace were both called "racists." Hitler killed in the millions, Wallace discriminated against blacks. What's the difference?

Wallace eventually changed his mind; Nazism ended only after history's greatest war.

Almost all societies have experienced the first. America seems intent on entering the second.

"Race" as a noun can describe differences between the multiple nationalities, tribes and populations that inhabit the earth. As such it can, and has been, both benevolent and hostile and has provoked, equally, both conflict and co-operation. In this sense it is merely descriptive, but, still, universal.

Derived from the noun, "racism" defies definition and remains a political spearpoint so elastic that it can be applied almost everywhere, and against everything. In this regard, racism is, in fact, a universal human concept, barely distinguishable from "opinion," "bias" or "prejudice." Thus the word "race" can adopt a far more comprehensive identification that, like sex, nation and patriot, becomes a dynamic and aggressive worldview attendant with an emotional appeal that goes far beyond identification. All one need do is attach an "ism."

Columbia professor John McWhorter, author of *Words On the Move*, has noted that "the spread of meanings that racism now covers can be confounding" and that "white supremacy is easing out racism" as a favored expression.

Journalist Isabel Wilkerson, author of the new book, *Caste, The Origins of Our Discontents*, has studied the infamous "caste" system of India and believes that the word offers a better description of modern America than racism. None other than Oprah has called it a "new way" to describe the reality while Harvard professor Kenneth Mack reviewed it as "likely to remain with us long after our current moment of racial reckoning is done."

Names and more names, "what's in a name"?

Ideologies are defined as "integrated assertions, theories and aims that constitute a sociopolitical program." Synonyms are "creed, doctrine, gospel, philosophy." Examples are "nazi," "communist," "liberal," "social," capital, all with "ism" attached.

Ideologies attempt to explain everything but, by the same token, they explain nothing, while demanding widespread accommodation from the rest of society. In this regard ideologies become revolutions, asking for total adherence regardless of reason or cost. Rather than explain life as "competitive," they explain it as "oppressive," borrowing directly from Karl Marx. Indeed, Marxism is the godfather of all modern ideologies insofar as it introduced the identity "group" as decisive in human development.

Ideologies are "deterministic" and simplify human behavior into convenient and attractive slogans, "proletariat," "aryan," "progressive," "peace loving" while masquerading as definitive profiles of humanity. Racist is meant, in this regard, to identify humanity into "oppressive" and "oppressed" divisions, thus, like Marx's "scientific revolution" into communism, turn human behavior into fixed and automatic categories. Like tunnels, the individual becomes lost and forbidden within the momentum of history. If "light" is seen at the end the revolution gathers momentum. If not it descends into greater "darkness."

The extent of the penetration of this idea can be found the moment one awakes. A casual read of a popular morning newspaper (unnamed) finds racism the dominate note of everyday life. One columnist wrote on classical literature, condemning its wholesale avoidance of contemporary American ideologies. Her conclusion was to urge readers, of Socrates to Aquinas, to find "ancient racism and sexism ... as topics to be explored thoughtfully than mindlessly celebrated." In other words, the classics are not classical but are judged on how they conform to American *clichés*.

Another, the next day, wrote on feminism and the upcoming midterm elections, examining that "suburban women do not like racist, sexist speech. I will tiptoe out further to say it's weird that racist, sexist speech would not also bother male voters" (implying that they don't even recognize it).

Recent top-ten "non-fiction" books have all (repeat "all") been on the subject "racism." *The New York Times* "project 1619" (when the first slave ship arrived) claims slavery as the definitive American identity and has been adopted in 4,500 school districts (claimed).

From where do such ridiculous oxymorons derive, and why do they absorb such an advanced society as this one? Racism is now almost a universally accepted identification of a country once called the "land of the free." There are, of course, contradictions in all societal metaphors, but the essence of each depends on what is *believed*. Today, racism has replaced liberty as America's historic identity. The American "cause" was once to advance something, now it is to erase something: replacing a future of opportunity with a history of remorse.

Color has always been an inaccurate, and thereby explosive, identification. All sides are guilty. The "yellow peril" against Chinese immigration in the nineteenth century, the identification of native Indians as "red" (and the Washington football team) are just cases in point. There are no yellow or red people. White, Black, Red, Yellow all mock human content and are the very origins of stereotyping.

Martin Luther King said that we should be judged not by color but by the content of our character. That means: how do people behave? Do they give to others what they have or do they take what others have? Are they stable? Do they obey the law? Do they respect their neighbors, families, and friends? Do they forgive their enemies? Do they plan, invest and build or do they live for today?

Keeping slogans and nametags will only worsen the issue; it's called "bumper sticker" thought. Names are also "lightning rods," deflecting all that comes at them. They also suffocate analysis, blaming everyone from Scandinavia to Detroit, Jefferson to Trump.

Ideologies are intellectual frauds, deceiving both users and bystanders alike. As such, they define humanity as "robotic," determined to behave through a single dimension (race) alone. As in "herd" it entirely removes the individual from consideration.

As Shakespeare once famously noted names are "full of sound and fury, signifying nothing."

The Hondurans are coming, the Hondurans are coming!

October 25, 2018

If you oppose the new Central American (mostly from Honduras) "caravan" of over 7,000 migrants, it's an "invasion;" if you support them it's a "right" of travel and citizenship. In colonial America, similar divisions dominated the political discourse. About half the country (then of three million) welcomed the British army as legitimate protectors of their way of life. They were "Tories," or Loyalists, and their tragic lot has been conveniently forgotten in the momentum of history. For them, America was British territory and, thus, "invasion" was an inappropriate expression.

To the other, and winning side, the Redcoats represented "tyranny," "taxation without representation" (a slogan still invoked today on DC license tags). England's rule was "oppressive," and these "Patriots" fought history's first and most important war for freedom and independence.

Perhaps the most memorable slogan from that first conflict for freedom was the cry, attributed to Paul Revere, around Boston that "The British are coming," warning Patriots of an imminent attack by the British army.

Fast forward nearly two and a half centuries, and the country, now 330 million, faces a crisis hauntingly similar — if not in kind at least in scope — with implications still ominous for freedom and future.

Throughout its history, the United States has represented the world's singular nation that was comprised of a public born elsewhere. These "hyphenated" Americans, who traveled, mostly from Europe, for months over turbulent waters, came to dominate what the late President Kennedy accurately called in his famous book, a "nation of immigrants." Most Americans proudly call themselves first by their heritage and, secondly by their "adopted" country. (Curiously, there is no identification as "English-American," the immigrants that created the country).

While still a nation of immigrants, American society increasingly kept a watchful eye on who came in and who was kept out. At first, it was akin to "open borders," with each state responsible for its own immigration. But as the country grew, along with the Federal government, regulations on immigration began to emerge. These also responded to the growing split between the old and the new, including riots, discrimination, persecution and violence. The movie *Gangs of New York* demonstrated this phenomenon graphically.

By the mid-nineteenth century, millions of beleaguered emigrants, almost all from Ireland and Germany, found refuge in America's "New World," for reasons similar to those found in today's caravan from Central America. They too were escaping poverty and persecution, both religious and political, and violence by home governments. Between 1847 and 1850, for example, almost two million Irish died of starvation as the ruling British government did next to nothing to alleviate the great potato famine. By any standard, there is very little — including Honduran poverty – that can approach such a tragic episode (dismissed now amidst "white privilege").

Subsequent to the famine, about four million Irish left for America. One difference between then and now is that those newcomers obeyed the law; now, they intend to break it even before they arrive. It does not bode well if one's very first act upon entry into another country is illegal. So much for a "nation of laws."

By the late nineteenth century, restrictions began to curtail even legal immigration. In 1882, the Chinese Exclusion Act banned all further immigration of Chinese into the country. Similar legislation against the Japanese had a powerful influence in both countries and remained an important resentment right up to Pearl Harbor. In 1890, the U.S. designated Ellis Island, next to the Statue of Liberty, as a federal immigration station responsible for the vetting of newcomers. More than twelve million immigrants, under careful supervision, passed legally until its closing in 1954. Obviously, America did not consider entry a contradiction of liberty, so long as it was supervised.

But the 1924 Immigration Act, and later legislation, served as the dominant restrictive force in American history. This act created the first quota system by limiting to two percent of the total number of immigrants per country as of the 1890 census. Aimed primarily against eastern and southern Europe, it also closed the doors to entire continents and regions, including Africa, Asia and the Arab World. Immigration from Italy, as one example, fell by ninety percent. The 1965 Immigration and Nationality Act finally lifted the quotas but allowed Americans to sponsor relatives from home countries, resulting in a shift of locale from Europe to Mexico and Central America.

Thus, American history has expressed both tolerance and intolerance in its immigration patterns. Two concepts, however, dominated: assimilation and legality. Both of these are now under severe challenge, with the potential to decide the future of the sovereign country. Will it become "balkanized" or stay united, issues that defined both its creation (1776) and the survival (1861)?

Much is at stake with the caravan. There is a powerful "open border" lobby in the media, entertainment, and government, that wishes sovereignty away and embraces a "globalized" world, without borders. Should this force win, it may well end sovereignty as we know it. After all this time, it is the new "Tories" that will have won.

Feminism On The March

September 27, 2018

The best, probably only, explanation for the wave of accusations and social upheaval between the two genders (biologically, not sociologically) that has swamped American culture lately lies in the concept of "ideology." The encyclopedic definition is tame enough: ideology is "a collection of normative beliefs and values that an individual or group holds for other than epistemic reasons." "Epistemic," from epistemology, means, in short, "logical discourse."

For sure, ideology is neither logical nor reasoned (i.e. rational).

Take a simple noun, innocent enough, such as sex, race, or nation. Add "ism," and, behold, you have a full-blown ideology on your hands, resplendent with all the characteristics of a "word in motion," i.e., a worldview, a comprehensive understanding of humanity and all its qualities. Ideology is nothing if not dynamic, a tsunami belief system at war with the world.

For one thing, ideology kills, even if it's stupid. Has anybody seen the "proletariat" rise up around the world, as Marx predicted? Then why have so many communist governments killed tens of millions of their own people? What about Hitler's "Thousand Year Reich," led by the "Aryan Race"? Just 988 years short of goal, with about 75 million left dead by 1945.

But ideology need not kill; it can even act as a positive force. To the British government in 1776, for example, George Washington must have appeared as a political sociopath. To the victorious allies in 1919 at the end of World War I, U.S. President Woodrow Wilson, with his League of Nations, also appeared a bit wacky. But it is the collective attributes of ideology that sets it apart from "rational discourse," and it is those traits that we must use to identify contemporary American social culture.

The famous "longshoreman" philosopher, Eric Hoffer, identified the attributes of ideology years ago in his classic, *The True Believer: Thoughts on the Nature of Mass Movements* (1951). The first indication of ideology is contained in the sub-title, "mass" and "movement." One cannot examine a case (harassment, rape, insult, income inequality, etc.) without engaging in wholesale indictment by societal groups *writ large*. In other words, group behavior is targeted. As a feminist U.S. Senator recently proclaimed, "Men, shut up or step up. Do something right for a change."

There must also be an elaboration on "mass movement," which involves no single cases, but general conditions expressed against society at large, or at least many. Also, a mass movement is considered to be dynamic, massive, moving toward comprehensive, societal behavior, new horizons. Indeed, the expanse is almost unlimited; the movement is "humanity's," nothing less.

That's just the tip of the proverbial "iceberg." Hoffer has identified several other qualities of the ideologue; many (if not all) can be observed in today's America (and not all belong only to feminists). First, and foremost, is "change," as a verb. There is no such thing as a reactionary ideologue. As such, history is not welcome. It is both dismissed (ahistorical) or abused (anti-historical). Either way, it doesn't belong. The indictment is wholesale: women were denied suffrage in America, and slavery existed as well. Verdict: American men guilty as charged (although both conditions were universal throughout history). Historians do not remove Lee's statue, they study rebellion.

Other traits identified by Hoffer and present in feminism (and other movements) include: the existence of evil: godless, "but never without belief in a devil;" imitation: "The less satisfaction we derive from being ourselves, the greater is the desire to be like others;" coercion: "it takes a fanatical faith" to rebel against your society; persuasion: "...a passionate search for something not yet found more than a desire to bestow something we already have;" leadership: "...vision of a breathtaking future, audacity, brazenness, iron will, fanatical conviction, passionate hatred, cunning....;" action: "unity, ...great projects, marches, exploration and industry;" and suspicions: "...prying and spying, tense watching, conformity, no dissent." (all quotations from Hoffer).

Such categories, of course, are general in nature and will cross a spectrum of behavior. But, if the "shoe" fits, feminism wears it. This is not (necessarily) an indictment, rather an identification. If the ideological component is removed, it becomes difficult to understand, and appreciate, what is going on.

In the current Kavanaugh case, for example, teenage behavior by itself cannot, rationally, rise to the occasion of judgment on the capacity to be on the Supreme Court. But as a symbol of the nature of an ideological society, it becomes monumental and, indeed, historic. Reason could argue that, say, the economy and national security are more critical for the country, but an ideologue wouldn't entertain that hypothesis. For one thing, such conditions lack a target to rally against, an ideological requirement.

For most feminists, "men" are the target, the whole gender. But, in conclusion, it should be noted that in today's America, women have greater rights, more money and privileges than in any other society in human history. For the most part, American males have built the society, its values and structures, wars, economies, privileges and opportunities. "Women and other minorities," (an ideological phrase) have profited therein.

Only men, incidentally, have returned home over time and by the millions from foreign wars in body bags. Is this (avoided) fact a form of "sexism"? Still, inequities must be addressed, even if you're not blown away. But please, when you cross country, recall it was the Wright Brothers, not the Sisters, who got you there.

Russian Summits (In Perspective)

July 24, 2018

Many in Congress and the media want to "censure" President Trump for his Helsinki performance with Putin. Go ahead, but allow for a little perspective. He made mistakes, but he is far from alone. We have been down this road before with decidedly mixed results. Perspective permits "cool heads," a rare concept in our current partisan atmosphere.

Going back to Franklin D. Roosevelt with Soviet dictator Josef Stalin during World War II, there have been a grand total of thirty-two Russian-American summits on a presidential level. Some were contentious, some were uneventful, some altered history, some were even comical, but none were so ominous as to cause censure for either of the principals. But if Trump's behavior was so far away from previous engagements, we have homework to do.

For those who appreciate perspective, all they need do is to hold up a photo of Franklin D. Roosevelt sitting next to Stalin at Yalta, February 1945, where the Democrat icon conceded Poland and most of east Europe to the Red Army. The results condemned that entire area to tragedy for nearly half a century. FDR needs censure first; then we can attack Trump with a good conscience.

If the public wants contention, we can go back to July 24, 1959, when a Republican, Vice President Richard Nixon, argued heatedly with Soviet Premier Nikita Khrushchev in the infamous "kitchen debate" held in the American exhibit in Moscow. The media had a circus, but little was accomplished, with Nixon later apologizing that he had "not been a very good host."

Then show another Democrat, John F. Kennedy, sparring with Nikita Khrushchev at Vienna, June 1961, where the results were so severe that Kennedy had to go on national TV, call up troop reinforcements for Berlin, add billions to the defense budget, and triple the draft. Privately, JFK told a *New York Times* reporter that "It was the worst thing in my life. He [Khrushchev] savaged me." In August, Khrushchev began building the Berlin Wall and announced that the Soviet Union was resuming nuclear weapons testing.

Horrible summit, but no censure.

As for innocuous summits, we have June 1967 at Glassboro, New Jersey, where Soviet Premier Alexi Kosygin met with President Lyndon Johnson to discuss the Vietnam War and the Middle East. After Trump's fiasco at Helsinki, much has been made on the secrecy of the talks, with only interpreters present. Such is common in most summits, where the heads of state prefer to avoid talking as though in some sort of "goldfish bowl." At Glassboro, for example, only interpreters were present, with special secured "drapes" installed to further insulate the two principals. Nobody seemed to complain.

Nothing concrete came of this meeting except a so-called "Spirit of Glassboro" and Johnson's comment that the summit "...made the world a little less dangerous." The following year, Johnson was out of office, and Kosygin had lost power to Leonid Brezhnev, while the wars in both Vietnam and the Middle East went on as before.

So much for "spirits."

Certainly the most prodigious and productive "summiteer" was Soviet Premier Mikhail Gorbachev, who co-hosted a total of twelve such meetings during the 1980s and 1990s, five with Reagan, seven with H.W. Bush. The results of these are far too numerous to list here, suffice it to note that they led to a number of historic accomplishments on issues like arms control, human rights, and the environment. The net result was the end of the Cold War itself, highlighted by Reagan's abrupt departure from the Reykjavik, Iceland 1986 meeting, vowing never to surrender the Strategic Defense Initiative (SDI) to Gorbachev's demands. But Reagan was never rude, just forceful.

The summits after the Cold War brought in a "spirit" of warmth and cordiality. Ironically, Trump today is vilified for treating Putin in similar ways, i.e., like a head of state, as if Trump instead was supposed to lecture Putin on Russia's political culture. Now Russia "meddles;" in the Soviet period, (most of the twentieth century) the operative word was "overthrow."

Perhaps another photo will suffice: President Bill Clinton in 1995 with his arm around Russian President Boris Yeltsin, laughing hysterically after their summit. The Russian leader was allegedly drunk during most of the meetings, once being mistaken by security as an intruder. Yeltsin called the U.S. media a "disaster." But Clinton was complimentary of Yeltsin: "As long as there is President Yeltsin in power in Russia, then definitely the reforms will continue." Clinton was equally generous, providing financial assistance to Russia's economy, including funds for nuclear scientists. Yeltsin went into rehab, while Clinton's wife took over the family business.

George W. Bush was about the same. In his first meeting with Putin, he announced comradeship: "I looked the man in the eye. I found him to be very straightforward and trustworthy... I was able to get a sense of his soul."

So why is Trump's behavior so universally condemned? Words have been unsparing: "disgusting," "disgraceful," "treasonous." Some pundits chose to use history, but lost all perspective. Calling the Helsinki summit a "Pearl Harbor" is a defiant abuse of history.

Within a historic context, this is ridiculous, but the American culture is increasingly "ahistoric." It's also deeply partisan, and getting even more so.

World Without Disorder

September 20, 2017

Of all the charges against the Trump Administration, including the President's obsessions and personal quirks, perhaps most damaging is the notion that he will eventually destroy world order as we know it. Nobody believes that he, like history's tyrants, Bonapartes and Hitlers, will send armies across borders to occupy neighbors. Most believe that this will simply be the natural result of his personality and experience. Typical is the following by Stewart Patrick, Director of the Global Governance Program at the Council on Foreign Relations: "U.S. President Donald Trump has promised a foreign policy that is national and transactional ... he has made clear that the pursuit of narrow advantage will guide his policies — apparently regardless of the impact on the liberal world order that the United States has championed since 1945" (*Foreign Affairs*, March/April 2017).

This is a reasonable and a rather consensus view by a reasonable and consensus intellectual. Yet the key word above is "apparently," implying at least a degree of uncertainty or hesitation. But if Donald Trump is anything, he is above all a surprise package. Unpredictable, unorthodox, unprepared, and unsophisticated, he is a businessman with a history of improvisation and the accumulation of vast wealth from his own mind and resources. If he can become a billionaire, why should world order be too far a reach? Others, with fewer talents, have done so, with a number of disparate results.

But world politics is anarchy by definition. This has always been so, especially when guided by a concept of the classic "balance of power." There has also always been some sort of balance; it just depends on who controls the pendulum. Since 1945, it has been the United States, but that is currently "under review." Does Trump's rhetoric to make America "great again" threaten this control? Apparently, or so most think. Is there a contradiction between nationalism and order? Again, apparently so.

But if the end of the "liberal" order is "apparent" why isn't it "inevitable"? World Order has a long and confused pedigree. Few leaders speak of it openly and those few saw only rack and ruin. Hitler talked of a "thousand year Reich;" he was only 988 years short. Lenin and Trotsky saw a permanent world proletariat rule. That idea never even got off the ground, and Trotsky was later axed to death by one of Stalin's men (Term Limits Soviet style). Napoleon's control of Europe fell at Waterloo. And so it goes. What do the Islamic terrorists want? They've waited hundreds of years to run the world, but flying airplanes into buildings will not bring Sharia Law to Nebraska.

Americans have announced their share of order. The Monroe Doctrine (1823) put an entire hemisphere under U.S. tutelage. Woodrow Wilson stunned the 1918 world by proclaiming World War I as a war "to end war" and to "make the world safe for democracy." His League of Nations was never endorsed by the Senate, but the idea of a "democratic peace" still resonates within the American political culture as the center of any renewed efforts to create order out of chaos.

Harry Truman was, like Trump, unprepared for the presidency. When FDR died, Truman was not even aware of the Manhattan Project to make an atom bomb. Four months later, he used both of them to end the Second World War. He was irascible, unpredictable, and unorthodox too, but created the Marshall Plan and NATO, the Korean War, and a treaty with Japan. The result was a world order still with us.

One of the brighter spots of the Bush I presidency came in 1990 when he told the UN General Assembly that the coming invasion of Iraq would introduce a "new world order." The phrase overnight became a rallying cry for support of the invasion and the "coalition of the willing." Needless to say, absolutely nothing came of it, and Bush lost the next election to the Governor of Arkansas (and his wife). So much for world order, as the Clinton presidency became absorbed with domestic priorities, "globalization," and ultimately sexual scandal and impeachment. As an acknowledgement toward at least the need for a rhetorical foreign policy, Clinton invented the phrase "Assertive Multilateralism," a term subject to probably a dozen interpretations. One of the frustrations from such emptiness came when then Senator Joe Biden told a 2001 audience:

"Before the end of the Cold War, we would say, if the Soviet Union does this, we'll do this. But who the hell can out-game Saddam Hussein? Who can out-game Slobodan Milosevic? Who the hell thinks they know what should have been done? Are you so sure about what was going to evolve?"

Bush II entered Iraq and Afghanistan as "nation building" experiments. Sixteen years later, we are still experimenting. Obama may have hit an all-time low by proclaiming that the U.S. would "lead from behind." Not only was this absurd, but it had the further indignity of being impossible.

It is easy to dismiss Trump as too far gone to behave intelligently on the world stage. But the historic record is mixed and, to say the least, he can't do much worse than his immediate predecessors.

The Immigration Imbroglio:

A Historical Perspective

August 21, 2017

"Give me your tired, your poor, your huddled masses yearning to breathe free," goes the first line of poetry etched on a plaque at the base of the Statue of Liberty. The poem was written in 1883 by Emma Lazarus (d. 1887) but wasn't placed there until 1903. The statue itself, a gift from France (but financed by American monies), originally had a confused meaning, being hailed both as a symbol of slave emancipation (the French design) and the open arms of the American people as the "land of the free."

According to the poet's biographer, Esther Shore, Lazarus "was the first American to make any sense of this statue" (2011). The notion that the statue symbolized a welcome to all comers who could make the voyage, in any case, has been the lasting importance of the image. In some sense, however, the confusion persists even today, as witnessed recently in the public argument between a CNN reporter (Acosta) and a Trump official (Miller) on the statue's lasting meaning.

Part of the meaning is accurate, ie. "land of the free," but part is also propaganda, masking the reality of a highly restrictive historic welcome both for and against outsiders.

The factual basis of a "nation of immigrants" (to use John Kennedy's famous book title) will reveal an open coast and borders for some outsiders and severely restrictive ones for others. Until the late nineteenth century, America was truly an "open" society, wherein immigrants, almost all from northern Europe, were allowed entrance with few or no restrictions. The arrival of English "pilgrims" in 1620 heralded the first influx of Europeans to arrive against a variety of oppressions in the "mother" country. In the mid-nineteenth century, over ten million newcomers from Germany and Ireland traveled to find homes in the Eastern and Midwestern cities, many of these impressed as "indentured servants," as soldiers in the Union Army, or facing a variety of restrictions forced by "nativist" and labor elements in the country. The American Party ("Know Nothings") had a brief but strong influence against immigration in the 1850s.

Until the late nineteenth century, immigration controls were administered by state and local officials. The hostility against these newcomers, however, led to a series of controls forced by the intervention of the Federal Government into the issue. The first restrictions in 1882, the Chinese Exclusion Act, was forced by Californians and banned all further emigration of Chinese laborers into the country. Similar legislation against the Japanese in California had a powerful influence on U.S. foreign policy and was an important resentment in Japan before Pearl Harbor. In 1890, the U.S. designated Ellis Island, near the Statue of Liberty, as a federal immigration station. More than twelve million immigrants, under careful control, passed through until its closing in 1954.

But the Immigration Act of 1924, and subsequent legislation, served as the definitive restrictive force in American history. This act created the first quota system by limiting to two percent of the total number of people from every nationality as of the 1890 census. Aimed primarily against eastern and southern Europe, it also severely closed off entire continents, all of Asia, the Arab world, and Africa. According to the State Department Office of the Historian, the 1924 law was passed "to preserve the ideal of American homogeneity." Immigration from Italy, for example, fell by ninety percent. After 1924, more Czechs, Yugoslavs, Greeks, Lithuanians, Hungarians, Portuguese, Romanians, Spaniards, Jews, Chinese and Japanese left the U.S. than entered. Between 1930 and 1950, America's foreign-born population fell from eleven to seven percent. The 1965 Immigration and Nationality Act finally removed the quotas and allowed Americans to sponsor relatives from their countries of origin. As a result, a shift in immigration patterns went to Mexico and Central America, an issue that dominated the 2016 election and still controls policy debate to this day.

From this brief sketch, it is apparent that the purpose of immigration to the United States, contrary to the Statue of Liberty, was not primarily to serve as the world's welfare state, but constructively to improve the home society. The key word has always been "assimilation," and if that verb cannot work, then the experiment fails. Enclaves of foreign-born populations who refuse the values of their host nations, as Europe will testify, can represent an authentic threat to the integrity and existence of any people. It is no accident that the issue of immigration has become dominant today.

In judging history, perspective is essential, an intellectual quality in scant supply within contemporary American culture.

Superpower Collapse

July 31, 2017

Less than a quarter-century ago, there were no competitors to the presence of American power on the world stage. The country had, unprecedentedly, won two of the greatest wars in world history and had prevailed over the Soviet Union, a land-based tyranny with over 40,000 nuclear weapons. According to Francis Fukuyama, history had "ended," and according to Charles Krauthammer, the "unipolar moment" in world politics had arrived.

Fast forward twenty-five years. On June 22, 2017, Defense Secretary Mattis told a Senate committee that, after sixteen years, the U.S. was "not winning" in Afghanistan. Sixteen years! That's four times the length of the Civil War, four times the length of the U.S. in World War II, and thirty-two times the length of American combat in World War I.

What happened to superpower? Since the end of the Cold War, it is fair to say that the United States has failed to devise new strategies and directions to meet the challenges of any "new world order." Nor do we seem to have the slightest interest in what exactly that concept may contain. Superpower has collapsed, replaced by an endless series of domestic struggles, scandals, celebrity, and vitriol between the various parts of the body politic. The result has been strategic isolation and domestic chaos.

In 1989, the focus of American interest was the Berlin Wall; ten years later it was Monica Lewinski. Now it is Donald Trump. Each image reflects the transition from a leader of the global order to an inward-looking public culture dominated by an aggressive coalition of racial, gender, media, and other identity sub-cultures. But this is not irreversible.

The American imbroglio in the quagmires of the Middle East is not necessarily fatal for a superpower. In 1781, Britain lost the American colonies, but continued to grow as the supreme colonial and naval power on earth. In 1975, the U.S. retreated from its twenty-five year tragedy in Vietnam. A few years later, the Soviet Union was gone with the U.S. left as the "sole remaining superpower."

In politics, it has been said, "two hours can be a lifetime" (attributed, Harold Wilson, British PM).

Such a moment took place right after Pearl Harbor, and the ensuing war provided probably the closest Americans have come to appreciate true unity. The near half-century of Cold War itself saw a general sense of purpose, but all that seems as ancient history today.

Without a powerful, existential threat, purpose and commitment are quickly lost in the American worldview. Soon after the Cold War, the Governor of Arkansas could ride to the White House on the slogan, "It's the economy, stupid." It's been downhill since, with any hope of exporting liberal democracy buried deeply under the ruins of places known as Iraq and Syria. Even post-Soviet Russia, once a powerful challenge for world order, has been now reduced to a computer hack allegedly changing votes in places like Michigan and Ohio. Without the release of evidence, this new threat depends on email leaks and the minutes of confidential meetings. Russia, as well, has certainly gone downhill.

Americans have never been comfortable with long and protracted excursions, just as they have equally condemned the centuries of European colonialism. Today, we are living through global experiments that contradict the kind of liberty inherent in America's original purpose. Democracy is not a product to be exported like machinery. The present decades-long efforts to rearrange centuries of cultural tribalism overseas have challenged the very fiber of the American political culture and have subverted the symbolism embedded in the same worldview.

Superpowers can be paralyzed by their own strength without clear and direct leadership. The problem is, in the final analysis, one of strategic culture.

Neither willpower, manpower, nor material resources are sufficient if there is a deficit in mental agility, imagination, and vision. Like most problems, thus, the issue is an intellectual one, over and above any defense budget or weapons system.

Can the Trump Administration overcome its quasi-isolationism and nationalistic impulses to rise above tweets and forge a genuine world order? Woodrow Wilson was a nationalist too and operated within an isolationist tradition. Wilson also created the first real comprehensive plan to "make the world safe for democracy." The League of Nations failed, but those same ideals resonate deeply within the American political soul. Harry Truman had some Trump-like qualities (to a degree): irascibility, uncultured in manners and diplomacy, a crude and often rude exterior, ignorance of foreign policy matters. Yet Truman had his own "two hours" in history, ended World War II, and produced a global order that is still largely intact.

Can Trump's time arrive as well? Hard as it is to believe, the present regime remains, for the moment, the sole remaining hope for the maintenance and ascendance of liberal democracy. Still, "hope springs eternal."

Can Trump Still Forge World Order?

G20 OSAKA SUMMIT 2019

December 31, 2019

Of all the critiques of the new President, certainly in foreign policy, none has been more pervasive than the notion that he will soon destroy the "world," at least that part of it known as the "liberal international order." As an assigned project, a student in my class listed a total of 43 articles published on Trump within weeks of his inaugural, all of which displayed the same message. Of course, this scratches the surface and, equally apparent, can hardly be blamed. In the 2016 campaign, candidate Trump made no bones about how he was uncomfortable with most of what had preceded him in all areas of life, including the world itself. Who could blame reporters for accepting his word at face value?

Yet, questions linger. President Trump has no formal experience in American foreign policy nor the order constructed over seventy years ago. He has criticized NATO and on occasion has been rude to foreign leaders. What does this mean? It could mean nothing; that this reflects the personality of a frustrated businessman. Or, does it mean a carefully constructed and organized plan to deconstruct the political globe, sort of an American *Mein Kampf*? But, from orchestrated campaign speeches plus off-the-cuff remarks and tweets, it is painfully obvious that, as a candidate, Trump displayed close to zero knowledge, and with the same degree of interest, in the nature of global order. Asking NATO members to recognize their statutory obligations is hardly a revolution in strategic thought. Hanging up on the Prime Minister of Australia is not nice either, but nobody said that Trump was diplomatic.

It is hardly unusual for a political campaign to display exaggerated or totally distorted expressions of reality or of future scenarios. In 1916, Woodrow Wilson campaigned against U.S. involvement in World War I; five months afterward, he was declaring war on Germany. In 1940, Franklin D. Roosevelt told Americans that "your boys are not going to be sent into any foreign wars." A year later, the U.S. was involved knee-deep in history's greatest war. Did these men both lie? Of course not; they simply were not prepared for the rush of events beyond human or political control. When he assumed the presidency in 1945, Vice President Harry Truman was so ill-informed that he did not even know about the Manhattan Project to build an atom bomb. Four months later, he dropped two of these over Japan to end the war. Within four years, Truman reconstructed war-torn Europe, with the Truman Doctrine, Marshall Plan, and NATO to develop the order that we still have today. In 1960, John Kennedy kept blasting Nixon and the Republicans against what he called a "missile gap" with the Soviet Union. After he won and was briefed on reality, he dropped the issue and its memory entirely.

So what do we do about campaign rhetoric versus strategic reality or the heat of the moment? Beyond electing candidates, probably very little. By what standard do we hold Trump accountable for all the extremes of his personality? Higher than all those who have preceded him?

Now the electorate has opted for "change" (but not by much). In domestic policy, this has already been manifested, especially in the health care bill. But what does it mean for "world order?" What indicators do we have by which to judge this president, minus a promise to get "tough" on terror and a stronger military? These are both clichés and hardly new in presidential parlance.

In terms of a real order in the world, we have next to nothing. Perhaps the greatest attack on Trump came after his "America First" speech, signaling a possible alignment back to a 1930's-style isolationism and an equal attachment to the virtues of a nineteenth century nation-state system. This collides against the "globalization" movement of Western businessmen and corresponds to Brexit and the rise of right-wing parties in continental Europe. The idea of Trump as "Fascist" frequently surfaces, and Hitler's ghost still haunts the modern world. But does this even approach reality?

World War I ended nearly one hundred years ago, and Trump bears as much relationship to Hitler as Charlie Chaplin. Do we really think that he will transform the highway of history and stand in the middle and yell "STOP?"

In his recent book *World Order* (1914), Dr. Kissinger reminds us that "America First" need not be taken literally: "Even as the lessons of challenging decades are examined, the affirmation of America's exceptional nature must be sustained." He also appreciates the enduring validity of the state system as the fundamental model for the future: "To achieve a genuine world order, its components, while maintaining their own values, need to acquire a second culture that is global, structural and juridical … At this moment in history, this would be a modernization of the Westphalian system informed by contemporary realities."

All his rhetoric aside, Trump may well turn out to resemble Metternich and Bismarck much more than the Hitler our media loves to resurrect. Sounds like *déjà vu* all over again.

National Security Candidates,

Then and Now

August 5, 2016

The 2016 presidential race has focused largely on personalities and domestic issues, especially the economy, with national security policies obscured amidst sustained recriminations on the Benghazi incident and Donald Trump's alleged reckless approach toward NATO, Russia and nuclear weapons. The personal nature of the campaign has no precedent in recent history and, at times, has taken on the spectacle of a comic opera, with both candidates ranking historic low numbers in the "unfavorable" column. Personality hysteria has reached new lows also, with Trump calling Mrs. Clinton "crooked Hillary," and columnists openly challenging Trump's capacity for office and, at bottom, his mental stability. Washington Post reporter Eugene Robinson has called Trump "just plain crazy," while leading "neocon" pundit Robert Kagan has written that "there really is something wrong with the man."

Former Secretary of State Clinton's email scandal has dominated any other national security news but this, at bottom, is a character issue remote from ongoing policies. Once asked what her greatest achievement as Secretary was, Clinton replied that she viewed her role "as a relay race. You run the best race you can, you hand off the baton. Some of what hasn't been finished may go on to be finished." This strongly suggests, as most see it, that a Clinton regime will, characteristically, continue in the mainstream of the Obama one, from whence she came.

This is logical thought, but there is no guarantee and, if history is any guide, may well be highly deceptive. Rare, indeed, has been a president-elect ever even remotely "qualified" to lead in national security areas. The adjective, properly, is a *non sequitur*.

Consider some of our great "foreign policy presidents" – how did they get that way? Woodrow Wilson is first. He coined the term "Wilsonianism" as a description of the quintessential American worldview on behalf of liberty and democracy. Yet there was no prior indication that he would carry that message to the Paris Peace Conference that ended World War I. Wilson had a profound political background: Governor (New Jersey), college president (Princeton) and a foremost scholar of American constitutional history and past-president of the American Political Science Association. Yet, when the war began, he proclaimed US neutrality and campaigned in 1916 that "he kept us out of war." Five months later, he declared war on Germany which, in turn, accepted an armistice based upon his own cherished Fourteen Points. Not only were those rejected by all U.S. allies but the linchpin of Wilson's message, the League of Nations, was rejected (twice) by the Senate.

Wilson's great experiment came and disappeared almost overnight, but his legacy remains symbolic of the American "cause" worldwide, then and now. A president who campaigned against war waged a holy global crusade against it, only to be rejected by all his own contemporaries. Yet his vision endures to this day, but there was little in his own background that prepared Americans, especially the European allies, for his crusades. Not only were both sides of the Atlantic confused and surprised by Wilson, but they were equally repulsed by him. Indeed, for his time Woodrow Wilson was an unwanted and disruptive surprise package.

Consider the next great Democratic foreign Policy president, Franklin D. Roosevelt. Although he had national security experience as Assistant Secretary of the Navy and Governor of New York, his entire presidential career in the

1930's was absorbed by the Great Depression and his New Deal domestic program. There was little in his political profile to indicate that he would challenge the prevailing doctrine of isolationism with a determined program to arm and support western Europe against Nazi Germany. In October 1940, he famously proclaimed that "your boys are not going to be sent into any foreign wars." Within little over a year, the US was in war across the globe. Roosevelt was another example of an abrupt departure from prevailing practice foreseen by practically no-one familiar with America's background and party platforms.

Still another, and more recent, foreign policy newcomer was Ronald Reagan, an actor and two-time Governor of California with absolutely no foreign policy credentials. In the 1980 campaign against Jimmy Carter, he proclaimed that it was "morning in America" and emphasized an optimistic domestic program of cutting taxes and reducing government with little or no offerings of what he privately sought: the dissolution of the Soviet Empire. Yet, that is exactly what the world got as Reagan and his staff engineered a revolutionary and abrupt reversal of existing policies, and by 1991 the USSR was gone. He had been widely portrayed by the media as a backward "cowboy" (as in many of his movies) who might pull the nuclear trigger against the Soviet Union. Yet, he turned out to be the most vigorous presidential champion of nuclear arms control and forged the famous Intermediate Nuclear Arms Control Treaty with the USSR.

So, where does this leave us with Trump and Clinton? If the past is any guide, hold all bets on their performance once ensconced in power. Since there is no real "experience" available for that particular job in that particular office, we are left with the unknowns of belief (as opposed to campaign theater), character (as opposed to rhetoric), vision (as opposed to record), and professional advisors (as opposed to politicians). Sit tight.

Casualties of War

August 19, 2016

On July 6, 2016, the British Government, under the leadership of former government civil service official, John Chilcot, issued its definitive summary of the six-year (2003-2009) British occupation of Iraq. The final result, twelve volumes, over 2.6 million words, seven years in the making, was a devastating critique of the adventure and of Prime Minister Tony Blair and his government. Concluding that the occupation was unnecessary, misdirected, and flawed from the beginning, the Chilcot report rocked the British public to its core and, coming shortly after the Brexit vote, made for one of the worst periods of modern British history.

Calling the aftermath "more hostile, protracted and bloody than ever we imagined," the report prompted former PM Blair to confess that his decision to support the U.S. in Iraq was "the hardest, most momentous, most agonizing decision I took in my ten years as Prime Minister."

The initial British invasion force consisted of 46,000 troops and support but dwindled down over the ensuing occupation. By the end in 2009, the U.S.

fatality list numbered about 4,500 amidst a force of about 160,000. The total British fatalities from this six-year mission: 179. That's right: 179 in six years, described as "more bloody than we ever imagined."

Is there a disconnect here? If so, there is certainly no perspective. Consider the following.

July 1, 1916: the British Expeditionary Force (BEF) charges from the river Somme in France over no-man's land toward German trenches just yards away, expecting to end World War I. They never made it. Hundreds of enemy machine guns and artillery cut them to pieces, averaging eight dead each second! By 2 PM on that same day, the BEF had suffered 60,000 casualties, 20,000 dead! The Battle of the Somme ended on November 18, with 92 more charges by the BEF (none as bad as the first). The war went on for two more years, taking tens of thousands of men from both sides on any given afternoon.

There was no "Chilcot Report" in 1916, and BEF Commander, Douglas Haig, remained as one of the bright stars in British military history, claiming that the Somme was, in fact, a British "victory." This battle took five miles of French ground and cost 420,000 British casualties total, but life went on in Whitehall. One searches in vain for words to compare this one hundred year gap between generational fantasy versus reality. They both can't be right.

A greater perspective than even the Somme would reveal a profound disparity between what our modern generation calls "suffering" and what earlier generations, around the globe, accepted as the price of war. Consider just World War II, within the lifespan of many readers, including this writer. A summary of that conflict's terrible battle statistics might serve to remind us of the nature of human "suffering" with a deeper appreciation of our current problems. The following list is characteristic (casualties in parentheses): Battle of Stalingrad (1.8 million), Berlin (1.3 million), Moscow (I million), Narva (550,000), France (469,000), Luzon (345,000), Kharkov (300,000), Kursk (388,000), and The Bulge (186,000). The list goes on, seemingly endless. If not sufficient, we can return to World War I after the Somme: The Hundred Days Offensive (1.8 million), The Spring Offensive (1.5 million), Verdun (976,000), and Passendale (848,000).

It's been said that a single death is a tragedy; a million is a statistic. The Chilcot Report in Britain diminishes the sacrifices of those British soldiers who gave their-all to keep that country alive.

A mature and stable society requires a perspective on its own identity or else it roams loose without compass or direction.

To Carry a Torch for Lady Liberty

August 1, 2016

There's a reason why she carries a torch, and there a reason why July 4th is associated with fire and fireworks. That reason is embedded within the fabric of American history and the cause of liberty which, from the beginning, was seen as the political "torch" that would light a fire worldwide. Fire, of course, is a destructive force of nature in the physical realm but a powerful and uplifting force in the political realm. It has been used throughout U.S. history in the latter mode and, indeed, the original Revolution was defined as a firestorm that carried political momentum far beyond a simple colonial revolt.

From the Revolution forward, the fire metaphor has been employed to define the nature of the original American experiment with political liberty. It is enshrined as "enlightening the world" in the statue that stands majestically in New York harbor. To appreciate the inner meaning of the term, it is necessary to go through history from the beginning, starting with the Inaugural Address of George Washington himself.

On April 30, 1789, the first president told the country that the American democratic experiment represented "the sacred fire of liberty." Thomas Jefferson spoke of America as "the sole depository of the sacred fire of freedom and self-government, from whence it is to be lighted up in other regions of the earth." A century and a half later, as though he was guided by some ghostlike speechwriter from the past, John F. Kennedy invoked a near-identical script: "The energy, the faith, the devotion which we bring to this endeavor will light our country and all who serve it – and the glow from that fire can truly light the world."

Closer to home, George W. Bush brought the past alive with his own interpretation of the same phenomenon: "By our efforts we have lit a fire as well – a fire in the minds of men. It warms those who feel its power, it burns those who fight its progress, and one day this untamed fire of freedom will reach the darkest corners of the world." The most recent reoccurrence of this theme came from Barack Obama in his first Inaugural, when he reminded the country that the ideals of the Founding Fathers "still light the world and we will not give them up for expedience' sake."

The term fire, of course, is rhetoric, but in a larger dimension, such rhetorical consistencies reflect the political personality of the American culture and rise high above the verbiage of succeeding generations. Fire also reflects the intangible elements of the intellect and instinct, the so-called "soft" elements of national power. They include will, maturity, vision, ambition, leadership, prudence, character, and consistency. While such qualities embedded in the statements of American political leaders may have served as only theoretical guides, they nonetheless represent efforts toward better and brighter futures, both domestic and global. That is the purpose of rhetoric, a design for the practical aspects of statesmanship toward horizons not yet attained. Such "fire" is essential for an ordered and free society.

At bottom, fire is the meaning of the fourth of July. It has revealed its essence through literally countless presidential and other political reflections on the American purpose or "cause." One such statement, perhaps characteristic of them all, was the war message of Woodrow Wilson to Congress, April 2, 1917, which seemed to embody all of the qualities of the metaphor in one salient paragraph: "Right is more precious than peace, and we shall fight for the things which we have always carried nearest our hearts – for democracy, for the rights of those who submit to authority to have a voice in their own governments, for the rights and liberties of small nations."

This wildly expansive declaration, which set the European world "on fire," properly exposes the unique American profile to "light a match" and enjoy the flames. This is arson, and it might righteously condemn the American democracy as the greatest "arsonist" of all time: most of the globe's dictators spend their time damping fires against this "spread."

They might be reminded of John Adam's admonition of 1821: "... the flames kindled on the fourth of July 1776 have been spread over too much of the globe to be extinguished by the feeble engines of despotism; on the contrary, they will consume these engines and all who work them."

Centuries later, world wars, cold war, ISIS and domestic terrorism, the flame of freedom still burns bright and still offers mankind the best hope for a "brave new world."

Brexit:

The second greatest British decision

June 20, 2016

On June 23, the British people will commit to the second greatest decision that they have been asked to make in over one hundred years: whether or not to remain in the European Union. "Brexit," ("British exit") has the potential to turn the entire international system on its head, including the very political/economic definition of Europe as we know it and the "special" American relationship with Britain, going back to the nineteenth century.

The stakes are truly historic and rise much higher than any temporal or technocratic gains or losses in the short run and even long run. The real stake is strategic and could redefine the character of world politics in any foreseeable future and, at bottom, issues of war or peace. These issues, as well, go far beyond Europe and will affect Asia, the Middle East, and Africa, in their turn.

This has always been the case, as it was in the "first" great decision. This occurred in August 1914, when Britain decided to join France in the war against Germany, despite no legal commitment to do so. The background to this decision goes to 1904 when the two countries signed the *Entente Cordiale*, which divided the Middle East between them (especially Egypt and Morocco) but contained no obligation to fight in Europe. In the ensuing years, both nations' militaries collaborated on theoretical defense plans against Germany, but when war broke out between France and Germany on August 3, Britain had to make a decision.

Just as now, the outcome was uncertain, and both the government and public were divided. In his war message to the House of Commons, Foreign Secretary Edward Grey appealed to British pride, profit, and patriotism in making the case. Citing British "interests ... honour ... [and] obligations," Grey pointed to the possible domination of Europe by Germany, the defense of Belgian independence (a "straw man" at best) and, in deference to France, he rejected "unconditional neutrality ... We cannot do that." In a passage that has haunted Britain since, Grey dismissed the consequences that nobody could foresee: "We are going to suffer ... terribly in this war, whether we are in it or whether we stand aside. Foreign trade is going to stop."

It was much more than foreign trade that stopped! It was the empire itself.

Years later, with nearly a million dead, a shattered empire, a Communist Russia, an isolated America, a politically paralyzed France, and a Nazi Germany, people would look back and wonder what it was "all about."

Grey himself had a premonition that something truly big was at stake. In drafting his message to Parliament, he noticed the lamplighter below dousing the streetlamps. Turning to his secretary, he uttered history's most prophetic insight: "The lamps are going out all over Europe, we shall not see them lit again in our lifetime." But unbeknown to Viscount Grey, he was in the process of putting them out himself, and with consequences that not even he could have foreseen.

Unlike Britain's upcoming decision, the Britain of 1914 went to war without either a referendum or full parliamentary participation. The ultimatum to Berlin was issued by the Foreign Office and came and went without any semblance of national debate. In the reflection on whether Europe was killed in 1914 or committed suicide, the answer remains academic. Either way, as a primary factor in world politics, Europe would soon be eclipsed by outside powers from North America and Eurasia. And that remains the case today, as Great Britain will go to the polls to determine if this long slide continues or ends.

For the supporters of Brexit, like Secretary of Justice Michael Gove, a British withdrawal from the EU will be a "galvanizing, liberating, empowering moment of patriotic renewal." But both opponents and supporters are at least united on one point, and that is the importance of the vote. As Prime Minister David Cameron (an opponent) has said, the issue is "perhaps the most important decision the British people will have to take at the ballot box in our lifetimes."

In terms of the international system and the momentum of history, any British rejection of the post-Cold War movement toward greater unity, "globalization," will have enormous consequences toward a future "world order." In his most recent book of the same name, Henry Kissinger posits a world order reminiscent of the "Westphalian" system that characterized Old Europe, leading to an order based upon a "concert" of free nations. Indeed, the rejection of the European Union by England might well be a profound restoration toward that order. The future may well hold a reverse movement away from unified nations into a system where geopolitics, culture, and sovereignty reign. On June 23rd, the stakes are high.

Memorial Day:

One Lucky Country

May 27, 2016

As we celebrate Memorial Day this weekend, it might be prudent to remember what we are celebrating. The holiday, originally called Decoration Day, began during the Civil War as a time to remember those who fell, on either side. The original name reflected the habit of "decorating" soldier's graves with flowers and may have begun as early as June 3, 1861 in Warrenton, VA. Another early claim was for 1862 in Savannah, GA and for July 4, 1864 in Boalsburg, PA. There are other claims for the original day, but Memorial Day historian David Bright has called all of these "apocryphal legends."

Bright also believes that the first widely publicized occurrence was on May 1, 1865 in Charleston, SC and was created primarily by recently freed slaves ("freedmen"). During the war, the graves of 257 Union POW's had been hastily covered inside the city and left to rot. A group of black freedmen, along with Union troops and white northern ministers, gathered to cover these sites with proper dignity and shelter. As Bright wrote, "This was the first Memorial

Day. African Americans invented Memorial Day in Charleston, South Carolina. What you have there is black Americans recently freed from slavery announcing to the world with their flowers, their feet and their songs what the war had been about."

The first official recognition of the practice is recorded on May 5, 1868, when General John A. Logan, Commander in Chief of the Grand Army of the Republic, proclaimed Decoration Day to be observed annually and nationally on May 30, a date chosen since it was not the anniversary of any major battle. That year, 183 cemeteries in 27 states celebrated the event; the next year there were 336.

The term "Memorial" Day began in 1882, but it was nearly a century later that it became official. On June 28, 1967, Congress gave it official status, and one year later to the day, they passed the Uniform Monday Holiday Act, moving it to the last Monday in May (ostensibly for a three-day weekend).

Of course, the significance of the day far transcends a vacation. The date was created to honor Americans killed in war from both sides of the Civil War and, subsequently, for all those who died in military service from the beginnings of the country. This covers a lot of ground, but America was never a militaristic society. From the start, America had opposed large standing armies in peacetime and had isolated the professional military to such an extent that it found itself usually removed from the body politic. The caricature of the infamous "man on horseback," representing a military coup or regime, so common elsewhere, was always a nightmare to the American political culture. So why a major day honoring the dead and their wars?

As with the rest of the political globe, the U.S. has engaged in numerous armed conflicts. America's military enemies, over time, would cover a sizable percentage of the nations on earth, some more than once. For a democracy opposed to the military in principle, and with an isolationist history, the U.S. armed services have been very busy. Consider these enemies: Native Americans from all tribes (about four centuries), Loyalists in the Revolution, England twice, The Confederacy (or Union, depending upon perspective), Mexico three times (1846, 1914, 1916), Germany twice, Spain, Russia twice (intervention 1918-20, Cold War vs. Soviet Russia), Austria-Hungary, Japan, East European Axis members, Italy, China, Korea, Vietnam, interventions in the Middle East since 1982 (nineteen), and Afghanistan.

That takes care of most of the major players, but there are also "little" wars against smaller countries and guerrillas, such as: naval/marine expeditions of the nineteenth century (about 100), interventions in Central America after 1898 (about 25, especially Panama, Haiti, Dominican Republic and Nicaragua), The Philippines (1899- 1913), plus such even lesser excursions as in Lebanon (1958) and Grenada (1983).

Characteristically, Memorial Day wasn't meant to honor all of these multiple military operations, but, as a matter of record, they deserve at least some recognition along with the great wars of the American past. These latter normally are confined to the "Big Three": the Civil War and both world wars. Thinking about American dead in war does not normally focus on, say, Nicaragua or The Philippines, but almost always on these climactic contests.

Throughout all of this, the United States has emerged not only quite fortunate but also politically stable, socially intact, safe from foreign invasion, and extremely prosperous. This is quite a record compared to the rest of the world which, except perhaps England, has suffered multiple invasions, occupations, revolutions, depressions and, to this day, large-scale departures of its own people to unknown places.

America has also been saved the wartime sufferings known elsewhere. World War II claimed 75 million lives; only 415,000 were Americans. During the 1940-41 air "blitz," England itself was bombed 76 days/nights in a row; that's 76 "9/11's" by our standards. The Cold War was won in 1991 without a single shot between the belligerents.

There are serious problems at home, but the symbolism of Memorial Day has persisted for a century and a half, namely: death, sacrifice, rebirth. This has been called the American "civil religion." May it prosper.

Erasing History

May 4, 2016

Driving down Virginia's John Mosby Highway recently, I wondered how long we will keep this name alive, given that Mosby was a fierce Confederate partisan during the Civil War. Should we rename the road? But if we remove Mosby, what do we do with the Jefferson Davis Highway? This is called a "slippery slope."

While it is appropriate to remove Confederate symbols from official sites, it is quite another matter to attempt a wholesale intellectual departure from any vestiges of history, however unpleasant they may be to current sentiments. It is also practically impossible. There are over 500 highway signs, monuments, statues and other fixed memories of the Confederacy in Virginia alone.

The first problem with this is: where do we stop? Having eliminated some relic of the past, say, from Harvard's flag or from someone's fraternity house, why not *all* of them? There's a built-in hypocrisy in removing some while leaving others.

A related problem is how to discern what to remove and what to keep? What is the criterion? Practically all of the removed items from our national landscape stem from the issue of slavery. The country once joined practically the rest of the globe in the historic institution of slaveholding. So we're not unique. And, what do we emphasize, the deaths of 750,000 white soldiers to eliminate the institution or its existence in the first place? If we remove all memories of this, why can't we insist on a total and global cleansing of the same everywhere, just as we have for all other aspects of "human rights"?

But where is slavery in the historical spectrum? Certainly better than genocide and probably worse than indentured service. But is a "wage slave" a form of the same institution? Do we remove America's corporate "robber barons" from memory? Was slavery worse than the forced removal of Native Americans from their ancestral homes, discrimination against the Irish, Italians, Jews, Germans, and other white "minorities," lack of voting rights for women, child labor, the Great Depression, the Vietnam War etc.? If we expand the point beyond slavery to simply "things we don't want to remember," then there is little history left to erase.

What about the draft and the unnecessary deaths of whole generations? Over 57,000 American servicemen were killed in Vietnam within several years for a now-lost cause. How many slaves were killed in a comparable period? We've seen more attention to Freddie Gray than the memory of Vietnam. Isn't justice supposed to be "even-handed"? Maybe we need a new movement, "Soldiers' Lives Matter."

What about our ally, England, that stood by while 1.5 million Irish starved to death from 1847 to 1850? The same country supervised 60,000 casualties of its young men in a single day (July 1, 1916). Their commander was Douglas Haig, so why is his name still honored?

If there are too many questions without answers here, I apologize but will not accept responsibility. It would be comical to watch our most fervent destroyers of the past wrestle with these and other such contradictions.

One who will not is Emerson College Professor Ted Gup, who wrote a recent editorial against those who are "waging war on the dead at Harvard" (*Washington Post*, March 20, 2016). Recently, the Harvard administration retired the Law School seal since it was inspired by a slave-owner some 200 years ago. With this logic, Gup writes, most of Harvard's other luminaries with properties in their name should also be retired. These included segregationists and racists of all stripes, anti-Catholics, anti-Semites, anti-women's-rights proponents, euthanasia advocates, anti-gay donors, famous Americans who fouled the environment, etc. Gup called the current ideologues to be on a "fool's errand," but why should an intelligent society suffer fools gladly? Or has the society lost its intelligence?

That is the heart of the issue. If we were to eliminate the past and judge it by current standards, whether they are correct or not, we would, in effect, have no history at all. On a larger scale, there would be no worth to a national society that condoned slavery or allowed slums. There is no room for understanding or perspective from a society fixated with tunnel vision. Abraham Lincoln was far ahead of his contemporaries in 1863; today he would probably be called an unapologetic "racist." Franklin Roosevelt led history's greatest war against global fascism, but he also imprisoned 120,000 Americans of Japanese ancestry. That fact alone would probably disqualify FDR from any claim to authority, much less greatness.

The American people are often dismissed as "ahistorical." Fair enough, but there should be a distinction between indifference and hostility. Otherwise, there's no George Washington, no dead soldiers, nothing worth celebrating.

That means no fourth of July.

"Doctrinaire" Foreign Policies

(1.) Realism: who are these people?

Hans J. Morgenthau
(1904-1980)
"Politics Among Nations:
The Struggle for Power
and Peace" (1948)

E.H. Carr (1882-1982)
"The Twenty Years Crisis,
1919–1939: an Introduction
to the Study of International
Relations" (1939)

Reinhold Niebuhr
(1892-1971)
"Moral Man and Immoral
Society: A Study of Ethics
and Politics" (1932)

May 3, 2016

Throughout history, nations have chosen to label their important policy objectives as "doctrinal" in scope, as though these were religious rather than merely secular in nature. A "doctrine," is, after all, a matter of faith and morals, not just a temporal reaction to some country's misdemeanors. In foreign policy, doctrinal status, like the Truman Doctrine beginning containment, or the Monroe Doctrine protecting Latin America from European encroachments, is revered and reflects high level interests.

A doctrine elevates state behavior to a much higher level, to an area where geopolitical strategy reaches untouchable limits, not to be crossed by either friend or foe. One is reminded of the symbolic flag of the American Revolution, a rattlesnake ready to strike. "Don't Tread On Me" was not technically a doctrine, but it had the same force: here, but no further!

Why do statesmen want to proclaim doctrines? Perhaps the greatest doctrine, Monroe in 1823, was not even given doctrinal status until much later and was twisted beyond all recognition by his successors. Not only was the U.S. unable to enforce the Monroe Doctrine as the British Navy patrolled the south Atlantic, but the basic idea was converted from a defensive shield against

European occupations in Latin America to an offensive sword. President James Polk reversed the original concept to a justification for American expansion in the 1840s, perhaps a good policy, but not because of James Monroe.

Polk, actually one of history's more successful leaders, invoked the doctrine to annex Texas, New Mexico, California, and Oregon into the greater U.S. His bold use of the idea was expanded in 1902 by Theodore Roosevelt with a "corollary" allowing for American intervention in Latin America against "chronic wrongdoing." The result was twenty-five American interventions in the region, finally stopped by Franklin Roosevelt's "Good Neighbor" Policy in the 1930s. Thus, doctrines can be both passive and active, depending upon circumstances and power.

Doctrines are customary in world statecraft, but not always with the same name. George Washington's Farewell Address urged a U.S. neutrality toward Europe, which largely held for 150 years, but was never called a "doctrine." The 1899-1900 "Open Door" notes sent by the U.S. to protect China against further interventions was largely ignored, but remained steadfast as U.S. policy for generations, finally producing a frustrated Japanese attack on Pearl Harbor in December 1941. But these notes were never given doctrinal status.

Doctrines are similar to the Shakespeare expression, "what's in a name." How serious is a country when it announces a doctrine? Over time, there have been many, but most U.S. political administrations have survived without a single one.

Let's survey the landscape. For the U.S. alone, the following doctrines have existed: Monroe, Tyler, Stimson, Truman, Eisenhower, Kennedy, Johnson, Nixon, Kirkpatrick, Weinberger, Reagan, Powell, Clinton, Bush, and Rumsfeld.

Aside from professional historians, there are few Americans who can recall the specifics of these. Except for the first, Monroe, most have left historical connections behind but, at the time, they at least had momentary interest. The "Bush Doctrine," which is what the press called it, is probably still in force but only sporadically.

Doctrines do not necessarily need enforcement. A doctrine by itself is a statement of purpose and no more. Enforcement is an entirely different matter and is not even required. The Monroe Doctrine was enforced by the British Navy. Secretary of State Stimson's doctrine condemned Japan in 1931 for taking Manchuria. Japan kept Manchuria until it lost the war.

Nor are doctrines confined to the United States. Other countries have announced their own, including Argentina (Calvo), Mexico (Estrada), and Britain (Palmerston). Perhaps the most important and most recent was the Brezhnev Doctrine, justifying Soviet interventions into Eastern Europe. Announced in 1968, it justified Soviet armed takeover of Czechoslovakia, but was forgotten after his death and the collapse of Soviet rule by 1989.

America's Monroe Doctrine was probably the longest standing in history, lasting 190 years if we are to believe Secretary of State John Kerry. On April 18, 2013, Kerry told an Organization of American States meeting that "the era of the Monroe Doctrine is over." According to one account, the point received "tepid applause," prompting Secretary Kerry to reply that it was "worth applauding." Many felt that Kerry was apologizing for history. Still, the news received little play in the U.S. media but much more in Latin America, where many papers mistook Kerry's word "era" for "error," reporting that, apparently, the U.S. was making its confession. They were probably right.

This point reflects the relatively new U.S. geopolitical role in the world. At one time, and even right up to Pearl Harbor and world war, Latin America was the most critical arena for the U.S. No longer. The new foreign policies, termed the Bush and Rumsfeld "Doctrines" by the press, are post-9/11 phenomena and were aimed against the "axis of evil," namely states that "harbored" terrorists.

Should these doctrines go on for 190 years, we may want to re-examine our strategies.

Is NATO Necessary?

May 4, 2016

April 4, 2016 — NATO is sixty-seven years old and has suddenly become a major bone of contention in the Republican primary fight. Although some may welcome the notion that, at long last, the remaining three in this contest are tackling a serious strategic issue, the rancor still remains. Front-runner Donald Trump has publically called the alliance "obsolete," and accused the European partners of "ripping off the United States."

Thus far, Trump has practically no support in this, certainly not from Europe. His chief rival, Senator Ted Cruz, proclaimed Trump to be "wrong," and that his ideas would mean that "America should withdraw from the world and abandon our allies." This also, Cruz went on, would provide "a major victory," both for Russia's Vladimir Putin and ISIS itself.

Predictably, the response from the media was equally apocalyptic. *The Washington Post's* Jackson Diehl warned against "chaos and dictatorship" among NATO's newest members and that western unity would face a "crumbling at the hands of populists and nationalists who would retreat behind refortified borders." Columnist Anne Applebaum called the Trump comments "... the end of liberal world order as we know it," while the *New York Times*, in one editorial, called his ideas, "unhinged, shockingly ignorant [and] bizarre."

This is all quite understandable. Since 1949, NATO has been the bedrock of American and European order that has carried the alliance through over forty years of Cold War, with an expansion of twelve new members since its end. One does not dismiss this record casually or without reflection, but that is what exactly what Trump has done. A reflection on NATO should not be dismissed outright. Nor should it indicate that the "grandfather" of western security may not be approaching retirement age or that his departure necessarily means a retreat to the First World War.

For the most part, this question depends on the circumstances prompting any reflection and the implications therein. Why should anything, including a military alliance, be sacrosanct or even permanent? In domestic political parlance, "change" is essential; few politicians promise a return to the past or the status quo (except Coolidge). Barack Obama won twice with the slogan "change we can believe in." That approach should be integral to foreign policy as well, with emphasis on what we "believe in" versus change for its own sake.

Alliances come and go, as do conditions in world politics. In 1954, for example, the United States led the creation of NATO's South Pacific counterpart, the Southeast Asia Treaty Organization (SEATO). With the American retreat from Vietnam in 1975, the purpose for SEATO quickly dissolved, and it ended finally two years later. In 1955, the Middle East Treaty Organization (METO) was formed by Britain and several Islamic nations. U.S. entry in 1958 made it the Central Treaty Organization (CENTO), but intermittent quarreling led to its demise in 1979. Thus, NATO is the last survivor among several Cold War coalitions whose life-span reflected the nature and momentum of strategic realities.

Thus, the question remains: does the strategic reality of 2016 require the continuation of an organization formed in 1949? Related questions involve the implications of change, especially what would emerge from any kind of change in a sixty-seven year-old structure, i.e. would it be an improvement?

The first, and most obvious issue, is the question of obsolesce. Obviously, the original purpose of NATO no longer exists. Created to safeguard Western Europe against the Red Army, at a time when the Soviet Union had no nuclear weapons, both the conditions of NATO's creation and its original purpose have long since disappeared. Article V, the heart of the Treaty, requires consultation in the event of a threat. Article V was never invoked in the entire span of the Cold War and was invoked for the first and only time after 9/11 when NATO troops were dispatched to Afghanistan. NATO has since been involved in a number of lesser roles in support of U.S. anti-terror operations, such as trainers in Iraq, enforcing no-fly zones, etc.

The second and more important issue is whether or not the alliance is needed in the global war on terrorism. The recent attacks in France and Belgium have, at the very least, to call into question the relevance of an alliance formed against a non-existent army in an age of irregular and clandestine terrorism. A related question is what any tampering with NATO might do to the security of member-states, particularly the new entrants. Does the United States, for example, still wish to guarantee the safety of Eastern Europe, including possibly the even newer ones to come, Bosnia and Herzegovina, Macedonia and Montenegro?

In 1953, Secretary of State John Foster Dulles sent shockwaves throughout NATO when he threatened an "agonizing reappraisal" of the American commitment should they refuse German rearmament. West Germany was rearmed and joined NATO. If a Senate Committee or a think tank proposed something similar, the pundits would be trampling over each other with supportive ideas. Money would flow, conferences held, books published.

A journey of a thousand steps starts with one. If NATO needs mending or replacing, what goes into its place? It depends on how one sees it: as an opportunity or a dilemma.

How to win a war without fighting

March 28, 2016

In the 1970s, the U.S. pursued a foreign policy of "détente," guided by Henry Kissinger, that had some success, especially with China, but failed to stop the surge of Soviet strategic nuclear power and Soviet advances across the globe. The ultimate purpose of détente was to "manage" relations between the two superpowers and to prevent nuclear war, which it did.

But the election of Ronald Reagan in 1980 began a new era in world politics and a new approach to the old geopolitics of containment. Before assuming office, Reagan, who had studied communism all his life, was determined to eradicate communism as a force in the world and to supervise the renewed ambitions of American power and purpose. At one point, he turned to his security advisor, Richard Allen, and said "Dick, my idea of American foreign policy toward the Soviet Union is simple and, some would say simplistic. It is this: We win and they lose." Yet from this elementary slogan, the Reagan Administration engineered such a historic, and still unappreciated, assault on the many vulnerabilities of Soviet society, that it ceased to exist within a decade. This was a geopolitical revolution of historic and unprecedented dimensions.

At the time, the USSR was one of history's largest and most powerful totalitarian regimes. Led by brutal leaders like Stalin and Brezhnev, it governed eleven time zones, over 300 million people, tens of thousands of nuclear weapons, total control of east and central Europe, and footholds throughout the political world from Cuba to Africa and the Middle East.

Yet this all came crashing down within a few years – without direct combat between the superpowers.

Nor was this understood even as it happened. Neither the American nor the Soviet people were aware that history was being made until December 1991 when Premier Gorbachev announced the end of his country. No parades, no military heroes, no "battles," no casualties, not even public acknowledgement. The United States, overnight, became the "sole remaining superpower." Few Americans knew how; most still don't.

But there were earlier signs, especially within the Republican Party, that "rollback," rather than containment, was needed. The 1952 Republican election platform called for this, and Barry Goldwater's campaign in 1964 did, as well. But the 1952 pledges went unfulfilled, and Goldwater lost his election.

But Reagan won and began changing U.S. military and diplomatic policy almost immediately. The Soviet Union had ten years to go.

In his first year alone, Reagan authorized a vast array of improvements in America's military posture: the B-1 bomber, a 600-ship navy, cruise and other new ballistic missiles including the M-X ICBM, Trident submarines, and new areas of R&D funds. Within six years of Reagan taking office, the U.S. had procured 3,000 new combat aircraft, 3,700 strategic missiles, and 10,000 tanks. A ranking member of Moscow's Institute for the Study of the USA later complained that "You Americans are trying to destroy our economy, to interfere with our trade, to overwhelm and make us inferior in the strategic field." Exactly!

None of these weapons were ever used in anger directly against the Soviet Bloc.

Major changes in direction in U.S. foreign policy began in 1982 and continued throughout the entire first term, producing a total of 135 NSDDs (National Security Decision Directives) that targeted the Soviet Bloc and brought about its downfall. The critical document in this process was NSDD 75, January 23, 1983, and was announced on March 8 in Toledo in Reagan's famous "Evil Empire" speech. Shortly thereafter, on March 23, he announced the equally famous Strategic Defense Initiative which, while never implemented, remained a symbolic threat to the Soviet economy. According to Cold War historian Derek Leebaert, SDI would "remain forever scattered between symbol, deception and real power ... by and large Moscow was fooled ... SDI was an inspired step in the war of attrition, whether or not Moscow tried to match it" (*The Fifty Year Wound*, 2002).

NSDD 75 drew upon a spectrum of economic, military, financial, and political initiatives. The creative product of National Security Council Soviet specialists Richard Pipes and John Lenczowski, the overall strategy developed a coordinated and comprehensive global assault from all quarters against the vulnerabilities of the Soviet Empire. With an antiquated economy decades behind the U.S. in computers and other technologies, the Soviets had no chance to compete with American resources. The Western allies were (reluctantly) persuaded to deny Soviet access to advanced technology and scientific data. The Soviets were unable to afford needed machine tools, electronics, and computers, and an ingenious campaign was begun to deny them worldwide access to these items. Pressure from Washington ended the highly anticipated Soviet gas pipeline to Western Europe. U.S. intelligence capabilities were greatly improved. The strategy was to challenge the Soviet Union's prevailing culture, via geopolitical and cultural initiatives; employing deceptive technical sales to the USSR; deploying Stinger missiles to Afghanistan; enlisting cooperation from global sources like Saudi Arabia and the Vatican; broadcasting to the Iron Curtain from Radio Free Europe, USIA, and Radio Liberty; exporting musical tapes and CDs to captive nations; and even promoting rock concerts and the sales of blue jeans.

In summary, the Reagan Administration employed a complete strategic geopolitical, economic, and cultural "invasion" to undermine a regime that had simply exhausted its term on earth. One can scan world history, but will find nothing comparable to this "assault." What has happened since is another story, in the next essay.

How to fight a war without winning

March 28, 2016

Having left Southeast Asia in 1975 in a disastrous condition, the United States vowed "No More Vietnams," the title of ex-President Nixon's 1985 book. Since Nixon had supervised about half of the war, his view on its legacy fairly summarizes a more general consensus: once bitten, twice shy. For the moment, or so it seemed, America was through with open-ended and lengthy occupations against ideological or unconventional opponents in far-flung parts of the globe.

Not so fast.

The starting point for the modern American involvement in the turmoils of the Middle East began in 1983. In April, the U.S. Embassy in Beirut, Lebanon was bombed, killing 17 Americans. But October 23 was the real beginning, when suicide truck bombers blew up the U.S. Marine barracks in Beirut, part of a larger peacekeeping force that was in place following the Israeli invasion of Lebanon in June 1982. In one of recent history's more prophetic asides, Marine Colonel Timothy Geraghty, commander of the U.S. 24th Marine Amphibious Unit, noted that the U.S. presence "… removed any lingering doubts of our neutrality, and I stated to my staff at the time that we were going to pay in blood for this decision." General Colin Powell, then assistant to Defense

Secretary Caspar Weinberger, said at the time that "When the shells started falling on the Shiites, they assumed that the American referee had taken sides." Although a group called "Islamic Jihad" took credit for the tragedy, subsequent investigations left no doubt that Iran, Syria, and Hezbollah were responsible. As if to publicize its complicity, Iran has erected a monument in Tehran honoring the Islamic "martyrs."

Due to a split between the Defense and State Departments, the U.S. reaction was limited. On February 8, 1984, the USS *New Jersey* rained down 300 shells in a nine hour period against enemy positions, but a complete withdrawal soon followed. The incident was not only typical of subsequent years, but served as the opening shot of American strategy in the area that has gone on to this day and symbolically still represents a strategic bankruptcy now into its third decade. The Civil War lasted four years, the U.S. fought in World War I for about six months, World War II lasted for about four years, Korea three, and Vietnam (considered our "longest" war) for about fifteen years. Why is the U.S. still debating the Middle East and "what to do about it" 33 years later?

The strategic genesis of all this was actually geopolitically sound. In January 1980, President Carter declared that "An attempt by any outside force to gain control of the Persian Gulf region will be regarded as an assault on the vital interests of the United States of America, and such an assault will be repelled by any means necessary, including military force." That was 36 years ago, but today the region has withstood decades of intermittent chaos, turmoil, terrorism, refugee escapes, and multiple American military interventions. The oil still flows, but with the rise of ISIS and the political disintegration of Syria and Iraq, the region is as unstable and dangerous as it has ever been. The implications of all this have now paralyzed much of Western Europe. Worse, there seems no end in sight.

The fundamental failure is neither lack of resources nor will but lack of focus, hesitant and incoherent strategies, and a glaring lack of even a shared definition or purpose. There is a breach between what the Obama Administration has defined as the enemy, where the use of the word "Islam" is banned, and the rest of the world, including the terrorists themselves. The first word in ISIS is "Islamic." When a nation cannot even coalesce behind an understanding of the issue nor the philosophical source of the opponent, then strategic anarchy will certainly follow.

Tragically, this conceptual problem undermines the best of American intentions in the Middle East, and, through six political administrations, despite bountiful resources, has been as serious as any strategic blunder in recent history. If "mission creep" means action without purpose, the American positions in the Middle East are unquestionably "creepy." They are also costly. Since the Carter administration, the U.S. has invaded, occupied, bombed or otherwise attacked a total of nineteen Islamic countries, from Kosovo in Europe, to Somalia in Africa, to the protracted wars in Afghanistan and Iraq. In those latter two wars alone, U.S. fatalities number almost seven thousand, with a cost estimated at three trillion dollars. The total cost of U.S. involvement in the entire Persian Gulf since 1980 is estimated at ten trillion dollars. The interventions, furthermore, have been sporadic and hesitant: three Iraq wars, in and out of Afghanistan, Syria, Pakistan, Sudan, Yemen, Lebanon, Somalia, etc. The highly politicized debate surrounding Hillary Clinton's role in the Benghazi affair illustrates the American public's focus on a microscopic tactical incident, terrible in itself, that is insignificant in comparison to the greater strategic picture.

The net result of all this is that U.S. strategy in the Middle East is murky and undefined, misunderstood, or ignored at home. There is no precedent in U.S. foreign policies for such a protracted and futile pursuit of objectives-however worthy in themselves-that, after three decades, simply carries its own momentum. By contrast, it took the Reagan Administration only a few years to terminate the vast empire of the Soviet Union. The U.S. in the Middle East appears closer to the historic wars against the many North American Indian tribes: wars that lasted decades with little coordinated direction. Lots of death and chaos; no closure. It is not much to look forward to.

American Involvement in Vietnam:

Geopolitics and Ideology

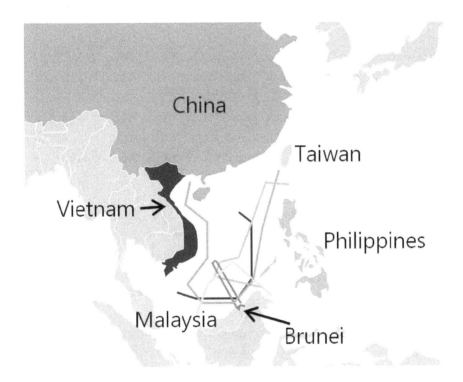

March 14, 2016

American involvement in Vietnam began quite early in the Cold War when, in 1950, the Truman Administration began financing the French effort to retain Indochina against the communist-nationalist "Vietminh" guerrillas led by Ho Chi Minh and based in Hanoi. But U.S. interest came very late in the Indochina game, which began long before anybody had ever heard of the Cold War. Ho Chi Minh was present at the 1919 Paris Peace Conference, where he petitioned Woodrow Wilson for Vietnamese independence based upon the Fourteen Points. Ironically, Ho would later use American history, including the Declaration of Independence and the Atlantic Charter, as supporting statements for his own cause. For the U.S., support for French colonialism contradicted the genesis of American purpose in the world from the inception, but was ignored for the global cause against communism.

From the start, American involvement in Vietnam reversed both ideology and geopolitics from any historic or strategic logic.

The battle of Dien Bien Phu, March-May 1954, was a turning point in world history, not only removing France from Indochina but also introducing the United States to the anti-communist cause of South Vietnam, which was left independent against the new communist regime in Hanoi. Dien Bien Phu, a historic French defeat, was covertly supported by the Eisenhower Administration, where American bombers flew over 600 sorties against the Vietminh. Two American pilots died, the first of nearly 58,000 Americans to die before the final retreat in 1975. From that point forward, Vietnam symbolized the global American crusade against communism, regardless of where or when it appeared on the map.

The geopolitical structure of the world defined such an interpretation of "life or death" policies. For over a thousand years Europe had been the epicenter of world politics, with all other members of global society either under direct domination or totally removed from any strategic interest in either global war or peace. But all that changed after World War II with Europe destitute and dependent upon outside resources just to survive. From a historic European "balance of power" consisting of ten or more "multipolar" interactive states in continuous territorial or dynastic struggles, the world, overnight, lapsed into a global contest between two continental behemoths in a "bipolar" contest for total world dominion. This, moreover, was an *ideological* struggle over "hearts and minds" more than it was strictly geopolitical.

In such an arena, relatively small and unimportant areas outside of Europe, i.e. Korea, Taiwan, Vietnam, took on an importance that mirrored the larger "cold" war between the giants. The contest became "zero sum," insofar as the loss of one seemed to amount to an equal gain for the other. Bipolarity allowed for little maneuver. As the U.S. Secretary of State said later in a memorable comment regarding the Soviet Union over Cuba: "we were eyeball to eyeball, and nobody blinked."

That was the context of America's obsession with Vietnam. The fall of China, one billion people apparently going over to the other side, without any serious American military involvement, provided the legend that China was "lost" because of the opinions of a handful of U.S. Foreign Service Officers in the field. The backlash was so severe that American officials could not possibly witness another similar debacle. Thus, in a reversal of all geopolitical logic, Vietnam, occupying a peninsula abutting southern China with only 30 million people, became host to over two million American military personnel in a decades-long fight to the finish. True to President Eisenhower's "domino" theory, Vietnam was seen as the key to victory or defeat in the Cold War, but it *wasn't* geopolitics.

As the Kennedy Administration began its entry into Southeast Asia in 1961, Premier Khrushchev of the Soviet Union introduced his own definition of ideological war into the equation. Based upon a speech on January 6, Khrushchev called for a global assault via "wars of national liberation," like the guerrilla campaigns waged by Ho Chi Minh and Fidel Castro, against western strongholds in the vast "Third World" areas of the globe.

This circular seemed to U.S. leaders to confirm the importance of Vietnam and other insurgencies in Africa and Asia in what was universally interpreted as a Soviet attempt to surround the West without the use of nuclear weapons. This encouraged U.S. leaders to dig even deeper inside Vietnam as the classic test case. As Defense Secretary Robert McNamara told a Senate Committee in 1965, "The stakes in South Vietnam are far greater than the loss of one small country to communism. ... Its loss would ... greatly complicate the task of preventing the further spread of militant Asian communism."

Echoes of that past are frequent today against the "spread" of "militant Islam." A generation ago, they led to millions of American troops inside a small outpost of Eurasia and the worst strategic defeat in American history. The false prophesies of the domino theory and the misplaced geopolitical theories of both sides are long since forgotten, but can still serve as powerful reminders that "ideas have consequences" and that warfare, at bottom, remains a clash of competing ideas.

Geopolitical Determinism:

Dominos

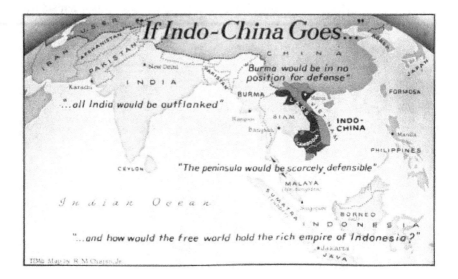

March 10, 2016

Traditional geopolitical theories have long concentrated on Europe as the center of their strategic universe, with the major exception of the sea power designs of the American naval officer, Alfred T. Mahan. But the classic geopoliticians have been Europeans. Halford Mackinder first introduced the subject in England in 1904 with his essay on the "Geographical Pivot of History," involving control of his so-called "Heartland," basically Eastern Europe and Eurasia, as the "pivot" for control of surrounding areas, termed the "World Island." Opposed to this conception came Yale professor (but from the Netherlands) Nicholas J. Spykman's later interpretation in 1943 in *The Geography of the Peace*. This theory stressed the importance of the "Rimlands" of western and southern Europe as the key to world power and is generally seen as the geopolitical foundation for the subsequent American foreign policy of "containment" against the Soviet Union.

But in a larger perspective, these competing interpretations of geopolitics mirror the actual shape and contour of most major wars and alliance systems that have dominated history over centuries. They also reflect the great geopolitical divide between armies versus navies, land power versus sea power, that have correspondingly divided the strategic world into two halves. World War I, pitting the armed strength of Germany and the Central powers versus Britain, the United States and France, was one example, but essentially the same geopolitical system dominated the strategic scenario of World War II, as well. The Soviet Union defeated Germany coming from the "Heartland," while the U.S. and Britain came from the ocean, through Normandy and France, i.e. the "Rimlands."

It is equally accurate to portray containment and the Cold War through a similar geopolitical lens, with NATO representing a continuation of Rimland power, i.e. maritime-air, and the Soviet Union, heartland power, Eurasia.

The dominant geopolitical interpretations of the twentieth century's focus on Europe reflect the political and strategic realities of that period of history. But the second half of that century witnessed a sharp turn in strategic focus, when Asia emerged to replace an exhausted and war-torn Europe. Compared to Europe, however, Asia was terra incognita, a geostrategic void.

While U.S. power created NATO and saved Western Europe from communist domination, there were neither the resources, historical perspective, nor geopolitical focus about how to save Asia, especially China, from a similar fate. The result was a series of disastrous and tragic situations in Asia beginning right after the Second World War and running throughout the remainder of the twentieth century.

During the war, it became President Roosevelt's "geopolitical assumption," as it was called then, that China under the Nationalist leader Chiang Kai-shek would stay unified and take its place as one of the great powers in the new world order. But as the civil war against the communists under Mao Tse-tung glaringly demonstrated the failures of nationalist rule, this assumption gradually crumbled and gave way to U.S. efforts to find a way to keep China unified and non-communist. Former Secretary of War George Marshall conducted negotiations between the sides from 1945 to 1947 but went home discouraged and braced for the eventual communist victory.

When that victory came in October 1949, the U.S. was completely unprepared as to how to combat the loss of the world's largest population to world communism and automatically assumed that Mao would align with Stalin against the West. This assumption proved wrong, but equally incorrect was the assumption that the U.S. had "lost" China by withholding massive support for the nationalists.

By 1950, after great success in Europe, American policies in Asia were in shambles, and Republicans were making political advances against the Truman Administration for the "loss" of China. In his infamous anti-communist crusade, Senator Joseph McCarthy blamed the U.S. for the fall of China in a "...a conspiracy so immense and an infamy so black so as to dwarf any previous such venture in the history of man."

The sudden outbreak of the Korean War in June 1950, only months after the fall of China, seemed to confirm Americans' fear of Asian communism and reinforced the conspiracy theories of the new Cold War, without any geopolitical ideas to guide policy. The election of war hero Dwight Eisenhower in 1952 helped end the Korean War in July 1953 but introduced a brand new interpretation of geopolitics as the communist threat shifted from China and Korea to Southeast Asia and, eventually, the tragedy of the Vietnam War.

America had been blindsided twice into Asian wars (Pearl Harbor and Korea) and had suffered the allegation that China was "lost" because of treason and lack of resolve. The Republicans swept into victory in 1952, determined not to repeat such fiascos. With the French evacuation of Indochina in 1954, it appeared that Southeast Asia was about to be added to this dismal list.

By 1954, the U.S. had firmly committed to South Vietnam as the new "last stand," and this commitment arrived with a revolutionary geopolitical interpretation, introduced by Eisenhower as the "domino" theory. Should South Vietnam fall, the president announced in April 1954, a "domino effect" will occur: "...you knock over the first one, and what will happen to the last one is the certainty that it will go over very quickly." The net result is the certain loss of the entire subcontinent, Indonesia, India and beyond – i.e. the loss of the Cold War itself.

Geopolitics had taken on a new and deterministic bent with, as Eisenhower stated, possibilities "incalculable to the free world."

IKE was playing the wrong game, Chess was the true metaphor: nothing automatic, players vastly different, calculation critical.

The Far East:

Geopolitics of the Open Door

March 2, 2016

The designation "Far East" for the United States is a geopolitical misnomer, a reflection of the powerful impact Great Britain has had upon the American worldview. If one would stand on the shores of San Francisco Bay, for example, and look across the Pacific, one would naturally be looking west. Yet, Americans have always referred to Asia and the Pacific as the "Far East." Conversely, if one would stand on the shores of New Jersey and look across the Atlantic one would naturally be looking east. Why, then, is NATO our "Western" alliance? Because these directions only correspond to the perspective of London and the British Empire. From Washington, they remain a convenient inheritance; their only problem is inaccuracy.

As far back as the mid-nineteenth century, the U.S. had interests in Asia, but lacked the resources to implement meaningful policies. The "China trade" of the nineteenth century was alive but small, consisting mostly of tea and silk, and, in 1853, Commodore Perry "opened" Japan to outside commerce. But the "Open Door" notes at the turn of the century remains the epitome of the triumph of principles over policy; ambition minus means.

With the end of the Spanish-American War in 1898 and the acquisition of The Philippines, the United States became a Pacific Ocean power but lacked the capacity to defend its interests against foreign encroachment. Japan, in particular, was the rising star of the region and had already defeated China (1895), occupied Taiwan and Korea, and would soon defeat Russia (1905). To assert itself in the region, the U.S. Secretary of State John Hay (who once was Abraham Lincoln's personal secretary), circulated a series of diplomatic notes in 1899-1900, requesting that several European states plus Japan (then in occupation of China) to respect that nation's territorial integrity and to maintain strict discipline in their approaches toward the government and people of China.

While Hays' notes were acknowledged, they accomplished very little, and, like the Monroe Doctrine earlier, remained abstract principles devoid of either the means or the will to force adherence. For the next forty years, this would remain American policy toward China and would result in a steady collision course with Japan that would only be settled by Pearl Harbor, the subsequent war in the Pacific, and the beginnings of the atomic age. Throughout this period, until Pearl Harbor, the United States would cling to policy pronouncements regarding Japanese invasions of China, of which there were several, but always minus the will and means required to support policy with force.

Within this long period, the only time that American geopolitical ambitions were matched by diplomatic policy came in the 1921-22 Washington Naval Disarmament Conference. A landmark in arms control history, the conference succeeded in limiting Japanese ambitions in the Pacific by prohibiting the expansion of naval bases, restricting the construction of new warships to a ratio lower than the U.S. and Britain (5 to 3, respectively) and by adhering to the original Open Door principles against further Japanese expansion against mainland China. The U.S. also succeeded in abrogating the 1902 Japan-British military alliance by replacing it with the new arrangements.

Hailed at the time as a new breakthrough in world politics, the Washington treaties did not even survive the decade. They remain as case studies in the futility of legalism versus reality and as the tragic effects of geopolitical ambitions unsupported by either will or means. The 1931 Japanese invasion of Manchuria (a Chinese province), for example, was condemned by the

League of Nations and the United States in the form of the "Stimson Doctrine" (named for the Secretary of State). Like future aggressions of the period by Fascist Italy and Nazi Germany, such legal declarations actually helped bring on war by allowing diplomatic processes to appear as ends in themselves rather than covers for aggression, as they actually were.

By 1936, both Germany and Japan were out of the League of Nations and the Washington treaties were only memories. Within a few years both Britain and the U.S. had their backs at the wall, without recourse than to defend themselves against the Luftwaffe and the Imperial Japanese Navy and Air Force.

World War II took 76 million lives and countless more were maimed and injured. The only serious geopolitical moves taken prior to war were by the Axis, leaving the democracies to rely on liberal internationalist thought, called "appeasement" in Europe. America's Open Door notes, like the Stimson Doctrine, the infamous Munich Conference of 1938, and the many other benign but misleading foreign policies remain to this day classic case studies of how *not* to conduct foreign policy against aggressive enemies.

Cold War Geopolitics:

Containment

March 3, 2016

With the end of world war and fascism erased from the globe, the United States followed its instincts and disarmed. Once war is over, peace begins, Americans thought, and there was nothing in between. With 16 million uniformed personnel by war's end in 1945, only 1.5 million remained by 1947. Not only did the rise of a new threat from the Soviet Union, a wartime ally, shock American belief systems, but the threat itself reversed centuries of faith in the oceans to protect them. The result was a strategic and geopolitical challenge unprecedented in U.S. history. Nor did the leadership have the slightest idea on what to do about it.

At first, there was little that the US *could* do. With 12 million Red Army soldiers in occupation of Eastern Europe, up to and including East Germany, and with powerful communist parties in France and Italy, the skeleton American army in West Germany was left without power or purpose. Americans were not used to strategic thought in foreign arenas in peacetime and were left bankrupt against Marshall Stalin and Soviet hostility toward the outside world. The potential of a communist Western Europe was real, as it appeared that that the West was about to turn the continent over to a new totalitarian, having just lost millions of lives against the original.

Into this void appeared George F. Kennan of the Moscow embassy with his "long" (8,000 words) telegram in 1946 that was about to turn American geopolitics on its head. Sent in February, Kennan identified the nature of the politico-military threat posed by the Soviet Union and outlined a broad set of policies that might counter it. Basically, this was the first comprehensive set of strategic principles to be applied, short of war, since the Farewell Address of 1796.

Acknowledging the revolutionary and totalitarian nature of the Soviet regime, Kennan distinguished between communist and fascist strategies, noting that the communist threat represented a spectrum of tactical maneuvers opposed to the largely military challenge of Hitler and the Nazis. To counter the communist threat, Kennan urged "...a long-term, patient but firm and vigilant containment of Russian expansive tendencies." From this point forward until the Reagan presidency, every successive U.S. political administration would adopt some variant of geopolitical "containment" against world communism, first in Europe, then everywhere.

Initially, Kennan advocated the "...adroit and vigilant application of counterforce at a series of constantly shifting geographical and political points," which, he predicted, would result in "either the break-up or gradual mellowing of Soviet power." Although nobody, including Kennan, could possibly have foreseen the geopolitical trajectory of the next-half-century of Cold War, that is exactly what happened: they mellowed; then they broke up. Or as Reagan put it before assuming the presidency: "We win, they lose."

This process began in theory with the Long Telegram and began in practice almost immediately. A month later came Churchill's historic Iron Curtain speech at Fulton, Missouri. With President Truman looking on favorably, the former Prime Minister (having been defeated for re-election) introduced Americans to the reality of Soviet rule in Eastern Europe and how it should be met. Advocating a permanent "settlement," Churchill drew upon his pre-war rhetoric for a coalition "by the whole strength of the English-speaking world and all its connections..." to establish "...an overwhelming assurance of security" for the Western allies. Although the text was not received favorably by the U.S. media, which still clung to an isolationist past, the net result, along with Kennan's cable, was to catapult the United States into a position of global leadership for the first time and, eventually, to a position of "sole remaining superpower," which is about where we are today. The entire revolution took about fifteen weeks.

On February 21, 1947 the British government sent a cable to the State Department that it could no longer provide support for Greece or Turkey, both of which appeared about to crumble against Moscow. Led by Undersecretary of State Dean Acheson and Senate Foreign Relations Committee Chairman Arthur Vandenberg (R-MI), the Truman Administration led an all-out bipartisan assault against world-wide communism and its home, the USSR. Acheson applied an original version of President Eisenhower's later "domino" theory by explaining to the Senate how the loss of Greece and Turkey would lead to the loss of nearby states such as Iran and India.

The key statement was Truman's March 12th address to Congress, the "Truman Doctrine," for $400 million of aid "...to support free peoples who are resisting attempted subjugation by armed minorities or by outside pressures." The rest of the package came swiftly: The Marshall Plan for the economic restoration of Western Europe (announced at Harvard on June 5th), the reorganization of the national security apparatus of the government, establishment of an independent Air Force and CIA in 1947, the Berlin airlift, 1948-49, and the crown jewel of the revolution, creation of NATO in 1949.

Thus, practically overnight, America moved from a sleepy isolationist outpost of Europe to undisputed champion of the Free World, responsible for the liberty of all "free peoples." Originally, this meant European peoples; but just as quickly it would literally mean "all," free or not. These were heady days, never to be seen again.

Europe First:

The Geopolitics of Global War

ALLIED STRATEGY
Europe first!

Hamburg

Dresden

Normandy

The Bulge

March 2, 2016

The transformation of American geopolitical direction was the result of the U.S. experience in World War II but was already in motion well before Pearl Harbor. Long before the first shot was fired, the Roosevelt Administration had already committed the country toward the liberation of Western Europe, a commitment that went far beyond the war and continues to this very day. In retrospect, Adolph Hitler was not only responsible for the end of the Great Depression, he was also chiefly responsible for the end of American isolationism and the historic shift of foreign policies from the Western Hemisphere to the remainder of the world. This may well be Hitler's lasting legacy.

The transformative impact of world war, in both domestic and foreign affairs, has not received the attention it deserves. Where would the women's movement be, for example, minus the experience of leaving home to build war machines in American factories while the men were fighting overseas? Similarly, where would U.S. peacetime foreign policies be without the experience of the Normandy beaches and the liberation of the continent from Nazism? This transformation began with Franklin D. Roosevelt and Winston Churchill, who collaborated to strengthen the geopolitical bonds between the English-speaking peoples. But the background lies deeply within the historic geopolitics of the American continent.

The priority of Europe in any wartime strategy was geopolitically as logical and consistent as the Farewell Address itself. By the twentieth century, the United States was the world's foremost industrial power, while the technological advances in air and sea power had made the country far more vulnerable to attack than ever before. The fact that most of American industry resided in the eastern and northeastern areas dictated concentration on Germany rather than Japan, while the companion fact that the Atlantic was much narrower a defensive shield than the Pacific reinforced this reality. This came home in the early years of the war, when bathers on the beaches of the eastern seaboard from Maine to Florida watched helplessly as hundreds of American cargo ships went down in clouds of smoke from German submarines. By contrast, the thousands of Japanese "balloon" bombs sent to the west coast had the combined effect of killing a family on picnic in an Oregon forest.

The close relationship of the British and U.S. navies in the Atlantic, furthermore, had a history going back to the 1823 Monroe Doctrine and had no counterpart in the Pacific, an area where the U.S. Navy operated practically alone.

From the early years of the twentieth century, the U.S. military had drawn up hypothetical war plans against potential enemies under color plans known as "Rainbow." Plan "Orange," for example, was war against Japan, "Red" against Britain, "Black" against Germany, etc. In the 1930s, such plans were revised to anticipate war against a European-Asian coalition, which was named Red-Orange and, in fact, became known as the "Axis." The geopolitical logic of such plans consistently dictated the priority of Europe over all others in the rainbow, setting a precedent that finally became real in the years right before Pearl Harbor. While the general public, outraged against Japan, demanded an all-out Pacific offensive, the die had long since been cast on behalf of "Europe First."

This became official policy more than a year before Pearl Harbor when Admiral Harold R. Stark, Chief of Naval operations, concluded with President Roosevelt after his third straight electoral victory that "Europe First" would be the priority in any future war (November 1940). This also confirmed the earlier view of the "Rainbow" plans (Plan "D" or "Dog") that, in any Pacific war, Germany would be the priority and that the U.S. would initially have to abandon everything west of Hawaii. While the Navy vigorously challenged this view and liberated the western Pacific, Europe became number one as the world war progressed.

In practical ways, the U.S. was already at war with Germany well before this time. In September 1940, the U.S. and Britain made their historic Destroyers for Bases deal, where 50 U.S. destroyers were transferred for U.S. bases on British Caribbean areas. In December 1940, Roosevelt made his classic "Arsenal of Democracy" broadcast; Germany was not included.

These continued in 1941. In March, Lend Lease was passed, providing aid to Britain and France. Starting in April, U.S. warships began escorting British convoys across the Atlantic, and, in August, the two signed the "Atlantic Charter," providing joint war aims. But only Britain was at war.

Almost immediately after Pearl Harbor, British Prime Minister Churchill came to the White House and stayed for several weeks. Now they both were at war. The meetings held then, known as "Arcadia," solidified earlier arrangements, announcing that "our view remains that Germany is still the prime enemy and her defeat is the key to victory."

Thus, the geopolitical policies of the United States, based upon location and power resources, had already replaced historic isolationism even before the reality of warfare. Seventy-five years later, they are still in place but multiplied a hundred-fold.

American Geopolitics: The Origins

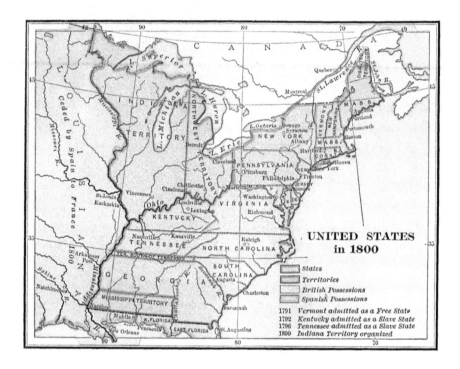

February 26, 2016

Among the great powers of history, the USA is unique insofar as it is separated from other land masses by the two greatest concentrations of water on earth, the Atlantic Ocean to the east, 41 million square miles and 20% of the earth's surface, and the Pacific Ocean to the west, 63 million square miles and 33% of the earth, respectively. Unlike nations in the rest of the world, which are bound to one another by endless borders and border wars, the US had no natural enemies east or west, and only native tribal clans on its western extensions. Neither Canada nor Mexico represented existential threats north or south, leaving the US, so to speak, "alone" to seek its "manifest" destiny as it saw fit. Even England, in its history of "splendid isolation" from Europe, was separated from the continent by only 26 miles of channel waters.

These simple facts, like the Swiss Alps, go a long way to discerning the direction and fate of history's foreign policies and destinies. Having no serious border challenges, for example, left the US free to develop naval power as opposed to standing armies, a critical fact in the pursuit of liberty and democracy. The country's first (and maybe only) geopolitician, Captain Alfred T. Mahan, wrote the classic *The Influence of Sea Power upon History* (1890).

Such geopolitical realities allowed the first president to lay down the marker for American foreign policies from the late eighteenth century to the mid twentieth, a fact that encouraged the phenomenal growth over time to "superpower" status. In his Farewell Address, Washington urged that America was to "steer clear of permanent alliances with any portion of the foreign world," a policy that remained a cornerstone of American political direction (with notable exceptions before World Wars I and II) until the beginnings of the Cold War in 1945. Geopolitics, thus, steered US foreign policies to such a point that Washington's advice grew into an article of faith until Europe finally exhausted itself in World War II. By that time, isolation was no longer an option.

But the vast majority of American history religiously adhered to this principle, based largely on the country's location. These policies, over time, were almost exclusively defensive, avoiding any form of offensive assertion, especially involving European powers. Both world wars, for example, began without US participation, and this country did very little to shape the nature of Europe's political formations prior to each conflict and, indeed, throughout the nineteenth century entirely.

The United States, however, was anything but pacifist and sent its military (mostly naval, marine) forces overseas on over 100 expeditions prior to World War I. Sometimes they would stay overnight, sometimes for years, but almost always removed from European involvement. These were undertaken within the confines of Washington's message of 1796 and scrupulously avoided the country being drawn into the incessant intermural rivalries of the "Old World."

The logical extension of America's geopolitical interests for most of history was the Western Hemisphere, and it was here, until only recently, that American overseas interests became assertive. This began in 1823 with the announcement of the Monroe Doctrine "that the American continents ... are henceforth not to be considered as subjects for future colonization by any European powers." Although this was largely a paper doctrine, the influence of the British navy prevented the return of Spain and Portugal to their Latin

American colonies. The US had the purpose but lacked the power to enforce its geopolitical ambitions, but this would change in the twentieth century and would control US peacetime foreign policies until replaced by the Cold War in the 1940s.

The Spanish-American War (1898) and the completion of the Panama Canal (1914) inaugurated a quasi-imperial American domination of the hemisphere that, less intrusively, continues to this day. This geopolitical imperative was best expressed in 1927 by an Assistant Secretary of State who articulated the Monroe Doctrine in classic geopolitical expressions:

"Geographical facts cannot be ignored. The Central American area down to and including the Isthmus of Panama constitutes a legitimate sphere of influence for the United States; if we are to have due regard for our safety and protection. Call it a sphere of influence ... we do control the destinies of Central America, and we do it for the simple reason that the national interest absolutely dictates such a course."

In subsequent years this "national interest" was extended throughout the hemisphere. In 1938, President Roosevelt publically promised to defend Canada against German aggression, and in 1941, the US occupied both Iceland and Greenland. By the end of the war, the US had established bases in sixteen Latin American countries and had bilateral lend-lease agreements with nineteen. By war's end, even pro-German Argentina was forced to declare war against the Axis.

Thus, the consolidation of the Western Hemisphere as an American geopolitical zone was complete, finalized by the establishment of the Organization of American States in 1948. But by then, US geopolitical interests had expanded to Western Europe and, subsequently, Asia and other far distant parts of the globe.

This global explosion of geopolitical interests will be taken up in subsequent essays.

Priorities:

The problem with shifting regional focus in American foreign policy

Worldmapper Regions

Territory size shows territorial land area.

North America
Western Europe
Eastern Europe
Middle East
Eastern Asia
Japan
Northern Africa
Southern Asia
South America
Central Africa
Asia Pacific
Southeastern Africa

February 19, 2016

Without warning, the U.S. had to prioritize its war aims, strategies and interests. Again, literally overnight, the U.S. had become the world's policeman, definitely against its own will. By war's end, the U.S. had come to adopt the "Europe First" strategy that acknowledged the priority of the Nazi threat to both the U.S. and Britain plus the longer-term threat that Hitler came to represent against the values of liberty, civilization and democracy. By 1945, almost 80 percent of total U.S. Army and Air Force resources were employed in Europe (although the Navy was dominant in the Pacific).

On December 7, 1941, Japan attacked Pearl Harbor. The next day, the U.S. declared war on Japan, and most men in the country lined up for city blocks on end to sign up for military duty against the Asian enemy. Literally overnight, America was on lockdown against Japan as never before and had no other purpose than to punish the enemy into oblivion (which it eventually did). Three days later, Nazi Germany, out of the blue, declared war against this country, throwing all the previous war plans and national fervor into chaos. Few in America anticipated a world war against both enemies, and Congress by itself would never have declared war against Hitler's regime while simultaneously fighting in the Pacific theater.

This transfer of commitment carried over well into the post-war years. The emergence of the Soviet threat amidst the Cold War, the fall of Eastern Europe and East Germany to the Red Army, and the political threat from communist parties in Italy and France dictated the continuity of a Europe First foreign policy. This was solidified in 1949 with the North Atlantic Treaty and carried over into the 1950's with the addition of Greece, Turkey, and West Germany to NATO.

While the fall of China to the communists in 1949 meant the extension of U.S. interests to East Asia, this fact alone was insufficient to offset the priority of Western Europe. Secretary of State George C. Marshall made this clear in his testimony shortly before the loss of China: the U.S., he said, "cannot afford, economically or militarily, to take over the continued failures of the present Chinese Government to the dissipation of our strength in more vital regions" (Europe). But these priorities slowly changed, beginning with the outbreak of the Korean War in 1950, and gradually extended into Southeast Asia, especially Vietnam, by the end of the decade.

The transfer of priorities from Europe to Southeast Asia, a transfer that would last for nearly twenty years, offers yet another example of the historic American penchant to move from area to global area, always seemingly near the disaster point, only either to resolve the issue or to retreat into another threatened region. During the first half of the twentieth century, nearly paranoid about the security of the Panama Canal, the U.S. committed troops in twenty-five separate interventions, some lasting as long as fifteen years (Haiti), constantly on the watch against overseas threats, first Germany and later Japan. It was not until 1979 that this paranoia came to an end, with the transfer of authority to Panama itself. The region has been comparatively quiet since.

A similar fate haunted U.S. interests in the long and tragic Vietnam War. After nearly twenty years of involvement, domestic revolutionary threats and over 57, 000 dead, the U.S. left the area in 1975. Today, Vietnam is poor, oppressed, and still committed to a communist regime, but it is also strategically neutral, a tourist center, and an American partner in the Pacific Trade Pact.

It is now the Middle East that has dominated American attention, into its third decade since the bombing of the Marine barracks in Lebanon in 1983. With seventeen separate military interventions, stretching from Lebanon, to Syria, Libya and Iraq, Americans are still obsessed with the region, and the current political debates offer no other strategic priority. It's as though the rest of the world does not even exist.

Like the rise and fall of previous geopolitical passions, these, too, will have a finish line. Then what or, more importantly, where?

This is not to argue that these regions did not deserve attention and even, at times, military attention. But strategy has to be governed by prudence, intellect and vision. America is deeply involved in the world but still lacks a coherent strategy for its policies and these include purpose and, above all, priorities.

In 1907 British foreign officer, Erye Crowe, sent a now-famous memorandum on the long-term priority and purpose of the country's foreign policies. Based upon the concept of the "balance of power," Crowe provided advice which can still resonate in the face of America's continuous search for its own strategic direction a century later:

"... History shows that the danger threatening the independence of this or that nation has generally arisen out of the momentary predominance of a neighboring state at once militarily powerful, economically efficient and ambitious ... the only check on the abuse of political predominance derived from such a position has always consisted in the opposition of an equally formidable rival ... The equilibrium established by such a grouping of forces is technically known as the balance of power, and it has become almost an historical truism to identify England's secular power with the maintenance of this balance, by throwing her weight now in this scale and now in that, but ever on the side opposed to the political dictatorship of the strongest single state or group at a given time."

It's called strategy, and it is beyond time the United States thought about one.

A "House Divided":

Wartime dissent in American history and today

February 1, 2016

Democracies are obviously much more fragile than their opponents in holding coalitions together or in keeping their domestic house in order while fighting on distant fronts. Since democracies have still yet to wage war against another, it remains true that democracy's wartime opponents have always been authoritarians. This is equally true today.

The American democracy is even more susceptible to dissent than most others, due to the vast openness of the political culture, the sanctity of free speech, and the importance placed on minority views, third parties and entertainment. The communications revolution in America has made stars of average people and has promoted TV personalities as arbiters of policies rather than just as reporters. Walter Cronkite was perhaps the most important American throughout the Vietnam War and solidified dissent against it.

The American tradition in wartime dissent was present from the beginning. Most colonists were either against breaking from Britain or were neutral. Less than one-third favored independence which was, of course, a treasonous act. In the War of 1812, the country was split between the so-called "War Hawks" of the south and southeast and the pro-British Federalists from the New England and mid-Atlantic states. In New England, dissension came close to secession, especially with the 1814 Hartford Convention, which demanded veto power against any future wars (never adopted).

The first modern opposition to a foreign war occurred after the Spanish-American War, when the McKinley Administration decided to keep Cuba, Puerto Rico and the Philippines as possessions. An insurrection against U.S. occupation in the Philippines forced a major troop intervention. Opposition to this conflict and expansionism in general split the country into bitter halves and dominated the 1900 election. Yale professor William Graham Sumner's essay of that time, "The Conquest of the United States by Spain," may still stand as the most important anti-war statement in American history. Sumner's thesis argued that, by keeping Spain's old empire, the United States had in effect come to resemble European despotism and imperialism, thus reversing the original purpose of the Revolution. In this respect, wartime dissent was seen as patriotism in the extreme.

Neither of the world wars were marked by significant protest, although there were serious divisions before World War II. April 6, 1917 and December 8, 1941, it should be noted, were the only times during the twentieth century when the U.S. formally declared war. A declaration of war certainly marks a powerful divide within the political culture, when dissent can lawfully be considered as treason. This formality has allowed anti-war opposition since then to thrive without crossing the line into treason, a legality that has continued to plague American conduct of foreign wars since. The late Colonel Harry Summers, probably the most insightful critic of the strategy employed by the U.S. in Vietnam, insisted that the failure of President Johnson to declare war was the biggest obstacle to a U.S. victory. Today, we hear cries that the country is "at war" with Islamic terrorism, but how and against whom do we expect a formal declaration?

Seen in its totality, the U.S. has been in deadly conflict against Islamic-driven terror since 1983, when 240 marines were blown up in their Lebanese barracks. More than a quarter century later, the political administration still cannot bring itself to identify properly the inspirational source for the "war." At the same time, volunteers have been deployed in at least seventeen Middle East locales against the non-state enemy and the home front has been riddled with dissent from political quarters, left and right. This occurs within an amorphous and ambiguous strategic arena, somewhere between war and peace, which to this day defies even a definition.

This strategic "no man's land" is the central reality of world politics. "Globalization" may unite the powerful economies of the developed world, but it simply offers opportunities for the millions of disaffected, who are supplied arms, support and sanctuary by rich suppliers. ISIS and its affiliates, contrasted with, say, Nazi Germany or Soviet Russia, by themselves have no military resources, but have benefitted from the largesse provided by the wealthy and oil-rich to terrorize society from Paris to San Bernardino to Baghdad. Imagine: the entire Western world, the one that defeated Nazi Germany, Imperial Japan and Soviet Russia, has recoiled in a defensive and confused mode against a gang of masked and barbaric thugs, guided by a truly otherworld vision, hopelessly beyond reason.

In today's social atmosphere, one wonders what is going on. There is neither war nor sustained dissent, just endless tragedy without strategic direction. The country is irreparably divided. For there to be unity, it may take a catastrophic event like Pearl Harbor — wherein unity ended debate. In the meantime, there are several America's, reminding one of Lincoln's comment that a "house divided against itself," cannot stand.

Is Banning Non-Americans Un-American?

December 22, 2015

There are several ways to critique Donald Trump's recent call for a "total and complete shutdown of Muslims entering the United States..." but "Un-American" has certainly summarized much of the emotional ire directed against his latest political bombshell. On December 10, the Senate Judiciary Committee voted 16-4 against the ban, stating that it was "contrary to the fundamental principles" of the US, ie. "Un-American." Where did this principle originate, from history or sentiment?

America has always prided itself on having the most open public borders of any significant nation in history, especially the Atlantic seaboard where the vast majority of new immigrants first touched shore. Aside from the core values of the political culture, liberty, democracy etc., the idea of a nation of immigrants may very well be the greatest and most lasting legacy that America has given to the world. Any challenge to this value would, indeed, be considered Un-American, while the testimony of presidents and political leaders throughout history has given substance to the claim.

George Washington recognized it from the start: "I had always hoped that this land might become a safe and agreeable asylum to the virtuous and persecuted part of mankind." Franklin D. Roosevelt reiterated it much later: "Remember,

remember always, that all of us, and you and I especially, are descended from immigrants and revolutionists." John F. Kennedy wrote the classic history of immigration in 1958, *A Nation of Immigrants*, while his successor Lyndon Johnson noted that "The land flourished because it was fed from so many sources – because it was nourished by so many cultures and traditions and peoples." More recently, George W. Bush, in proposing immigration reform, reminded Americans that "We're ... a nation of immigrants, and we must uphold that tradition, which has strengthened our country in so many ways."

Given such a perspective, it is small wonder that any challenge to America's perceived tradition, especially a wholesale ban, must be considered beyond the pale. But the pale is incomplete and popularly misunderstood. The true story of America's immigration history will reveal a number of retreats and restrictions that demonstrate that emigration to the New World was never a blank check and that the road to citizenship was full of political pitfalls and human tragedies. The illusion that immigration was either a right or an obligation is contradicted by the historical record.

Entry to the United States was frequently restricted, especially as the population grew. As a general rule, many Americans, especially "nativist" Protestants and labor unions, resented and fought against immigration, despite being immigrants themselves. The Know Nothing movement of the mid-nineteenth century was the first major challenge to the right of minority religions to arrive here and compete with Anglo Protestantism as America's dominant religion.

The target of the "Know Nothings," formally the American Party, was Roman Catholicism, and the movement was spiked by the large numbers of Irish and German immigrants in the mid nineteenth century. The party came to control the Massachusetts legislature (where most Irish settled) and dominated politics in states with large Catholic populations, Ohio especially. Milliard Fillmore represented the American Party in the 1856 presidential election, where he received 900,000 votes, of four million cast. At the bottom of one party flier ran the motto: "Eternal hostility to Foreign and Roman Catholic influence." But disputes over slavery crippled the party's influence and the Civil War ended it permanently. But the scars of resentment lingered for decades, and powerful anti-immigrant influences, security, religious, cultural, political and economic, influenced American politics thereafter.

The first major restrictive legislation against immigration was the Page Act of 1875 (named after Rep. Horace Page, R-CA), which basically restricted immigration from China, the world's most populous country, and classified as "undesirable" any Chinese who was a "forced laborer," a prostitute or considered to be a convict. This act was reinforced in 1882 by the Chinese Exclusion Act, which prohibited all immigration of Chinese laborers. Amendments to the Act in 1884 and 1888 tightened it and prohibited reentry of Chinese ethnics after leaving the U.S. (there were no "sanctuary cities" in 1888).

In 1924 the Immigration Act was passed by the U.S. Congress, with virtually no opposition. This was the most sweeping restrictive law in US history, banning all Japanese, Africans, and Arabs and limiting the number of European immigrants to 2% of their total inside the U.S. This drastically reduced immigration from southern and eastern Europe, including Jews. Italian immigration dropped 90% in what the State Department Historian wrote was meant to "preserve the ideal of American homogeneity."

Over time, these laws were revised or repealed, but Donald Trump's ban against Muslims, ignorant or brilliant, self-destructive or necessary, is closer to the record than the ideal.

December 7, 2015

Nearly three quarters of a century later, the words "Pearl Harbor" still have a unique meaning to the American people. The image of the sunken USS Arizona, where half of the 2,400 casualties remain, still conveys one of the country's most lasting symbols. But what does the image symbolize, and why is it lasting?

In his address to Congress the day after December 7, 1941, President Franklin D. Roosevelt accurately prophesied that Pearl Harbor Day would live "in infamy," but he underestimated the symbolism. Infamy implies treachery, and the immediate impact certainly emphasized that characteristic of the "unprovoked and dastardly" attack. Pearl Harbor came without warning and was accompanied by simultaneous Japanese attacks across the Pacific against both U.S. and British territories: Hong Kong, Guam, Wake, Midway, the Philippines, and Malaya. The immediate national anger against the nature of the treachery slowly gave way to the deeper realization that Pearl Harbor was a turning point in national history and that no looking back was possible.

The first realization struck immediately that the safety and security of the country behind two oceans was a thing of the past. Since Washington's Farewell Address in 1796, Americans grew accustomed to the ingrained geopolitical belief that their "isolationism" was guaranteed by their location. The young Abe Lincoln spoke for most Americans in 1836 with these penetrating reflections on national security: "Shall we expect some transatlantic military giant to step the ocean and crush us at a blow? Never! All the armies of Europe, Asia and Africa combined with all the treasure of the earth, with a Bonaparte for a commander, could not by force take a drink from the Ohio or make a track on the Blue Ridge in a trial of a thousand years."

That history lay buried next to the Arizona.

With isolationism gone, the logical sequence saw the United States join in a grand global coalition of nations against the Axis. Literally overnight, the United States became the defender of most of humanity, democracy, liberty, and all of the value systems cherished by free peoples going back centuries. Like Pearl Harbor itself, this was not an American decision. Four days after the attack, December 11, 1941, both Hitler and Mussolini declared war, sparing the American Congress the agony of deciding on a two front war and, in the process, forcing the U.S. to accept leadership of what later came to be known as the "Free World." After centuries of isolation, this country became a "superpower" within a few days.

This responsibility has been with the U.S. since. Within the wartime coalition, which began in peacetime with NATO in 1949, the U.S. solidified its "special" relationship with Great Britain, which fulfilled Winston Churchill's cherished goal going back to American involvement in World War I. The fact of Pearl Harbor and the subsequent reality of Anglo-American strategic cooperation not only won the Second World War but continued throughout the century, including the Thatcher-Reagan alliance that ended the Cold War. This relationship, which would not have been realized without Pearl Harbor, made the political trajectory of the twentieth century a by-product of the English-speaking peoples, a fact that can be considered as the outstanding reality of the entire period.

This, also, is ongoing into the twenty-first century and the war against Islamic terrorism.

Domestic unity is another direct result of the Pearl Harbor attack, but the effects of this are far more elusive than the effects upon the political world. Prior to the attack, American society had been bitterly split in half between the isolationists, represented mostly in Congress and the Midwest, and interventionists, led by President Roosevelt and eastern constituents. There seemed to be no resolution between this split until Pearl Harbor closed all debate and produced a unity, an energy, and a momentum not seen before or since. The greatest isolationist group of U.S. history, *America First*, which included the aviator hero Charles Lindbergh, the Ambassador to Britain Joseph Kennedy, and his young son John, abruptly closed its doors shortly after Pearl Harbor. Such a show of unity embraced all walks of domestic life, media and theatrical, unions, management, both political parties, all interest groups, women, men, the literati, Christians, Jews, and denominations of all stripes. From 1942 on, there was no commercial construction, from cars to dishwashers; all food was rationed and travel restricted. Indeed, America was on lockdown, but the war lasted less than four years.

Fast forward to the present. The U.S. has been involved against Islamic terrorism since 1983 when 240 Marines were killed in a bombing in Lebanon. Decades later, there is still no resolution. The political system is divided between "reds" and "blues," and the country is widely accused of all kinds of social abuses, sexism and racism among others.

But Pearl Harbor remains sacrosanct.

The Best or Worst of Times

IT WAS THE BEST OF TIMES, IT WAS THE WORST OF
TIMES, IT WAS THE AGE OF WISDOM, IT WAS THE
AGE OF FOOLISHNESS, IT WAS THE EPOCH OF
BELIEF, IT WAS THE EPOCH OF INCREDULITY, IT WAS
THE SEASON OF LIGHT, IT WAS THE SEASON OF
DARKNESS, IT WAS THE SPRING OF HOPE, IT WAS
THE WINTER OF DESPAIR.

- CHARLES DICKENS -

LIBQUOTES.COM

December 2, 2015

With the growth of ISIS, the recent Paris attacks, the threats to the American homeland, not to mention the racial unrest at home, plus practically everything else since September 11th, one could easily believe that the world has suddenly plunged into unprecedented chaos and violence.

That's a reasonable presumption. However, while these may not be comforting times, they may not be the worst either.

It's easy to forget that our ancestors, while living in smaller cities and countries, experienced their own problems, but history's comparisons might be a bit awkward for those who believe that our modern issues are paramount, urgent or unprecedented.

Take war. The U.S. has been in and out of Iraq and Afghanistan since 2001. Total battle deaths so far are about 6,717. Granting that a single casualty, dead, wounded or missing, is someone's tragedy, numbers cannot be ignored. The U.S. population is about 330 million and can absorb these overseas combats.

But what about history? Let's take the Civil War for example. In 1861, the U.S. had a white population of 31 million. The Civil War ended four years later and took 750,000 of those lives, almost all white soldiers. That is approximately 2.5 percent of their population. If similar percentages were absorbed today, we would have lost about eight million soldiers. How would those numbers fit into MSNBC?

Closer to "modern" times, consider World War II. In 1940, the world had about 2.3 billion people; compared with today's give or take 7 billion. The war lasted exactly six years and a day. Within that span, total fatalities, all theaters, combat, disease, men, women and children, totaled approximately 76 million (consensus). That's about 35,000 killed every day for the duration! If these percentages were suffered in today's world, we would have witnessed around 100,000 dead bodies every day since 2009. We may not know it, but our generation, with all its violence, has actually been "spared" what our fathers and grandfathers knew. (And their memories will soon be gone; about 800 veterans of that war die each day.)

None of this should minimize the individual, with each life sacred and unique, but perspective is an intellectual necessity. The American people rightly remember Pearl Harbor and 9/11 as profound historical landmarks, or, as FDR put it, "infamy." At Pearl Harbor, the country lost 2,403, mostly sailors; on 9/11 the toll was 2,977, most but not all Americans. These were heavy tolls, with each event over in minutes or hours. Pearl Harbor led to U.S. entry in the Second World War and 407,000 more battle deaths; 9/11 has not (yet) been repeated. These were national tragedies but certainly not unprecedented.

Take the Battle of Britain. Formally it went on from July 10 to October 31, 1940 — that's 57 consecutive days (and sometimes nights) in which as many as 800 German planes pounded London and other cities each day. Total fatalities, almost all civilian, were 40,000, half in London. In U.S. terms, that would be 57 straight "9/11's." What would the country do?

But the "Blitz," as it was called, actually continued until June 1941 when Hitler gave up any idea of invading Britain and attacked the Soviet Union. Yet, compare Britain, with 45 million people, absorbing nearly a year of continuous terror from the skies, ending the raids and then fighting the Axis for five more years on all fronts.

One wonders how these people went on, especially considering that they had just finished four years of World War I. By contrast, modern America goes ballistic if a single black man is killed, especially by a policeman. The event is headline news for weeks.

The group "Black Lives Matter," a distant cousin of the 1960's "Black Panthers," has led the assault against both the Police and society at large.

Co-founder Alica Garza has vocally committed the group against "black poverty and genocide."

But genocides throughout history may have taken more lives than even war. The greatest dictators of history were mainly twentieth century tyrants. Mao Zedong leads them all with an estimated 60 million of his own people killed during his reign. Stalin is not far behind, killing more Russians than Hitler, including over 10 million private farmers ("Kulaks") in the late 1920's alone. Stalin also engineered the great mass starvation in 1931-32 against the Ukraine, killing as many as 7.5 million Ukrainians. Going deeper into history, the Irish Potato famine of the mid-nineteenth century starved fifteen percent of the population (1.5 million) and forced emigration (mostly to America) of 25 percent. Great Britain stood by and watched.

We're sorry about Freddie Gray. Tragedies and injustices happen every day, but perspective tells us that this is not the worst of times.

What's In a Name?

November 30, 2015

The refusal of President Obama to use the "Islamist" or Muslim name to define global terror confuses and annoys many Americans. His supporters dismiss this as a trivial sideshow, claiming that names are distracting as long as tactics work. But are names relevant when waging war against enemies who mow down civilians without shame or guilt, invoking "Allah Akbar" and releasing hostages who can recite the Koran?

The reader must pause. What's going on here?

Are these just semantics, mere words without content? No.

Names matter. A Nazi is not a Kaiser and a Bolshevik is not a Czar. These are not trivial differences, they are profound and defined differences between life and death for millions.

Perhaps the chief issue separating the two sides on this are the complexities between the architects or "activists" of the movement and the socio/political environment from whence they came. This is a universal problem, no exceptions. Nothing comes from a vacuum.

Take the American Revolution. George Washington led a relatively small percentage of Americans against British rule, with over three-fourths either loyal ("Tories") or ambivalent. The British were aware of this distinction and, in addition to 57,000 Redcoats, used the Tories against the Patriots throughout the war. Similar distinctions dominated most modern revolutions.

In 1917 a handful of Bolsheviks took over millions of Russians and ruled them for the next seventy-five years. Using this base, they terrorized most of the world, occupied half of Europe, created a bipolar world that always seemed on the brink of disaster and built thousands of nuclear weapons that could have wiped out the US many times over. Most Americans had no problem making the distinction between the Russian people and Bolshevism. Nor did the distinction stop the United States from waging total political warfare, including nuclear deterrence, against them for nearly half a century. Neither is there a substantial record of a President or Secretary of State who refused to call the Communists what they, in fact, were, or to identify where they came from.

But the Bolsheviks weren't the only terrorists that we have met. With fewer than 200 official members the National Socialist German Workers Party, the "Nazis" came to rule and terrorize eighty million German citizens between 1933 and 1945 while, in the world at large, successfully instigated total military war that took around 75 million lives. The fact that the Nazis represented a minutia of the German population was small comfort to the millions of soldiers who faced their forces around the globe any more than it excused those millions more who fought for them and served as the popular culture and territory from whence they came.

On the beaches of Normandy Americans faced Germans. That's what they were and that's what they looked like and the hierarchy back home in Berlin was nowhere in sight. But the Nazis undoubtedly pulled the strings.

The distinctions that have reflected practically all historical movements such as these are present again in the Jihads that have convulsed this country since 240 Marines were killed by a suicide bomber in Lebanon in 1983. Since then, US military forces have bombed, occupied or otherwise intervened in 19 Islamic countries in what has been known as the Global War On Terror (GLOT). That's over a quarter century ago, seemingly sufficient time for our elite leadership to arrive at a common consensus as to what, on earth, we are fighting.

In the ongoing debate as to this question there is actually no winner and no loser. To use a favorite cliché it is actually academic and it is a wonder how such an intelligent country as this, cannot decide who to fight after more than twenty-five years of fighting them.

Is it the Germans or the Nazis, the Communists or the Russians, the Chinese or Mao, Washington or the Americans, Napoleon or France, the south or Lee? The answer, now as before, is *both* and it is high time we arrived at a simple intellectual consensus able to distinguish between the soldiers and the culture behind them.

November 24, 2015

I often open my class on U.S. foreign policy by asking the following (trick) question: In history, what is the Capital city that has come closest to an existential defeat of the United States? Hands go up: Moscow, Berlin, Tokyo, even London. After discussion I reveal the answer: it's Richmond. I emphasize that Richmond is only 90 miles away from where we are all sitting in Washington, D.C. And although these graduate students are well versed in the Civil War, the fact that our once-mortal enemy was so close is always a revelation.

This, I announce, is meant to emphasize a theme of the class, that is, the most likely scenario for the end of America as we know it is more than likely to come from within, rather than without. That, at least, is historically accurate. I then show the 1943 Frank Capra propaganda film, *Why We Fight*, which shows fictitious Japanese soldiers marching up Pennsylvania Avenue toward the Capitol, bringing on raucous laughter from the class. But, historically, it is funny.

Indeed, the political divide between "blue" and "red" states, the campus unrest infecting the country, the riots in the cities and the ongoing, seemingly endless racial, ethnic and geographic disturbances reminds me of the notion, often cited, that a nation "divided against itself cannot stand." But is Lincoln's 1858 warning still valid? I think so.

It is instructive to know that many of our most important political leaders insisted that a stable home society was critical to American security, more critical even than foreign policies. This began with Washington's Farewell Address, which emphasized this point at the very beginning: "The unity of government which constitutes you one people is also now dear to you. It is justly so, for it is a main pillar in the edifice of your real independence, the support of your tranquility at home, your peace abroad; of your safety; of your prosperity; of that very liberty which you so highly prize."

This same theme was repeated by Walter Lippmann the chief spokesman for U.S. foreign policy in the first half of the twentieth century. Fearing a postwar domestic split, Lippmann wrote in 1943 in *The Shield of the Republic*, that "The spectacle of this great nation which does not know its own mind is as humiliating as it is dangerous. It casts doubt on the capacity of the people to govern themselves. It will be a profound humiliation [...], if once again we fail to form a national policy, and the acids of this failure will be with us for ages to come."

At the beginning of the Cold War, George Kennan, the author of containment, reiterated this point. To succeed against the Soviet Union, he wrote that it would be "... a question of the degree to which the United States can create among the people of the world [...] the impression of a country which knows what it wants, which is coping successfully with the problem of its internal life and with the responsibilities of a World Power." In addition, he continued, "exhibitions of indecision, disunity and internal disintegration within this country have an exhilarating effect on the whole Communist movement."

The renowned theologian, John Courtney Murray, once put the self-identification of Americans as a moral and spiritual issue: "Self-understanding is the necessary condition of a sense of self-identity and self-confidence. [...] The complete loss of one's identity is, with all propriety of theological definition, *hell*. In diminished forms, it is insanity. And it would not be well for the American giant to go lumbering about the world today, lost and mad."

But is that not about where we are now? Nobody will argue that it is 1861 all over again. But the divides and acrimonies among the people has approached crisis, with "Balkanization" a real possibility, either formally or, as now, informally but real enough.

Unity shows in our wartime efficiency. A united "Union" beat the Confederacy in four years, US combat in World War I lasted six months, in World War II less than four years. It's been downhill since then and the divisions have grown wide open.

The social divides that occurred during the Vietnam War, including closing over 250 universities, lasted about fifteen years and resulted in abject defeat. The US has been involved in the Middle East since 1983 when 240 Marines were killed by a suicide bomber. American forces have intervened in 19 Islamic countries since then, including long occupations of several. The area is now worse than ever and ISIS has hit Paris. Washington and New York are now on alert.

Is America committing suicide or being murdered? Either way, it's an inside job.

Liberty:

America's gift to the world

"GIVE ME LIBERTY, OR GIVE ME DEATH !"

November 18, 2015

The name "America" may mean a number of things to the seven billion people living on planet earth. Both good and bad. The word "superpower" comes first to mind, and many do not like the world's policeman (both at home and abroad). With about 800 military facilities overseas, including at least 140 "bases," the American presence is virtually everywhere. But do people remember the American military and financial contribution to both world wars, the Cold War, and the billions of aid dollars from the Marshall Plan to development assistance?

Yet, the primary contribution of this country abroad should not even be measured in "hard" power resources and cannot even be defined by empirical designs. It is an abstraction but separates nations that live through law and order, however imperfectly, and those, that rule through fear, terror and the iron fist. The former, led by the US, are few and far between; the latter, sadly, represent almost all the rest of the political globe. The American "gift" is liberty, and there has been no other political authority in history that represents this concept more than the United States of America.

How, then, one might ask, can this be a "contribution" if most of the world rejects it? The answer does not lie in what the country does in its foreign policies, whether it is isolationist or interventionist, whether it has bases or not, how powerful or wealthy it is. The answer lies in what the United States stands for in the world, its political culture, its values.

These began with the observation, *circa* 1630, by the future Puritan Governor of Massachusetts, John Winthrop, when he observed that "We shall be as a city upon a hill, the eyes of all people are upon us." This force of example has guided America throughout the intervening centuries and remains the essential difference between this country and the remainder of the world. Nearly two centuries later, the fifth president, James Monroe, concurred: "Our country may be likened to a new house. We lack many things, but we possess the most precious of all — liberty."

The central role of liberty has been enshrined in almost every major event surrounding US political culture from the beginnings of the Republic. Political Scientist Paul Seabury reflected upon this reality in the bicentennial issue of *Orbis*:

"A concern about the relations between morals and politics is not uniquely American. But few nations take philosophic purpose in foreign affairs as seriously as Americans do … For better or worse, since the beginnings of the Republic Americans have displayed strong sentiments about their country's role in world affairs. Liberty occupies a central thematic place among them. Emblazoned on monuments, sung about in anthems, stamped on coinage and expressed on placards, it still dominates our civic thought and language. Even as aspiration, the American view extends the hope that freedom may spill over into other lands, and from time to time this view affects America's international activities in momentous ways."

Almost all American politicians have reflected on this central reality. Consider the presidents. Many of them have alluded to the "fire" of liberty as representing a powerful force that would engulf all before it.

Start with George Washington in the first official statement of the new Republic. The new democratic experiment, he proclaimed in his Inaugural Address, represented "the sacred fire of liberty." In 1809, Thomas Jefferson spoke of America as "the sole depository of the sacred fire of freedom and self-government, from hence it is to be lighted up in other regions of the earth."

As if guided by the invisible hand of the same speechwriter, a century and a half later, John Kennedy echoed the same sentiments in his historic Inaugural: "The energy, the faith, the devotion which we bring to this endeavor will light our country and all who serve it — and the glow from that fire can truly light the world." Coming full circle, George W. Bush brought the past alive with his own version of the fire of liberty: "By our efforts, we have lit a fire as well — a fire in the minds of men. It warms those who feel its power, it burns those who fight its progress, and one day this untamed fire of freedom will reach the darkest corners of our world." In his first Inaugural, President Obama repeated this theme, noting that the ideals of the Founding Fathers "still light the world, and we will not give them up for expedience' sake."

Should this flame expire, for whatever reason, the world could well descend into what Churchill called during World War II "a new dark age."

In 1998, journalist Tom Brokaw wrote *The Greatest Generation*, describing how Americans preserved liberty against Fascism in that same war. The question remains: Will the current generation keep the torch of liberty alive? The jury is out.

Anarchy

October 21, 2015

In 1990, columnist Charles Krauthammer first pronounced the coming demise of the Soviet Union as the beginning of what he termed the political globe's "unipolar moment."

The term was not Krauthammer's invention, nor were the implications new to history. Indeed, most of world history to this day has consisted of imperial regimes, from Rome to China, which governed their regions from a singular source, or "pole." However, with the end of the European "multipolar" order after World War II, the world entered nearly a half-century of "bipolar" struggle between the forces of democracy and totalitarian communism. In 1990, that "bipolar" period was closing, and a new dawn, with The United States in the ascendancy, was about to emerge.

But the moment lingered. A decade later, Krauthammer revised his estimate, and wrote, the "unipolar moment" was in fact a "unipolar era," one, "unlike anything ever seen," and an order likely to last for decades to come, (*National Interest*, Winter 2002).

Anarchy has always been the essential condition of world politics, particularly under the European order, insofar as there was never a hierarchical structure or a common culture to control events, as in all domestic political systems. But the term was qualified by the existence of an amorphous conceptual entity called the "balance of power" which was able to provide at least a mechanism, often given as automatic, which enabled member states to live within a rational political universe.

The best definition of this historic entity was provided by the British Foreign Office over a hundred years ago as Britain began aiming its foreign policy against a rising Germany. The "only check on the abuse of political predominance" by a rival, the author Eyre Crowe wrote, "has always consisted in the opposition of an equally formidable rival, or a combination of several countries forming leagues of defense. The equilibrium established by such a grouping of forces is technically known as the balance of power...."

In today's atmosphere, such strategic calculations have been lost to history. The political climate of world politics, especially from the Obama Administration, concentrates on "world community," the environment, and social equality as the cutting edges of foreign policies for the new century. The rise of the European Union, while providing peace after centuries of war, has demonstrated a similar mindset with regard to security and, led by Germany, has welcomed the dangerously large wave of refugees into its borders. Such actions reflect the new anarchy infecting contemporary world politics and provides an accurate forecast of times to come.

Unlike the balance of power, when there was a semblance of structure and coherence, today there is no recognized balance of power nor, like Britain in the past, no "balancer" to check revolutionary states or global movements. The last definitive time that the United States provided such leadership was early in the Cold War under the doctrine of containment and the formation of NATO. Containment ultimately led to the Reagan Doctrine of "rollback" with its global coalition including the Vatican, Saudi Arabia and the Afghanistan Mujahedeen (1980s).

Since September 11th, 2001, fourteen years ago, the United States has been actively fighting insurrection, jihad, violence and political unrest in the Middle East and Afghanistan. The results, after thousands killed or wounded, the rise of new entities (ISIS) and the destruction of whole states and geopolitical arenas have seemed to send the region into a new dark age, another description of anarchy. Russia is now an active competitor in the region.

The U.S. won World War II in three and a half years, World War I in about six months. Today, the Middle East festers for decades while the President recently told 60 Minutes that "My definition of leadership would be leading on climate change."

The primary campaigns for 2016 reflect the same nonchalance: the main war now being fought, it seems, is against "women," while a single incident, Benghazi, has been the focus of almost all strategic attention.

The French have a saying, *sauve qui peut*, "save yourself if you can." There may have been a unipolar moment for the United States, but nobody seemed to have told the politicians.

Where's the Fire?

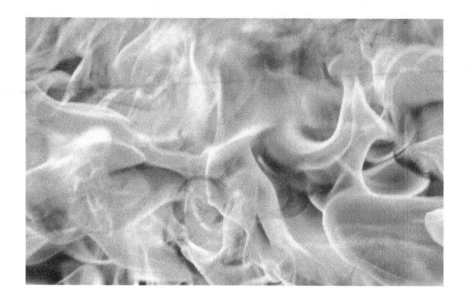

September 9, 2015

California is not the only part of America now burning. So is the political system. The metaphor "fire" has served a number of purposes for human endeavor, mostly positive. Out West, the fire is tragic, but in human affairs, fire has indicated resolve, purpose, and dogmatic sense of mission, also hard to "put out."

The political arena is where fire has burned the brightest and where it has played its most dominant role. Today, in the Republican primary campaign, fire is evident. Donald Trump is on fire, and he is burning the rest of the pack into ashes. Turn on the TV; all you get is Trump.

Fire explains failure, success and "burning" desire. In 1996, Colin Powell dropped out of the presidential race, claiming that he lacked "fire in the belly." Going deeper into history, fire has often been ascribed to America in the world – the *weltanschauung*. The first official statement of the new Republic offered fire. On April 30, 1789, President Washington's first Inaugural Address told the country that the American experiment represented "the sacred fire of liberty." This theme would repeat into the future as though there were a single grey-bearded speechwriter for the ages. In 1809, President Thomas Jefferson told a Washington audience that the United States was "the sole depository of the sacred fire of freedom and self-government, from hence it is to be lighted up into other regions of the earth." A century and a half later, John Kennedy electrified the country with nearly-identical rhetoric: "The energy, the faith, the devotion which we bring to this endeavor will light our country and all who serve it – and the glow from that fire can truly light the world." Closer to home, George W. Bush, in preparing the war against terrorism, invoked the same image: "By our efforts, we have lit a fire as well – a fire in the minds of men. It warms those who feel its power, it burns those who fight its progress, and one day this untamed fire of freedom will reach the darkest corners of our world." Not to be outdone, President Obama in his first Inaugural, provided *almost* the same. The American Founding Fathers, he said, "still light the world, and we will not give them up for expedience sake."

Thus, from the beginning, the greatness of American liberty has been associated with fire. Is the same phenomenon still present today? Does Donald Trump represent the flame of American greatness? He certainly thinks so, his numbers eclipse all the sixteen others, but most political pundits hesitate … and wait.

The image is totally absent from the current campaign, but every Trump comment seems only to "fan the flames." The rest of the field, in the meantime, seems transfixed, scrambling for recognition and uncertain as to how to fight fire. The Republican leadership, plus Fox News, does not appear comfortable with the specter of a Trump ticket, and even less comfortable with the candidate using his time to bully one of the media's star anchors. The adolescence of this should be embarrassing to the candidate, but the fire rages. This dominates despite the absence of most of the traditional qualities of candidacy: governing experience, nuanced talking points, measured conversation, respect for others, sophisticated policy options, etc. While, admittedly, few other people are billionaires, calling the remainder of the American government "stupid" and calling analysts such as George Will and Charles Krauthammer "losers" should not be a political virtue. But it is and the fire rages and the numbers climb.

Using the metaphor introduced herein, there are at least three main options available to face the current challenge to the political system as most appreciate it.

First, "fight fire with fire." The voters are "angry," and Trump, it is said, has "tapped in" to this. So, therefore, should the rest of the field. Get angry, loosen your language, shout at the camera and identify with the dissonance that, apparently, has provided the "spark" for the current unrest. Have little respect for authority and less for other opinions.

Second, call the Fire Department. Sixteen polished candidates, with combined years of experience and expertise, watching their poll numbers rise and fall a few points does not bode well for the campaign. A concerted effort to expose and diminish a singular appeal might serve to resurrect honest debate and throw "cold water" on the source of the flames. All it takes is one spark (is it Carson?).

Third, let the fire "burn out." The final resolution of all fires is that they inevitably expire by themselves, with no help from anyone. But the path of the destruction is terrible.

Finally, there is one last option: the eternal flame such as the one that presides over John Kennedy's grave in Arlington Cemetery. But that is reserved for posterity only. The Donald must wait.

The Real Meaning of D-Day

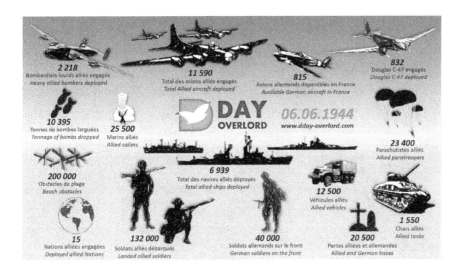

2 218
Bombardiers lourds alliés engagés
Heavy allied bombers deployed

11 590
Total des avions alliés engagés
Total Allied aircraft deployed

815
Avions allemands disponibles en France
Available German aircraft in France

832
Douglas C-47 engagés
Douglas C-47 deployed

10 395
Tonnes de bombes larguées
Tonnage of bombs dropped

25 500
Marins alliés
Allied sailors

DAY OVERLORD · 06.06.1944 · www.dday-overlord.com

23 400
Parachutistes alliés
Allied paratroopers

200 000
Obstacles de plage
Beach obstacles

6 939
Total des navires alliés déployés
Total allied ships deployed

12 500
Véhicules alliés
Allied vehicles

1 550
Chars alliés
Allied tanks

15
Nations alliées engagées
Deployed allied Nations

132 000
Soldats alliés débarqués
Landed allied soldiers

40 000
Soldats allemands sur le front
German soldiers on the front

20 500
Pertes alliées et allemandes
Allied and German losses

June 6, 2004

Over the past week the media has showered us with newsreels and testimonies regarding the importance and meaning of D-Day. The President is in Normandy, as are dignitaries from all over the world, and the 60th anniversary which we celebrate today has been heralded by many as the most important single day for Americans in the Twentieth Century. The festivities were somewhat interrupted yesterday by the news of the death of Ronald Reagan. But upon reflection, most will probably agree that his passing may give the day an even greater impact, given the importance he attached to D-Day and the fact of his presence there at the 40th anniversary. Reagan, in fact, probably symbolizes the meaning of D-Day more than any other American leader of the post-1945 period save Ike himself.

    D-Day, then, has a virtue far beyond its significance as the greatest amphibious military operation in history. It was by no means the largest battle of the war, and there were many battles throughout history, including the American Civil War, which were equally or more decisive and which took many more casualties. But D-Day has a meaning that integrates both the virtue of hope and the concept of political liberty, ideas which reinforce each other.

If Pearl Harbor meant The Beginning, D-Day meant The Beginning of the End. D-Day was a true turning point in history, as was Gettysburg in the Civil War and Midway in the Pacific. Yet, unlike these others, everybody knew D-Day was coming: it was not an accidental happening. Thus, the worldwide spotlight on Normandy that morning served to highlight the purpose and meaning of D-Day unlike any other event in historical memory. The note announcing failure which General Eisenhower carried in his pocket, just in case, would have doomed both hope and liberty for the continent of Europe for an unforeseeable future, perhaps for a time too long to bear.

The symbolism of political liberty for the continent, which the bright hope of D-Day resurrected, stands today as one of the truly liberating moments in human history. None compares, even after six decades. The memory of the thousands of open-arm welcomes which were offered to the Pathfinders, Beachmasters, Paratroopers and ordinary soldiers and sailors by French villagers after D-Day offers a lasting tribute to liberty as shared across the ocean, and across the sands of time.

The giants who stormed the beach that day, and the people they set free, reflect a lasting tribute to the unity of the new and the old worlds, far beyond the petty differences which politicians and pundits seem to have imposed today. D-Day rises above it all.

Shackled to a Corpse

June 9, 2008

Into its fifth year, with no end in sight, the war in Iraq has consumed the American people in ways similar to the Vietnam War a generation ago. Many see the war as open-ended, with a commitment lasting one hundred years if needed. The U.S. attempt at democratic transformation is still raging in a place that has never experienced representative rule in a history stretching over four thousand years. Apart from the human cost, both local and American, this conflict is costing the American taxpayer $12 billion each month!

Now we are faced with the possibility of yet another combat against Iran, a country with about three times the population of Iraq and with a potential nuclear capacity. Has the United States become obsessed with fighting such conflicts, in areas with only a distant and obscured national interest at stake? There are historical precedents.

By 1914, when World War I began, Balkan intrigues against the Habsburg Empire (Austria-Hungary) had been ongoing for years but Germany had always resisted the temptation to engage, prompting Chancellor Otto von Bismarck to quip that the Balkans "weren't worth the bones of a Pomeranian grenadier."

As the war went on, Germany hoped that its Hapsburg ally could secure the Balkans. But the political chaos of the Empire and its military weakness became a major problem. The endemic need to rescue Austria-Hungary both from itself and its enemies caused Germany to belatedly view the Habsburgs as a strategic liability. Inside Germany, the phrase "shackled to a corpse" symbolized her view of the entanglement.

The current conflict with Iraq, amidst the maze of other zones of contention in the Middle East, may well represent America's version of the Hapsburg alliance, draining this country's global strategic ability to pursue its interests elsewhere, especially in the Far East, Russia, eastern and western Europe, China, India, Pakistan, and the Western Hemisphere. Domestically, this concentration, particularly with Iraq, has produced an increasingly bitter public, a "house divided," and has eroded both our treasury and the public's willingness to engage abroad.

Al Qaeda and other Muslim terrorists, of course, use the overall pattern of the U.S. presence in the Middle East as one of the main reasons for their aggressive hostilities. The official Bush Administration "line" dismisses these explanations as transparent and phony, instead proffering as terrorist motivations "hatred" of freedom and American values. Yet, we may be dangerously self-deceptive if we dismiss our enemies' statements out-of-hand. This also has a precedent in history. The western world had Hitler's Mein Kampf years before World War II but failed to take his rantings seriously until it was too late. Is it too late for the United States to self-examine its interests in the Middle East, in balance with strategic dangers and opportunities throughout the rest of the world?

There are a billion Muslims in the world, but American foreign policies have reflected little if any appreciation of their sensitivities or interests. To a large degree, we have been too parochial and generally have failed to appreciate the "otherness" of other cultures and religions. U.S. public diplomacy has not yet figured out a way to make our cultural and political system palatable to these people, while it is commonplace for our country to be labeled "the great Satan."

Does this mean that the Middle East and Iraq/Iran are of no significance, that radical Islam is no threat, that the United States abandon the Middle East altogether and evacuate our military out of the area? Of course not! But on the other hand, it is past time for a wholesale re-evaluation of American global strategic policies. A prioritization of interests and commitments is absolutely essential if we are to have geopolitical balance – and success – in foreign policy and national security.

By and large, this fixation on transforming Iraq has developed without serious input from the body politic, while presidential candidates scurry away in denial of their earlier votes on Iraq. Nor is the problem an original American one, as it was imperial Britain and France which dismissed Lawrence of Arabia and carved up the Middle East for their own interests. But as the world's only "superpower," the United States has inherited Europe's imperial adventures. This may have left America, the world's greatest advocate of human freedom, on the wrong side of history.

The "corpse" metaphor, of course, is neither literal nor preordained. The U.S. spent over twelve years before finally leaving Vietnam, with barely any long-term side effects upon its range of global interests. Indeed, the country prospered, and, within years, had achieved the status as the world's "sole superpower," leaving the Soviet Union as a failed state. In the larger issue of Middle East oil, choices were – and still are – available. Persian Gulf oil constitutes only about 15% of the U.S. total. Can we find other regions, off-shore, like Alaska? Can we find non-military solutions to the conflicts endemic throughout the area? Can the U.S. act as an honest broker, with cultural understanding and diplomatic pursuits? Can we conform to the brilliant image as the "city on a hill," offering hope in contrast to the endemic failures of Islamic nativism?

But the most serious problem is how the war in Iraq has created a strategic imbalance. In trying to "drain the swamp" of terrorism, the U.S. has only created more swamps, while others fester on the geopolitical map. Just imagine if the Chinese attacked Taiwan, or if the North Koreans threatened South Korea, or Venezuela threatened Colombia or any number of other contingencies that would command Washington's immediate attention. America's strategic focus on the scores of flash-points and larger interests throughout the rest of the world has been diverted for too long a time period.

Future generations will have to pay for this strategic error, but for the moment we remain politically paralyzed, shackled to a corpse.